LENIN

COLLECTED WORKS

4

VERSO

London · New York

V. I. LENIN

COLLECTED WORKS

VOLUME
4

1898 – April 1901

The typeset files we have used in these editions were created by David J. Romagnolo and are taken from *www.marx2mao.com*. They represent years of work, meticulously re-creating a stunningly high resolution, re-type-set digital archive of Lenin's *Collected Works* and the PDFs are free to download. Verso gratefully acknowledges the invaluable work of Mr Romagnolo, who has kindly granted permission to reproduce his typesetting in the volumes of this series.

This English edition of V. I. Lenin's *Collected Works* is a translation of the fourth, enlarged Russian edition prepared by the Institute of Marxism-Leninism, Central Committee of the C.P.S.U.

Corrections have been made to some of the texts and notes in accordance with the fifth Russian edition, and some further editorial comments have been added.

This paperback edition first published by Verso 2023
First published in English by Progress Publishers 1960
© Verso 2023

1 3 5 7 9 10 8 6 4 2

Verso
UK: 6 Meard Street, London W1F 0EG
US: 388 Atlantic Ave, Brooklyn, NY 11217
versobooks.com

Verso is the imprint of New Left Books

ISBN-13: 978-1-839767-807
ISBN-13: 978-1-839767-814 (UK EBK)
ISBN-13: 978-1-839767-821 (US EBK)

British Library Cataloguing in Publication Data
A catalogue record for this book is available from the British Library

Library of Congress Cataloging-in-Publication Data
A catalog record for this book is available from the Library of Congress

Printed in the United States

CONTENTS

1901

ILLUSTRATIONS

PREFACE

Volume Four of the *Collected Works* contains Lenin's writings for the period February 1898-February 1901. These writings are devoted to the struggle for the victory of revolutiollary Marxism in the working-class movement and to the exposure of the anti-revolutionary views of the Narodniks, "legal Marxists," and "economists."

"A Note on the Question of the Market Theory (Apropos of the Polemic of Messrs. Tugan-Baranovsky and Bulgakov)," "Once More on the Theory of Realisation," and "Capitalism in Agriculture (Kautsky's Book and Mr. Bulgakov's Article)" were directed against the "legal Marxists," who sought to subordinate and adapt the working-class movement to the interests of the bourgeoisie.

This volume contains Lenin's first writings against "economism": "A Protest by Russian Social-Democrats," articles for the third issue of *Rabochaya Gazeta*, "A Retrograde Trend in Russian Social-Democracy," and "Apropos of the *Profession de foi*," in which he laid bare the opportunism of the "economists" and showed "economism" to be a variety of international opportunism ("Bernsteinism on Russian soil"). Against the anti-Marxist positions adopted by the "economists," Lenin contraposed the plan of the unity of socialism with the working-class movement.

Several of the articles in this volume are models of the journalism of social and political exposure to which Lenin attached great significance in the struggle against the lawlessness of the tsarist officials, the struggle to awaken the consciousness of the broad masses of the people. These articles are: "Beat—but Not to Death!", "Why Accelerate the Vicissitude of the Times?" and "Objective Statistics," published under the general heading of "Casual Notes": "The Drafting of 183 Studeuts into the Army," the preface to the pamphlet on the famous Kharkov May Day celebration, 1900, *May Days in Kharkov,* and the article, "Factory Courts," written in connection with the granting of police functions to the Factory Inspectorate.

The volume also contains writings relating to the organisation of the all-Russian illegal Marxist newspaper *Iskra*: "Draft of a Declaration of the Editorial Board of *Iskra* and *Zarya*," "How the 'Spark' Was Nearly Extinguished," and "Declaration of the Editorial Board of *Iskra*."

These documents, as well as the articles, "Our Programme," "A Draft Programme of Our Party," "The Urgent Tasks of Our Movement," and "The Workers' Party and the Peasantry," define the tasks confronting the Marxist organisations and the working-class movement of Russia at the moment when Lenin set about the actual formation of a party to fight under the unitary banner of revolutionary Marxism against opportunism, amateurishness in work, ideological disunity, and vacillation.

The present volume also contains the "Draft Agreement" with the Plekhanovist Emancipation of Labour group on the publication of the newspaper *Iskra* and the magazine *Zarya*, which appears for the first time in a collected edition of Lenin's writings. *Iskra* was launched on the basis of the "Draft Agreement."

ON THE QUESTION OF OUR FACTORY STATISTICS

(PROFESSOR KARYSHEV'S NEW STATISTICAL EXPLOITS)[1]

The Russian reading public displays a lively interest in the question of our factory statistics and in the chief conclusions to be drawn from them. This interest is quite understandable, for the question is connected with the more extensive one of the "destiny of capitalism in Russia." Unfortunately, however, the state of our factory statistics does not correspond to the general interest in their data. This branch of economic statistics in Russia is in a truly sad state, and still sadder, perhaps, is the fact that the people who write about statistics often display an astounding lack of understanding of the nature of the figures they are analysing, their authenticity and their suitability for drawing certain conclusions. Such precisely is the estimate that must be made of Mr. Karyshev's latest work, first published in *Izvestia Moskovskovo Selskokhozyaistvennovo Instituta* (4th year, Book 1) and then as a separate booklet with the high-sounding title *Material on the Russian National Economy. I. Our Factory Industry in the Middle Nineties* (Moscow, 1898). Mr. Karyshev tries, in this essay, to draw conclusions from the latest publication of the Department of Commerce and Manufactures on our factory industry.* We shall make a detailed analysis of Mr. Karyshev's conclusions and, especially, of his methods. We think that an analysis of this sort will have significance, not only in determining the way in which the material is treated by Pro-

---

* Ministry of Finance. Department of Commerce and Manufactures. The Factory Industry of Russia. *List of Factories and Works*, St. Petersburg, 1897, pp. 63 + vi + 1047.

fessor So-and-So (for this a review of a few lines would suffice), but also in determining the degree of reliability of our factory statistics, for which deductions they are suitable and for which they are unsuitable, what the most important requirements of our factory statistics are and the tasks of those who study them.

As its name implies, the source used by Mr. Karyshev contains a list of factories in the Empire for the year 1894-95. The publication of a full list of all factories (i.e., of *relatively* large industrial establishments, with varying conceptions of what is to be considered large) is not new to our literature. Since 1881 Messrs. Orlov and Budagov have compiled a *Directory of Factories and Works* the last (third) edition of which was issued in 1894. Much earlier, in 1869, a list of factories was printed in the notes accompanying the statistical tables on industry in the first issue of the *Ministry of Finance Yearbook*. The reports which factory owners are by law obliged to submit annually to the Ministry provided the material for all these publications. The new publication of the Department of Commerce and Manufactures differs from former publications of this type in its somewhat more extensive information, but at the same time it has tremendous shortcomings from which the earlier ones did not suffer and which greatly complicate its utilisation as material on factory statistics. In the introduction to the *List* there is a reference to the unsatisfactory condition of these statistics in the past which thereby defines the purpose of the publication to serve precisely as material for statistics and not merely as a reference book. But the *List*, as a statistical publication, amazes one by the complete absence of any sort of summarised totals. It is to be hoped that a publication of this sort, the first of its kind, will also be the last statistical publication without summaries. The huge mass of raw material in the form of piles of figures is useless ballast in a reference book. The introduction to the *List* sharply criticises the reports previously submitted to the Ministry by factory owners on the grounds that they "consisted of confusing information, always one and the same, which was repeated from year to year and did not allow even the quantity of goods produced to be accurately determined, whereas production figures as complete and reliable as possible are an urgent necessity" (p. 1). We shall certainly not say a word in defence of the absolutely outmoded system of our former factory statistics that were purely pre-Reform,* both as to organisation and as to quality. But, unfortunately, there is *scarcely any noticeable* improvement in their present condition. The gigantic *List* just published still does not give us the right to speak of any serious changes in the old system admitted by all to be useless. The reports "did not allow even the quantity of goods produced to be accurately determined."... Indeed, in the latest *List* there is no information whatsoever on the quantity of goods, although Mr. Orlov's *Directory*, for example, gave this information for a very large number of factories, and in some branches of industry for almost all factories, so that in the summarised table there is information on the quantity of the product (for the leather, distilling, brick, cereals, flour milling, wax, lard, flax-scutching, and brewery industries). And it was from the old reports that the *Directory* material was compiled. The *List* does not give any information on machinery employed, although the *Directory* gave this information for some branches of industry. The introduction describes the changes that have occurred in our factory statistics in this way: formerly, factory owners supplied information through the police according to "a brief and insufficiently clear programme" and no one checked the information. "Material was obtained from which no more or less precise conclusions could be drawn" (p. 1). Now a new and much more detailed programme has been compiled and the gathering and checking of factory statistical information have been entrusted to the factory inspectors. At first glance one might think that we now have the right to expect really acceptable data, since a correct programme and provision for checking the data are two very important conditions for successful statistics. In actual fact, however, these two features are still in their former primitively chaotic state. The detailed programme with an explanation is not published in the introduction to the *List* although statistical methodology requires the publication of the programme according to which the data were gathered. We

---

* The Reform of 1861 which abolished serfdom in Russia.—*Ed.*

shall see from the following analysis of the *List* material that the basic questions of programme for factory statistics still remain entirely unclarified. With regard to checking the data, here is a statement by a person engaged in the practical side of this process—Mr. Mikulin, Senior Factory Inspector of Kherson Gubernia,* who has published a book containing an analysis of statistical data gathered according to the new system in Kherson Gubernia.

"It proved impossible to make a factual check of all the figures in the reports submitted by owners of industrial establishments and they were, therefore, returned for correction only in those cases when comparison with the data of similar establishments or with information obtained during an inspection of the establishments showed obvious inconsistencies in the answers. *In any case, responsibility for the correctness of the figures for each establishment contained in the lists rests with those who submitted them*" (*Factory and Artisan Industry in Kherson Gubernia*, Odessa, 1897, preface. Our italics). And so, responsibility for the accuracy of the figures, as before, still rests with the factory owners. Representatives of the Factory Inspectorate were not only unable to check all the figures, but, as we shall see below, were even unable to ensure that they were uniform and could be compared.

Later, we shall give full details of the shortcomings of the *List* and the material it uses. Its chief shortcoming, as we have noted, is the complete absence of summaries (private persons who compiled the *Directory* drew up summaries and expanded them with each edition). Mr. Karyshev, availing himself of the collaboration of two other people, conceived the happy idea of filling this gap, at least in part, and of compiling summaries on our factory industry according to the *List*. This was a very useful undertaking, and every one would have been grateful for its achievement, if ... if Mr. Karyshev, firstly, had published even a few of

---

* *Gubernia, uyezd, volost*—Russian administrative-territorial units. The largest of these was the gubernia, which had its subdivisions in uyezds, which in turn were subdivided into volosts. This system of districting continued under the Soviet power until the introduction of the new system of administrative-territorial division of the country 1929-30.—*Ed*.

the obtained results in their entirety and if, secondly, he had not displayed, in his treatment of the material, a lack of criticism bordering on high-handedness. Mr. Karyshev was in a hurry to draw conclusions before he had studied the material attentively and before his statistical processing was anything like "thorough,"* so that naturally he made a whole series of the most curious errors.

Let us begin with the first, basic question in industrial statistics: what establishments should come under the heading of "factories"? Mr. Karyshev does not even pose this question; he seems to assume that a "factory" is something quite definite. As far as the *List* is concerned, he asserts, with a boldness worthy of better employment, that in contrast to former publications this one registers not only *large* establishments but *all* factories. This assertion, which the author repeats twice (pp. 23 and 34), *is altogether untrue*. Actually the reverse is the case; the *List* merely registers *larger* establishments as compared with former publications on factory statistics. We shall now explain how it is that Mr. Karyshev could "fail to notice" such a "trifle"; but first let us resort to historical reference. Prior to the middle eighties our factory statistics did not include *any* definitions or rules that limited the concept of factory to the larger industrial establishments. Every type of industrial (and artisan) establishment found its way into "factory" statistics; this, it goes without saying, led to terrific chaos in the data, since the full registration of all such establishments, by the employment of existing forces and means (i.e., without a correct industrial census), is absolutely out of the question. In some gubernias or in some branches of industry hundreds and thousands of the tiniest establishments were included, while in others only the larger "factories" were listed. It was, therefore, natural that the people who first tried to make a scientific analysis of the data contained in our factory statistics (in the sixties) turned all their attention to this question and directed all their efforts to separating the

---

* Contrary to the opinion of the reviewer in *Russkiye Vedomosti*[2] (1898, No. 144), who, apparently, was as little capable of a critical attitude to Mr. Karyshev's conclusions as was Mr. Karyshev of a critical attitude to the *List*'s figures.

branches for which there were more or less reliable data from those for which the data were absolutely unreliable, to separating establishments large enough to enable the obtainment of satisfactory data from those too small to yield satisfactory data. Bushen,* Bok,** and Timiryazev*** provided such valuable criteria on all these questions that, had they been carefully observed and developed by the compilers of our factory statistics, we should now have, in all probability, some very acceptable data. But in actual fact all these criteria remained, as usual, a voice crying in the wilderness, and our factory statistics have remained in their former chaotic state. From 1889 the Department of Commerce and Manufactures began its publication of the *Collection of Data on Factory Industry in Russia* (for 1885 and the following years). A slight step forward was made in this publication: the small establishments, i.e., those with an output valued at less than 1,000 rubles, were excluded. It goes without saying that this standard was too low and too indefinite; it is ridiculous even to think of the *full* registration of *all* industrial establishments with an output valued at more than that amount as long as the information is collected by the police. As before, some gubernias and some branches of industry included a mass of small establishments with outputs ranging in value from 2,000 to 5,000 rubles, while other gubernias and other branches of industry omitted them. We shall see instances of this further on. Finally, our latest factory statistical system has introduced a completely different formula for defining the concept "factory." It has been recognised that "all industrial establishments" (of those "*under the jurisdiction*" *of the Factory Inspectorate*) are subject to registration "if they employ no fewer than 15 workers, as are also those employing fewer than 15 workers, if they have a steam-boiler, a steam-engine, *or other mechanical motive power and*

---

* *Ministry of Finance Yearbook*. First issue. St. Petersburg, 1869.
** *Statistical Chronicle of the Russian Empire*. Series II, Issue 6, St. Petersburg, 1872. Material for the factory statistics of European Russia, elaborated under the editorship of I. Bok.
*** *Statistical Atlas of Main Branches of Factory Industry of European Russia, with List of Factories and Works*. Three issues St. Petersburg, 1869, 1870, and 1873.

machines or factory installations."* We must examine this
definition in detail (the points we have stressed are particularly unclear), but let us first say that this concept of "factory" is something quite new in our factory statistics; until
now no attempt has been made to limit the concept "factory"
to establishments with a definite number of workers, with
a steam-engine, etc. In general, the strict limitation of the
concept "factory" is undoubtedly necessary, but the definition
we have cited suffers, unfortunately, from its extreme lack
of precision, from its unclarity and diffusion. It provides the
following definitions of establishments subject to registration as "factories" in the statistics: 1) The establishment must
come within the jurisdiction of the Factory Inspectorate.
This, apparently, excludes establishments belonging to the
state, etc., metallurgical plants and others. In the *List*,
however, there are many state and government factories
(see Alphabetical List, pp. 1-2), and we do not know whether
they were registered in all gubernias or whether the data pertaining to them were subject to checking by the Factory
Inspectorate, etc. It must be said, in general, that as long
as our factory statistics are not freed from the web of various
"departments" to which the different industrial establishments
belong, they *cannot be* satisfactory; the areas of departmental
jurisdiction frequently overlap and are subject to changes;
even the implementation of similar programmes by different
departments will never be identical. The rational organisation of statistics demands that complete information
on all industrial establishments be concentrated in one
purely statistical institution to ensure careful observation
of identical methods of gathering and analysing data. So
long as this is not done, the greatest caution must he exercised in dealing with factory statistics that now include and
now exclude (at different times and in different gubernias)
establishments belonging to "another department." Metallurgical plants, for instance, have long been excluded from
our factory statistics; but Orlov, nevertheless, included in

---

* Circular of June 7, 1895, in Kobelyatsky (*Handbook for Members
of the Factory Inspectorate, etc.*, 4th edition. St. Petersburg, 1897,
p. 35. Our italics). This circular is not reprinted in the introduction
to the *List*, and Mr. Karyshev, in analysing the *List* material, did not
go to the trouble of discovering what the *List* meant by "factories"!!

the last edition of his *Directory* quite a number of metallurgical plants (almost all rail production, the Izhevsk and Votkinsk factories in Vyatka Gubernia, and others) that are not included in the *List*, although the latter records metallurgical plants in other gubernias that were previously not included in "factory" statistics (e.g., the Siemens copper-smelting plant in Elisavetpol Gubernia, p. 330). In Section VIII of the introduction to the *List*, iron-working, iron-smelting, iron and copper-founding and other establishments are mentioned (p. iii), but no indication at all is given of the way in which metallurgical plants are separated from those "subordinated" to the Department of Commerce and Manufactures. 2) Only *industrial* establishments are subject to registration. This definition is not as clear as it seems to be at first glance; the separation of artisan and agricultural establishments requires detailed and clearly defined rules applicable to each branch of industry. Below we shall see confusion in abundance arising out of the absence of these rules. 3) The number of workers in an establishment must be no less than 15. It is not clear whether only workers actually employed in the establishment are counted or whether those working outside are included; it has not been explained how the former are to be distinguished from the latter (this is also a difficult question), whether auxiliary workers should be counted, etc. In the above-mentioned book Mr. Mikulin quotes instances of the confusion arising out of this unclarity. The *List* enumerates many establishments that employ *only* outside workers. It stands to reason that an attempt to list *all* establishments of this type (i.e., all shops giving out work, all people in the so-called handicraft industries who give out work, etc.) can only raise a smile under the present system, of gathering information, while fragmentary data for some gubernias and some branches of industry are of no significance and merely add to the confusion. 4) All establishments possessing a steam-boiler or a steam-engine are called "factories." This definition is the most accurate and most happily chosen, because the employment of steam is really typical for the development of large-scale machine industry. 5) Establishments possessing "other" (non-steam) "mechanical motive power" are regarded as factories. This definition is very inaccurate and exceedingly broad; by this definition, establishments employing water, horse, and wind power, even treadmills, may be called factories. Since the registration of all such establishments is not even feasible, there must be confusion, examples of which we shall soon see. 6) Under the heading "factories" are included establishments having "factory installations." This most indefinite and hazy definition negates the significance of all definitions given previously and makes the data chaotic and impossible to compare. This definition will inevitably be understood differently in different gubernias, and what sort of definition is it in reality? A factory is an establishment having factory installations.... Such is the last word of our newest system of factory statistics. No wonder these statistics are so unsatisfactory. We shall give examples from *all* sections of the *List* in order to show that in some gubernias and in some branches of industry the tiniest establishments are registered, which introduces confusion into factory statistics, since there can be no question of recording all such establishments. Let us take Section I: "cotton processing." On pp. 10-11 we come across five "factories" in the villages of Vladimir Gubernia which, for payment, dye yarn and linen belonging to others (*sic*!). In place of the value of the output the sum paid for dyeing is given as from 10 rubles (?) to 600 rubles, with the number of workers from zero (whether this means that there is no information on the number of workers or that there are no *hired* workers, is not known) to three. There is no mechanical motive power. These are peasant dye-houses, i.e., the most primitive artisan establishments that have been registered by chance in one gubernia and, it goes without saying, omitted in others. In Section II (wool processing), in the same Vladimir Gubernia, we find hand "factories" that card wool belonging to others for the payment of 12-48 rubles a year and employ 0 or 1 worker. There is a hand silk factory (Section III, No. 2517) in a village; it employs three workers and has an output valued at 660 rubles. Then more village dye-houses in the same Vladimir Gubernia, employing 0-3 workers for hand work and receiving 150-550 rubles for the treatment of linen (Section IV, treatment of flax, p. 141). There is a bast-mat "factory" in Perm Gubernia, on a hand-work level, employing six workers (Section V), with an output valued at 921 rubles (No. 3936). It goes without saying that there are more than a few such establishments in other gubernias (Kostroma, for instance), but they were not counted as factories. There is a printing-works (Section VI) with one worker and an output value of 300 rubles (No. 4167): in other gubernias only the big printing-works were included, and in still others, none at all. There is a "sawmill" with three workers sawing barrel staves for the payment of 100 rubles (Section VII, No. 6274), and a metal-working hand establishment employing three workers with an output valued at 575 rubles (No. 8962). In Section IX (processing of mineral products) there are very many of the tiniest establishments, brickworks especially, with, for example, only one worker and an output valued at 48-50 rubles, and so on. In Section X (processing of livestock products) there are petty candle, sheepskin processing, leather and other establishments employing hand labour, 0-1-2 workers, with an output valued at a few hundred rubles (pp. 489, 507, et al.). More than anywhere else there are numerous establishments of a purely artisan type in Section XI (processing of foodstuffs), in the oil-pressing and, especially, the flour-milling branches. In the latter industry the strict division of "factories" from petty establishments is most essential; but so far this has not been done and utter chaos reigns in all our factory statistical publications. An attempt to introduce order into the statistics on the factory-type flour-milling establishments was made by the first congress of gubernia statistical committee secretaries (in May 1870),* but it was in vain, and up to the present day the compilers of our factory statistics do not seem to be concerned about the utter uselessness of the figures they print. The *List*, for example, included among the factories windmills employing one worker and realising from 0 to 52 rubles, etc. (pp. 587, 589, *et passim*); water-mills with one wheel, employing one worker and earning 34-80 rubles, etc. (p. 589, *et passim*); and so on. It goes without saying that such "statistics" are simply ridiculous, because another and even several other volumes could be filled with such mills without giving

---

* According to the draft rules drawn up by the congress on the gathering of industrial data, all mills equipped with less than 10 pairs of millstones, but not roller mills, were excluded from the list of factories. *Statistical Chronicle*, Series II, Issue 6, Introduction, p. xiii.

a complete list. Even in the section dealing with the chemical industry (XII) there are tiny establishments such as village pitch works employing from one to three workers, with an output valued at 15-300 rubles (p. 995, et al.). Such methods can go so far as to produce "statistics" similar to those published in the sixties in the well-known *Military Statistical Abstract* that for European Russia listed 3,086 pitch and tar "factories," of which 1,450 were in Archangel Gubernia (employing 4,202 workers, with a total output valued at 156,274 rubles, i.e., an average of fewer than three workers and a little more than 100 rubles per "factory"). Archangel Gubernia seems to have been deliberately left out of this section of the *List* altogether, as though the peasants there do not distil pitch and make tar! We must point out that all the instances cited concern registered establishments that do not come under the definitions given in the circular of June 7, 1895. Their registration, therefore, is *purely fortuitous*; they were included in some gubernias (perhaps, even, in some uyezds*), but in the majority they were omitted. Such establishments were omitted in former statistics (from 1885 onwards) as having an output valued at less than 1,000 rubles.

Mr. Karyshev did not properly understand this basic problem of factory statistics; yet he did not hesitate to make "deductions" from the figures he obtained by his calculations. The first of these deductions is that the number of factories in Russia is decreasing (p. 4, et al.). Mr. Karyshev arrived at this conclusion in a very simple way: he took the number of factories for 1885 from the data of the Department of Commerce and Manufactures (17,014) and deducted from it the number of factories in European Russia given in the *List* (14,578). This gives a reduction of 14.3%—the professor even calculates the percentage and is not bothered by the fact that the 1885 data did not include the excise-paying factories; he confines himself to the remark that the addition of excise-paying establishments would give a greater "reduction" in the number of factories. And the author undertakes to discover in which part of Russia this "process of diminution in the number of establishments" (p. 5) is evolving "most rapidly." In actual fact *there is no process of diminution, the number of*

---

* See footnote on p. 15.—*Ed.*

factories in Russia is increasing and not decreasing, and the figment of Mr. Karyshev's imagination came from the learned professor's having compared data that are not at all comparable.* The incomparability is by no means due to the absence of data on excise-paying factories for 1885. Mr. Karyshev could have taken figures that included such factories (from Orlov's cited *Directory* that was compiled from the same Department of Commerce and Manufactures lists), and in this way could have fixed the number of "factories" in European Russia at *27,986* for 1879, *27,235* for 1884, *21,124* for 1890, and the "reduction" by 1894-95 (14,578) would have been incomparably greater. The only trouble is that all these figures are quite unsuitable for comparison, because, frst, there is no uniform conception of "factory" in old and present-day factory statistical publications, and, secondly, very small establishments are included in the number of "factories" fortuitously and indiscriminately (for certain gubernias, for certain years), and, with the means at the disposal of our statistics, it would be ridiculous even to assume that they could be registered in full. Had Mr. Karyshev taken the trouble to study the definition of "factory" in the *List*, he would have seen that in order to compare the number of factories in that publication with the number of factories in others it would be *necessary to take only establishments employing 15 or more workers, because it is only this type* of establishment that the *List* registered *in toto* and without any limitations for all gubernias and all branches of industry. Since such establishments are among the relatively large ones, their registration in previous publications was also more satisfactory. Having thus assured the uniformity of data to be compared, let us compute the number of factories in European Russia employing sixteen** or

---

* In 1889 Mr. Karyshev took data for 1885 (*Yuridichesky Vestnik*,[3] No. 9) drawn from the most loyal reports of the governors, data that included the very smallest flour-mills, oil-presses, brickyards, potteries, leather, sheepskin, and other handicraft establishments, and fixed the number of "factories" in European Russia at *62,801*! We are amazed that he did not calculate the percentage of "reduction" in the number of factories today in relation to this figure.

** We are taking 16 and not 15 workers, partly because the computation of factories with 16 and more workers has already been made

more workers, taking them from the *Directory* for 1879 and
from the *List* for 1894-95. We get the following instructive
figures:

| | | | Number of Factories in European Russia | |
Source	Year	Total	Employing 16 or more workers	Employing fewer than 16 workers
Directory, 1st edition	1879	27,986*	4,551	23,435
Directory, 3rd edition	1890	21,124	6,013	15,111
List	1894-95	14,578	6,659 (without print-shops 6,372)	7,919

Therefore, the comparison of those figures which alone can
be considered relatively uniform, comparable, and complete
shows that *the number of factories in Russia is increasing*, and
at a fairly rapid rate: in fifteen or sixteen years (from 1879 to
1894-95) it has increased from 4,500 to 6,400, i.e., by 40 per
cent (in 1879 and 1890 print-shops were not included in the
number of factories). As far as the number of establishments
employing fewer than 16 workers is concerned, it would be
absurd to compare them for these years, since different definitions of "factory" and different methods of excluding
small establishments were employed in all these publications. In 1879 *no* small establishments were excluded; *on
account of this*, the very smallest establishments in branches
closely connected with agriculture and peasant industries
(flour milling, oil pressing, brickmaking, leather, potteries,
and others) were included, but they were omitted in later
publications. By 1890 some small establishments (those with
an output valued at less than 1,000 rubles) were omitted;
this left fewer small "factories." And lastly, in 1894-95, the
mass of establishments employing fewer than 15 workers was
omitted, which resulted in the immediate reduction in the
number of small "factories" to about a half of the 1890 figure.
The number of factories for 1879 and 1890 can be made
comparable in another way—by selecting the establishments

---

in the *Directory* for 1890 (3rd edition, p. x), and partly because the
explanations of the Ministry of Finance sometimes adopt this standard
(see Kobelyatsky, *loc. cit.*, p. 14).

  * Some gaps in the information have been filled in approximately:
see *Directory*, p. 695.

with an output valued at no less than 2,000 rubles. This is possible because the totals from the *Directory*, as quoted above, refer to all registered establishments, whereas the *Directory* entered in its *name index* of factories only those with an output valued at no less than 2,000 rubles. The number of establishments of this type may be considered approximately comparable (although there can never be a complete list of these establishments as long as our statistics are in their present state), with the exception, however, of the flour-milling industry. Registration in this branch is of a completely fortuitous character in different gubernias and for different years both in the *Directory* and in the *Collection* of the Department of Commerce and Manufactures. In some gubernias only steam-mills are counted as "factories," in others big water-mills are added, in the third case hundreds of windmills, and in the fourth even horse-mills and treadmills are included, etc. Limitation on the basis of the value of output does not clear up the chaos in statistics on factory-type mills, because, instead of that value the quantity of flour milled is taken, and this, even in very small mills, frequently amounts to more than 2,000 poods a year. The number of mills included in factory statistics, therefore, makes unbelievable leaps from year to year on account of the lack of uniformity in registration methods. The *Collection*, for example, listed 5,073, 5,605 and 5,201 mills in European Russia for the years 1889, 1890, and 1891 respectively. In Voronezh Gubernia the number of mills, 87 in 1889, suddenly increased to 285 in 1890 and 483 in 1892 as a result of the accidental inclusion of windmills. In the Don region the number of mills increased from 59 in 1887 to 545 in 1888 and 976 in 1890, then dropping to 685 in 1892 (at times windmills were included, while at others they were not), etc., etc. The employment of such data is clearly impermissible. We, therefore, take only steam-mills and add to them establishments in other branches of industry with an output value of no less than 2,000 rubles, and the number of factories we get for European Russia in 1879 is about 11,500 and in 1890 about 15,500.* From this, again, it follows that there is *an increase*

---

* It is impossible to obtain the required figure from the data in the *List*, first, because it omits a mass of establishments with an output valued at 2,000 rubles and more owing to their employing fewer than

in the number of factories and not the decrease invented by Mr. Karyshev. Mr. Karyshev's theory of the "process of diminution in the number of establishments" in the factory industry of Russia is a pure fable, based on a worse than insufficient acquaintance with the material he undertook to analyse. Mr. Karyshev, as long ago as 1889 (*Yuridiehesky Vestnik*, No. 9), spoke of the number of factories in Russia, comparing absolutely unsuitable figures taken from the loyal reports of the governors and published in the *Returns for Russia for 1884-85* (St. Petersburg, 1887, Table XXXIX) with the strange figures of the *Military Statistical Abstract* (Issue IV. St. Petersburg, 1871), which included among the "factories" thousands of tiny artisan and handicraft establishments, thousands of tobacco plantations (*sic!* see pp. 345 and 414 of the *Military Statistical Abstract* on tobacco "factories" in Bessarabia Gubernia), thousands of rural flour-mills and oil-presses, etc., etc. Small wonder that in this way the *Military Statistical Abstract* recorded over 70,000 "factories" in European Russia in 1866. The wonder is that a man was found who was so inattentive and uncritical with regard to every printed figure as to take it as a basis for his calculations.*

Here a slight diversion is necessary. From his theory of the diminution of the number of factories Mr. Karyshev deduces the existence of a process of the concentration of industry. It goes without saying that, in rejecting his theory, we do not by any means reject the conclusion, since it is only Mr. Karyshev's way of arriving at it that is wrong. To demonstrate this process, we must isolate the biggest establishments. Let us take, for example, establishments employing 100 or more workers. Comparing the number of such establishments, the number of workers they employ, and the total value of their output with data on all establishments, we get this table:

---

15 workers. Secondly, because the *List* counted the total value of the output without excise (in which it differed from former statistics). Thirdly, because the *List*, in some cases, registered, not the total value of the output, but payment for the processing of raw material.

* Dealing with the question of the number of factory workers, Mr. Tugan-Baranovsky has shown the utter uselessness of the *Military Statistical Abstract* data (see his book, *The Factory, etc.*, St. Petersburg, 1898, p. 336, et seq., and *Mir Bozhy*,[4] 1898, No. 4), and Messrs. N. —on and Karyshev have responded with silence to his direct challenge. They really cannot do anything else but remain silent.

See footnote*	1879			1890			1894-95		
	Number of		Value of output (thous. rubles)	Number of		Value of output (thous. rubles)	Number of		Value of output (thous. rubles)
	Factories	Workers		Factories	Workers		Factories	Workers	
All "factories"	27,986	763,152	1,148,134	21,124	875,764	1,500,871	14,578	885,555	1,345,346
Establishments with 100 or more workers	21,238	509,643	629,926	1,431	623,146	855,588	1,468	655,670	955,233
Percentage of total	—	66.8	54.8	—	71.1	57.2	—	74	70.8

* The same sources. Some data for 1879, as already mentioned, have been added approximately. The general data of the *Directory* and the *List* are incomparable with each other, but here we compare *only percentages* of the total number of workers and of the total value of output, and these data in their totals are much more reliable (as we shall show later) than the data on the total number of factories. The estimate of large establishments is taken from *Capitalism in Russia*, which the present writer is preparing for print.[5]

It can be seen from this table that the number of very large establishments is increasing, as well as the number of workers employed and the value of the output, which constitute an ever greater proportion of the total number of workers and the total value of the output of officially registered "factories." The objection may be raised that if a concentration of industry is taking place, it means that big establishments are squeezing out the smaller, whose number and, consequently, the total number of establishments, is decreasing. But, firstly, this last deduction is not made in respect of "factories" but refers to *all industrial establishments*, and of these we have no right to speak because we have no statistics on industrial establishments that are in the least reliable and complete. Secondly, and from a purely theoretical standpoint, it cannot be said *a priori* that the number of industrial establishments in a developing capitalist society must inevitably and always diminish, since, simultaneous with the process of the concentration of industry, there is the process of the population's withdrawal from farming, the process of growth in the number of small industrial establishments in the backward parts of the country as a result of the break-up of the semi-natural peasant economy, etc.*

Let us return to Mr. Karyshev. He pays almost the greatest attention of all to those data that are the least reliable (i.e., the data on the number of "factories"). He divides up the gubernias into groups according to the number of "factories," he designs a cartogram on which these groups are plotted, he compiles a special table of gubernias having the greatest number of "factories" in each branch of industry (pp. 16-17); he presents a mass of calculations in which the number of factories in each gubernia is shown as a percentage of the total (pp. 12-15). In doing this Mr. Karyshev overlooked a mere bagatelle: he forgot to ask himself *whether the numbers of factories in different gubernias are comparable*. This is a question that must be answered in the negative and, consequently, the greater part of Mr. Karyshev's calculations,

---

* The handicraft census for 1894-95 in Perm Gubernia showed, for example, that with every decade of the post-Reform period more and more small industrial establishments are being opened in the villages. See *Survey of Perm Territory. A Sketch of the State of Handicraft Industry in Perm Gubernia.* Perm, 1896.

comparisons, and arguments must he relegated to the sphere
of innocent statistical exercises. If the professor had acquainted himself with the definition of "factory" given in the circular of June 7, 1895, he would easily have concluded that
such a vague definition *cannot* be applied uniformly in
different gubernias, and a more attentive study of the *List*
itself could have led him to the same conclusion. Let us cite
some examples. Mr. Karyshev selects Voronezh, Vyatka, and
Vladimir gubernias (p. 12) for the number of establishments
in Section XI (processing of food products; this group
contains the greatest number of factories). But the abundance
of "factories" in these gubernias is to be explained primarily
by the *purely fortuitous* registration, specifically in these
gubernias, of small establishments such as were not included
in other gubernias. In Voronezh Gubernia, for instance, there
are many "factories" simply because small flour-mills were
included (of 124 mills only 27 are steam-mills; many of them
are water-mills with 1-2-3 wheels; such mills were not included
in other gubernias, and, indeed, they could not be listed in
full), as well as small oil-presses (mostly horse-driven), which
were not included in other gubernias. In Vyatka Gubernia only
3 out of 116 mills are steam-driven, in Vladimir Gubernia a
dozen windmills and 168 oil-presses were included, of which
the majority were wind- or horse-driven or were worked by
hand. The fact that there were fewer establishments in other gubernias, does not, of course, mean that these gubernias
were devoid of windmills, small water-mills, etc. They were
simply not included. In a large number of gubernias steam-
mills were included almost exclusively (Bessarabia, Ekaterinoslav, Taurida, Kherson, et al.), and the flour-milling
industry accounted for 2,308 "factories" out of 1,233 in
European Russia, according to Section XI. It was absurd
to speak of the distribution of factories by gubernias without
investigating the *dissimilarity* of the data. Let us take Section
IX, the processing of minerals. In Vladimir Gubernia, for
example, there are 96 brickworks and in the Don region, 31,
i.e., less than a third of the number. The *Directory* (for
1890) showed the opposite: 16 in Vladimir and 61 in the Don
region. It now turns out that, according to the *List*, out of
the 96 brickworks in Vladimir Gubernia only 5 employ 16 or
more workers, while the analogous figures for the Don region

are 26 out of 31. The obvious explanation of this is that in the Don region small brickworks were not so generously classified as "factories" as in Vladimir Gubernia, and that is all (the small brickworks in Vladimir Gubernia are all run on hand labour). Mr. Karyshev does not see any of this (p. 14). In respect of Section X (processing of livestock products) Mr. Karyshev says that the number of establishments is small in almost all gubernias but that "an outstanding exception is Nizhni-Novgorod Gubernia with its 252 factories" (p. 14). This is primarily due to the fact that very many small hand establishments (sometimes horse- or wind-driven) were included in this gubernia and not in the others. Thus, for Mogilev Gubernia the *List* includes only two factories in this section; each of them employs more than 15 workers. Dozens of small factories processing livestock products could have been listed in Mogilev Gubernia, in the same way as they were included in the *Directory* for 1890, which showed 99 factories processing livestock products. The question then arises: What sense is there in Mr. Karyshev's calculations of the distribution by percentages of "factories" so differently understood?

In order to show more clearly the different conceptions of the term "factory" in different gubernias, we shall take two neighbouring gubernias: Vladimir and Kostroma. According to the *List*, there are 993 "factories" in the former and 165 in the latter. In all branches of industry (sections) in the former there are tiny establishments that swamp the large ones by their great number (only 324 establishments employ 16 or more workers). In the latter there are very few small establishments (112 factories out of 165 employ 16 or more workers), although everybody realises that more than a few windmills, oil-presses, small starch, brick, and pitch works, etc., etc., could be counted in this gubernia.*

---

* We have here another instance of the arbitrary determination of the number of "factories" in our "newest" system of factory statistics. The *List* for 1894-95 records 471 factories for Kherson Gubernia (Mr. Karyshev, op. cit., p. 5), but for 1896 Mr. Mikulin suddenly lists as many as 1,249 "factory establishments" (op. cit., p. xiii), among them 773 with mechanical motive power and 109 without, employing more than 15 workers. With this unclarity in the definition of "factory" such leaps are inevitable.

Mr. Karyshev's light-minded attitude towards the authenticity of the figures he uses reaches its peak when he compares the number of "factories" per gubernia for 1894-95
(according to the *List*) with that for 1885 (according to the
Collection). There is a serious dissertation on the increased
number of factories in Vyatka Gubernia, on the "considerably decreased" number in Perm Gubernia, and on the substantially increased number in Vladimir Gubernia, and so on (pp.
6-7). "In this we may see," concludes our author profoundly,
"that the above-mentioned process of diminution in the number of factories affects places with a more developed and older
industry less than those where industry is younger" (p. 7).
Such a deduction sounds very "scientific"; the greater the
pity that it is merely nonsensical. The figures used by
Mr. Karyshev are quite fortuitous. For example, according to
the *Collection*, for 1885-90 the number of "factories" in Perm
Gubernia was 1,001, 895, 951, 846, 917, and 1,002 respectively, following which, in 1891, the figure suddenly dropped to
585. One of the reasons for these leaps was the inclusion of
469 mills as "factories" in 1890 and 229 in 1891. If the *List*
gives only 362 factories for that gubernia, it must be borne in
mind that it now includes only 66 mills as "factories." If
the number of "factories" has increased in Vladimir Gubernia, the *List*'s registration of small establishments in that
gubernia must be remembered. In Vyatka Gubernia, the *Collection* recorded 1-2-2-30-28-25 mills from 1887 to 1892 and
the *List*, 116. In short, the comparison undertaken by
Mr. Karyshev demonstrates over and over again that he is
quite incapable of analysing figures from different sources.

In giving the numbers of factories in different sections
(groups of industrial branches) and in computing their ratio
to the total number, Mr. Karyshev once again fails to notice
that there is no uniformity in the number of small establishments included in the various sections (there are, for example, fewer in the textile and metallurgical industries than
elsewhere, about one-third of the total number for European
Russia, whereas in the industries processing livestock and
food products they constitute about two-thirds of the total
number). It stands to reason that in this way he is comparing
non-comparable magnitudes, with the result that his percentages (p. 8) are devoid of all meaning. In short, on the entire

question of the number of "factories" and their distribution Mr. Karyshev has displayed a complete lack of understanding of the nature of the data he has employed and their degree of reliability.

As we go over from the number of factories to the number of workers, we must say, in the first place, that the figures for the total number of workers recorded in our factory statistics are much more reliable than those given for the factories. Of course, there is no little confusion here, too, and no lack of omissions and reductions of the actual number. But in this respect we do not find such great divergence in the type of data used, and the excessive variations in the number of small establishments, which are at times included in the number of factories and at others not, have very little effect on the total number of workers, for the simple reason that even a very large percentage of the smallest establishments gives a very small percentage of the total number of workers. We have seen above that for the year 1894-95, 74 per cent of the workers were concentrated in 1,468 factories (10 per cent of the total number). The number of small factories (employing fewer than 16 workers) was 7,919 out of 14,578, i.e., more than a half, and the number of workers in them was (even allowing an average of 8 workers per establishment) something like 7 per cent of the total. This gives rise to the following phenomenon: while there is a tremendous difference in the number of factories in 1890 (in the *Directory*) and in 1894-95, the difference in the number of workers is insignificant: in 1890 the figure was 875,764 workers for fifty gubernias of European Russia, and in 1894-95 it was 885,555 (counting only workers employed inside the establishments). If we deduct from the first figure the number of workers employed in the rail manufacturing (24,445) and salt-refining (3,704) industries, not included in the *List*, and from the second figure the number of workers in print-shops (16,521), not included in the *Directory*, we get 847,615 workers for 1890 and 869,034 workers for 1894-95, i.e., 2.5 per cent more. It goes without saying that this percentage cannot express the actual increase, since many small establishments were not included in 1894-95, but, in general, the closeness of these figures shows the relative suitability of the over-all data on the total number of workers and their relative reliability. Mr. Karyshev, from whom we have taken the total number of workers, does not make an accurate analysis of precisely which branches of industry were included in 1894-95 as compared with former publications, nor does he point out that the *List* omits many establishments that were formerly included in the number of factories. For his comparison with former statistics he takes the same absurd data of the *Military Statistical Abstract* and repeats the same nonsense about the alleged reduction in the number of workers relative to the population which has already been refuted by Mr. Tugan-Baranovsky (see above). Since the data on the number of workers are more authentic, they are deserving of a more thorough analysis than the data on the number of factories, but Mr. Karyshev has done just the opposite. He does not even group factories together according to the number of workers employed, which is what he should have done in the first place, in view of the fact that the *List* regards the number of workers as an important distinguishing feature of the factory. It can be seen from the data cited above that the concentration of workers is very great.

Instead of grouping factories according to the number of workers employed in them, Mr. Karyshev undertook a much simpler calculation, aimed at determining the average number of workers per factory. Since the data on the number of factories are, as we have seen, particularly unreliable, fortuitous, and dissimilar, the calculations are full of errors. Mr. Karyshev compares the average number of workers per factory in 1886 with the figure for 1894-95 and from this deduces that "the average type of factory is growing larger" (pp. 23 and 32-33), not realising that in 1894-95 only the larger establishments were listed, so that the comparison is incorrect. There is a very strange comparison of the number of workers per factory in the different gubernias (p. 26); Mr. Karyshev obtains the result, for instance, that "Kostroma Gubernia turns out to have a bigger average type of industry than all other gubernias"—242 workers per factory as compared with, for example, 125 in Vladimir Gubernia. It does not enter the learned professor's head that this is due merely to different methods of registration, as we have explained above. Having allowed the difference between the number of large and small establishments in different gubernias to pass unnoticed, Mr. Karyshev invented a very simple way of *evading* the difficulties encountered in this question. Precisely put, he multiplied the average number of workers *per factory for the whole of European Russia* (and then for Poland and the Caucasus) by the number of factories in each gubernia and indicated the groups he thus obtained on a special cartogram (No. 3). This, indeed, is really so simple! Why group factories according to the number of workers they employ, why examine the relative number of large and small establishments in different gubernias, when we can so easily *artificially level out* the "average" size of the factories in various gubernias according to one standard? Why try to find out whether there are many or few small and petty establishments included in the number of factories in Vladimir or Kostroma Gubernia, when we can "simply" take the average number of workers per factory *throughout* European Russia and multiply it by the number of factories in *each* gubernia? What matters it if such a method equates hundreds of fortuitously registered windmills and oil-presses with big factories? The reader, of course, will not notice it, and who knows—he may even believe the "statistics" invented by Professor Karyshev!

In addition to workers employed in the establishment, the *List* has a special category of workers "outside the establishment." This includes not only those working at home to the orders of the factory (Karyshev, p. 20), but also auxiliary workers, and so on. The number of these workers given in the *List* (66,460 in the Empire) must not be regarded as "an indication of how far advanced in Russia is the development of the so-called outside department of the factory" (Karyshev, p. 20), since there can be no question of anything like a complete registration of such workers under the present system of factory statistics. Mr. Karyshev says very thoughtlessly: "66,500 for the whole of Russia with her millions of handicraftsmen and artisans is but a few" (*ibid.*). Before writing this he had to forget that, if not the greater part, at least a very large part of these "millions of handicraftsmen," as is confirmed by all sources, work for jobbers, i.e., are the selfsame "outside workers." One has only to glance at those pages of the *List* devoted to districts known for their handicraft industries to be convinced of the thoroughly fortuitous and fragmentary nature of the registration of

"outside workers." Section II (wool processing) of the *List*,
for example, for Nizhni-Novgorod Gubernia counts only 28
outside workers in the town of Arzamas and in the suburban
Viyezdnaya Sloboda (p. 89), whereas we know from the
*Transactions of the Commission of Inquiry into Handicraft
Industry in Russia* (Issues V and VI) that many hundreds
(up to a thousand) "handicraftsmen" work there for masters.
The *List* does not record any outside workers at all in Semyo-
nov Uyezd, whereas we know from the Zemstvo[6] statistics
that over 3,000 "handicraftsmen" work there for masters in
the felt boot and insole branches. The *List* records only one
"factory" employing 17 outside workers in the accordion industry of Tula Gubernia (p. 395), whereas the cited *Transactions of the Commission*, etc., as early as 1882, listed between
2,000 and 3,000 handicraftsmen working for accordion factory
owners (Issue IX). It is, therefore, obvious that to regard the
figure of 66,500 outside workers as being in any way authentic and to discuss their distribution by gubernias and branches
of industry, as Mr. Karyshev does, and even to compile a
cartogram, is simply ridiculous. The real significance of
these figures lies not at all in the determination of the extent
to which capitalist work is done in the home (which is deter-
minable only from a complete industrial census that includes
all shops and other establishments, as well as individuals
giving out work to be done at home), but in the separation of
the workers in the establishments, i.e., factory workers in the
strict sense from outside workers. Hitherto these two types of
workers have often been confounded; frequent instances of
such confusion are to be found even in the *Directory* for 1890.
The *List* is now making the first attempt to put an end to
this state of affairs.

The *List*'s figures relating to the annual output of the
factories have been analysed by Mr. Karyshev most satisfac-
torily of all, mainly because that author at last introduced
the grouping of factories by the magnitude of their output
and not by the usual "averages." It is true that the author
still cannot rid himself of these "averages" (the magnitude
of output per factory) and even compares the averages for
1894-95 with those for 1885, a method that, as we have repeatedly said, is absolutely incorrect. We would note that the
total figures for the annual output of factories are much more

authentic than the total figures for the number of factories, for the reason, already mentioned, of the minor role of the small establishments. According to the *List*, there are, for example, only 245 factories in European Russia with an output valued at more than one million rubles, i.e., only 1.9 per cent, but they account for 45.6 per cent of the total annual output of all factories in European Russia (Karyshev, p. 38), while factories with an output valued at less than 5,000 rubles constitute 30.8 per cent of the total number, but account for only 0.6 per cent of the total output, i.e., a most insignificant fraction. We must here note that in these calculations Mr. Karyshev ignores the difference between the value of the total output (= value of the product) and payment for the processing of raw material. This very important distinction is made for the first time in our factory statistics by the *List*.* It goes without saying that these two magnitudes are absolutely incomparable with each other and that they should have been separated. Mr. Karyshev does not do this, and it is to be supposed that the low percentage of annual output of the small establishments is partly due to the inclusion of establishments that showed only the cost of processing the product and not its value. Below we shall give an example of the error into which Mr. Karyshev falls through ignoring this circumstance. The fact that the *List* differentiates between payment for processing and the value of the product and that it does not include the sum of the excise in the price of production makes it impossible to compare these figures with those of previous publications. According to the *List*, the output of all the factories of European Russia amounts to 1,345 million rubles, while according to the *Directory* for 1890 it amounted to 1,501 million. But if we subtract the sum of the excise from the second figure (250 million rubles in the distilling industry alone), then the first figure will be considerably greater.

---

* The only thing is that, unfortunately, we have no guarantee that the *List* made this distinction strictly and consistently, i.e., that the value of the product is shown *only* for those factories that actually sell their product, and payment for processing raw material only for those that process material belonging to others. It is possible, for example, that in the flour-milling industry (where the above-mentioned distinction is most frequently met with) the mill owners should have shown either of the figures indiscriminately. This is a problem that requires special analysis.

In the *Directory* (2nd and 3rd editions) factories were distributed in groups according to the amount of annual output (without any indication of the share of each group in the total output), but this distribution cannot he compared with the data in the *List* because of the differences in registration methods mentioned above and in the determining of the magnitude of annual output.

We have yet another fallacious argument of Mr. Karyshev to examine. Here, too, in quoting data on the total annual output of factories in each gubernia, he could not refrain from making comparisons with the data for the years 1885 to 1891, i.e., with the data of the *Collection*. Those data contain no information on productions subject to excise, and for that reason Mr. Karyshev looks only for gubernias in which the total output for 1894-95 is *less* than in previous years. Such gubernias are to be found to the number of eight (pp. 39-40), and apropos of this Mr. Karyshev argues about "the retrograde movement in industry" in the "less industrial" gubernias and says that this "may serve as an indication of the difficult position of the small establishments in their competition with big establishments," and so on. All these arguments would probably be very profound if—if they were not all completely fallacious. And here, too, Mr. Karyshev did not notice that he was comparing absolutely noncomparable and dissimilar data. Let us demonstrate this incomparability by data on each of the gubernias indicated by Mr. Karyshev.* In Perm Gubernia the total output in 1890 was 20.3 million rubles (Directory), while in 1894-95 it was 13.1 million rubles; this includes the flour-milling industry, 12.7 million (at 469 mills!) in 1890, and 4.9 million (at 66 mills) in 1894-95. The seeming "reduction," therefore, is simply a matter of the fortuitous registration of different numbers of mills. The number of steam-mills, for example, increased from 4 in 1890 and 1891 to 6 in 1894-95. The "reduction" of

---

* In this case we do not take the data of the *Collection* but those of the *Directory* for 1890, *deducting industries subject to excise*. With the exception of these industries, the *Directory* data do not differ from those of the *Collection*, since they are based on the same reports of the Department of Commerce and Manufactures. In order to expose Mr. Karyshev's error we need detailed data for individual factories and not only for individual industries.

output in Simbirsk Gubernia is to be explained in the same way (1890: 230 mills with an output of 4.8 million rubles; 1894-95: 27 mills with an output of 1.7 million rubles. Steam-mills, 10 and 13 respectively). In Vyatka Gubernia the total output was 8.4 million rubles in 1890 and 6.7 million in 1894-95, a reduction of 1.7 million rubles. Here, in 1890, two metallurgical works, the Votkinsk and the Izhevsk, were included, with a combined output valued at precisely 1.7 million rubles; in 1894-95 they were not included because they were "subordinated" to the Department of Mines and Metallurgy. Astrakhan Gubernia: 2.5 million rubles in 1890 and 2.1 million in 1894-95. But in 1890 the salt-refining industry (346,000 rubles) was included, while in 1894-95 it was not, because it belongs to the "mining" industries. Pskov Gubernia: 2.7 million rubles in 1890 and 2.3 million in 1894-95; but 45 flax-scutching establishments with a total output of 1.2 million rubles were counted in 1890, and in 1894-95 only four *flax-spinning* establishments with an output valued at 248,000 rubles. It stands to reason that the flax-scutching establishments in Pskov Gubernia have not disappeared but were simply not included in the list (perhaps because the majority of them are hand-worked and employ less than 15 workers). In Bessarabia Gubernia the output of the flour-mills was registered in different ways, although a similar number of mills was recorded both in 1890 and in 1894-95 (97 in each case); in 1890 the quantity of flour milled was computed—4.3 million poods valued at 4.3 million rubles, while in 1894-95 the majority of the mills recorded *only payment for milling*, so that their total output (1.8 million rubles) cannot be compared with the figure for 1890. The following instances will illustrate the difference. Levenson's two mills recorded an output of 335,000 rubles in 1890 (*Directory*, p. 424), and in 1894-95 recorded only 69,000 rubles *payment for milling* (*List*, No. 14231-2). Schwartzberg's mill, on the contrary, showed the value of the product in 1890 as 125,000 rubles (*Directory*, p. 425), and in 1894-95 as 175,000 rubles (*List*, No. 14214); out of the total sum for the flour-milling industry in 1894-95, 1,400,000 rubles are accounted for by the value of the product and 0.4 million rubles as payment for milling. The same is true of Vitebsk Gubernia: in 1890—241 mills with a total output figure of 3.6 million rubles, and in 1894-95—82 mills with a total output figure of 120,000 rubles, the majority of the mills showing only payment for milling (the number of steam-mills in 1890 was 37, in 1891, 51, and in 1894-95, 64), so that *more than a half* of this sum of 120,000 rubles does not represent the value of the product but payment for milling. And, finally, in the last gubernia, Archangel, the "retrograde movement in industry" discovered by Mr. Karyshev is explained simply by a strange error in his calculations: in actual fact the total value of the output of the Archangel factories, according to the *List*, is not the 1.3 million rubles twice quoted by Mr. Karyshev (pp. 40 and 39, as compared with 3.2 million rubles in 1885-91), but *6.9 million rubles*, of which 6.5 million rubles was accounted for by 18 sawmills (*List*, p. 247).

Summarising what has been said above, we come to the conclusion that Mr. Karyshev's approach to the material he was analysing was astonishingly inattentive and devoid of criticism, so that he committed a whole series of the crudest errors. With regard to the calculations based on the *List* figures that he made together with his colleagues, it must be said that they lose much in statistical value from the fact that Mr. Karyshev did not publish full totals, i.e., total numbers of factories, workers, value of output for all gubernias and all branches of industry (although he apparently made these calculations, which, had he published them in full, would, on the one hand, have made verification possible and, on the other, have proved of great benefit to those who use the *List*). The purely statistical analysis of the material, therefore, proved extremely fragmentary, incomplete, and unsystematic, and Mr. Karyshev's deductions, made in too great a hurry, serve, for the most part, as an example of how not to work with figures.

Returning to the question raised above on the present state of our factory statistics, we must say, first of all, that if "complete and reliable production figures" are an "urgent necessity" (as the introduction to the *List* says, with which one cannot but agree), then, to obtain them, a correctly organised industrial census is essential, one that will register each and every industrial establishment, enterprise, and kind of work, and that will be taken regularly at definite intervals of time. If the data on occupations in the first census[7] of the population, taken on January 28, 1897, prove satisfactory and if they are analysed in detail, they will greatly facilitate the taking of an industrial census. As long as there are no such censuses it can only be a question of registering some of the big industrial establishments. It must be conceded that the present system of collecting and processing statistical information on such big establishments ("factories and workers" in the prevailing terminology) is unsatisfactory in the highest degree. Its first shortcoming is the division of factory statistics among various "departments" and the absence of a special, purely statistical institution that centralises the collecting, checking, and classifying of all information on all types of factories. When you analyse the data of our present-day factory statistics you find yourself on territory that is intersected in all directions by the boundaries of various "departments" (which employ special ways and means of registration, and so on). It sometimes happens that these boundaries pass through a certain factory, so that one section of a factory (the iron foundry, for example) comes under the Department of Mines and Metallurgy, while another section (the manufacture of ironware, for example) comes under the Department of Commerce and Manufactures. It can be understood how this makes the use of the data difficult and into what errors those investigators risk falling (and fall) who do not pay sufficient attention to this complicated question. With regard to the checking of the information, it must be said in particular that the Factory Inspectorate will, naturally, never be in a position to check the extent to which all information supplied by all factory owners corresponds to reality. Under a system of the present-day type (i.e., under which the information is not gathered by means of a census conducted by a special staff of agents but by means of questionnaires circulated among factory owners), the chief attention should be paid to ensuring that the central statistical institution have *direct* contact with all factory owners, systematically control the *uniformity* of the returns, and see to their completeness and to the dispatch of questionnaires to *all* industrial centres of any importance—that it thus prevent the fortuitous inclusion of dissimilar data, or different applications and interpretations of the programme. The second basic shortcoming of present-day statistics lies in the fact that the programme for the gathering of information has not been elaborated. If this programme is prepared in offices and is not submitted to the criticism of specialists and (what is particularly important) to an all-round discussion in the press, the information *never can be* in any way complete and uniform. We have seen, for example, how unsatisfactorily even the basic programmatic question—what is a "factory"?—is being solved. Since there is no industrial census, and the system employed is that of gathering information from the industrialists themselves (through the police, the Factory Inspectorate, etc.), the concept "factory" should most certainly be defined with complete accuracy and limited to big establishments of such size as to warrant our expectation that they will be registered *everywhere and in their entirety without omissions.* It appears that the fundamental elements of the definition of a "factory establishment" as at present accepted have been quite well chosen: 1) the number of workers employed *in the establishment* to be no fewer than 15 (the question of separating auxiliary workers from factory workers in the true sense of the word, of determining the average number of workers for the year, etc., to be elaborated); and 2) the presence of a steam-engine (even when the number of workers is smaller). Although extreme caution should be exercised in extending this definition, it is an unfortunate fact that to these distinguishing characteristics have been added other, quite indeterminate ones. If, for instance, the bigger establishments employing water power must not be omitted, it should be shown with absolute accuracy what establishments of this type are subject to registration (using motive power of not less than so many units, or employing not less than a certain number of workers and so on). If it is considered essential to include smaller establishments in some branches, these branches must be listed very precisely and other definite features of the concept "factory establishments" must be given. Those branches in which "factory" establishments merge with "handicraft" or "agricultural" establishments (felt, brick, leather, flour milling, oil pressing, and many others) should be given special attention. We believe that the two characteristics we have given of the concept "factory" should in no case be extended, because even such relatively big establishments can scarcely be registered without omissions under the existing system of gathering information. A reform of the system may be expressed either in partial and insignificant changes or in the introduction of full industrial censuses. As far as the extent of the information is concerned, i.e., the number of questions asked the industrialists, here, too, a radical distinction has to be made between an industrial census and statistics of the present-day type. It is only possible and necessary to strive for complete information in the first case (questions on the history of the establishment, its relations to neighbouring establishments and the neighbourhood population, the commercial side of affairs, raw and auxiliary materials, quantity and type of the product, wages, the length of the working day, shifts, nightwork and overtime, and so on and so forth). In the second case great caution must be exercised: it is better to obtain relatively little reliable, complete, and uniform information than a lot of fragmentary, doubtful information that cannot be used for comparisons. The only addition undoubtedly necessary is that of questions on machinery in use and on the amount of output.

In saying that our factory statistics are unsatisfactory in the highest degree, we do not by any means wish to imply that their data are not deserving of attention and analysis. Quite the contrary. We have examined in detail the shortcomings of the existing system in order to stress the necessity for a particularly thorough analysis of the data. The chief and basic purpose of this analysis should be the separation of the wheat from the chaff, the separation of the relatively useful material from the useless. As we have seen, the chief mistake made by Mr. Karyshev (and many others) consists precisely in the failure to make such a separation. The figures on "factories" are the least reliable, and under no circumstances can they be used without a thorough preliminary analysis (the separate listing of the bigger establishments, etc.). The number of workers and the output values are much more reliable in the grand totals (it is, however, still necessary to make a strict analysis of which productions were included and in which way, how the output value was computed, etc.). If the more detailed totals are taken, it is possible that the data will prove unsuited for comparison and their use conducive to error. The fables of the reduction of the number of factories in Russia and of the number of factory workers (relative to the population)—fables that have been so zealously disseminated by the Narodniks[8]—can only be explained as due to the ignoring of all these circumstances.

As far as the analysis of the material itself is concerned, it must undoubtedly be based on information on each separate factory, i.e., card-index information. The cards must, first and foremost, be grouped by territorial units. The gubernia is too big a unit. The question of the distribution of industry is so important that the classification must be for individual cities, suburbs, villages, and groups of villages that form industrial centres or districts. Further, grouping by branches of industry is essential. In this respect our latest factory statistical system has, in our opinion, introduced an undesirable change, causing a radical rupture with the old subdivision into branches of industry that has predominated right from the sixties (and earlier). The *List* made a new grouping of industries in twelve sections: if the data are taken by sections only, we get an excessively broad framework embracing branches of production of the most diverse character and throwing them together (felt cloth and rough felt, sawmills and furniture manufacture, notepaper and printing, iron-founding and jewellery, bricks and porcelain, leather and wax, oil-pressing and sugar-refining, beer-brewing and tobacco, etc.). If these sections are subdivided in detail into separate branches we get groups that are far too detailed (see Mikulin, op. cit.), *over three hundred* of them! The old system that had ten sections and about a hundred branches of production (91 in the *Directory* for 1890) seems to us to have been much happier. Furthermore, it is essential to group the factories *according to the number of workers, the type of motive power*, as well as *according to the amount of output*. Such a grouping is particularly necessary from the purely theoretical standpoint for the study of the condition and development of industry and for the separation of relatively useful from useless data in the material at hand The absence of such a grouping (necessary within the territorial groups and the groups of branches of production) is the most significant shortcoming of our present publications on factory statistics, which allow only "average figures" to be determined, quite often absolutely false and leading to serious errors. Lastly, grouping under all these headings should not be limited to a determination of the number of establishments in each group (or sub-group) but must be accompanied by a calculation of the number of workers and aggregate output in each group, in establishments employing both machine and hand labour, etc. In other words, *combined* tables are necessary as well as *group* tables.

It would be a mistake to think that such an analysis involves an inordinate amount of labour. The Zemstvo statistical bureaus with their modest budgets and small staffs carry out much more complicated work for each uyezd; they analyse 20,000, 30,000 and 40,000 separate cards (and the number of relatively big, "factory" establishments throughout the whole of Russia would probably not be more than 15,000-16,000); moreover, the volume of information on each card is incomparably greater: there are several hundred columns in the Zemstvo statistical abstracts, whereas in the *List* there are less than twenty. Notwithstanding this, the best Zemstvo statistical abstracts not only provide group tables under various headings, but also combined tables, i.e., those showing a combination of various features.

Such an analysis of the data would, firstly, provide the requisite material for economic science. Secondly, it would fully decide the question of separating relatively useful from useless data. Such an analysis would immediately disclose the fortuitous character of data on some branches of industry, some gubernias, some points of the programme, etc. An opportunity would be provided to extract relatively full, reliable, and uniform material. Valuable indications would be obtained of the way in which these qualities can be assured in the future.

Written in August 1898

Published in 1898 in the collection,
Economic Studies and Essays,
by Vladimir Ilyin

Published according to
the text in the collection

REVIEW

A. Bogdanov. *A Short Course of Economic Science.* *Moscow, 1897. Publ. A. Murinova's Bookshop. 290 pp. Price 2 rubles.*

Mr. Bogdanov's book is a remarkable manifestation in our economic literature; not only is it "no superfluous" guide among a number of others (as the author "hopes" in his preface), it is by far the best of them. In this note, therefore, we intend to call the reader's attention to the outstanding merits of the book and to indicate a few minor points which could, in our opinion, be improved upon in future editions; in view of the lively interest displayed by our reading public in economic questions, it is to be expected that further editions of this useful book will soon be forthcoming.

The chief merit of Mr. Bogdanov's *Course* is the strict adherence to a definite line from the first page to the last, in a book that treats of many and very extensive problems. From the outset the author gives a clear-cut and precise definition of political economy as "the science that studies the social relations of production and distribution in their development" (3), and he never deviates from this point of view, one that is often but poorly understood by learned professors of political economy who lapse from "the social relations of production" to production in general and fill their ponderous courses with a pile of empty banalities and examples that have nothing to do with social science. Alien to the author is the scholasticism that often impels compilers of textbooks to indulge in "definitions" and in an analysis of every aspect of each definition; the clarity of his exposition, actually gains, rather than loses, by this, and the reader gets a clear conception, for example, of such a category as *capital*, both in the social and in the historical sense. In his *Course*, Mr. Bogdanov bases the sequence of his exposition on the view that political economy is the science of the historically developing systems of social production. He begins his *Course* with a brief exposition of "general concepts" (pp. 1-19) of the science and ends with a brief "history of economic views" (pp. 235-90), outlining the subject of the science in Section C: "The Process of Economic Development"; he does not give his outline dogmatically (as is the case with the majority of textbooks), but by means of a characteristic of the periods of economic development in their proper sequence: the periods of primitive clan communism, slavery, feudalism and guilds, and, finally, capitalism. This is precisely what an exposition of political economy should be. The objection may be raised that under these circumstances the author is inevitably compelled to break up one and the same theoretical division (e.g., money) between different periods and thereby repeat himself. But this purely formal shortcoming is more than compensated by the fundamental merits of the historical exposition. And is it really a shortcoming? The repetitions are quite insignificant and are of benefit to the beginner because he is better able to grasp the more important postulates. The treatment of the various functions of money in the various periods of economic development, for example, shows the student clearly that the theoretical analysis of these functions is not based on abstract speculation but on a precise study of what actually happened in the course of the historical development of mankind. It provides a more complete conception of the particular, historically determined, systems of social economy. The whole task of a handbook of political economy is, of course, to give the student of that science the fundamental concepts of the different systems of social economy and of the basic features of each system; the whole task is one of placing in the hands of the student who has mastered the elementary handbook a reliable guide to the further study of the subject, so that, having understood that the most important problems of contemporary social life are intimately bound up with problems of economic science, he may acquire an interest in this study. In ninety-nine cases out of a hundred this is precisely what is lacking in handbooks of political economy. Their shortcoming is due not so much to the fact that they are usually limited to one system of social economy (i.e., the capitalist system) as to their inability to focus the reader's attention on the basic features of that system; they are unable to give a clear definition of its historical significance and to show the process (and the conditions) of its emergence, on the one hand, and the tendencies of its further development, on the other; they are unable to represent the different aspects and different manifestations of contemporary economic life as component parts of a definite system of social economy, as manifestations of the basic features of that system; they are unable to give the reader reliable guidance, because they do not usually adhere to one particular line with complete consistency; and, lastly, they are unable to interest the student, because they have an extremely narrow and incoherent conception of the significance of economic questions and present economic, political, moral, and other "factors" in "poetic disorder." Only the *materialist conception of history* can bring light into this chaos and open up the possibility for a broad, coherent, and intelligent view of a specific system of social economy as the foundation of a specific system of man's entire social life.

The outstanding merit of Mr. Bogdanov's *Course* is that the author adheres consistently to historical materialism. In outlining a definite period of economic development in his "exposition" he usually gives a sketch of the political institutions, the family relations, and the main currents of social thought *in connection* with the basic features of the economic system under discussion. The author explains how the particular economic system gave rise to a certain division of society into classes and shows how *these classes* manifested themselves in the political, family, and intellectual life of that historical period, and how the interests of these classes were reflected in certain schools of economic thought, for example, how the interests of developing capitalism were expressed by the school of free competition and how, at a later period, the interests of the same

class were expressed by the school of vulgar economists
(284), the apologist school. The author rightly points
out the connection between the position of definite classes
and the historical school (284), as well as the school of
Katheder-reformers[9] (the "realistic" or "historico ethical" school), which, with its empty and false conception of
the "non-class" origin and significance of juridico-political
institutions (288), etc., must be characterised as the school
of "compromise" (287). The author connects the theories
of Sismondi and Proudhon with the development of capitalism and with good reason relegates them to the category of
petty-bourgeois economists; he shows the roots of their
ideas in the interests of a specific class in capitalist society,
the class that occupies the "middle, transitional place"
(279), and recognises without circumlocution the reactionary
import of such ideas (280-81). Thanks to the consistency
of his views and his ability to examine the different aspects
of economic life in their relation to the fundamental features of the economic system under discussion, the author has
given a correct assessment of such phenomena as the participation of the workers in the profits of an enterprise (one
of the "forms of wages" that "can very rarely prove profitable for the employer" [pp. 132-33]) or the production
associations which, "being organised within capitalist
relations," "in reality serve only to increase the petty bourgeoisie" (187).

We know that it is precisely these features of Mr. Bogdanov's *Course* that will give rise to more than a few reproaches. It stands to reason that representatives and supporters of the "ethico-sociological" school in Russia[10]
will be dissatisfied. Among the dissatisfied there will also
be those who assume that "the question of the economic
conception of history is purely academic,"* and many others.... But apart from this, one might say partisan, dissatisfaction, the objection will be raised that the posing of
questions so extensively has led to the extraordinarily
condensed exposition of the *Short Course* which, in the brief

---

* This is the opinion of the *Russkaya Mysl*[11] reviewer (1897; November, bibliographical section, p. 517). And to think that there are
such comedians in the world!

space of 290 pages, deals with all periods of economic development, from the clan community and savagery to capitalist cartels and trusts, as well as the political and family life of the world of antiquity and the Middle Ages, and with the history of economic views. Mr. A. Bogdanov's exposition really is condensed to the highest degree, as he himself states in his preface, wherein he says plainly that his book is a "conspectus." There is no doubt that some of the author's terse notes, dealing mostly with facts of a historical character, but sometimes with more detailed problems of theoretical economics, will not be understood by the beginner who wishes to learn something of political economy. We, however, do not think that the author should be blamed for this. We would even say, without fear of being accused of paradoxes, that such notes should be regarded as a merit and not a shortcoming of the book under review. For, indeed, were the author to think of giving a detailed exposition, explanation and basis for every such note, his book would have attained immeasurable dimensions quite out of keeping with the purposes of a short guide. And it would be impossible to outline, in any course, no matter how extensive, all the data of modern science on all periods of economic development and on the history of economic views from Aristotle to Wagner. Had he discarded all such notes, his book would positively have been worsened by the reduction of the scope and significance of political economy. In their present form these terse notes will, we think, be of great benefit both to teachers and students who use the book. Concerning the former this is more than true. The latter will see from the sum total of these notes that political economy cannot be studied carelessly, *mir nichts dir nichts*,* without any previous knowledge, and without making the acquaintance of very many and very important problems in history, statistics, etc. Students will see that they cannot become acquainted with problems of social economy in its development and its influence on social life from one or even from several textbooks or courses that are often distinguished by their "facility of exposi-

---

* As Kautsky aptly remarked in the preface to his well-known book, *Marx's Oekonomische Lehren*. (*Marx's Economic Teachings.—Ed.*)

tion" as well as by their amazing emptiness, their meaningless phrase-mongering; that the most vitally important questions of history and present-day reality are indissolubly bound up with economic questions and that the roots of the latter are to be found in the social relations of production. Such, indeed, is the chief purpose of any guidebook—to give the basic concepts of the subject under discussion and to show in what direction it is to be studied in greater detail and why such a study is important.

Let us now turn to the second part of our remarks and point out those places in Mr. Bogdanov's book that, in our opinion, stand in need of correction or expansion. We hope the respected author will not demur at the trivial and even hole-picking nature of these remarks: in a conspectus individual phrases and even individual words have incomparably greater significance than in an extensive and detailed exposition.

Mr. Bogdanov, in general, uses only the terminology of the school of economics to which he adheres. But when he speaks of the form of value he replaces that term by the expression "formula of exchange" (p. 39, et seq.). This seems to us to be an unfortunate expression; the term "form of value" is really inconvenient in a brief handbook, and it would probably be better to say instead: form of exchange or stage of development of exchange, since, otherwise, we get such expressions as "predominance of the second formula of exchange" (43) (?). In speaking of capital, the author was mistaken in omitting the general formula of capital which would have helped the student to master the fact that trading and industrial capital are of the same kind.

In describing capitalism, the author omitted the question of the growth of the commercial-industrial population at the expense of the agricultural population and that of the concentration of the population in the big cities; this gap is felt all the more because the author, in speaking of the Middle Ages, dealt in detail with the relations between countryside and town (63-66), while in respect of the modern town he said only a couple of words about the countryside being subordinated to it (174).

In discussing the history of industry, the author determinedly placed the "domestic system of capitalist production"* "mid-way between artisan production and manufacture" (p. 156, *Thesis* 6). This simplification does not seem to us, in the present case, to be very convenient. The author of *Capital* described capitalist domestic industry in the section on machine industry and attributed it directly to the transforming effect which the latter exerts on old forms of labour. Actually those forms of domestic labour that prevail, both in Europe and in Russia, in the dressmaking industry, for example, cannot by any means be placed "mid-way between artisan production and manufacture." They come *later* than manufacture in the historical development of capitalism and it would have been worth while, we think, to say a few words about this.

In the chapter on the machine period of capitalism,** a noticeable gap is the absence of a paragraph on the reserve army and capitalist over-population, engendered by machine industry, on its significance in the cyclical development of industry, and on its chief forms. The very scanty mention the author makes of these phenomena on pages 205 and 270 are clearly insufficient.

The author's statement that "during the past fifty years" "profit has been increasing more rapidly than rent" (179) is too bold an assertion. Not only Ricardo (against whom Mr. Bogdanov mentions the point), but Marx as well affirms the general tendency of rent to increase with particular rapidity under all and any circumstances (rent may even increase when the price of grain is decreasing). That reduction in grain prices (and in rent under certain circumstances), brought about recently by the competition of the virgin fields of America, Australia, etc., became acute only in the seventies, and Engels' note to the section on rent (*Das Kapital*, III, 2, 259-60[12]), devoted to the present-day agrarian crisis, is formulated with much greater caution. Engels here postulates the "law" of the growth of rent in civi-

---

* Pp. 93, 95, 147, 156. It seems to us that this term is a successful substitution for the expression "domestic system of large-scale production" that was introduced into our literature by Korsak.

** The strict division of capitalism into a period of manufacture and a period of machine industry is one of the most valuable features of Mr. Bogdanov's *Course*.

lised countries, which explains the "amazing vitality of the class of big landlords," and further says only that this vitality "is gradually being exhausted" (*allmählig sich erschöpft*).

The paragraphs devoted to farming are also marked by excessive brevity. The paragraph on (capitalist) rent shows only in the barest outline that it is conditioned by capitalist farming ("In the period of capitalism land remains private property and takes on the role of capital," 127—and that is all!). In order to avoid all sorts of misunderstandings, a few words, in greater detail, should have been said about the emergence of the rural bourgeoisie, the condition of the farm labourers, and the difference in their condition and that of the factory workers (a lower standard of living and requirements, remnants of their attachment to the land or of various *Gesindeordnungen*,* etc.). It is also a pity that the author did not touch on the genesis of capitalist rent. After the mention he made of the *coloni*[13] and dependent peasants and, further, of the rent paid by our peasants, he should have given a brief characteristic of the course taken by the development of rent from labour rent (*Arbeitsrente*) to rent in kind (*Produktenrente*), then to money rent (*Geldrente*), and finally to capitalist rent (cf. *Das Kapital*, III, 2, *Kap.* 47[14]).

In treating of the supplanting of subsidiary industries by capitalism and the resultant loss of stability experienced by peasant economy, the author expresses himself as follows: "In general the peasant economy becomes poorer—the sum total of values produced decreases" (148). This is most inexact. The process of the ruination of the peasantry by capitalism consists in its dispossession by the rural bourgeoisie, which derives from that same peasantry. Mr. Bogdanov could hardly, for example, describe the decline of peasant farming in Germany without mentioning the *Vollbauer*.** In the place mentioned the author speaks of the peasantry in general, and follows this up immediately with an example from Russian reality; well, to speak of the

---

* Legal injunctions fixing the relations between landowners and serfs.—*Ed.*

** A peasant who is in possession of a full (undivided) plot of land.—*Ed.*

Russian peasantry "in general" is a more than risky business. On the same page the author says: "The peasant either
engages in farming alone or he goes to the manufactory,"
that is, we add on our own part, be becomes either a
rural bourgeois or a proletarian (with a tiny piece of land).
Mention should have been made of this two-sided process.

Lastly, we must mention the absence of examples from
Russian life as a general drawback of the book. On very
many questions (for instance, on the organisation of production in the Middle Ages, the development of machine industry and railways, the growth of the urban population,
crises and syndicates, the difference between manufacto-
ries and factories, etc.) such examples taken from our economic literature would have been of great importance, since
the absence of examples with which he is familiar makes it
much more difficult for the beginner to master the subject.
It seems to us that the filling of these gaps would not greatly
increase the size of the book and would not increase the difficulty of distributing it widely, which is very desirable
in all respects.

Written in February 1898

Published in April 1898
in the magazine *Mir Bozhy*, No. 4

Published according to
the text in the magazine

A NOTE ON THE QUESTION OF THE MARKET THEORY

(APROPOS OF THE POLEMIC of Messrs. TUGAN-BARANOVSKY AND BULGAKOV)

The question of markets in capitalist society, it will be remembered, occupied a highly important place in the theory of the Narodnik economists headed by Messrs. V. V. and N.—on. It is, therefore, perfectly natural that economists who adopt a negative attitude towards the Narodnik theories should deem it essential to call attention to this problem and to explain, first and foremost, the basic, abstract-theoretical points of the "market theory." An attempt to offer such an explanation was undertaken by Mr. Tugan-Baranovsky in 1894 in his book, *Industrial Crises in Modern England*, Chapter 1, Part 2, "The Market Theory"; last year, Mr. Bulgakov devoted his book, *Markets under Capitalist Production* (Moscow, 1897), to the same problem. The two authors are in agreement in their basic views; the central feature of both is an exposition of the noteworthy analysis, "the circulation and reproduction of the aggregate social capital," an analysis made by Marx in the third section of Volume II of *Capital*. The two authors agree that the theories propounded by Messrs. V. V. and N.—on on the market (especially the internal market) in capitalist society are completely erroneous and are due either to an ignoring or a misunderstanding of Marx's analysis. Both authors recognise the fact that developing capitalist production creates its own market mainly for *means of production and not for articles of consumption*; that the realisation of the product in general and of surplus-value in particular is fully explicable without the introduction of a foreign market; that the necessity of a foreign market for a capitalist country is not due to the conditions of realisation (as Messrs. V. V. and N.—on assumed), but to historical conditions, and so on. It would seem that Messrs. Bulgakov and Tugan-Baranovsky, being in such complete accord, would have nothing to argue about and that they could direct their joint efforts to a further and more detailed criticism of Narodnik economics. But in actual fact a polemic arose between these two writers (Bulgakov, op. cit., pages 246-57, *et passim*; Tugan-Baranovsky in *Mir Bozhy*, 1898, No. 6, "Capitalism and the Market," apropos of S. Bulgakov's book). In our opinion both Mr. Bulgakov and Mr. Tugan-Baranovsky have gone a bit too far in their polemic and have given their remarks too personal a character. Let us try and discover whether there is any real difference between them and, if there is, which of them has the greater right on his side.

To begin with, Mr. Tugan-Baranovsky charges Mr. Bulgakov with possessing "little originality" and with liking too much *jurare in verba magistri** (*Mir Bozhy*, 123). "The solution I set forth as regards the question of the role of the foreign market for a capitalist country," says Mr. Tugan-Baranovsky, "adopted *in toto* by Mr. Bulgakov, is not taken from Marx at all." We believe this statement to be untrue, for it was *precisely from Marx* that Mr. Tugan-Baranovsky took his solution to the question; Mr. Bulgakov no doubt also took it from the same source, so that the argument should not be about "originality" but about the understanding of a certain postulate of Marx, about the need to expound Marx in one way or in another. Mr. Tugan-Baranovsky says that Marx "does not touch at all on the question of the foreign market in the second volume" (*loc. cit.*). This is not true. In that same (third) section of the second volume, wherein he analyses the realisation of the product, Marx very definitely explains the relationship of foreign trade and, consequently, of the foreign market, to this question. He says the following:

"Capitalist production does not exist at all without foreign commerce. But when one assumes normal annual reproduction on a given scale one also assumes that foreign commerce *only replaces home products* [*Artikel*—

---

* To swear by the words of the master.—*Ed.*

goods]* *by articles of other use- or bodily form,* without affecting value-relations, hence without affecting either the value-relations in which the two categories 'means of production' and 'articles of consumption' mutually exchange, or the relations between constant capital, variable capital, and surplus-value, into which the value of the product of each of these categories may be divided. The involvement of foreign commerce in analysing the annually reproduced value of products can therefore only confuse without contributing any new element of the problem, or of its solution. For this reason it must be entirely discarded" (*Das Kapital,* II[1], 469.[15] Our italics). Mr. Tugan-Baranovsky's "solution of the question," namely, "...in any country importing goods from abroad there may be a surplus of capital; a foreign market is absolutely essential to such a country" (*Industrial Crises,* p. 429. Quoted in *Mir Bozhy, loc. cit.,* 121)—is merely a paraphrase of Marx's postulate. Marx says that in analysing realisation foreign trade must not be taken into consideration, since it only replaces one article by another. In analysing the question of realisation (Chapter I of the second part of *Industrial Crises*), Mr. Tugan-Baranovsky says, that a country importing goods must export them, that is, must have a foreign market. One may ask, can it be said after this that Mr. Tugan-Baranovsky's "solution of the question" is "not taken from Marx at all"? Mr. Tugan-Baranovsky says further that "Volumes II and III of *Capital* constitute a far from finished rough draft" and that "for this reason we do not find in Volume III conclusions drawn from the splendid analysis given in Volume II" (op. cit., 123). This statement too is inaccurate. In addition to individual analyses of social reproduction (*Das Kapital,* III, 1, 289),[16] there is an explanation of how and to what extent the realisation of constant capital is "independent" of individual consumption and "we find in Volume III" a special chapter (the 49th, "Concerning the Analysis of the Process of Production") devoted to conclusions drawn from the splendid analysis given in Volume II, a chapter in which the results of the analysis

---

* Interpolations in square brackets (within passages quoted by Lenin) have been introduced by Lenin, unless otherwise indicated.—*Ed.*

are applied to the solution of the exceedingly important question of the forms of social revenue in capitalist society. Lastly, we must point out the equal inaccuracy of Mr. Tugan-Baranovsky's assertion that "Marx, in Volume III of *Capital* speaks in a quite different manner on the given question," and that in Volume III we "can even find statements that are decisively refuted by that analysis" (op. cit., 123). On page 122 of his article Mr. Tugan-Baranovsky quotes two such passages from Marx that allegedly contradict the basic doctrine. Let us examine them closely. In Volume III Marx says: "The conditions of direct exploitation, and those of realising it, are not identical. They diverge not only in place and time, but also logically. The first are only limited by the productive power of society, the latter by the proportional relation of the various branches of production and the consumer power of society.... The more productiveness develops, the more it finds itself at variance with the narrow basis on which the conditions of consumption rest" (III, 1, 226. Russian translation, p. 189).[17] Mr. Tugan-Baranovsky interprets these words as follows: "The mere proportional distribution of national production does not guarantee the possibility of marketing the products. The products may not find a market even if the distribution of production is proportional—this is apparently the meaning of the above-quoted words of Marx." No, this is not the meaning of those words. There are no grounds for seeing in them some sort of a *correction* to the theory of realisation expounded in Volume II. Marx is here merely substantiating that contradiction of capitalism which he indicated in other places in *Capital*, that is, the contradiction between the tendency toward the *unlimited* expansion of production and the inevitability of *limited* consumption (as a consequence of the proletarian condition of the mass of the people). Mr. Tugan-Baranovsky will, of course, not dispute the fact that this contradiction is *inherent* in capitalism; and since Marx points to this in the passage quoted, we have no right to look for some other meaning in his words. "The consumer power of society" and the "proportional relation of the various branches of production"—these are not conditions that are isolated, independent of, and unconnected with, each other. On the contrary, a definite condition of consumption is one of the elements of proportionality. In actual fact, the analysis of realisation showed that the formation of a home market for capitalism owes less to articles of consumption than to means of production. From this it follows that Department I of social production (the production of means of production) can and must develop more rapidly than Department II (the production of articles of consumption). Obviously, it does not follow from this that the production of means of production can develop *in complete independence* of the production of articles of consumption and *outside of all connection with it*. In respect of this, Marx says: "As we have seen [Book II, Part III], continuous circulation takes place between constant capital and constant capital.... It is at first independent of individual consumption because it never enters the latter. But this consumption definitely (*definitiv*) limits it nevertheless, since constant capital is never produced for its own sake but solely because more of it is needed in spheres of production whose products go into individual consumption"- (III, 1, 289. Russian translation, 242).[18] In the final analysis, therefore, productive consumption (the consumption of means of production) is always bound up with individual consumption and is always dependent on it. Inherent in capitalism, on the one hand, is the tendency toward the limitless expansion of productive consumption, toward the limitless expansion of accumulation and production, and, on the other, the proletarisation of the masses of the people that sets quite narrow limits for the expansion of individual consumption. It is obvious that we have here a contradiction in capitalist production, and in the above-quoted passage Marx simply reaffirms this contradiction.*

---

* The other passage quoted by Mr. Tugan-Baranovsky has precisely the same meaning (III, 1, 231, cf. S. [*Seite*—German for page.— *Ed.*] 232 to the end of the paragraph),[19] as well as the following passage on crises: "The ultimate cause of all real crises always remains the poverty and limited consumption of the masses as opposed to the drive of capitalist production to develop the productive forces as though only the absolute consuming power of society constituted their limit" (*Das Kapital*, III, 2, 21. Russian translation, p. 395).[20] The following observation by Marx expresses the same idea: "Contradiction in the capitalist mode of production: the labourers as buyers of commodities are important for the market. But as sellers of their own commodity—

The analysis of realisation in Volume II does not in any
way refute this contradiction (Mr. Tugan-Baranovsky's opinion notwithstanding); it shows, on the contrary, the connection between productive and personal consumption. It
stands to reason that it would be a serious error to conclude
from this contradiction of capitalism (or from its other
contradictions) that capitalism is impossible or unprogres-
sive as compared with former economic regimes (in the way
our Narodniks like doing). Capitalism cannot develop except
in a whole series of contradictions, and the indication of
these contradictions merely explains to us the historically
transitory nature of capitalism, explains the conditions and
causes of its tendency to go forward to a higher form.

Summarising all that has been said above, we arrive at
the following conclusion: the solution of the question of the
role of the foreign market as expounded by Mr. Tugan-Baranovsky was taken precisely from Marx; there is no contradiction whatsoever on the question of realisation (or on
the theory of markets) between Volumes II and III of
Capital.

Let us proceed. Mr. Bulgakov accuses Mr. Tugan-Baranovsky of an incorrect assessment of the market theories of
pre-Marxian economists. Mr. Tugan-Baranovsky accuses
Mr. Bulgakov of uprooting Marx's ideas from the scientific
soil in which they grew and of picturing matters as though
"Marx's views had no connection with those of his predeces-
sors." This last reproach is absolutely groundless, for
Mr. Bulgakov not only did not express such an absurd opinion
but, on the contrary, cited the views of representatives of
various pre-Marxian schools. In our opinion, both Mr. Bulgakov and Mr. Tugan-Baranovsky, in outlining the history
of the question, were wrong in paying too little attention to
Adam Smith, who absolutely should have been treated in
the greatest detail in a *special* exposition of the "market

labour-power—capitalist society tends to keep them down to the
minimum price (*Das Kapital*, II, 303).[21] We have already spoken of
Mr. N.—on's incorrect interpretation of this passage in *Novoye Slovo*,[22]
1897, May. (See present edition, Vol. 2, *A Characterisation of Economic
Romanticism*, pp. 168-69.—*Ed.*) There is no contradiction whatsoever
between all these passages and the analysis of realisation in Section
III of Volume II.

theory"; "absolutely" because it was precisely Adam Smith who was the founder of that fallacious doctrine of the division of the social product into variable capital and surplus-value (wages, profit and rent, in Adam Smith's terminology), which persisted until Marx and which, not only prevented the solution of the question of realisation, but did not even pose it correctly. Mr. Bulgakov says in all justice that "with incorrect premises and a false formulation of the problem itself, these disputes [on the market theory, that arose in economic literature] could only lead to empty, scholastic discussions" (op. cit., p. 21, note). The author, incidentally, devoted only one page to Adam Smith, omitting the brilliant, detailed analysis of Adam Smith's theory given by Marx in the 19th chapter of Volume II of *Capital* (§ II, S. 353-83),[23] and instead dwelt on the theories of the secondary and unoriginal theoreticians, J. S. Mill and von Kirchmann. As far as Mr. Tugan-Baranovsky is concerned, he *ignored Adam Smith altogether* and, as a result, in his outline of the views of later economists *omitted their fundamental error* (that of repeating Adam Smith's above-mentioned error). It goes without saying that under these circumstances the exposition could must be satisfactory. We shall confine ourselves to two examples. Having outlined his Scheme No. 1 that explains simple reproduction, Mr. Tugan-Baranovsky says: "But the case of simple reproduction assumed by us does not, of course, give rise to any doubts; the capitalists, according to our assumption, consume all their profits, so it is obvious that the supply of commodities will not exceed the demand" (*Industrial Crises*, p. 409). This is wrong. It was not at all "obvious" to former economists, for they could not explain even the simple reproduction of social capital, and, indeed, it cannot be explained unless it is understood that the value of the social product is divided into *constant capital* + variable capital + surplus-value, and in its material form into two great departments—means of production and articles of consumption. For this reason even this case gave Adam Smith cause for "doubts," in which, as Marx showed, he got tangled up. If the later economists repeated Smith's *error* without sharing his *doubts*, this only shows that they had taken a step backwards in theory as far as the present ques-

tion is concerned. It is likewise incorrect for Mr. Tugan-
Baranovsky to state: "The Say-Ricardo doctrine is correct
theoretically; if its opponents had taken the trouble to make
numerical computations of the way commodities are distributed in capitalist economy, they would easily have understood that their refutation of this theory contains a logical
contradiction" (*loc. cit.*, 427). No. The Say-Ricardo doctrine is
incorrect theoretically—Ricardo repeated Smith's error (see
his *Works*, translated by Sieber, St. Petersburg, 1882,
p. 221), and Say put the finishing touches to it by maintaining
that the difference between the gross and the net product of
society is fully subjective. And however hard Say-Ricardo
and their opponents had applied themselves to "numerical
computations," they would never have reached a solution,
because this is not merely a matter of figures, as Bulgakov
has rightly remarked in respect of another passage in Mr.
Tugan-Baranovsky's book (Bulgakov, *loc. cit.*, p. 21, note).

We now come to another subject for dispute between
Messrs. Bulgakov and Tugan-Baranovsky—the question of
numerical schemes and their significance. Mr. Bulgakov maintains that Mr. Tugan-Baranovsky's Schemes, "owing to their
departure from the model [i.e., from Marx's Schemes, to a
great extent lose their power of conviction and do not explain the process of social reproduction" (*loc. cit.*, 248); and
Mr. Tugan-Baranovsky says that "Mr. Bulgakov does not
properly understand what such schemes are intended for"
(*Mir Bozhy*, No. 6 for 1898, p. 125). In our opinion the truth
in this case is entirely on Mr. Bulgakov's side. It is more
likely that Mr. Tugan-Baranovsky "does not properly understand what the schemes are intended for" when he assumes
that they "prove the deduction," (*ibid.*). Schemes alone cannot prove anything: they can only *illustrate* a process, *if
its separate elements have been theoretically explained*.
Mr. Tugan-Baranovsky compiled his own Schemes which
differed from Marx's (and which were incomparably less
clear than Marx's), at the same time omitting a theoretical
explanation of those elements of the process that they
were supposed to illustrate. The basic postulate of
Marx's theory, that the social product does not consist of
only variable capitall + surplus-value (as Adam Smith,
Ricardo, Proudhon, Rodbertus, and others thought), but of

constant capital+the above two parts—this postulate is
not explained at all by Mr. Tugan-Baranovsky, although he
adopted it in his Schemes. The reader of Mr. Tugan-Baranovsky's book is *unable to understand* this basic thesis of
the new theory. Mr. Tugan-Baranovsky did not in any way
show why it is essential to divide social production into two
departments (I: means of production and II: articles of consumption), although, as Mr. Bulgakov justly remarked, "in
this one division there is greater theoretical meaning than
in all former arguments about the market theory" (*loc. cit.*,
p. 27). This is why Mr. Bulgakov's exposition of the Marxian theory is much clearer and more correct than Mr. Tugan-
Baranovsky's.

In conclusion, examining Mr. Bulgakov's book in greater
detail, we must note the following. About a third of the
book is devoted to questions of the "differences in the turnover of capital" and of the "wages fund." The sections under these headings seem to us to be the least successful. In
the first of these the author tries to add to Marx's analysis (see p. 63, note) and delves into very intricate computations and schemata to illustrate how the process of realisation takes place with differences in the turnover of capital. It seems to us that Mr. Bulgakov's final conclusion
(that, in order to explain realisation with differences in the
turnover of capital, it is necessary to assume that the capitalists in both departments have reserves, cf. p. 85) follows naturally from the general laws of the production and
circulation of capital, so that there was no need to assume
different cases of relations of the turnover of capital in
Departments I and II and to draw up a whole series of
diagrams. The same must be said of the second of the above-
mentioned sections. Mr. Bulgakov correctly points out
Mr. Herzenstein's error in asserting that he had found a contradiction in Marx's theory on this question. The author rightly says that "if the turnover period of all individual capitals
is made to equal one year, at the beginning of the given year
the capitalists will be the owners both of the entire product
of the preceding year and of a sum of money equal to its value" (pp. 142-43). But Mr. Bulgakov was entirely wrong to
take (p. 92, et seq.) the purely scholastic presentation of
the problem by earlier economists (whether wages are derived

from current production or from the production of the preceding working period); he created additional difficulties
for himself in "dismissing" the statement by Marx, who
"seems to contradict his basic point of view," "arguing as
though" "wages are not derived from capital but from current production" (p. 135). But Marx did not pose the question
in this way at all. Mr. Bulgakov found it necessary to "dis-
miss" Marx's statement because he tried to apply to Marx's
theory a completely alien formulation of the question. Once
it has been established how the entire process of social production takes place in connection with the consumption of
the product by different classes of society, how the capitalists contribute the money necessary for the circulation of
the product—once all this has been explained, the question
of whether wages are derived from current or preceding production loses all serious significance. Engels, publisher of
the last volumes of *Capital*, therefore, said in the preface to
Volume II that arguments like that of Rodbertus, for example, as to "whether wages are derived from capital or income,
belong to the domain of scholasticism and are definitely settled in Part III of the second book of *Capital*" (*Das Kapital*,
II, *Vorwort*, *S*. xxi).[24]

Written at the end 1898

Published in January 1899
in the magazine *Nauchnoye
Obozreniye*,[25] No. 1
Signed: *Vladimir Ilyin*

Published according to the
text in the magazine

REVIEW

Parvus. *The World Market and the Agricultural Crisis.*
Economic essays. Translated from the German by L. Y. St. Pe-
tersburg, 1898. Publ O. N. Popova (Educational Library, Series 2,
No. 2). 142 pp. Price 40 kopeks.

This book, by the gifted German journalist who writes
under the pseudonym of Parvus, consists of a number of essays describing some of the phenomena of modern world
economy, with the greatest attention paid to Germany. Parvus' central theme is the development of the world market
and he describes mainly the recent stages of this development
in the period of the decline of England's industrial hegem-
ony. Of the greatest interest are his remarks on the role
being played by the old industrial countries that serve as
a market for the younger capitalist countries: England, for
example, swallows up an ever-growing amount of German
manufactured goods and at the present time takes from one-
fifth to a quarter of the total German export. Parvus employs
the data of commercial and industrial statistics to describe
the peculiar division of labour between the various capitalist countries, some of whom produce mainly for the colonial
market and others for the European market. In the chapter
headed "Towns and Railways" the author makes an extremely interesting attempt to describe the most important
"forms of capitalist towns" and their significance in the general system of capitalist economy. The remaining and greater part of the book (pp. 33-142) is devoted to questions
concerning the contradictions in present-day capitalist
agriculture and the agrarian crisis. Parvus first explains
the influence of industrial development on grain prices, on
ground rent, etc. He then outlines the theory of ground rent
developed by Marx in Volume III of *Capital* and explains

the basic cause of capitalist agrarian crises from the standpoint of this theory. Parvus adds data on Germany to the
purely theoretical analysis of this question and comes to
the conclusion that "the last and basic cause of the agrarian
crisis is increased ground rent due exclusively to capitalist
development and the consequent increased price of land."
"Eliminate these prices," says Parvus, "and European
agriculture will again be able to compete with the Russian
and American." "Its [private property's] only weapon against
the agrarian crisis is, with the exception of fortuitous favourable combinations on the world market, the auctioning of
all capitalist landed properties" (141). The conclusion drawn
by Parvus, therefore, coincides, by and large, with Engels'
opinion; in Volume III of *Capital* Engels pointed to the fact
that the present-day agricultural crisis makes the ground
rents formerly obtained by European landowners impossible.[26] We strongly recommend to all readers who are interested
in the questions mentioned above to acquaint themselves
with Parvus' book. It is an excellent reply to the current
Narodnik arguments on the present agricultural crisis which
are constantly to be met with in the Narodnik press and which
suffer from a most essential shortcoming: the fact of the crisis is examined in disconnection from the general development of world capitalism; it is examined, not from the standpoint of definite social classes, but solely for the purpose of
deducing the petty-bourgeois moral on the viability of small
peasant farming.

The translation of Parvus' book, can, on the whole, be
considered satisfactory, although in places awkward and
heavy turns of speech are to be met with.

Written in February 1899   Published according to
Published in March 1899   the text in the magazine
in the magazine *Nachalo*,[27] No. 3
   Signed: *Vl. Ilyin*

REVIEW

R. Gvozdev. *Kulak Usury, Its Social and Economic Significance.* St. Petersburg, 1899. Publ. N. Garin.

Mr. Gvozdev's book sums up data gathered by our economic literature on the interesting question of kulak usurers. The author mentions a number of indications of the development of commodity circulation and production in the pre-Reform period that brought about the emergence of trading and usurer's capital. He then reviews the material on usury in grain production, on kulakism, in connection with migration, handicraft industries, and peasants' auxiliary employments, as well as in connection with taxation and credit. Mr. Gvozdev rightly points out that representatives of Narodnik economics have held a wrong view of kulakism, regarding it as some sort of an "excrescence" on the organism of "people's production" and not as one of the forms of capitalism, closely and indivisibly bound up with the entire Russian social economy. The Narodniks ignored the connection between kulakism and the differentiation of the peasantry, the closeness of the village usurer "bloodsuckers" and others to the "enterprising muzhiks," those representatives of the rural petty bourgeoisie in Russia. The survivals of medieval institutions that still weigh down on our countryside (social-estate seclusion of the village commune,[28] the tying of the peasant to his allotment,[29] collective liability,[30] the social-estate inequality of taxation) create tremendous barriers against the investment of small amounts of capital in production, against their employment in agriculture and industry. The natural result of all this is the tremendous prevalence of *the lowest and worst forms of capital*, viz., trading and usurer's capital. In the midst of a mass of "economically weak" peasants dragging out an existence of semi-starvation on their small allotments, the small group of prosperous peasants inevitably turns into exploiters of the worst type, enslaving the poor by money loans, winter hiring,[31] etc., etc. Outdated institutions hindering the growth of capitalism both in agriculture and in industry thereby reduce the demand for labour-power but, at the same time, do not protect the peasant from the most shameless and uncurbed exploitation or even from starving to death. A rough estimate of the sums paid by indigent peasants to the kulaks and usurers, quoted by Mr. Gvozdev in his book, shows clearly the groundlessness of the usual comparison made between the Russian allotment-holding peasantry and the West-European proletariat. In actual fact the masses of that peasantry are in a far worse condition than is the rural proletariat in the West; in actual fact our indigent peasants are paupers and the years in which it is necessary to take extraordinary measures of help for millions of starving peasants occur with over-growing frequency. If the fiscal institutions did not artificially lump together the prosperous and poor peasantry, the latter would undoubtedly have to be officially regarded as paupers, which would more accurately and more truthfully define the attitude of modern society to those strata of the population. Mr. Gvozdev's book is valuable because it gives a summary of data on the process of "non-proletarian impoverishment"* and very justly describes this process as the lowest and worst form of the differentiation of the peasantry. Mr. Gvozdev is apparently well acquainted with Russian economic literature, but his book would have gained had he given less space to quotations from various magazines and allowed more space for an independent study of the material. The Narodnik analysis of the available material usually leaves untouched the aspects of the given question that are most important from the theoretical point of view. Furthermore, Mr. Gvozdev's

---

* Parvus, *The World Market and the Agricultural Crisis*. St. Petersburg, 1898, p. 8, footnote.

own arguments are frequently too sweeping and general. This must be said, in particular, of the chapter on handicraft industries. The style of the book suffers, at times, from mannerisms and haziness.

Written in February 1899

Published in March 1899
in the magazine *Nachalo,* No. 3
Signed: *Vl. Ilyin*

Published according to
the text in the magazine

REVIEW

Commercial and Industrial Russia. Handbook for Merchants
and Factory Owners. Compiled under the editorship of A. A. Blau,
Head of the Statistical Division of the Department of Commerce
and Manufactures. St. Petersburg, 1899. Price 10 rubles.

The publishers of this gigantic tome set themselves the
aim of "filling a gap in our economic literature" (p. i), that is,
to give at one and the same time the addresses of commercial
and industrial establishments throughout Russia and information on the "condition of the various branches of industry."
No objection could be made to such a combination of reference and scientific-statistical material, were both the one
and the other sufficiently complete. In the book named above,
unfortunately, the directory completely overwhelms the
statistical material, the latter being incomplete and insufficiently analysed. First of all, this publication compares un-
favourably with previous publications of the same nature,
since it does not give statistical data for *each individual*
establishment or enterprise included in its lists. As a result,
the lists of establishments and enterprises, occupying 2,703
huge columns of small print, lose all their scientific significance. In view of the chaotic state of our commercial and
industrial statistics it is extremely important to have data
precisely on each individual establishment or enterprise,
since our official statistical institutions never make anything like a tolerable analysis of these data but confine
themselves to announcing totals in which relatively reliable
material is mixed up with absolutely unreliable material.
We shall now show that this last remark applies equally to

the book under review; but first let us mention the following original method employed by the compilers. Printing the addresses of establishments and enterprises in each branch of production, they gave the number of establishments and the sum of their turnover for the whole of Russia only; they calculated the average turnover for one establishment in each branch and indicated with a special symbol those having a turnover greater or less than the average. It would have been much more to the purpose (if it was impossible to print information on each individual establishment) to fix a number of categories of establishments and enterprises that are similar for each branch of commerce and industry (according to the amount of turnover, the number of workers, the nature of the motive power, etc.) and to distribute all establishments according to these categories. It would then at least have been possible to judge the completeness and comparability of the material for different gubernias and different branches of production. As far as factory statistics, for example, are concerned, it is enough to read the phenomenally vague definition of this concept on page 1 (footnote) of the publication under review and then glance over the lists of factory owners in some branches to become convinced of the heterogeneity of the statistical material published in the book. It is, therefore, necessary to exercise great caution in dealing with the summarised factory statistics in Section I, Part I of *Commercial and Industrial Russia* (Historical-Statistical Survey of Russian Industry and Trade). We read here that in 1896 (partly also in 1895) there were, throughout the Russian Empire, 38,401 factories with an aggregate output of 2,745 million rubles, employing 1,742,181 workers; these data include excise-paying and non-excise-paying industries and mining and metallurgical enterprises. We are of the opinion that this figure cannot, without substantial verification, be compared with the figures of our factory statistics for previous years. In 1896 a number of branches of production were registered that formerly (until 1894-95) had not come under the heading of "factories": bakeries, fisheries, abattoirs, print-shops, lithograph shops, etc., etc. The value of the total output of all mining and metallurgical establishments in the Empire was fixed at 614 million rubles by original methods about which we are told only that the value of pig-iron is, apparently, repeated in the value of iron and steel. The total number of workers in the mining and metallurgical industries is, on the contrary, apparently underestimated: the figure for 1895-96 was given as 505,000. Either this is an error or many branches have been omitted. From the figures scattered throughout the book it can be seen that for only a few branches in this department the number of workers is 474,000, not including those engaged in coal-mining (about 53,000), salt-mining (about 20,000), stone-quarrying (about 10,000), and in other mining industries (about 20,000). There were more than 505,000 workers in all the mining and metallurgical industries of the Empire in 1890, and precisely these branches of production have developed particularly since that time. For example: in five branches of this division for which historical-statistical data are given in the text of the book (iron founding, wire drawing, machine building, gold- and copper-ware manufacturing) there were, in 1890, 908 establishments, with a total output valued at 77 million rubles and employing 69,000 workers, while in 1896 the figures were—1,444 establishments, with a total output valued at 221.5 million rubles, employing 147,000 workers. By assembling the historical-statistical data scattered throughout the book, which, unfortunately, do not cover all branches of production but only a certain number (cotton processing, chemical production, and more than 45 other branches), we can obtain the following information for the Empire as a whole. In 1890 there were 19,639 factories, with a total output valued at 929 million rubles, employing 721,000 workers, and in 1896 there were 19,162 factories, with a total output valued at 1,708 million rubles, employing 985,000 workers. If we add two branches subject to excise—beet-sugar and distilling—(1890-91—116,000 workers and 1895-96—123,000 workers), we get the number of workers as 837,000 and 1,108,000 respectively, *an increase of nearly one-third in a period of six years*. Note that the decrease in the number of factories is due to the differences in the registration of flour-mills: in 1890, among the factories, 7,003 mills were included (156 million rubles, 29,638 workers), while in 1896 only 4,379 mills (272 million rubles, 37,954 workers) were included.

Such are the data that can be extracted from the publication under review and which allow us to get some conception of the industrial boom in Russia in the nineties. It will be possible to deal with this question in greater detail when the full statistical data for 1896 have been published.

Written in February 1899

Published in March 1899
in the magazine *Nachalo*, No. 3
Signed: *Vl. Ilyin*

Published according to the
text in the magazine

ONCE MORE ON THE THEORY OF REALISATION

My "Note on the Question of the Market Theory (Concerning the Polemic of Messrs. Tugan-Baranovsky and Bulgakov)" was published in the number of *Nauchnoye Obozreniye* for January of the present year (1899) and was followed by P. B. Struve's article, "Markets under Capitalist Production (Apropos of Bulgakov's Book and Ilyin's Article)." Struve "rejects, to a considerable extent, the theory proposed by Tugan-Baranovsky, Bulgakov, and Ilyin" (p. 63 of his article) and expounds his own conception of Marx's theory of realisation.

In my opinion, Struve's polemic against the above-mentioned writers is due not so much to an essential difference of views as to his mistaken conception of the content of the theory he defends. In the first place, Struve confuses the market theory of bourgeois economists who taught that products are exchanged for products and that production, therefore, should correspond to consumption, with Marx's theory of realisation which showed by analysis *how* the reproduction and circulation of the aggregate social capital, i.e., the realisation of the product in capitalist society, takes place.* Neither Marx nor those writers who have expounded his theory and with whom Struve has entered into a polemic deduced the harmony of production and consumption from this analysis, but, on the contrary, stressed forcefully the contradictions that are inherent in capitalism and that are bound to make their appearance in the course of capitalist

---

* See my *Studies*, p. 17, et al. (See present edition, Vol. 2, *A Characterisation of Economic Romanticism*, p. 151, et al.—*Ed.*)

realisation.* Secondly, Struve confuses the abstract theory of realisation (with which his opponents dealt exclusively) with concrete historical conditions governing the realisation of the capitalist product in some one country and some one epoch. This is just the same as confusing the abstract theory of ground rent with the concrete conditions of the development of capitalism in agriculture in some one country. These two basic delusions of Struve engendered a whole series of misunderstandings which can only be cleared up by an analysis of the individual propositions of his article.

1. Struve does not agree with me when I say that in expounding the theory of realisation we must give Adam Smith special emphasis. "If it is a matter of going back to Adam," he writes, "then we should not stop at Smith but at the physiocrats."[32] But this is not so. It was precisely Adam Smith who did not confine himself to admitting the truth (known also to the physiocrats) that products are exchanged for products but raised the question of how the different component parts of social *capital* and the product are replaced (realised) according to their value.** For this reason Marx, who fully recognised that in the theory of the physiocrats, i.e., in Quesnay's *Tableau économique*, some postulates were, "for their time, brilliant"***; who recognised that in the analysis of the process of reproduction Adam Smith had, in some respects, taken a step backwards as compared with the physiocrats (*Das Kapital*, I 2, 612, Anm. 32[34]), nevertheless devoted only about a page and a half to the physiocrats in his review of the history of the question of realisation (*Das Kapital*, II 1, S. 350-51[35]), whereas he devoted

---

* *Ibid.*, pp. 20, 27, 24, et al. (See present edition, Vol. 2, pp. 155, 163-64, 160-61.—*Ed.*)

** Incidentally, in my article in *Nauchnoye Obozreniye* the term "stoimost" (value) was everywhere changed to "tsennost." This was not my doing, but the editor's. I do not regard the use of any one term as being of particularly great importance, but I deem it necessary to state that I used and always use the word "stoimost."

*** Frederick Engels, *Herrn E. Dühring's Umwälzung der Wissenschaft, Dritte Auflage* (Frederick Engels, *Herr Eugen Dühring's Revolution in Science* [*Anti-Dühring*], third ed.—*Ed.*), p. 270,[33] from the chapter written by Marx.

over thirty pages to Adam Smith (*ibid.*, 351-83[36]) and
analysed in detail Smith's basic error which was inherited
by the entire subsequent political economy. It is, therefore,
necessary to pay greater attention to Adam Smith in order
to explain the bourgeois economists' theory of realisation,
since they all repeated Smith's mistake.

2. Mr. Bulgakov quite correctly says in his book that
bourgeois economists confuse simple commodity circulation with capitalist commodity circulation, whereas Marx
established the difference between them. Struve believes
that Mr. Bulgakov's assertion is based on a misunderstanding. In my opinion it is just the opposite, the misunderstanding is not Mr. Bulgakov's but Struve's. And how, indeed, has Struve refuted Mr. Bulgakov? In a manner most
strange: he refutes his postulate by repeating it. Struve says:
Marx cannot be regarded as a champion of that theory
of realisation according: to which the product can be realised inside the given community, because Marx "made a sharp
distinction between simple commodity circulation and
capitalist circulation" (!! p. 48). But that is precisely what Mr.
Bulgakov said! This is precisely why Marx's Theory is not
confined to a repetition of the axiom that products are exchanged for products. That is why Mr. Bulgakov is correct in
regarding the disputes between bourgeois and petty-bourgeois economists on the possibility of over-production to be
"empty and scholastic discussions": the two disputants
confused commodity and capitalist circulation; both of
them repeated Adam Smith's error.

3. Struve is wrong in giving the theory of realisation
the name of the theory of proportional distribution. It is
inaccurate and must inevitably lead to misunderstandings.
The theory of realisation is an abstract* theory that shows
how the reproduction and circulation of the aggregate social capital takes place. The essential premises of this
abstract theory are, firstly, the exclusion of foreign trade,
of the foreign markets. But, by excluding foreign trade, the
theory of realisation does not, by any means, postulate
that a capitalist society has ever existed or could ever

---

* See my article in *Nauchnoye Obozreniye*, p. 37. (See p. 55 of this
volume.—*Ed.*)

exist without foreign trade.* Secondly, the abstract theory
of realisation assumes and must assume the proportional distribution of the product between the various branches of
capitalist production. But, in assuming this, the theory
of realisation does not, by any means, assert that in a capitalist society products are always distributed or could
be distributed proportionally.** Mr. Bulgakov rightly compares the theory of realisation with the theory of value.
The theory of value presupposes and must presuppose the
equality of supply and demand, but it does not by any means
assert that this equality is always observed or could be
observed in capitalist society. The law of realisation, like
every other law of capitalism, is "implemented only by
not being implemented" (Bulgakov, quoted in Struve's article, p. 56). The theory of the average and equal rate of
profit assumes, in essence, the same proportional distribution of production between its various branches. But surely
Struve will not call it a theory of proportional distribution
on these grounds.

4. Struve challenges my opinion that Marx justly
accused Ricardo of repeating Adam Smith's error. "Marx
was wrong," writes Struve. Marx, however, quotes directly
a passage from Ricardo's work (II¹, 383).[37] Struve ignores
this passage. On the next page Marx quotes the opinion of

---

* *Ibid.*, p. 38. (See p. 56 of this volume.—*Ed.*) Cf. *Studies*, p. 25
(see present edition, Vol. 2, p. 162.—*Ed.*): "Do we deny that capitalism
needs a foreign market? Of course not. But the question of a foreign
market has absolutely nothing to do with the question of realisation.
** "Not only the products ... which replace surplus-value, but
also those which replace variable ... and constant capital ... all these
products are realised in the same way, in the midst of 'difficulties,'
in the midst of continuous fluctuations, which become increasingly
violent as capitalism grows" [*Studies*, p. 27 (see present edition, Vol.
2, p. 164.—*Ed.*)]. Perhaps Struve will say that this passage is contradicted by other passages, e.g., that on p. 31 (see present edition, Vol.
2, p. 169.—*Ed.*): "... the capitalists can realise surplus-value"? This
is only a seeming contradiction. Since we take an abstract theory of
realisation (and the Narodniks put forward precisely an abstract theory
of the impossibility of realising surplus-value), the deduction that
realisation is possible becomes inevitable. But while expounding the
abstract theory, it is necessary to indicate the contradictions that
are inherent in the actual process of realisation. This was done in
my article.

Ramsay, who had also noted Ricardo's error. I also indicated another passage from Ricardo's work where he says forth-
rightly: "The whole produce of the land and labour of every
country is divided into three portions: of these, one portion is devoted to wages, another to profits, and the other to
rent" (here constant capital is erroneously omitted. See
Ricardo's Works, translated by Sieber, p. 221). Struve also
passes over this passage in silence. He quotes only one of
Ricardo's comments which points out the absurdity of
Say's argument on the difference between gross and net
revenue. In Chapter 49, Volume III of *Capital*, where
deductions from the theory of realisation are expounded,
Marx quotes precisely this comment of Ricardo, saying the
following about it: "By the way, we shall see later"—apparently, this refers to the still unpublished Volume IV of *Capital*[38]—"that Ricardo nowhere refuted Smith's false analysis of commodity-price, its reduction to the sum of the
values of the revenues (*Revenuen*). He does not bother
with it, and accepts its correctness so far in his analysis
that he 'abstracts' from the constant portion of the value of
commodities. He also falls back into the same way of looking
at things from time to time" (i.e., into Smith's way of looking at things. *Das Kapital*, III, 2, 377. Russian translation,
696).[39] We shall leave the reader to judge who is right:
Marx, who says that Ricardo repeats Smith's error,* or
Struve, who says that Ricardo "knew perfectly well [?]
that the whole social product is not exhausted by wages,
profit, and rent," and that Ricardo "unconsciously [!] wandered away from the parts of the social product that constitute production costs." Is it possible to know *perfectly well*
and at the same time *unconsciously* wander away?

5. Struve not only did not refute Marx's statement
that Ricardo had adopted Smith's error, but repeated that
very error in his own article. "It is strange ... to think,"

---

* The correctness of Marx's assessment is also seen with particular
clarity from the fact that Ricardo shared Smith's fallacious views on
the accumulation of an individual capital. Ricardo thought that the
accumulated part of the surplus-value is expended entirely on wages,
whereas it is expended as: 1) constant capital and 2) wages. See *Das
Kapital*, I[2], 611-13, Chapter 22, § 2.[40] Cf. *Studies*, p. 29, footnote. (See
present edition, Vol. 2, p. 167.—*Ed.*)

he writes, "that any one division of the social product into categories could have substantial importance for the general comprehension of realisation, especially since all portions of the product that is being realised actually take on the form of revenue (gross) in the process of realisation and the classics regarded them as revenues" (p. 48). That is precisely the point—*not* all the portions of the product in realisation take on the form of revenue (gross); it was precisely this mistake of Smith that Marx explained when he showed that a part of the product being realised does not and cannot ever take on the form of revenue. That is the part of the social product which replaces the constant capital that serves for the production of means of production (the constant capital in Department I, to use Marx's terminology). Seed grain in agriculture, for instance, never takes on the form of revenue; coal used for the extraction of more coal never takes on the form of revenue, etc., etc. The process of the reproduction and circulation of the aggregate social capital cannot be understood unless that part of the gross product which can serve only as capital, the part that can never take on the form of revenue, is separated from it.*
In a developing capitalist society this part of the social product must necessarily grow more rapidly than all the other parts of the product. Only this law will explain one of the most profound contradictions of capitalism: the growth of the national wealth proceeds with tremendous rapidity, while the growth of national consumption proceeds (if at all) very slowly.

6. Struve "cannot at all understand" why Marx's differentiation between constant and variable capital "is essential to the theory of realisation" and why I "particularly insist" on it.

Struve's lack of comprehension is, on the one hand, the result of a simple misunderstanding. In the first place, Struve himself admits one point of merit in this differentiation—that it includes not only revenues, but the whole product. Another point of merit is that it links up the analysis of the process of realisation logically with the

* Cf. *Das Kapital*, III, 2, 375-76 (Russian translation, 696),[41] on distinguishing the gross product from gross revenue.

analysis of the process of production of an individual capital. What is the aim of the theory of realisation? It is to show *how* the reproduction and circulation of the aggregate social capital takes place. Is it not obvious from the first glance that the role of variable capital must be radically different from that of constant capital? Products that replace variable capital must be exchanged, in the final analysis, for *articles of consumption* for the workers and meet their usual requirements. The products that replace constant capital must, in the final analysis, be exchanged for *means of production* and must be employed as capital for fresh production. For this reason the differentiation between constant and variable capital is absolutely essential for the theory of realisation. Secondly, Struve's misunderstanding is due to his having, here also, arbitrarily and erroneously understood the theory of realisation as showing that the products are distributed proportionally (see, especially, pp. 50-51). We have said above and say again that such a conception of the content of the theory of realisation is fallacious.

Struve's failure to understand is, on the other hand, due to the fact that he deems it necessary to make a distinction between "sociological" and "economic" categories in Marx's theory and makes a number of general remarks against that theory. I must say, first, that none of this has anything whatsoever to do with the theory of realisation, and, secondly, that I consider Struve's distinction to be vague and that I see no real use for it. Thirdly, that I consider not only debatable, but even directly incorrect, Struve's assertions that "it is indisputable that the relation of the sociological principles" of his theory to the analysis of market phenomena "was not clear to Marx himself," that "the theory of value, as expounded in Volumes I and III of *Capital*, undoubtedly suffers from contradiction."* All these statements of Struve

---

* In opposition to this last statement of Struve let me quote the latest exposition of the theory of value made by K. Kautsky, who states and proves that the law of the average rate of profit "does not abolish the law of value but merely modifies it" (*Die Agrarfrage*, S. 67-68). (*The Agrarian Question*, pp. 67-68.—*Ed.*) We would point out, incidentally, the following interesting statement made by Kautsky in the introduction to his excellent book: "If I have succeeded in developing new and fruitful ideas in this work I am grateful, first and

are mere empty words. They are not arguments but decrees.
They are the anticipated results of the criticism of Marx
which the Neo-Kantians[42] intend to undertake.* If we live
long enough we shall see what the criticism brings. In the
meantime we assert that this criticism has provided nothing
on the theory of realisation.

---

foremost, to my two great teachers for this; I stress this the more readily since there have been, for some time, voices heard even in our
circles that declare the viewpoint of Marx and Engels to be obsolete....
In my opinion this scepticism depends more on the personal peculiarities of the sceptics than on the qualities of the disputed theory. I
draw this conclusion, not only from the results obtained by analysing
the sceptics' objections, but also on the basis of my own personal experience. At the beginning of my ... activities I did not sympathise with
Marxism at all. I approached it quite as critically and with as much
mistrust as any of those who now look down with an air of superiority
on my dogmatic fanaticism. I became a Marxist only after a certain
amount of resistance. But then, and later, whenever I had doubts
regarding any question of principle, I always came to the ultimate
conclusion that it was I who was wrong and not my teachers. A more
profound study of the subject compelled me to admit the correctness of
their viewpoint. Every new study of the subject, therefore, every attempt to re-examine my views served to strengthen my conviction, to
strengthen in me my recognition of the theory, the dissemination and
application of which I have made the aim of my life."

* Incidentally, a few words about this (future) "criticism," on
which Struve is so keen. Of course, no right-minded person will, in
general, object to criticism. But Struve, apparently is repeating his
favourite idea of fructifying Marxism with "critical philosophy." It
goes without saving that I have neither the desire nor the opportunity
to deal here at length with the philosophical content of Marxism and
therefore confine myself to the following remark. Those disciples of
Marx who call, "Back to Kant," have so far produced exactly nothing to
show the necessity for such a turn or to show convincingly that Marx's
theory gains anything from its impregnation with Neo-Kantianism.
They have not even fulfilled the obligation that should be a priority
with them—to analyse in detail and refute the negative criticism
of Neo-Kantianism made by Engels. On the contrary, those disciples
who have gone back to pre-Marxian materialist philosophy and not to
Kant, on the one hand, and to dialectical idealism, on the other, have
produced a well-ordered and valuable exposition of dialectical materialism, have shown that it constitutes a legitimate and inevitable
product of the entire latest development of philosophy and social science. It is enough for me to cite the well-known work by Mr. Beltov
in Russian literature and *Beiträge zur Geschichte des Materialismus*
(Stuttgart, 1896)[43] [*Essays on the History of Materialism* (Stuttgart,
1896).—*Ed.*] in German literature.

7. On the question of the significance of Marx's Schemes

In the third section of *Capital* II, Struve maintains that the abstract theory of realisation can be well explained by the most varied methods of dividing the social product. This amazing assertion is to be fully explained by Struve's basic misunderstanding—that the theory of realisation "is completely exhausted" (??!) by the banality that products are exchanged for products. Only this misunderstanding could have led Struve to write such a sentence: "The role played by these masses of commodities [those being realised] in production, distribution, etc., whether they represent capital (*sic*!!) and what sort of capital, constant or variable, is of absolutely no significance to the essence of the theory under discussion" (51). It is of no significance to Marx's theory of realisation, a theory that consists in the analysis of the reproduction and circulation of the aggregate social *capital*, whether or not commodities constitute capital!! This amounts to saying that as far as the essence of the theory of ground rent is concerned, there is no significance in whether or not the rural population is divided into landowners, capitalists, and labourers, since the theory is reduced, as it were, to an indication of the differing fertility of the different plots of land.

Only because of the same misunderstanding could Struve have asserted that the "natural relations between the elements of social consumption—social *metabolism*—can best be shown," not by the Marxian division of the product, but by the following division: means of production+articles of consumption+surplus-value (p. 50).

What is this social metabolism? Primarily it is the exchange of means of production for articles of consumption. How can this exchange be shown if surplus-value is especially *separated from* means of production and *from* articles of consumption? After all, surplus-value is embodied either in means of production or in articles of consumption! Is it not obvious that such a division, which is logically groundless (in that it confuses division according to the natural form of the product with division by elements of value), *obscures* the process of social metabolism?*

---

* Let us remind the reader that Marx divides the aggregate social product into two departments according to the natural form of the

8. Struve says that I ascribed to Marx the bourgeois-apologetic theory of Say-Ricardo (52), the theory of harmony between production and consumption (51), a theory that is in howling contradiction to Marx's theory of the evolution and eventual disappearance of capitalism (51-52); that, therefore, my "perfectly correct argument" that Marx, in both the second and third volumes, stressed the contradiction, inherent in capitalism, between the unlimited expansion of production and the limited consumption on the part of the masses of the people, "jettisons that theory of realisation ... whose defender" I am "in other cases."

This statement of Struve is likewise untrue and derives likewise from the above-mentioned misunderstanding to which he has become subject.

Whence comes Struve's assumption that I do not understand the theory of realisation as an analysis of the process of reproduction and circulation of the aggregate social capital, but as a theory which says only that products are exchanged for products, a theory which preaches the harmony of production and consumption? Struve could not have shown by an analysis of my articles that I understand the theory of realisation in the second way, for I have stated definitely and directly, that I understand it in the first way. In the article "A Characterisation of Economic Romanticism," in the section devoted to an explanation of Smith's and Sismondi's error, I say: "The whole question is *how* realisation takes place—*that is*, the replacement of all parts of the social product. Hence, the point of departure in discussing social capital and revenue—or, what is the same thing, the realisation of the product in capitalist society—must be the distinction between ... *means of production* and *articles of consumption*" (*Studies*, 17).* "The problem of realisation consists in analysing the *replacement* of all parts of the social product in terms of value and in terms of material form" (*ibid.*, 26).** Is not Struve repeating this when he

---

product: I—means of production and II—articles of consumption. In each of these departments the product is divided into three parts according to elements of value: 1) constant capital, 2) variable capital, and 3) surplus-value.

* See present edition, Vol. 2, p. 152.—*Ed.*
** *Ibid.*, p. 162.—*Ed.*

says—supposedly against me—that the theory which
interests us "shows the mechanism of realisation ... insofar as
that realisation is effected" *(Nauchnoye Obozreniye,* 62)?
Am I contradicting *that* theory of realisation which I defend when I say that realisation is effected "in the midst of
difficulties, in the midst of continuous fluctuations, which
become increasingly violent as capitalism grows, in the midst
of fierce competition, etc."? *(Studies,* 27)*; when I say
that the Narodnik theory "not only reveals a failure to understand this realisation, but, in addition, reveals *an extremely
superficial understanding of the contradictions inherent in
this realisation"* (26-27)**; when I say that the realisation of the product, effected not so much on account of
articles of consumption as on account of means of production, "is, of course, a contradiction, but the sort of contradiction that exists in reality, that springs from the very
nature of capitalism" (24),*** a contradiction that "fully
corresponds to the historical mission of capitalism and to
its specific social structure: the former" (the mission) "is to
develop the productive forces of society (production for
production); the latter" (the social structure of capitalism)
"precludes their utilisation by the mass of the population"
(20)****?

9. Apparently there are no differences of opinion between
Struve and me on the question of the relations between
production and consumption in capitalist society. But if
Struve says that Marx's postulate (which asserts that consumption is not the aim of capitalist production) "bears the
obvious stamp of the polemical nature of Marx's whole
system in general," that "it is tendentious" (53), then I most
decidedly challenge the appropriateness and justification of
such expressions. It is a fact that consumption is not the aim
of capitalist production. The contradiction between this fact
and the fact that, in the final analysis, production is bound
up with consumption, that it is also dependent on consumption in capitalist society—this contradiction does not spring
from a doctrine but from reality. Marx's theory of realisation

---

* See present edition, Vol. 2, p. 164.—*Ed.*
** *Ibid.,* p. 163.—*Ed.*
*** *Ibid.,* p. 160.—*Ed.*
*** *Ibid.,* p. 156.—*Ed.*

has, incidentally, tremendous scientific value, precisely because it shows how this contradiction occurs, and because it puts this contradiction in the foreground. "Marx's system" is of a "polemical nature," not because it is "tendentious,"* but because it provides an exact picture, in theory, of all the contradictions that are present in reality. For this reason, incidentally, all attempts to master "Marx's system" without mastering its "polemical nature" are and will continue to be unsuccessful: the "polemical nature" of the system is nothing more than a true reflection of the "polemical nature" of capitalism itself.

10. "What is the real significance of the theory of realisation?" asks Mr. Struve and answers by quoting the opinion of Mr. Bulgakov, who says that the possible expansion of capitalist production is actually effected even if only by a series of crises. "Capitalist production is increasing throughout the world," says Mr. Bulgakov. "This argument," objects Struve, "is quite groundless. The fact is that the real 'expansion of capitalist production' is not by any means effected in that ideal and isolated capitalist state which Bulgakov presupposes and which, by his assumption, is sufficient unto itself, but in the arena of world economy where the most differing levels of economic development and differing forms of economic existence come into collision" (57).

Thus, Struve's objection may be summed up as follows: In actual fact realisation does not take place in an isolated, self-sufficing, capitalist state, but "in the arena of world economy," i.e., by the marketing of products in other countries. It is easy to see that this objection is based on an error. Does the problem of realisation change to any extent if we do not confine ourselves to the home market ("self-sufficing" capitalism) but make reference to the foreign market, if we take several countries instead of only one? If we do not think that the capitalists throw their goods into the sea or give them away gratis to foreigners—if we do not take individual, exceptional cases or periods, it is obvious that we must accept a certain equilibrium of export and import.

---

* The classical example of gentlemen à la A. Skvortsov who sees tendentiousness in Marx's theory of the average rate of profit could serve as a warning against the use of such expressions.

If a country exports certain products, realising them "in
the arena of world economy," it imports other products in
their place. From the standpoint of the theory of realisation
it must necessarily be accepted that "foreign commerce only
replaces home products [*Artikel*—goods] by articles of other
use- or bodily form" (*Das Kapital*, II, 469.[44] Quoted by me in
Nauchnoye Obozreniye, p. 38*). Whether we take one country
or a group of countries, the essence of the process of realisation does not change in the slightest. In his objection to
Mr. Bulgakov, therefore, Struve repeats the old error of the
Narodniks, who connected the problem of realisation with
that of the foreign market.**

In actual fact these two questions have nothing in common.
The problem of realisation is an abstract problem that is
related to the general theory of capitalism. Whether we take
one country or the whole world, the basic laws of realisation, revealed by Marx, remain the same.

The problem of foreign trade or of the foreign market is
an historical problem, a problem of the concrete conditions
of the development of capitalism in some one country and
in some one epoch.***

11. Let us dwell for a while on the problem that has "long
interested" Struve: what is the real scientific value of the
theory of realisation?

It has exactly the same value as have all the other postulates of Marx's abstract theory. If Struve is bothered by
the circumstance that "perfect realisation is the ideal of
capitalist production, but by no means its reality," we must
remind him that all other laws of capitalism, revealed by
Marx, also depict only the ideal of capitalism and not its
reality. "We need present," wrote Marx, "only the inner organisation of the capitalist mode of production, in its ideal
average (*in ihrem idealen Durchschnitt*), as it were" (*Das
Kapital*, III, 2, 367; Russian translation, p. 688).[45] The
theory of capital assumes that the worker receives the full
value of his labour-power. This is the ideal of capitalism,

---

* See present volume, pp. 56-57.—*Ed.*
** I analysed this error of the Narodniks in my *Studies*, pp. 25-29.
(See present edition, Vol. 2, pp. 161-66.—*Ed.*)
*** Ibid., cf. *Nauchnoye Obozreniye*, No. 1, p. 37 (see present
volume, p. 55.—*Ed.*)

but by no means its reality. The theory of rent presupposes that the entire agrarian population has been completely divided into landowners, capitalists, and hired labourers. This is the ideal of capitalism, but by no means its reality. The theory of realisation presupposes the proportional distribution of production. This is the ideal of capitalism, but by no means its reality.

The scientific value of Marx's theory is its explanation of the process of the reproduction and circulation of the aggregate social capital. Further, Marx's theory showed how the contradiction, inherent in capitalism, comes about, how the tremendous growth of production is definitely not accompanied by a corresponding growth in people's consumption. Marx's theory, therefore, not only does not restore the apologetic bourgeois theory (as Struve fancies), but, on the contrary, *provides a most powerful weapon against apologetics*. It follows from the theory that, *even* with an ideally smooth and proportional reproduction and circulation of the aggregate social capital, the contradiction between the growth of production and the narrow limits of consumption is inevitable. But in reality, *apart from this*, realisation does not proceed in ideally smooth proportions, but only amidst "difficulties," "fluctuations," "crises," etc.

Further, Marx's theory of realisation provides a most powerful weapon against the petty-bourgeois reactionary criticism of capitalism, as well as against apologetics. It was precisely this sort of criticism against capitalism that our Narodniks tried to substantiate with their fallacious theory of realisation. Marx's conception of realisation inevitably leads to the recognition of the historical progressiveness of capitalism (the development of the means of production and, consequently, of the productive forces of society) and, thereby, it not only does not obscure the historically transitory nature of capitalism, but, on the contrary, explains it.

12. "In relation to an ideal or isolated, self-sufficing capitalist society," asserts Struve, extended reproduction would be impossible, "since the necessary additional workers can nowhere be obtained."

I certainly cannot agree with Struve's assertion. Struve has not proved, and it cannot be proved, that it is impossible

to obtain additional workers from the reserve army. Against
the fact that additional workers can be obtained from
the natural growth of the population, Struve makes the un-
substantiated statement that "extended reproduction, based
on the natural increase in the population, may not be arith-
metically identical with simple reproduction, but from the
practical capitalist standpoint, i.e., economically, may
fully coincide with it." Realising that the impossibility of
obtaining additional workers cannot be proved theoretically,
Struve evades the question by references to historical and
practical conditions. "I do not think that Marx could solve
the historical [?!] question on the basis of this absolutely
abstract construction." ... "Self-sufficing capitalism is the
historically [!] inconceivable limit." ... "The intensification
of the labour that can be forced on a worker is extremely
limited, not only in actual fact, but also logically." ... "The
constant raising of labour productivity cannot but weaken
the very compulsion to work." ...

The illogicality of these statements is as clear as daylight! None of Struve's opponents has ever or anywhere
given voice to the absurdity that an historical question can
be solved with the aid of abstract constructions. In the
present instance Struve himself did not propound an historical question, but one that is an absolute abstraction, a
purely theoretical question, "in relation to an ideal capitalist society" (57). Is it not obvious that he is simply evading the question? I, of course, would not dream of denying
that there exist numerous historical and practical conditions
(to say nothing of the immanent contradictions of capitalism)
that are leading and will lead to the destruction of capitalism rather than to the conversion of present-day capitalism
into an ideal capitalism. But on the purely theoretical
question "in relation to an ideal capitalist society" I still
retain my former opinion that there are no theoretical
grounds for denying the possibility of extended reproduction
in such a society.

13. "Messrs. V. V. and N.—on have pointed out the
contradictions and stumbling-blocks in the capitalist development of Russia, but they are shown Marx's Schemes
and told that capital is always exchanged for capital..."
(Struve, op. cit., 62).

This is sarcasm in the highest degree. The pity is that matters are depicted in an absolutely false light. Anyone who reads Mr. V. V.'s *Essays on Theoretical Economics* and Section XV of the second part of Mr. N. —on's *Sketches* will see that both these writers raised precisely the abstract-theoretical question of realisation—the realisation of the product in capitalist society in general. This is a fact. There is another circumstance which is also a fact; other writers, those who opposed them, "deemed it essential to explain, *first and foremost*, the basic, *abstract-theoretical* points of the market theory" (as is stated in the opening lines of my article in *Nauchnoye Obozreniye*). Tugan-Baranovsky wrote on the theory of realisation in the chapter of his book on crises, which bears the subtitle, "The Market Theory." Bulgakov gave his book the subtitle, "A Theoretical Study." It is therefore a question of who confuses abstract-theoretical and concrete-historical questions, Struve's opponents or Struve himself?

On the same page of his article Struve quotes my statement to the effect that the necessity for a foreign market is not due to the conditions of realisation but to historical conditions. "But," Struve objects (a very typical "but"!), "Tugan-Baranovsky, Bulgakov, and Ilyin have examined only the abstract conditions of realisation and have not examined the historical conditions" (p. 62).

The writers mentioned did not explain historical conditions for the precise reason that they took it upon themselves to speak of abstract-theoretical and not concrete-historical questions. In my book, *On the Question of the Development of Capitalism in Russia* ("The Home Market for Large-Scale Industry and the Process of Its Formation in Russia"),* the printing of which has now (March 1899) been completed, I did not raise the question of the market theory but of a home market for Russian capitalism. In this case, therefore, the abstract truths of theory play only the role of guiding principles, a means of analysing concrete data.

---

* The reference is to *The Development of Capitalism in Russia* (see present edition, Vol. 3).—*Ed.*

14. Struve "wholly supports" his "point of view" on the theory of "third persons" which he postulated in his *Critical Remarks*. I, in turn, wholly support what I said in this connection at the time *Critical Remarks* appeared.[46]

In his *Critical Remarks* (p. 251) Struve says that Mr. V. V.'s argument "is based on a complete theory, an original one, of markets in a developed capitalist society." "This theory," says Struve, "is correct insofar as it confirms the fact that surplus-value cannot be realised by consumption, either by the capitalists or the workers, and presupposes consumption by third persons." By these third persons "in Russia" Struve "presumes the Russian agricultural peasantry" (p. 61 of the article in *Nauchnoye Obozreniye*).

And so, Mr. V. V. propounds a complete and original theory of markets in a developed capitalist society, and the Russian agricultural peasantry is pointed out to him! Is this not confusing the abstract-theoretical question of realisation with the concrete-historical question of capitalism in Russia? Further, if Struve acknowledges Mr. V. V.'s theory to be even partly correct, he must have overlooked Mr. V. V.'s basic theoretical errors on the question of realisation, he must have overlooked the incorrect view that the "difficulties" of capitalist realisation are confined to surplus-value or are specially bound up with that part of the value of the product—he must have overlooked the incorrect view that connects the question of the foreign market with the question of realisation.

Struve's statement that the Russian agricultural peasantry, by the differentiation within it, creates a market for our capitalism is perfectly correct (in the above-mentioned book I demonstrated this thesis in detail by an analysis of Zemstvo statistical data). The theoretical substantiation of this thesis, however, relates in no way to the theory of the realisation of the product in capitalist society, but to the theory of the formation of capitalist society. We must also note that calling the peasants "third persons" is not very fortunate and is likely to cause a misunderstanding. If the peasants are "third persons" for capitalist industry, then the industrial producers, large and small, the factory owners and workers, are "third persons" for capitalist farming. On the other hand, the peasant farmers ("third persons") create a market for capitalism only to the extent that they are differentiated into the classes of capitalist society (rural bourgeoisie and rural proletariat), i.e., only insofar as they cease to be *third* persons and become *active* persons in the capitalist system.

15. Struve says: "Bulgakov makes the very subtle remark that no difference in principle can be discerned between the home and the foreign market for capitalist production." I fully agree with this remark: in actual fact a tariff or political frontier is very often quite unsuitable as aline drawn between the "home" and "foreign" markets. But for reasons just indicated I cannot agree with Struve that "the theory asserting the necessity for third persons ... arises out of this." One demand does arise directly out of this: do not stop at the traditional separation of the home and foreign markets when analysing the question of capitalism. This distinction, groundless from a strictly theoretical point of view, is of particularly little use for such countries as Russia. It could be replaced by another division which distinguishes, for instance, the following aspects of capitalist development: 1) the formation and development of capitalist relations within the bounds of a certain fully populated and occupied territory; 2) the expansion of capitalism to other territories (in part completely unoccupied and being colonised by emigrants from the old country, and in part occupied by tribes that remain outside the world market and world capitalism). The first side of the process might be called the development of capitalism in depth and the second its development in breadth.* Such a division would include the whole process of the historical development of capitalism: on the one hand, its development in the old countries, where for centuries the forms of capitalist relations up to and including large-scale machine industry have

---

* It goes without saying that the two sides of the process are actually closely united, and that their separation is a mere abstraction, merely a method of investigating a complicated process. My book mentioned above is devoted entirely to the first side of the process. See Chapter VIII, Section V.

been built up; on the other hand, the mighty drive of developed capitalism to expand to other territories! to populate and plough up new parts of the world, to set up colonies and to draw savage tribes into the whirlpool of world capitalism. In Russia this last-mentioned capitalist tendency has been and continues to be seen most clearly in our outlying districts whose colonisation has been given such tremendous impetus in the post-Reform, capitalist period of Russian history. The south and south-east of European Russia, the Caucasus, Central Asia, and Siberia serve as something like colonies for Russian capitalism and ensure its tremendous development, not only in depth but also in breadth.

Finally, the division proposed is convenient because it clearly determines the range of questions which precisely is embraced by the theory of realisation. It is clear that the theory applies only to the first side of the process, only to the development of capitalism in depth. The theory of realisation (i.e., the theory which examines the process of the reproduction and circulation of the aggregate social capital) must necessarily take an isolated capitalist society for its constructions, i.e., must ignore the process of capitalist expansion to other countries, the process of commodity exchange between countries, because this process does not provide anything for the solution of the question of realisation and only transfers the question from one country to several countries. It is also obvious that the abstract theory of realisation must take as a prerequisite an ideally developed capitalist society.

In regard to the literature of Marxism, Struve makes the following general remark: "The orthodox chorus still continues to dominate, but it cannot stifle the new stream of criticism because true strength in scientific questions is always on the side of criticism and not of faith." As can be seen from the foregoing exposition, we have satisfied ourselves that the "new stream of criticism" is not a guarantee against the repetition of old errors. No, let us better remain "under the sign of orthodoxy"! Let us not believe that orthodoxy means taking things on trust, that orthodoxy precludes critical application and further development, that it permits historical problems to be obscured by abstract schemes. If there are orthodox disciples who are guilty of these truly grievous sins, the blame must rest entirely with those disciples and not by any means with orthodoxy, which is distinguished by diametrically opposite qualities.

Written at the end 1898

Published in January 1899 in the magazine *Nauchnoye Obozreniye,* No. 8 Signed: *V. Ilyin*

Published according to the text in the magazine

REVIEW

Karl Kautsky. *Die Agrarfrage. Eine Uebersicht über die Tendenzen der modfernen Landwirtschaft und die Agrarpolitik u.s.w.* *
Stuttgart, Dietz, 1899.

Kautsky's book is the most important event in present-day economic literature since the third volume of *Capital*. Until now Marxism has lacked a systematic study of capitalism in agriculture. Kautsky has filled this gap with "The Development of Agriculture in Capitalist Society," the first part (pp. 1-300) of his voluminous (450-page) book. He justly remarks in his preface that an "overwhelming" mass of statistical and descriptive economic material on the question of agricultural capitalism has been accumulated and that there is an urgent need to reveal the "basic tendencies" of economic evolution in this branch of the economy in order to demonstrate the varied phenomena of agricultulal capitalism as "partial manifestations of one common [integral] process" (*eines Gesammtprozesses*). It is true that agricultural forms and the relations among the agricultural population in contemporary society are marked by such tremendous variety that there is nothing easier than to seize upon a whole mass of facts and pointers taken from any inquiry that will "confirm" the views of the given writer. This is precisely the method used in a large number of arguments by our Narodnik press which tries to prove the viability of petty peasant economy or even its superiority over large-scale production.

---

* Karl Kautsky. *The Agrarian Question.* A Review of the Tendencies in Modern Agriculture and Agrarian Policy, etc.—*Ed.*

in agriculture. A distinguishing feature of all these arguments is that they isolate individual phenomena, cite individual cases, and do not even make an attempt to connect them with the general picture of the whole agrarian structure of capitalist countries in general and with the basic tendencies of the entire present-day evolution of capitalist farming. Kautsky does not make this usual mistake. He has been studying the problem of capitalism in agriculture for over twenty years and is in possession of very extensive material; in particular, Kautsky bases his inquiry on the data of the latest agricultural censuses and questionnaires in England, America, France (1892), and Germany (1895). He never loses his way amidst piles of facts and never loses sight of the connection between the tiniest phenomenon and the general structure of capitalist farming and the general evolution of capitalism.

Kautsky does not confine himself to any one particular question, e.g., the relations between large-scale and small-scale production in agriculture, but deals with tha general question of whether or not capital is bringing agriculture under its domination, whether it is changing forms of production and forms of ownership in agriculture and how this process is taking place. Kautsky gives every recognition to the important rola played by pre-capitalist and non-capitalist forms of agriculture in modern society and to the necessity of examining ths relationship of these forms to the purely capitalist forms; he begins his investigation with an extremely brilliant and precise characterisation of the patriarchal peasant economy and of agriculture in the feudal epoch. Having thus established the starting-points for the development of capitalism in agriculture, he proceeds to characterise "modern agriculture." The description is given first of all from the technical standpoint (the crop rotation system, division of labour, machinery, fertilisers, bacteriology), and the reader is given a splendid picture of the great revolution capitalism has wrought in the course of a few decades by making agriculture a *science* instead of a routine craft. Further comes the investigation of "the capitalist character of modern agriculture"—a brief and popularly written, but extremely precise and talented, exposition of Marx's theory of profit and rent. Kautsky shows that the tenant farmer system

and the mortgage system are merely two sides of one and the
same process, noted by Marx, of separating the agricultural
producers from the landowners. The relations between large-
scale and small-scale production are then examined and it is
shown that the technical superiority of the former over the
latter is beyond doubt. Kautsky effectively demonstrates
this thesis and explains in detail how the stability of petty
production in agriculture does not depend in any way on its
technical rationality but on the fact that the small peasants
work far harder than hired labourers and reduce their vital
necessities to a level lower than that of the latter.
The supporting data which Kautsky cites are in the
highest degree interesting and clear-cut. An analysis of
the question of associations in agriculture leads Kautsky
to the conclusion that associations are undoubtedly
indicative of progress but that they are a transition to
capitalism and not to communal production; associations
do not decrease but increase the superiority of large-scale
over small-scale agricultural production. It is absurd to think
that the peasant in modern society can go over to communal
production. Reference is usually made to statistical data
which do not show that the small producer is ousted by the
big producer, but which merely serve to show that the development of capitalism in agriculture is much more complicated
than in industry. In industry, too, such manifestations as the
spread of capitalist work in the home, etc., are not infrequently interconnected with the basic tendency development.
But in agriculture the ousting of the small producer is hampered, primarily, by the limited size of the land area; the
buying-up of small holdings to form a big holding is a very
difficult matter; with intensified farming an increase in the
quantity of products obtained is sometimes compatible with
a reduction in the area of the land (for which reason statistics
operating exclusively with data on the size of the farm have
little evidential significance). The concentration of production takes place through the buying-up of many holdings by
one proprietor; the latifundia thus formed serve as a basis
for one of the higher forms of large-scale capitalist farming.
Lastly, it would not even be advantageous for the big landowners to force out the small proprietors completely: the
latter provide them with hand[s]! For this reason the landown-

ers and capitalists frequently pass laws that artificially maintain the small peasantry. Petty farming becomes stable when it ceases to compete with large-scale farming, when it is turned into a supplier of labour-power for the latter. The relations between large and small landowners come still closer to those of capitalists and proletarians. Kautsky devotes a special chapter to the "proletarisation of the peasantry," one that is rich in data, especially on the question of the "auxiliary employments" of the peasants, i.e., the various forms of hired labour.

After elucidating the basic features of the development of capitalism in agriculture, Kautsky proceeds to denuonstrate the historically transitory character of this system of social economy. The more capitalism develops, the greater the difficulties that commercial (commodity) farming encounters. The monopoly in land ownership (ground rent), the right of inheritance, and entailed estates[47] hamper the rationalisation of farming. The towns exploit the countryside to an ever greater extent, taking the best labour forces away from the farmers and absorbing an ever greater portion of the wealth produced by the rural population, whereby the rural population is no longer able to return to the soil that which is taken from it. Kautsky deals in particularly great detail with the depopulating of the countryside and acknowledges to the full that it is the middle stratum of farmers which suffers least of all from a shortage of labour-power, and he adds that "good citlzens" (we may also add: and the Russian Narodniks) are mistaken in rejoicing at this fact, in thinking that they can see in it the beginnings of a rebirth of the peasantry which refutes the applicability of Marx's theory to agriculture. The peasantry may suffer less than other agricultural classes from a shortage of hired labour, but it suffers much more from usury, tax oppression, the irrationality of its economy, soil exhaustion, excessive toil, and underconsumption. The fact that not only agricultural labourers, but even the children of the peasants, flee to the towns is a clear refutation of the views of optimistically-minded pettybourgeois economists! But the biggest changes in the condition of European agriculture have been brought about by the competition of cheap grain imported from America, the Argentine, India, Russia, and other countries. Kautsky made

a detailed study of the significance of this fact that arose out
of the development of industry in quest for markets. He
describes the decline in European grain production under the
impact of this competition, as well as the lowering of rent,
and makes a particularly detailed study of the "industrialisation of agriculture" which is manifested, on the one hand,
in the industrial wage-labour of the small peasants and, on the
other, in the development of agricultural technical production
(distilling, sugar refining, etc.), and even in the elimination of some branches of agriculture by manufacturing industries. Optimistic economists, says Kautsky, are mistaken in
believing that such changes in European agriculture can save
it from crisis; the crisis is spreading and can only end in a
general crisis of capitalism as a whole. This, of course, does
not give one the least right to speak of the ruin of agriculture,
but its conservative character is gone for ever; it has entered
a state of uninterrupted transformation, a state that is typical of the capitalist mode of production in general. "A
large area of land under large-scale agricultural production,
the capitalist nature of which is becoming more and more
pronounced; the growth of leasing and mortgaging, the industrialisation of agriculture—these are the elements that
are preparing the ground for the socialisation of agricultural
production...." It would be absurd to think, says Kautsky in
conclusion, that one part of society develops in one direction
and another in the opposite direction. In actual fact "social
development in agriculture is taking the same direction as in
industry."

Applying the results of his theoretical analysis to questions
of agrarian policy, Kautsky naturally opposes all attempts
to support or "save" peasant economy. There is no reason
even to think that the village commune, says Kautsky,
could go over to large-scale communal farming (p. 338,
section, "Der Dorfkommunismus"*; cf. p. 339). "The
protection of the peasantry (der Bauernschutz) does not mean
protection of the person of the peasant (no one, of course,
would object to such protection), but protection of the
peasant's property. Incidentally, it is precisely the peasant's
property that is the main cause of his impoverishment and

---

* Village communism.—Ed.

his degradation. Hired agricultural labourers are now quite frequently in a better position than the small peasants. The protection of the peasantry is not protection from poverty but the protection of the fetters that chain the peasant to his poverty" (p. 320). The radical transformation of agriculture by capitalism is a process that is only just beginning, but it is one that is advancing rapidly, bringing about the transformation of the peasant into a hired labourer and increasing the flight of the population from the countryside. Attempts to check this process would be reactionary and harmful: no matter how burdensome the consequences of this process may be in present-day society, the consequences of checking the process would be still worse and would place the working population in a still more helpless and hopeless position. Progressive action in present-day society can only strive to lessen the harmful effects which capitalist advance exerts on the population, to increase the consciousness of the people and their capacity for collective self-defence. Kautsky, therefore, insists on the guarantee of freedom of movement, etc., on the abolition of all the remnants of feudalism in agriculture (e.g., *die Gesindeordnungen,** which place farm workers in a personally dependent, semi-serf position), on the prohibition of child labour under the age of fourteen, the establishment of an eight-hour working day, strict sanitary police to exercise supervision over workers' dwellings, etc., etc.

It is to be hoped that Kautsky's book will appear in a Russian translation.[48]

Written in March 1899
Published in April 1899
in the magazine *Nachalo,* No. 4
Signed: *Vl. Ilyin*

Published according to
the text in the magazine

---

* Legislation defining relations between landowners and serfs.— *Ed.*

REVIEW

J. A. Hobson. *The Evolution of Modern Capitalism.* Translated
from the English. St. Petersburg, 1898. Publ. O. N. Popova.
Price 1 rb. 50 kop.

Hobson's book is, strictly speaking, not a study of the evolution of modern capitalism, but a series of sketches, based
mainly on English data, dealing with the most recent industrial development. Hence, the title of the book is somewhat
broad: the author does not touch upon agriculture at all and
his examination of industrial economics is far from complete.
Like the well-known writers Sidney and Beatrice Webb,
Hobson is a representative of one of the advanced trends of
English social thought. His attitude towards "modern capitalism" is critical; he fully admits the necessity of replacing
it by a higher form of social economy and treats the problem
of its replacement with typically English reformist practi-
cality. His conviction of the need for reform is, in the main,
arrived at empirically, under the influence of the recent
history of English factory legislation, of the English labour
movement, of the activities of the English municipalities,
etc. Hobson lacks well-knit and integral theoretical views
that could serve as a basis for his reformist programme and
elucidate specific problems of reform. He is, therefore, at his
best when he deals with the grouping and description of the
latest statistical and economic data. When, on the other
hand, he deals with the general theoretical problems of political economy, he proves to be very weak. The Russian reader
will even find it strange to see a writer with such extensive

knowledge and practical aspirations deserving of full sympathy helplessly labouring over questions like, what is
"capital," what is the role of "savings," etc. This weak side of
Hobson is fully explained by the fact that he regards John
Stuart Mill as a greater authority on political economy than
Marx, whom he quotes once or twice but whom he evidently
does not understand at all or does not know. One cannot but
regret the vast amount of unproductive labour wasted by
Hobson in an attempt to get clear on the contradictions of
bourgeois and professorial political economy. At best he
comes close to the solutions given by Marx long ago; at worst
he borrows erroneous views that are in sharp contradiction
to his attitude towards "modern capitalism." The most unfortunate chapter in his book is the seventh: "Machinery and
Industrial Depression." In this chapter Hobson tried to analyse the theoretical problems of crises, of social capital and
revenue in capitalist society, and of capitalist accumulation.
Correct ideas on the disproportionateness of production and
consumption in capitalist society and on the anarchic character of capitalist economy are submerged in a heap of scholastic arguments about "saving" (Hobson confuses accumulation
with "saving"), amidst all sorts of Crusoeisms (suppose "a man
working with primitive tools, discovers an implement ...
saving food,"etc.), and the like. Hobson is very fond of diagrams, and in most cases he uses them very ably for graphic
illustration of his exposition. But the idea of the "mechanism
of production" given in his diagram on page 207 (Chap. VII)
can only elicit a smile from the reader who is at all acquainted with the real "mechanism" of *capitalist* "production."
Hobson here confuses production with the social system of
production and evinces an extremely vague understanding
of what capital is, what its component parts are, and into
what classes capitalist society is necessarily divided. In Chapter VIII he cites interesting data on the composition of the
population according to occupation, and on the changes in
this composition in the course of time, but the great flaw in
his theoretical arguments on "machinery and the demand for
labour" is that he ignores the theory of "capitalist over-
population" or the reserve army. Among the more happily
written chapters of Hobson's book are those in which he
examines modern towns and the position of women in modern

industry. Citing statistics on the growth of female labour and describing the extremely bad conditions under which this labour is performed, Hobson justly points out that the only hope of improving these conditions lies in the supplanting of domestic labour by factory labour, which leads to "closer social intercourse" and to "organisation." Similarly, on the question of the significance of towns, Hobson comes close to Marx's general views when he admits that the antithesis between town and country contradicts the system of collectivist society. Hobson's conclusions would have been much more convincing had he not ignored Marx's teaching on this question too. Hobson would then, probably, have emphasised more clearly the historically progressive role of the cities and the necessity of combining agriculture with industry under the collectivist organisation of economy. The last chapter of Hobson's book, "Civilisation and Industrial Development," is perhaps the best. In this chapter the author proves by a number of very apt arguments the need to reform the modern industrial system along the line of expanding "public control" and the "socialisation of industry." In evaluating Hobson's somewhat optimistic views regarding the methods by which these "reforms" can be brought about, the special features of English history and of English life must be borne in mind: the high development of democracy, the absence of militarism, the enormous strength of the organised trade unions, the growing investment of English capital outside of England, which weakens the antagonism between the English employers and workers, etc.

In his well-known book on the social movement in the nineteenth century, Prof. W. Sombart notes among other things a "tendency towards unity" (title of Chapter VI), i.e., a tendency of the social movement of the various countries, in its various forms and shades, towards uniformity and along with it a tendency towards the spread of the ideas of Marxism. In regard to England Sombart sees this tendency in the fact that the English trade unions are increasingly abandoning "the purely Manchester standpoint." In regard to Hobson's book we can say that under pressure of the demands of life, which is increasingly corroborating Marx's "prognosis," progressive English writers are beginning to realise the unsoundness of traditional bourgeois political economy and, freeing themselves from its prejudices, are involuntarily approaching Marxism.

The translation of Hobson's book has substantial short-comings.

Written in April 1899
Published in May 1899
in the magazine *Nachalo*, No. 5
Signed: *Vl. Ilyin*

Published according to
the text in the magazine

CAPITALISM IN AGRICULTURE

(KAUTSKY'S BOOK AND
MR. BULGAKOV'S ARTICLE)

Written in April-May 1899

Published in January-February
1900 in the magazine *Zhizn*[49]
Signed: *Vl. Ilyin*

Published according to the
text in the magazine

Cover of the magazine *Zhizn* in which Lenin's "Capitalism in Agriculture" was published in 1900

Reduced

FIRST ARTICLE

Nachalo, No. 1-2 (Section II, pp. 1-21), contains an article by Mr. S. Bulgakov entitled: "A Contribution to the Question of the Capitalist Evolution of Agriculture," which is a criticism of Kautsky's work on the agrarian question. Mr. Bulgakov rightly says that "Kautsky's book represents a whole world outlook," that it is of great theoretical and practical importance. It is, perhaps, the first systematic and scientific investigation of a question that has stimulated a heated controversy in all countries, and still continues to do so, even among writers who are agreed on general views and who regard themselves as Marxists. Mr. Bulgakov "confines himself to negative criticism," to criticism of "individual postulates in Kautsky's book" (which he "briefly"—too briefly and very inexactly, as we shall see—reviews for the readers of *Nachalo*). "Later on," Mr. Bulgakov hopes "to give a systematic exposition of the question of the capitalist evolution of agriculture" and thus "also present a whole world outlook" in opposition to Kautsky's.

We have no doubt that Kautsky's book will give rise to no little controversy among Marxists in Russia, and that in Russia, too, some will oppose Kautsky, while others will support him. At all events, the writer of these lines disagrees most emphatically with Mr. Bulgakov's opinion, with his appraisal of Kautsky's book. Notwithstanding Mr. Bulgakov's admission that *Die Agrarfrage** is "a remarkable work," his appraisal is astonishingly sharp, and is written in a tone unusual in a controversy between authors of

---

* *The Agrarian Question.—Ed.*

related tendencies. Here are samples of the expressions Mr. Bulgakov uses: "extremely superficial" ... "equally little of both real agronomics and real economics" ... "Kautsky employs *empty phrases* to evade serious scientific problems" (Mr. Bulgakov's italics!!), etc., etc. We shall therefore carefully examine the expressions used by the stern critic and at the same time introduce the reader to Kautsky's book.

I

Even before Mr. Bulgakov gets to Kautsky, he, in passing, takes a shot at Marx. It goes without saying that Mr. Bulgakov emphasises the enormous services rendered by the great economist, but observes that in Marx's works one "sometimes" comes across even "erroneous views ... which have been sufficiently refuted by history." "Among such views is, for example, the one that in agriculture variable capital diminishes in relation to constant capital just as it does in manufacturing industry, so that the organic composition of agricultural capital continuously rises." Who is mistaken here, Marx or Mr. Bulgakov? Mr. Bulgakov has in mind the fact that in agriculture the progress of technique and the growing intensity of farming often lead *to an increase* in the amount of labour necessary to cultivate a given plot of land. This is indisputable; but it is very far from being a refutation of the theory of the diminution of variable capital *relatively* to constant capital, *in proportion* to constant capital. Marx's theory merely asserts that the ratio $\frac{v}{c}$ (v=variable capital, c=constant capital) in general has a tendency to diminish, even when v increases per unit of area. Is Marx's theory refuted if, simultaneously, c increases still more rapidly? Agriculture in capitalist countries, taken by and large, shows a diminution of v and an increase of c. The rural population and the number of workers employed in agriculture are diminishing in Germany, in France, and in England, whereas the number of machines employed in agriculture is increasing. In Germany, for example, from 1882 to 1895, the rural population diminished from 19,200,000 to 18,500,000 (the number of wage-workers in agriculture diminished from 5,900,000 to 5,600,000), whereas the number of machines

employed in agriculture increased from 458,369 to 913,391*;
the number of steam-driven machines employed in agriculture increased from 2,731 (in 1879) to 12,856 (in 1897),
while the total horse power of the steam-driven machinery
employed increased still more. The number of cattle increased from 15,800,000 to 17,500,000 and the number of pigs
from 9,200,000 to 12,200,000 (in 1883 and 1892 respectively).
In France, the rural population diminished from 6,900,000
("independent") in 1882 to 6,600,000 in 1892; and the number
of agricultural machines increased as follows: 1862—132,784;
1882—278,896; 1892—355,795. The number of cattle was as
follows: 12,000,000; 13,000,000; 13,700,000 respectively;
the number of horses: 2,910,000; 2,840,000; 2,790,000 respectively (the reduction in the number of horses in the period
1882-92 was less significant than the reduction in the rural
population). Thus, by and large, the history of modern capitalist countries has certainly not refuted, but has *confirmed*
the applicability of Marx's law to agriculture. The mistake
Mr. Bulgakov made was that he too hastily raised certain
facts in agronomics, without examining their significance, to
the level of *general* economic laws. We emphasise "general,"
because neither Marx nor his disciples ever regarded this
law otherwise than as the law of the general tendencies of
capitalism, and not as a law for all individual cases. Even
in regard to industry Marx himself pointed out that periods
of technical change (when the ratio $\frac{v}{c}$ diminishes) are followed by periods of progress on the given technical basis (when
the ratio $\frac{v}{c}$ remains constant, and in certain cases may even
increase). We know of cases in the industrial history of capitalist countries in which this law is contravened by entire
branches of industry, as when large capitalist workshops
(incorrectly termed factories) are broken up and supplanted
by capitalist domestic industry. There cannot be any doubt
that in agriculture the process of development of capitalism
is immeasurably more complex and assumes incomparably
more diverse forms.

---

* Machines of various types are combined. Unless otherwise stated,
all figures are taken from Kautsky's book.

Let us now pass to Kautsky. The outline of agriculture in the feudal epoch with which Kautsky begins is said to be "very superficially compiled and superfluous." It is difficult to understand the motive for such a verdict. We are sure that if Mr. Bulgakov succeeds in realising his plan to give a systematic exposition of the capitalist evolution of agriculture, he will have to outline the main features of the *precapitalist* economics of agriculture. Without this the character of *capitalist* economics and the transitional forms which connect it with feudal economics cannot be understood. Mr. Bulgakov himself admits the enormous importance of "the form which agriculture assumed *at the beginning* [Mr. Bulgakov's italics] of its capitalist course." It is precisely with "the beginning of the capitalist course" of European agriculture that Kautsky begins. In our opinion, Kautsky's outline of feudal agriculture is excellent; it reveals that remarkable distinctness and ability to select what is most important and essential without becoming submerged in details of secondary importance which, in general, are characteristic of this author. In his introduction Kautsky first of all gives an extremely precise and correct presentation of the question. In most emphatic terms he declares: "There is not the slightest doubt—we are prepared to accept this *a priori* (*von vornherein*)—that agriculture does not develop according to the same pattern as industry: it is subject to special laws" (S. 5-6). The task is "to investigate whether capital is bringing agriculture under its domination and how it is dominating it, how it transforms it, how it invalidates old forms of production and forms of property and creates the need for new forms" (S. 6). Such, and only such, a presentation of the question can result in a satisfactory explanation of "the development of agriculture in capitalist society" (the title of the first, theoretical, part of Kautsky's book).

At the beginning of the "capitalist course," agriculture was in the hands of the *peasantry*, which, as a general rule, was subordinated to the feudal regime of social economy. Kautsky first of all characterises the *system* of peasant farming, the combining of agriculture with domestic industry, and further the elements of decay in this paradise of pettybourgeois and conservative writers (*à la* Sismondi), the significance of usury and the gradual "penetration into the countryside, deep into the peasant household itself, of the class antagonism which destroys the ancient harmony and community of interests" (S. 13). This process, which began as far back as the Middle Ages, has not completely come to an end to this day. We emphasise this statement because it shows immediately the utter incorrectness of Mr. Bulgakov's assertion that Kautsky did not even raise the question of who was the carrier of technical progress in agriculture. Kautsky raised and answered that question quite definitely; anyone who reads his book carefully will grasp the truth (often forgotten by the Narodniks, agronomists, and many others) that the carrier of technical progress in modern agriculture is the *rural bourgeoisie*, both petty and big; and (as Kautsky has shown) the big bourgeoisie plays a more important role in this respect than the petty bourgeoisie.

II

After describing (in Chapter III) the main features of feudal agriculture: the predominance of the three-field system, the most conservative system in agriculture; the oppression and expropriation of the peasantry by the big landed aristocracy; the organisation of feudal-capitalist farming by the latter; the transformation of the peasantry into starving paupers (*Hungerleider*) in the seventeenth and eighteenth centuries; the development of bourgeois peasants (*Grossbauern*, who cannot manage without regular farm labourers and day labourers), for whom the old forms of rural relations and land tenure were unsuitable; the abolition of these forms and the paving of the way for "capitalist, intensive farming" (S. 26) by the forces of the bourgeois class which had developed in the womb of industry and the towns—after describing all this, Kautsky goes on to characterise "modern agriculture" (Chapter IV).

This chapter contains a remarkably exact, concise, and lucid outline of the gigantic revolution which capitalism brought about in agriculture by transforming the routine craft of peasants crushed by poverty and ignorance into the scientific application of agronomics, by disturbing the age-long stagnation of agriculture, and by giving (and continuing to give) an impetus to the rapid development of the productive forces of social labour. The three-field system gave way to the crop rotation system, the maintenance of cattle and the cultivation of the soil were improved, the yield increased and specialisation in agriculture and the division of labour among individual farms greatly developed. Pre-capitalist uniformity was replaced by increasing diversity, accompanied by technical progress in all branches of agriculture. Both the use of machinery in agriculture and the application of steam power were introduced and underwent rapid development; the employment of electric power, which, as specialists point out, is destined to play an even greater role in this branch of production than steam power, has begun. The use of access roads, land improvement schemes, and the application of artificial fertilisers adapted to the physiology of plants have been developed; the application of bacteriology to agriculture has begun. Mr. Bulgakov's assertion that "Kautsky's data"* are not accompanied by an *economic* analysis" is completely groundless. Kautsky shows precisely the connection between this revolution and the growth of the *market* (especially the growth of the towns), and the subordination of agriculture to *competition* which *forced* the changes and specialisation. "This revolution, which has its origin in urban capital, increases the dependence of the farmer on the market and, moreover, constantly changes market conditions of importance to him. A branch of production that was profitable while the local market's only connection with the world market was a high road becomes unprofitable and must necessarily be superseded by another branch of production when a railway is run through the locality. If, for example, the railway brings cheaper grain, grain production

---

* "All these data," thinks Mr. Bulgakov; "can be obtained from any (*sic!*) handbook of the economics of agriculture." We do not share Mr. Bulgakov's roseate views on "handbooks." Let us take from "any" of the Russian books those of Messrs. Skvortsov (*Steam Transport*) and N. Kablukov (*Lectures*, half of them reprinted in a "new" book *The Conditions of Development of Peasant Economy in Russia*). Neither from the one nor from the other would the reader be able to obtain a picture of that transformation which was brought about by *capitalism* in agriculture, because neither even sets out to give a general picture of the transition from feudal to capitalist economy.

becomes unprofitable; but at the same time a market for milk is created. The growth of commodity circulation makes it possible to introduce new, improved varieties of crops into the country," etc. (*S.* 37-38). "In the feudal epoch," says Kautsky, "the only agriculture was small-scale agriculture, for the landlord cultivated his fields with the peasant's implements. Capitalism first created the possibility for large-scale production in agriculture, which is technically more rational than small-scale production." In discussing agricultural machinery, Kautsky (who, it should be said in passing, points precisely to the specific features of agriculture in this respect) explains the *capitalist* nature of its employment; he explains the influence of agricultural machinery upon the workers, the significance of machinery as a factor of progress, and the "reactionary utopianism" of schemes for restricting the employment of agricultural machinery. "Agricultural machines will continue their transformative activity: they will drive the rural workers into the towns and in this way serve as a powerful instrument for raising wages in the rural districts, on the one hand, and for the further development of the employment of machinery in agriculture, on the other" (*S.* 41). Let it be added that in special chapters Kautsky explains in detail the capitalist character of modern agriculture, the relation between large- and small-scale production, and the proletarisation of the peasantry. As we see, Mr. Bulgakov's assertion that Kautsky "does not raise the question of knowing why all these wonder-working changes were necessary" is entirely untrue.

In Chapter V ("The Capitalist Character of Modern Agriculture") Kautsky expounds Marx's theory of value, profit, and rent. "Without money, modern agricultural production is impossible," says Kautsky, "or, what is the same thing, it is impossible *without capital*. Indeed, under the present mode of production any sum of money which does not serve the purpose of individual consumption can be transformed into capital, i.e., into a value begetting surplus-value and, as a general rule, actually is transformed into capital. Hence, modern agricultural production is capitalist production" (*S.* 56). This passage, incidentally, enables us to appraise the following statement made by Mr. Bulgakov: "I employ this term (capitalist agriculture) in the ordinary sense

(Kautsky also employs it in the same sense), i.e., in the sense of large-scale production in agriculture. Actually, however (*sic!*), when the *whole* of the national economy is organised on capitalist lines, there is no *non*-capitalist agriculture, the *whole* of it being determined by the general conditions of the organisation of production, and only within these limits should the distinction be made between large-scale, entrepreneur farming and small-scale farming. For the sake of clarity a new term is required here also." And so it seems, Mr. Bulgakov *is correcting* Kautsky.... "Actually, however," as the reader sees, Kautsky *does not employ* the term "capitalist agriculture" in the "ordinary," inexact sense in which Mr. Bulgakov employs it. Kautsky understands perfectly well, and says so very precisely and clearly, that under the capitalist mode of production all agricultural production is "as a general rule" capitalist production. In support of this opinion he adduces the simple fact that in order to carry on modern agriculture money is needed, and that in modern society money which does not serve the purpose of individual consumption becomes capital. It seems to us that this is somewhat clearer than Mr. Bulgakov's "correction," and that Kautsky has fully proved that it is possible to dispense with a "new term."

In Chapter V of his book Kautsky asserts, *inter alia*, that both the tenant farmer system, which has developed so fully in England, and the mortgage system, which is developing with astonishing rapidity in continental Europe, express, in essence, one and the same process, viz., *the separation of the land from the farmer*.* Under the capitalist tenant farmer system this separation is as clear as daylight. Under the mortgage system it is "less clear, and things are not so simple; but in essence it amounts to the same thing" (*S.* 86). Indeed, it is obvious that the mortgaging of land is the mortgage, or sale, of ground rent. Consequently, under the mortgage system, as well as under the tenant farmer system, the recipients of rent (=the landowners) are separated from the

---

* Marx pointed to this process in Volume III of *Capital* (without examining its various *forms* in different countries) and observed that this separation of "land as an instrument of production from landed property and landowner" is "one of the major results of the capitalist mode of production" (III, 2, *S.* 156-57; Russian translation, 509-10).[50]

recipients of the profit of enterprise (= farmers, rural entrepreneurs). "In general, the significance of this assertion of
Kautsky is unclear" to Mr. Bulgakov. "It can hardly be considered as proved that the mortgage system expresses the separation of the land from the farmer." "Firstly, it cannot be proved
that debt absorbs the *whole* rent; this is possible only by
way of exception...." To this we reply: There is no need to
prove that interest on mortgage debts absorbs the *whole*
rent, just as there is no need to prove that the *actual amount*
paid for land leased coincides with rent. It is sufficient to
prove that mortgage debts are growing with enormous rapidity; that the landowners strive to mortgage all their land,
to sell the whole of the rent. The existence of this tendency—
a theoretical economic analysis can, in general, deal only
with tendencies—cannot be doubted. Consequently, there
can be no doubt about the process of separation of the land
from the farmer. The combination of the recipient of rent and
the recipient of the profit of enterprise in one person is, "from
the historical point of view, an exception" (*ist historisch eine
Ausnahme, S.* 91).... "Secondly, the causes and sources of the
debt must be analysed in each separate case for its significance to be understood." Probably this is either a misprint
or a slip. Mr. Bulgakov cannot demand that an economist
(who, moreover, is dealing with the "development of agriculture in capitalist society" *in general*) should investigate
the causes of the debt "*in each separate case*" or even expect
that he would be able to do so. If Mr. Bulgakov wanted
to say that it is necessary to analyse the causes of debt in
different countries at different periods, we cannot agree with
him. Kautsky is perfectly right in saying that too many
monographs on the agrarian question have accumulated, and
that the urgent task of modern theory is not to add new monographs but to "investigate the main trends of the capitalist
evolution of agriculture as a whole" (*Vorrede, S.* vi*). Among
these main trends is undoubtedly the separation of the land
from the farmer in the form of an increase in mortgage debts.
Kautsky precisely and clearly defined the real significance of
mortgages, their progressive historical character (the separation of the land from the farmer being one of the condi-

---

* Foreword, p. vi.—*Ed.*

tions for the socialisation of agriculture, S. 88), and the
essential role they play in the capitalist evolution of agriculture.* All Kautsky's arguments on this question are extremely valuable theoretically and provide a powerful
weapon against the widespread bourgeois talk (particularly
in "any handbook of the economics of agriculture") about
the "misfortune" of debts and about "measures of assistance."
... "Thirdly," concludes Mr. Bulgakov, "land leased out may,
in its turn, be mortgaged; and in this sense it may assume the
same position as land not leased out." A strange argument!
Let Mr. Bulgakov point to at least one economic phenomenon, to at least one economic category, that is not interwoven
with others. The fact that there are cases of combined leasing
and mortgaging does not refute, does not even weaken, the
theoretical proposition that the separation of the land from
the farmer is expressed in two forms: in the tenant farmer
system and in mortgage debts.

Mr. Bulgakov also declares that Kautsky's statement
that "countries in which the tenant farmer system is developed are also countries in which large land ownership predominates" (S. 88) is "still more unexpected" and "altogether untrue." Kautsky speaks here of the concentration of
land ownership (under the tenant farmer system) and the
concentration of mortgages (under the system in which the
landowners manage their own farms) as conditions that facilitate the abolition of the private ownership of land. On the
question of concentration of land ownership, continues Kautsky, there are no statistics "which would enable one to trace
the amalgamation of several properties in single hands";
but "in general it may be taken" that the increase in the number of leases and in the area of the leased land proceeds
side by side with concentration of land ownership. "Countries in which the tenant farmer system is developed are
also countries in which large land ownership predominates."

---

* The increase in mortgage debts does not always imply that
agriculture is in a depressed state.... The progress and prosperity of
agriculture (as well as its decline) "should find expression in an increase
in mortgage debts—firstly, because of the growing need of capital
on the part of progressing agriculture, and, secondly, because of the
increase in ground rent, which facilitates the expansion of agricultural
credit" (S. 87).

It is clear that Kautsky's entire argument applies only to countries in which the tenant farmer system is developed; but Mr. Bulgakov refers to East Prussia, where he "hopes to show" an increase in the number of leases side by side with the break-up of large landed properties—and he thinks that by means of this single example he is refuting Kautsky! It is a pity, however, that Mr. Bulgakov forgets to inform his readers that Kautsky himself points to the break-up of large estates and the growth of peasant tenant farming in the East Elbe province and, in doing so, explains, as we shall see later, the real significance of these processes.

Kautsky points to the concentration of mortgage institutions as proof that the concentration of land ownership is taking place in countries in which mortgage debts exist. Mr. Bulgakov thinks that this is no proof. In his opinion, "It might easily be the case that the deconcentration of capital (by the issue of shares) is proceeding side by side with the concentration of credit institutions." Well, we shall not argue with Mr. Bulgakov on this point.

III

After examining the main features of feudal and capitalist agriculture, Kautsky passes on to the question of "large- and small-scale production" in agriculture (Chapter VI). This chapter is one of the best in Kautsky's book. In it he first examines the "technical superiority of large-scale production." In deciding the question in favour of large-scale production, Kautsky does not give an abstract formula that ignores the enormous variety of agricultural relations (as Mr. Bulgakov, altogether groundlessly, supposes); on the contrary, he clearly and precisely points to the necessity of taking this variety into account in the practical applications of the theoretical law. In the first place, *"it goes without saying"* that the superiority of large-scale over small-scale production in agriculture is inevitable only when *"all other conditions are equal"* (S. 100. My italics). In industry, also, the law of the superiority of large-scale production is not as absolute and as simple as is sometimes thought; there, too, it is the equality of *"other conditions"* (not always existing in reality) that ensures the full applicability of the law. In agriculture, however, which is distinguished for the incomparably greater complexity and variety of its relations, the full applicability of the law of the superiority of large-scale production is hampered by considerably stricter conditions. For instance, Kautsky very aptly observes that on the borderline between the peasant and the small landlord estates "quantity is transformed into quality": the big peasant farm may be "economically, if not technically, superior" to the small landlord farm. The employment of a scientifically educated manager (one of the important advantages of large-scale production) is too costly for a small estate; and the management by the owner himself, is very often merely "Junker," and by no means scientific, management. Secondly, large-scale production in agriculture is superior to small production only up to a certain limit. Kautsky closely investigates this limit further on. It also goes without saying that this limit differs in different branches of agriculture and under different social-economic conditions. Thirdly, Kautsky does not in the least ignore the fact that "*so far,*" there are branches of agriculture in which, as experts admit, small-scale production can compete with large-scale production; for example, vegetable gardening, grape growing, industrial crops, etc. (*S.* 115). But these branches occupy a position quite subordinate to the decisive (*entscheidenden*) branches of agriculture, viz., the production of grain and animal husbandry. Moreover, "even in vegetable gardening and grape growing there are already fairly successful large-scale enterprises" (*S.* 115). Hence, "taking agriculture as a whole (*in Allgemeinen*), those branches in which small-scale production is superior to large-scale production need not be taken into account, and it is quite permissible to say that large-scale production is decidedly superior to small-scale production" (*S.* 116).

After demonstrating the technical superiority of large-scale production in agriculture (we shall present Kautsky's arguments in greater detail later on in examining Mr. Bulgakov's objections), Kautsky asks: "What can small production offer against the advantages of large-scale production?" And he replies: "The greater diligence and greater care of the worker, who, unlike the hired labourer, works for himself, and the low level of requirements of the small independent farmer, which is even lower than that of the agricultural labourer" (*S.* 106); and, by adducing a number of striking facts concerning the position of the peasants in France, England, and Germany, Kautsky leaves no doubt whatever about "overwork and under-consumption in small-scale production." Finally, he points out that the superiority of large-scale production also finds expression in the striving of farmers to form *associations*: "Associated production is large-scale production." The fuss made by the ideologists of the petty bourgeoisie in general, and the Russian Narodniks in particular (e.g., the above-mentioned book by Mr. Kablukov), over the small farmers' associations is well known. The more significant, therefore, is Kautsky's excellent analysis of the role of these associations. Of course, the small farmers' associations are a link in economic progress; but they express *a transition to capitalism* (*Fortschritt zum Kapitalismus*) *and not toward collectivism*, as is often thought and asserted (*S.* 118). Associations do not diminish but enhance the superiority (*Vorsprung*) of large-scale over small-scale production in agriculture, because the big farmers enjoy greater opportunities of forming associations and take greater advantage of these opportunities. It goes without saying that Kautsky very emphatically maintains that communal, collective large-scale production is superior to capitalist large-scale production. He deals with the experiments in collective farming made in England by the followers of Robert Owen* and with analogous communes in the United States of North America. All these experiments, says Kautsky, *irrefutably prove* that it is quite possible for workers to carry on large-scale modern farming collectively, but that for this possibility to become a reality "a number of definite economic, political, and intellectual conditions" are necessary. The transition of the small producer (both artisan and peasant) to collective production is hindered by the extremely low development of solidarity and discipline, the isolation, and the "property-owner fanaticism," noted not only among West-European peasants, but, let us add,

---

* On pages 124-26 Kautsky describes the agricultural commune in Ralahine, of which, incidentally, Mr. Dioneo tells his Russian readers in *Russkoye Bogatstvo*,[51] No. 2, for this year.

also among the Russian "commune" peasants (recall
A. N. Engelhardt and G. Uspensky). Kautsky categorically declares that "it is absurd to expect that the peasant in *modern society* will go over to communal production"
(*S*. 129).

Such is the extremely rich content of Chapter VI of
Kautsky's book. Mr. Bulgakov is particularly displeased
with this chapter. Kautsky, we are told, is guilty of the
"fundamental sin" of confusing various concepts; "technical
advantages are confused with economic advantages." Kautsky
"proceeds from the false assumption that the *technically*
more perfect mode of production is also *economically* more
perfect, i.e., more viable." Mr. Bulgakov's emphatic statement is altogether groundless, of which, we hope, the reader
has been convinced by our exposition of Kautsky's line of
argument. Without in the least confusing technique with
economics,* Kautsky rightly investigates the question of
the relation of large-scale to small-scale production in agriculture, *other conditions being equal*, under the capitalist
system of production. *In the opening sentence of the first
section of Chapter VI Kautsky points precisely to this con-*

----

* The only thing Mr. Bulgakov could quote in support of his
claim is the *title* Kautsky gave to the first section of his Chapter VI:
"(a) The *Technical* Superiority of Large-Scale Production," although
this section deals with both the technical and the economic advantages
of large-scale production. But does this prove that Kautsky *confuses*
technique with economics? And, strictly speaking, it is still an open
question as to whether Kautsky's title is inexact. The point is that
Kautsky's object was to contrast the content of the first and second
sections of Chapter VI: in the first section (a) he deals with the technical
superiority of large-scale production in capitalist agriculture, and
here, in addition to machinery, etc., he mentions, for instance, credit.
"A peculiar sort of technical superiority," says Mr. Bulgakov ironically.
But *Rira bien qui rira le dernier!* (He laughs best who laughs last.—*Ed.*)
Glance into Kautsky's book and you will see that he has in mind, prin-
cipally, the progress made in the *technique* of credit business (and
further on in the technique of trading), which is accessible *only* to
the big farmer. On the other hand, in the second section of this chapter
(b) he compares the quantity of labour expended and the rate of consumption by the workers in large-scale production with those in small-
scale production. Consequently, in this part Kautsky examines *the
purely economic difference* between small- and large-scale production.
The *economics* of credit and commerce is the same for both; but the
technique is different.

*nection between the level of development of capitalism and the
degree of the general applicability of the law of the superiority of large-scale agriculture*: "The more capitalist agriculture becomes, the more it develops the qualitative difference between the techniques of small- and large-scale production" (*S.* 92). This qualitative difference did not exist in
pre-capitalist agriculture. What then can be said of this
stern admonition to which Mr. Bulgakov treats Kautsky:
"In point of fact, the question should have been put as
follows: what significance in the competition between
large- and small-scale production can any of the specific
features of either of these forms of production have *under
the present social-economic conditions*?" This "correction"
bears the same character as the one we examined above.

Let us see now how Mr. Bulgakov refutes Kautsky's arguments in favour of the technical superiority of large-scale
production in agriculture. Kautsky says: "One of the most
important features distinguishing agriculture from industry
is that in agriculture production in the proper sense of the
word [*Wirtschaftsbetrieb*, an economic enterprise] is usually
connected with the household (*Haushalt*), which is not the
case in industry." That the larger household has the advantage over the small household in the saving of labour and
materials hardly needs proof.... The former purchases (note
this! *V. I.*) "kerosene, chicory, and margarine wholesale;
the latter purchases these articles retail, etc." (*S.* 93).
Mr. Bulgakov "corrects": "Kautsky did not mean to say that
this was technically more advantageous, but that it cost
less"!... Is it not clear that in this case (as in all the others)
Mr. Bulgakov's attempt to "correct" Kautsky was more than
unfortunate? "This argument," continues the stern critic, "is
also very questionable in itself, because under certain conditions the value of the product may not include the value of
the scattered huts, whereas the value of a common house is
included, even with the interest added. This, too, depends
upon social-economic conditions, which—and not the alleged
technical advantages of large-scale over small-scale production—should have been investigated."... In the first place,
Mr. Bulgakov forgets the trifle that Kautsky, after comparing the significance of large-scale production with that of
small-scale production, *all other conditions being equal*,

proceeds to examine these conditions in detail. Consequently, Mr. Bulgakov wants to throw different questions together. Secondly, how is it that the value of the peasants' huts does not enter into the value of the product? Only because the peasant "does not count" the value of the timber he uses or the labour he expends in building and repairing his hut. Insofar as the peasant still conducts a natural economy, he, of course, may "not count" his labour; there is no justification for Mr. Bulgakov's not telling his readers that *Kautsky very clearly and precisely points this out on pp. 165-67 of his book* (Chapter VII, "The Proletarisation of the Peasant"). But we are now discussing the "social-economic condition" of capitalism and not of natural economy or of simple commodity production. Under capitalist social conditions "not to count" one's labour means to work for nothing (for the merchant or another capitalist); it means to work for incomplete remuneration for the labour power expended; it means to lower the level of consumption below the standard. As we have seen, Kautsky fully recognised and correctly appraised *this* distinguishing feature of small production. In his objection to Kautsky, Mr. Bulgakov repeats the usual trick and the usual mistake of the bourgeois and petty-bourgeois economists. These economists have deafened us with their praises of the "viability" of the small peasant, who, they say, need not count his own labour, or chase after profit and rent, etc. These good people merely forget that such arguments confuse the "social-economic conditions" of natural economy, simple commodity production, and capitalism. Kautsky excellently explains all these mistakes and *draws a strict distinction* between the various systems of social-economic relations. He says: "If the agricultural production of the small peasant is not drawn into the sphere of commodity production, if it is merely a part of household economy, it also remains outside the sphere of the centralising tendencies of the modern mode of production. However irrational his parcellised economy may be, no matter what waste of effort it may lead to, he clings to it tightly, just as his wife clings to her wretched household economy, which likewise produces infinitely miserable results with an enormous expenditure of labour-power, but which represents the only sphere in which she is not subject to another's rule and is free from exploitation" (S. 165). The situation changes when natural economy is supplanted by commodity economy. The peasant then has to sell his produce, purchase implements, and *purchase land*. As long as the peasant remains *a simple commodity producer*, he can be satisfied with the standard of living of the wage-worker; he needs neither profit nor rent; he can pay a higher price for land than the capitalist entrepreneur (S. 166). But simple commodity production is supplanted by *capitalist production*. If, for instance, the peasant has mortgaged his land, he must also obtain the rent which he has sold to the creditor. At this stage of development the peasant can only formally be regarded as a simple commodity producer. *De facto*, he usually has to deal with the *capitalist*—the creditor, the merchant, the industrial entrepreneur—from whom he must seek "auxiliary employment," i.e., to whom he must sell his labour-power. At this stage— and Kautsky, we repeat, compares large-scale with small-scale farming in capitalist society—the possibility for the peasant "not to count his labour" means only one thing to him, namely, to work himself to death and continually to cut down his consumption.

Equally unsound are the other objections raised by Mr. Bulgakov. Small-scale production permits of the employment of machinery within narrower limits; the small proprietor finds credit more difficult to obtain and more expensive, says Kautsky. Mr. Bulgakov considers these arguments false and refers to—peasant associations! He completely ignores the evidence brought forward by Kautsky, whose appraisal of these associations and their significance we quoted above. On the question of machinery, Mr. Bulgakov again reproaches Kautsky for not raising the "more general economic question: What, upon the whole, is the economic role of machinery in agriculture [Mr. Bulgakov has forgotten Chapter IV of Kautsky's book!] and is it as inevitable an instrument in agriculture as in manufacturing industry?" Kautsky clearly pointed to the capitalist nature of the use of machinery in modern agriculture (S. 39, 40, et seq.); noted the specific features of agriculture which create "technical and economic difficulties" for the employment of machinery in agriculture (S. 38, et seq.); and adduced data on the growing employment of machinery (S. 40), on its technical significance (42, et seq.), and on the role of steam and electricity. Kautsky indicated the size of farm necessary, according to agronomic data, for making the fullest use of various machines (94), and pointed out that according to the German census of 1895 the employment of machinery steadily and rapidly increases from the small farms to the big ones (2 per cent in farms up to two hectares, 13.8 per cent in farms of 2 to 5 hectares, 45.8 per cent in farms of 5 to 20 hectares, 78.8 per cent in farms of 20 to 100 hectares, and 94.2 per cent in farms of 100 and more hectares). Instead of these figures, Mr. Bulgakov would have preferred "general" arguments about the "invincibility" or non-invincibility of machines!...

"The argument that a larger number of draught animals per hectare is employed in small-scale production is unconvincing ... because the relative intensity of animal maintenance per farm ... is not investigated"—says; Mr. Bulgakov. We open Kautsky's book at the page that contains this argument and read the following: "The large number of cows in small-scale farming [per 1,000 hectares] is to no small extent are determined by the fact that the peasant engages more in animal husbandry and less in the production of grain than the big farmer; but this does not explain the difference in the number of horses maintained" (page 96, on which are quoted figures for Saxony for 1860, for the whole of Germany for 1883, and for England for 1880). We remind the reader of the fact that in Russia the Zemstvo statistics reveal the same law expressing the superiority of large-scale over small-scale farming: the big peasant farms manage with a smaller number of cattle and implements per unit of land.*

Mr. Bulgakov gives a far from complete exposition of Kautsky's arguments on the superiority of large-scale over small-scale production in capitalist agriculture. The superiority of large-scale farming does not only lie in the fact that there is less waste of cultivated area, a saving in livestock and implements, fuller utilisation of implements,

---

* See V. Y. Postnikov, *Peasant Farming in South Russia*. Cf. V. Ilyin, *The Development of Capitalism*, Chapter II, Section I. (See present edition, Vol. 3.—*Ed.*)

wider possibilities of employing machinery, and more opportunities for obtaining credit; it also lies in the commercial
superiority of large-scale production, the employment in
the latter of scientifically trained managers (Kautsky, *S*.
104). Large-scale farming utilises the co-operation of workers
and division of labour to a larger extent. Kautsky attaches
particular importance to the scientific, agronomic education
of the farmer. "A scientifically well-educated farmer can be
employed only by a farm sufficiently large for the work of
management and supervision to engage fully the person's
labour-power" (*S*. 98: "The size of such farms varies, according
to the type of production," from three hectares of vineyards
to 500 hectares of extensive farming). In this connection
Kautsky mentions the interesting and extremely characteristic fact that the establishment of primary and secondary
agricultural school benefits the big farmer and not the
peasant by providing the former with employees (the same
thing is observed in Russia). "The higher education that is
required for fully rationalised production is hardly compatible with the peasants' present conditions of existence. This,
of course, is a condemnation, not of higher education, but
of the peasants' conditions of life. It merely means that peasant production is able to exist side by side with large-scale
production, not because of its higher productivity, but because of its lower requirements" (*S*. 99). Large-scale production must employ, not only peasant labourers, but also
urban workers, whose requirements are on an incomparably
higher level.

Mr. Bulgakov calls the highly interesting and important
data which Kautsky adduces to prove "overwork and under-
consumption in small-scale production" "a few[!] casual[??]
quotations." Mr. Bulgakov "undertakes" to cite as many
"quotations of an opposite character." He merely forgets to
say whether he also undertakes to make *an opposite assertion* which he would prove by "quotations of an opposite
character." This is the whole point! Does Mr. Bulgakov
undertake to assert that large-scale production in capitalist
society differs from peasant production in the prevalence
of overwork and the lower consumption of its workers?
Mr. Bulgakov is too cautious to make such a ludicrous assertion. He considers it possible to avoid the fact of the peasants'

overwork and lower consumption by remarking that "in some
places peasants are prosperous and in other places they are
poor"!! What would be said of an economist who, instead of
generalising the data on the position of small- and large-
scale production, began to investigate the difference in the
"prosperity" of the population of various "places"? What
would be said of an economist who evaded the overwork and
lower consumption of handicraftsmen, as compared with
factory workers, with the remark that "in some places handicraftsmen are prosperous and in other places they are poor"?
Incidentally, a word about handicraftsmen. Mr. Bulgakov
writes: "Apparently Kautsky was mentally drawing a parallel with *Hausindustrie*,* where there are no technical limits
to overwork [as in agriculture], but this parallel is unsuitable here." Apparently, we say in reply, Mr. Bulgakov
was astonishingly inattentive to the book he was criticising, for Kautsky did not "mentally draw a parallel" with
Hausindustrie, but *pointed to it directly and precisely on the
very first page of that part of the chapter* which deals with the
question of overwork (Chapter VI, b, *S.* 106): "As in domestic
industry (*Hausindustrie*), the work of the children of the
family in small peasant farming is even more harmful than
wage-labour for others." However emphatically Mr. Bulgakov decrees that this parallel is unsuitable here, his opinion is nevertheless entirely erroneous. In industry, overwork has no technical limits; but for the peasantry it is
"limited by the technical conditions of agriculture," argues
Mr. Bulgakov. The question arises: who, indeed, confuses
technique with economics, Kautsky or Mr. Bulgakov?
What has the technique of agriculture, or of domestic industry, to do with the case when facts prove that the small
producer in agriculture and in industry drives his children
to work at an earlier age, works more hours per day, lives
"more frugally," and cuts down his requirements to such a
level that he stands out in a civilised country as a real "bar-
barian" (Marx's expression)? Can the economic similarity of
such phenomena in agriculture and in industry be denied on
the grounds that agriculture has a large number of specific
features (which Kautsky does not forget in the least)? "The

---

* Domestic industry.—*Ed.*

small peasant could not put in more work than his field requires even if he wanted to," says Mr. Bulgakov. But the small peasant can and does work fourteen, and not twelve, hours a day; he can and does work with that super-normal intensity which wears out his nerves and muscles much more quickly than the normal intensity. Moreover, what an incorrect and extreme abstraction it is to reduce all the peasant's work to field work! You will find nothing of the kind in Kautsky's book. Kautsky knows perfectly well that the peasant also works in the household, works on building and repairing his hut, his cowshed, his implements, etc., *"not counting"* all this additional work, for which a wage-worker on a big farm would demand payment at the usual rate. Is it not clear to every unprejudiced person that overwork has *incomparably wider limits* for the peasant—for the small farmer— than for the small industrial producer if he is *only* such? The overwork of the small farmer is strikingly demonstrated as a universal phenomenon by the fact that all bourgeois writers unanimously testify to the "diligence" and "frugality" of the peasant and accuse the workers of "indolence" and "extravagance."

The small peasants, says an investigator of the life of the rural population in Westphalia quoted by Kautsky, overwork their children to such an extent that their physical development is retarded; working for wages has not such bad sides. A small Lincolnshire farmer stated the following to the parliamentary commission which investigated agrarian conditions in England (1897): "I have brought up a family and nearly worked them to death." Another said: "I and my children have been working eighteen hours a day for several days and average ten to twelve during the year." A third: "We work much harder than labourers, in fact, like slaves." Mr. Read described to the same commission the conditions of the small farmer, in the districts where agriculture in the strict sense of the word predominates, in the following manner: "The only way in which he can possibly succeed is this, in doing the work of two agricultural labourers and living at the expense of one ... as regards his family, they are worse educated and harder worked than the children of the agricultural labourers" (Royal Commission on Agriculture, Final Report, pp. 34, 358. Quoted by Kautsky,

S. 109). Will Mr. Bulgakov assert that not less frequently a day labourer does the work of two peasants? Particularly characteristic is the following fact cited by Kautsky showing that "the peasant art of starvation (*Hungerkunst*) may lead to the economic superiority of small production": a comparison of the profitableness of two peasant farms in Baden shows a deficit of 933 marks in one, *the large one*, and a surplus of 191 marks in the other, which was *only half the size* of the first. But the first farm, which was conducted exclusively with the aid of hired labourers, had to feed the latter properly, at a cost of nearly one mark (about 45 kopeks) per person per day; whereas the smaller farm was conducted exclusively with the aid of the members of the family (the wife and six grown-up children), whose maintenance *cost only half the amount* spent on the day labourers: 48 pfennigs per person per day. If the family of the small peasant had been fed as well as the labourers hired by the big farmer, the small farmer would have suffered a deficit of 1,250 marks! "His surplus came, not from his full corn bins, but from his empty stomach." What a huge number of similar examples would be discovered, were the comparison of the "profitableness" of large and small farms accompanied by calculation of the consumption and work of peasants and of wage-workers.* Here is another calculation of the higher profit of a small farm (4.6 hectares) as compared with a big farm (26.5 hectares), a calculation made in one of the special magazines. But how is this higher profit obtained?—asks Kautsky. It turns out that the small farmer is assisted by his children, assisted from the time they begin to walk; whereas the big farmer has to spend money on his children (school, *gymnasium*). In the small farm even the old people, over 70 years of age, "take the place of a full worker." "An ordinary day labourer, particularly on a big farm, goes about his work and thinks to himself: 'I wish it was knocking-off time.' The small peasant, however, at all events in all the busy seasons, thinks to himself: 'Oh, if only the day were an hour or two longer.'" The small producers, the author of this article in the agricultural magazine says didactically, make

---

* Cf. V. Ilyin, *The Development of Capitalism in Russia*, pp. 112, 175, 201. (See present edition, Vol. 3, pp. 168-70, 244-46, 273-75.—*Ed.*)

better use of their time in the busy seasons: "They rise earlier, retire later and work more quickly, whereas the labourers employed by the big farmer do not want to get up earlier, go to bed later or work harder than at other times." The peasant is able to obtain a net income thanks to the "simple" life he leads: he lives in a mud hut built mainly by the labour of his family; his wife has been married for 17 years and has worn out only one pair of shoes; usually she goes barefoot, or in wooden sabots; and she makes all the clothes for her family. Their food consists of potatoes, milk, and on rare occasions, herring. Only on Sundays does the husband smoke a pipe of tobacco. "These people did not realise that they were leading a particularly simple life and did not express dissatisfaction with their position.... Following this simple way of life, they obtained nearly every year a small surplus from their farm."

IV

After completing his analysis of the interrelations between large- and small-scale production in capitalist agriculture, Kautsky proceeds to make a special investigation of the "limits of capitalist agriculture" (Chapter VII). Kautsky says that objection to the theory that large-scale farming is superior to small-scale is raised mainly by the "friends of humanity" (we almost said, friends of the people...) among the bourgeoisie, the pure Free Traders, and the agrarians. Many economists have recently been advocating small-scale farming. The statistics usually cited are those showing that big farms are not eliminating small farms. And Kautsky quotes these statistics: in Germany, from 1882 to 1895, it was the area of the medium-sized farms that increased most; in France, from 1882 to 1892, it was the area of the smallest and biggest farms that increased most; the area of the medium-sized farms diminished. In England, from 1885 to 1895, the area of the smallest and the biggest farms diminished; it was the area of the farms ranging from 40 to 120 hectares (100 to 300 acres), i.e., farms that cannot be put in the category of small farms, which increased most. In America, the average area of farms is diminishing: in 1850 it was 203 acres; in 1860—199 acres; in 1870—153 acres; in 1880—134

acres; and in 1890—137 acres. Kautsky makes a closer examination of the American statistics and, Mr. Bulgakov's
opinion notwithstanding, his analysis is extremely important from the standpoint of *principle*. The main reason for
the diminution in the average farm area is the break-up
of the large plantations in the South after the emancipation
of the Negroes; in the Southern States the average farm area
diminished by more than one-half. "Not a single person who
understands the subject will regard these figures as evidence
of the victory of small-scale over *modern* [= capitalist] large-
scale production." In general, an analysis of American statistics *by regions* shows a large variety of relations. In the
principal "wheat states," in the northern part of the Middle
West, the average farm area *increased* from 122 to 133 acres.
"Small-scale production becomes predominant only in those
places where agriculture is in a state of decline, or where
pre-capitalist, large-scale production enters into competition with peasant production" (135). This conclusion of Kautsky is very important, for it shows that if certain conditions
are not adhered to, the handling of statistics may become
merely *mishandling*: a distinction must be drawn between
capitalist and pre-capitalist large-scale production. A
detailed analysis must be made for separate districts that
differ materially from one another in the forms of farming
and in the historical conditions of its development. It is
said, "Figures prove!" But one must analyse the figures to
see what they prove. They only prove *what they directly
say*. The figures do not speak directly of the scale on which
production is carried on, but of the *area* of the farms. It is
possible, and in fact it so happens, that "with intensive farming, production can be carried on upon a larger scale on
a small estate than on a large estate extensively farmed."
"Statistics that tell us only about the area of farms tell us
nothing as to whether the diminution of their area is due to
the actual diminution of the scale of farming, or to its intensification" (146). Forestry and pastoral farming, these
first forms of capitalist large-scale farming, permit of the
largest area of estates. Field cultivation requires a smaller
area. But the various systems of field cultivation differ
from one another in this respect: the exhaustive, extensive
system of farming (which has prevailed in America up to

now) permits of huge farms (up to 10,000 hectares, such as the *bonanza farms** of Dalrymple, Glenn, and others. In our steppes, too, peasant farms, and particularly merchants' farms, attain such dimensions). The introduction of fertilisers, etc., necessarily leads to a diminution in the area of farms, which in Europe, for instance, are smaller than in America. The transition from field farming to animal husbandry again causes a diminution in the area of farms: in England, in 1880, the average size of livestock farms was 52.3 acres, whereas that of field farms was 74.2 acres. That is why the transition from field farming to animal husbandry which is taking place in England *must* give rise to a tendency for the area of farms to diminish. "But it would be judging very superficially if the conclusion were drawn from this that there has been a decline in production" (149). In East Elbe (by the investigation of which Mr. Bulgakov hopes some time to refute Kautsky), it is precisely the introduction of intensive farming that is taking place: the big farmers, says Sering, whom Kautsky quotes, are increasing the productivity of their soil and are selling or leasing to peasants the remote parts of their estates, since with intensive farming it is difficult to utilise these remote parts. "Thus, large estates in East Elbe are being reduced in size and in their vicinity small peasant farms are being established; this, however, is not because small-scale production is superior to large-scale, but because the former dimensions of the estates were adapted to the needs of extensive farming" (150). The diminution in farm area in all these cases usually leads to an increase in the quantity of products (per unit of land) and frequently to an increase in the number of workers employed, i.e., to an actual *increase* in the scale of production.

From this it is clear how little is proved by general agricultural statistics on the *area* of farms, and how cautiously one must handle them. In industrial statistics we have *direct* indices of the scale of production (quantity of goods, total value of the output, and the number of workers employed), and, besides, it is easy to distinguish the different branches. Agricultural statistics hardly ever satisfy these necessary conditions of evidence.

---

* These words are in English in the original.—*Ed*.

Furthermore, the monopoly in landed property limits agricultural capitalism: in industry, capital grows as a result of *accumulation*, as a result of the conversion of surplus-value into capital; *centralisation*, i.e., the amalgamation of several small units of capital into a large unit, plays a lesser role. In agriculture, the situation is different. The whole of the land is occupied (in civilised countries), and it is possible to enlarge the area of a farm only by *centralising* several lots; this must be done in such a way as to form *one continuous area*. Clearly, enlarging an estate by purchasing the surrounding lots is a very difficult matter, particularly in view of the fact that the small lots are partly occupied by agricultural labourers (whom the big farmer needs), and partly by small peasants who are masters of the art of maintaining their hold by reducing consumption to an unbelievable minimum. For some reason or other the statement of this simple and very clear fact, which indicates the limits of agricultural capitalism, seemed to Mr. Bulgakov to be a mere "phrase" (??!!) and provided a pretext for the most groundless rejoicing: "And so [!], the superiority of large-scale production comes to grief [!] at the very first obstacle." First, Mr. Bulgakov misunderstands the law of the superiority of large-scale production, ascribing to it excessive abstractness, from which Kautsky is very remote, and then turns his misunderstanding into an argument against Kautsky! Truly strange is Mr. Bulgakov's belief that he can refute Kautsky by referring to Ireland (large landed property, but without large-scale production). The fact that large landed property is one of the conditions of large-scale production does not in the least signify that it is a sufficient condition. Of course, Kautsky could not examine the historical and other causes of the specific features of Ireland, or of any other country, in a general work on capitalism in agriculture. It would not occur to anyone to demand that Marx, in analysing the general laws of capitalism in industry, should have explained why small industry continued longer in France, why industry was developing slowly in Italy, etc. Equally groundless is Mr. Bulgakov's assertion that concentration "could" proceed gradually: it is not as easy to enlarge estates by purchasing neighbouring lots as it is to add new premises to a factory for an additional number of machines, etc.

In referring to this purely fictitious possibility of the gradual concentration, or renting, of land for the purpose of forming large farms, Mr. Bulgakov paid little attention to the really specific feature of agriculture in the process of concentration—a feature which Kautsky indicated. This is the latifundia, the concentration of several estates in the hands of a single owner. Statistics usually register the number of individual estates and tell us nothing about the process of concentration of various estates in the hands of big landowners. Kautsky cites very striking instances, in Germany and Austria, of such concentration which leads to a special and higher form of large-scale capitalist farming in which several large estates are combined to form a single economic unit managed by a single central body. Such gigantic agricultural enterprises make possible the combination of the most varied branches of agriculture and the most extensive use of the advantages of large-scale production.

The reader will see how remote Kautsky is from abstractness and from a stereotyped understanding of "Marx's theory," to which he remains true. Kautsky warned against this stereotyped understanding, even inserting a special section on the doom of small-scale production in industry in the chapter under discussion. He rightly points out that even in industry the victory of large-scale production is not so easy of achievement, and is not so uniform, as those who talk about Marx's theory being inapplicable to agriculture are in the habit of thinking. It is sufficient to point to capitalist domestic industry; it is sufficient to recall the remark Marx made about the extreme variety of transitional and mixed forms which obscure the victory of the factory system. How much more complicated this is in agriculture! The increase in wealth and luxury leads, for example, to millionaires purchasing huge estates which they turn into forests for their pleasures. In Salzburg, in Austria, the number of cattle has been declining since 1869. The reason is the sale of the Alps to rich lovers of the hunt. Kautsky says very aptly that if agricultural statistics are taken in general, and uncritically, it is quite easy to discover in the capitalist mode of production a tendency to transform modern nations into hunting tribes!

Finally, among the conditions setting the limits to capitalist agriculture, Kautsky also points to the fact that the shortage of workers—due to the migration of the rural population—compels the big landowners to allot land to labourers, to create a small peasantry to provide labour-power for the landlord. An absolutely propertyless agricultural labourer is a rarity, because in agriculture rural economy, in the strict sense, is connected with household economy. Whole categories of agricultural wage-workers own or have the use of land. When small production is eliminated too greatly, *the big landowners try to strengthen or revive it* by the sale or lease of land. Sering, whom Kautsky quotes, says: "In all European countries, a movement has recently been observed towards ... settling rural labourers by allotting plots of land to them." Thus, within the limits of the capitalist mode of production it is impossible to count on small-scale production being entirely eliminated from agriculture, for the capitalists and agrarians themselves strive to revive it when the ruination of the peasantry has gone too far. Marx pointed to this rotation of concentration and parcellisation of the land in capitalist society as far back as 1850, in the *Neue Rheinische Zeitung.*[52]

Mr. Bulgakov is of the opinion that these arguments of Kautsky contain "an element of truth, but still more of error." Like all Mr. Bulgakov's other verdicts, this one has also extremely weak and nebulous grounds. Mr. Bulgakov thinks that Kautsky has "constructed a theory of proletarian small-scale production," and that this theory is true for a very limited region. We hold a different opinion. The agricultural wage-labour of small cultivators (or what is the same thing, the agricultural labourer and day labourer with an allotment) is *a phenomenon characteristic, more or less, of all capitalist countries.* No writer who desires to describe capitalism in agriculture can, without violating the truth, leave this phenomenon in the background.* Kautsky, in Chapter VIII of his book, viz., "The Proletarisation of the Peasant," adduces extensive evidence to prove that in Germany, in

---

* Cf. *The Development of Capitalism in Russia*, Chapter II, Section XII, p. 120. (See present edition, Vol. 3, p. 178.—*Ed.*) It is estimated that in France about 75 per cent of the rural labourers own land. Other examples are also given.

particular, proletarian small-scale production is general. Mr. Bulgakov's statement that other writers, including Mr. Kablukov, have pointed to the "shortage of workers" *leaves the most important thing in the background*—the enormous difference in principle between Mr. Kablukov's theory and Kautsky's theory. Because of his characteristically *Kleinbürger** point of view, Mr. Kablukov "constructs" out of the shortage of workers the theory that large-scale production is unsound and that small-scale production is sound. Kautsky gives an accurate description of the facts and indicates their true significance in modern class society: the class interests of the landowners compel them to strive to allot land to the workers. As far as class position is concerned, the agricultural wage-workers with allotments are situated between the petty bourgeoisie and the proletariat, but closer to the latter. In other words, Mr. Kablukov develops one side of a complicated process into a theory of the unsoundness of large-scale production, whereas Kautsky analyses the special forms of social-economic relations created by the interests of large-scale production at a certain stage of its development and under certain historical conditions.

V

We shall now pass to the next chapter of Kautsky's book, the title of which we have just quoted. In this chapter Kautsky investigates, firstly, the "tendency toward the parcellisation of landholdings," and, secondly, the "forms of peasant auxiliary employments." Thus, here are depicted those extremely important trends of capitalism in agriculture that are typical of the overwhelming majority of capitalist countries. Kautsky says that the break-up of landholdings leads to an increased demand for small plots on the part of small peasants, who pay a higher price for the land than the big farmers. Several writers have adduced this fact to prove that small-scale farming is superior to large-scale farming. Kautsky very appropriately replies to this by comparing the price of land with the price of houses: it is well known that small and cheap houses are *dearer* per unit of

---

* Petty-bourgeois.—*Ed.*

capacity (per cubic foot, etc.) than large and costly houses. The higher price of small plots of land is not due to the superiority of small-scale farming, but to the particularly oppressed condition of the peasant. The enormous number of dwarf farms that capitalism has called into being is seen from the following figures: in Germany (1895), out of 5,500,000 farms, 4,250,000, i.e., more than three-fourths, are of an area of less than five hectares (58 per cent are less than two hectares). In Belgium, 78 per cent (709,500 out of 909,000) are less than two hectares. In England (1895), 118,000 out of 520,000 are less than two hectares. In France (1892), 2,200,000 (out of 5,700,000) are less than one hectare; 4,000,000 are less than five hectares. Mr. Bulgakov thinks that he can refute Kautsky's argument that these dwarf farms are very irrational (insufficient cattle, implements, money, and labour-power which is diverted to auxiliary occupations) by arguing that "very often" (??) the land is spade-tilled "with an incredible degree of intensity," although ... with "an extremely irrational expenditure of labour-power." It goes without saying that this objection is totally groundless, that individual examples of excellent cultivation of the soil by small peasants are as little able to refute Kautsky's general characterisation of this type of farming as the above-quoted example of the greater profitableness of a small farm is able to refute the thesis of the superiority of large-scale production. That Kautsky is quite right in placing these farms, *taken as a whole*,* in the proletarian category is seen from the fact, revealed by the German census of 1895, that very many of the small farmers cannot dispense with subsidiary earnings. Of a total of 4,700,000 persons obtaining an independent livelihood in agriculture, 2,700,000, or *57 per cent*, have subsidiary earnings. Of 3,200,000 farms of less than two hectares each, only 400,000, or *13 per cent*, have no subsidiary incomes! In the whole of Germany, out of

---

* We emphasise "taken as a whole," because it cannot, of course, be denied that in certain cases even these farms having an insignificant area of land can provide a large quantity of products and a large income (vineyards, vegetable gardens, etc.). But what would we say of an economist who tried to refute the reference to the lack of horses among Russian peasants by pointing, for instance, to the vegetable growers in the suburbs of Moscow who may sometimes carry on rational and profitable farming without horses?

5,500,000 farms, *1,500,000* belong to agricultural and industrial wage-workers (+704,000 to artisans). And after this
Mr. Bulgakov presumes to assert that the theory of proletarian small landholdings was "constructed" by Kautsky!*
Kautsky thoroughly investigated the forms assumed by the
proletarisation of the peasantry (the forms of peasant auxiliary employment) (*S.* 174-93). Unfortunately, space does
not permit us to deal in detail with his description of these
forms (agricultural work for wages, domestic industry—
Hausindustrie, "the vilest system of capitalist exploitation"—
work in factories and mines, etc.). Our only observation is
that Kautsky makes the same appraisal of *auxiliary employ-*
ment as that made by Russian economists. Migratory workers

* In a footnote to page 15, Mr. Bulgakov says that Kautsky, believing that grain duties were not in the interest of the overwhelming
majority of the rural population, repeats the mistake committed by
authors of the book on grain prices.[53] We cannot agree with this opinion either. The authors of the book on grain prices made a large number of mistakes (which I indicated repeatedly in the above-mentioned
book), but there is no mistake whatever in admitting that high grain
prices are not in the interests of the mass of the population. What is a
mistake is the *direct* deduction that the interests of the masses coincide with the interests of the whole social development. Messrs. Tugan-
Baranovsky and Struve have rightly pointed out that the *criterion* in
appraising grain prices must be whether, more or less rapidly, through
capitalism, they eliminate labour-service, whether they stimulate social development. This is a question of fact which I answer differently
from the way Struve does. I do not at all regard it as proved that the
development of capitalism in agriculture is retarded by low prices. On
the contrary, the particularly rapid growth of the agricultural machinery industry and the stimulus to specialisation in agriculture which
was given by the reduction of grain prices show that low prices *stimu-*
late the development of capitalism in Russian agriculture (cf. *The*
Development of Capitalism in Russia, Chapter III, Section V, p. 147,
footnote 2). (See present edition, Vol. 3, pp. 212-13.—*Ed.*) The reduction of grain prices has a profound transforming effect upon all other
relations in agriculture.

Mr. Bulgakov says: "One of the important conditions for the intensification of farming is the raising of grain prices." (The same opinion
is expressed by Mr. P. S. in the "Review of Home Affairs" column,
p. 299 in the same issue of *Nachalo*.) This is inexact. Marx showed in
Part VI of Volume III of *Capital*[54] that the productivity of additional
capital invested in land may diminish, *but may also increase*; with a
reduction in the price of grain, rent may fall, *but it may also rise*.
Consequently, intensification may be due—in different historical
periods and in different countries—to altogether different conditions,
irrespective of the level of grain prices.

are less developed and have a lower level of requirements than urban workers; not infrequently, they have a harmful effect on the living conditions of the urban workers. "But for those places from which they come and to which they return they are pioneers of progress.... They acquire new wants and new ideas" (S. 192), they awaken among the backwoods peasants consciousness, a sense of human dignity, and confidence in their own strength.

In conclusion we shall deal with the last and particularly sharp attack Mr. Bulgakov makes upon Kautsky. Kautsky says that in Germany, from 1882 to 1895 it was the smallest (in area) and the largest farms that grew most in number (so that the parcellisation of the land proceeded at the expense of the medium farms). Indeed, the number of farms under one hectare increased by 8.8 per cent; those of 5 to 20 hectares increased by 7.8 per cent; while those of over 1,000 hectares increased by 11 per cent (the number of those in the intervening categories hardly increased at all, while the total number of farms increased by 5.3 per cent). Mr. Bulgakov is extremely indignant because the percentage is taken of the biggest farms, the number of which is insignificant (515 and 572 for the respective years). Mr. Bulgakov's indignation is quite groundless. He forgets that these farms insignificant in number, are the largest in size and that they *occupy nearly as much land as* 2,300,000 to 2,500,000 dwarf farms (up to one hectare). If I were to say that the number of very big factories in a country, those employing 1,000 and more workers, increased, say, from 51 to 57, by 11 per cent, while the total number of factories increased 5.3 per cent, would not that show an increase in large-scale production, notwithstanding the fact that the *number* of very large factories may be insignificant as compared with the total number of factories? Kautsky is fully aware of the fact that it was the peasant farms of from 5 to 20 hectares which grew most in total area (Mr. Bulgakov, p. 18), and he deals with it in the ensuing chapter.

Kautsky then takes the changes in area in the various categories in 1882 and 1895. It appears that the largest increase (+563,477 hectares) occurred among the peasant farms of from 5 to 20 hectares, and the next largest among the biggest farms, those of more than 1,000 hectares (+94,014), where as the area of farms of from 20 to 1,000 hectares *diminished* by 86,809 hectares. Farms up to one hectare increased their area by 32,683 hectares, and those from 1 to 5 hectares, by 45,604 hectares.

And Kautsky draws the following conclusion: the diminution in the area of farms of from 20 to 1,000 hectares (more than balanced by an increase in the area of farms of 1,000 hectares and over) is due, not to the decline of large-scale production, but to its intensification. We have already seen that intensive farming is making progress in Germany and that it frequently requires a diminution in the area of farms. That there is intensification of large-scale production can be seen from the growing utilisation of steam-driven machinery, as well as from the enormous increase in the number of agricultural non-manual employees, who in Germany are employed only on large farms. The number of estate managers (inspectors), overseers, bookkeepers, etc., increased from 47,465 in 1882 to 76,978 in 1895, i.e., by 62 per cent; the percentage of women among these employees increased from 12 to 23.4.

"All this shows clearly how much more intensive and more capitalist large-scale farming has become since the beginning of the eighties. The next chapter will explain why simultaneously there has been such a big increase in the area of middle-peasant farms" (S. 174).

Mr. Bulgakov regards this description as being "in crying contradiction to reality," but the arguments he falls back on again fail to justify such an emphatic and bold verdict, and not by one iota do they shake Kautsky's conclusion. "In the first place, the intensification of farming, if it took place, would not in itself explain the relative and absolute diminution of the cultivated area, the diminution of the total proportion of farms in the 20- to 1,000-hectare group. The cultivated area could have increased simultaneously with the increase in the number of farms. The latter need merely (*sic!*) have increased somewhat faster, so that the area of each farm would have diminished."*

---

* Mr. Bulgakov adduces data, in still greater detail, but they add nothing whatever to Kautsky's data, since they show the same increase in the number of farms in one group of big proprietors and a reduction in the land area.

We have deliberately quoted in full this argument, from which Mr. Bulgakov draws the conclusion that "the diminution in the size of farms owing to the growth of intensive farming is pure fantasy" (*sic!*), because it strikingly reveals the very mistake of mishandling "statistics" against which Kautsky seriously warned. Mr. Bulgakov puts ridiculously strict demands upon the statistics of the *area* of farms and ascribes to these statistics a significance which they never can have. Why, indeed, should the cultivated area have increased "somewhat"? Why "should not" the intensification of farming (which, as we have seen, sometimes leads to the sale and renting to peasants of parts of estates remote from the centre) have shifted a certain number of farms from a higher category to a lower? Why "should it not" have diminished the cultivated area of farms of from 20 to 1,000 hectares?* In industrial statistics a reduction in the *output* of the very big factories would have indicated a decline in large-scale production. But the diminution in *area* of large estates by 1.2 per cent does not and *cannot indicate* the volume of production, which very often increases with a decrease in the area of the farm. We know that the process of livestock breeding replacing grain farming, particularly marked in England, is going on in Europe as a whole. We know that sometimes this change causes a decrease in the farm area; but would it not be strange to draw from this the conclusion that the smaller farm area implied a decline in large-scale production? That is why, incidentally, the "eloquent table" given by Mr. Bulgakov on page 20, showing the reduction in the number of large and small farms and the increase in the number of medium farms (5 to 20 hectares) possessing animals for field work, proves nothing at all. This may have been due to a change in the system of farming.

That large-scale agricultural production in Germany has become more intensive and more capitalist is evident, firstly, from the increase in the number of *steam-driven* machines employed: from 1879 to 1897 their number increased

---

* There was a reduction in this category from 16,986,101 hectares to 16,802,115 hectares, i.e., by a whole ... 1.2 per cent! Does not this speak in favour of the "death agony" of large-scale production seen by Mr. Bulgakov?

fivefold. It is quite useless for Mr. Bulgakov to argue in his objection that the number of *all* machines *in general* (and not steam-driven machines only) owned by small farms (up to 20 hectares) is much larger than that owned by the large farms; and also that in America machines are employed in extensive farming. We are not discussing America now, but Germany, where there are no *bonanza farms.** The following table gives the percentage of farms in Germany (1895) employing steam ploughs and steam threshing machines:

Farms	Per cent of farms employing	
	steam ploughs	steam threshing machines
Under 2 hectares	0.00	1.08
2 to 5 "	0.00	5.20
5 to 20 "	0.01	10.95
20 to 100 "	0.10	16.60
100 hectares and over	5.29	61.22

And now, if the total number of steam-driven machines employed in agriculture in Germany has increased fivefold, does it not prove that large-scale farming has become more intensive? Only it must not be forgotten, as Mr. Bulgakov forgets on page 21, that an increase in the size of enterprises in agriculture is not always identical with an increase in the area of farms.

Secondly, the fact that large-scale production has become more capitalist is evident from the increase in the number of agricultural non-manual employees. It is useless for Bulgakov to call this argument of Kautsky a "curiosity": "an increase in the number of officers, side by side with a reduction of the army"—with a reduction in the number of agricultural wage-workers. Again we say: *Rira bien qui rira le dernier!*** Kautsky not only does not forget the reduction in the number of agricultural labourers, but shows it

---

* These words are in English in the original.—*Ed.*
** What is indeed a curiosity is Mr. Bulgakov's remark that the increase in the number of non-manual employees testifies, perhaps, to the growth of agricultural industry, *but not*(!) to the growth of intensive large-scale farming. Until now we have thought one of the most important forms of increased intensification to be the growth of industry in agriculture (*described in detail and appraised by Kautsky in Chapter X*).

in detail in regard to a number of countries; only this fact
has absolutely nothing to do with the matter in hand, because the rural population as a whole is diminishing, while
the number of proletarian small farmers is increasing. Let us
assume that the big farmer abandons the production of grain
and takes up the production of sugar-beet and the manufacture of sugar (in Germany in 1871-72, 2,200,000 tons of
beets were converted into sugar; in 1881-82, 6,300,000
tons; in 1891-92, 9,500,000 tons, and in 1896-97,
13,700,000 tons). He might even sell, or rent, the remote
parts of his estate to small peasants, particularly if he
needs the wives and children of the peasants as day labourers
on the beet plantations. Let us assume that he introduces a
steam plough which eliminates the former ploughmen (on
the beet plantations in Saxony—"models of intensive farming"*—steam ploughs have now come into common use).
The number of wage-workers diminishes. The number of
higher grade employees (bookkeepers, managers, technicians,
etc.) necessarily increases. Will Mr. Bulgakov deny that
we see here an increase in intensive farming and capitalism
in large-scale production? Will he assert that nothing of
the kind is taking place in Germany?

To conclude the exposition of Chapter VIII of Kautsky's
book, viz., on the proletarisation of the peasants, we
need to quote the following passage. "What interests us
here," says Kautsky, after the passage we have cited above,
quoted also by Mr. Bulgakov, "is the fact that the proletarisation of the rural population is proceeding in Germany,
as in other places, notwithstanding the fact that the tendency to parcellise medium estates has ceased to operate there.
From 1882 to 1895 the total number of farms increased by
281,000. By far the greater part of this increase was due to
the greater number of proletarian farms up to one hectare in
area. The number of these farms increased by 206,000.

"As we see, the development of agriculture is quite a
special one, quite different from the development of industrial and trading capital. In the preceding chapter we pointed
out that in agriculture the tendency to centralise farms
does not lead to the complete elimination of small-scale pro-

* Kärger, quoted by Kautsky, S. 45.

CAPITALISM IN AGRICULTURE

duction. When this tendency goes too far it gives rise to an opposite tendency, so that the tendency to centralise and the tendency to parcellise alternate with each other. Now we see that both tendencies can operate side by side. There is an increase in the number, of farms whose owners come into the commodity market as proletarians, as sellers of labour-power.... All the material interests of these small farmers as sellers of the commodity labour-power are identical with the interests of the industrial proletariat, and their land owner-ship does not give rise to antagonism between them and the proletariat. His land more or less emancipates the peasant small holder from the dealer in food products; but it does not emancipate him from the exploitation of the capitalist entrepreneur, whether industrial or agricultural" (*S.* 174).

In the following article we shall deal with the remain-ing part of Kautsky's book and give the work a general ap-praisal; in passing, we shall examine the objections Mr. Bulgakov raises in a later article.

SECOND ARTICLE

I

In Chapter IX of his book ("The Growing Difficulties of Commercial Agriculture") Kautsky proceeds to analyse the *contradictions* inherent in capitalist agriculture. From the objections which Mr. Bulgakov raises against this chapter, which we shall examine later, it is evident that the critic has not quite properly understood the general significance of these "difficulties." There are "difficulties" which, while being an "obstacle" to the full development of rational agriculture, at the same time *stimulate the development* of capitalist agriculture. Among the "difficulties" Kautsky points, for example, to the depopulation of the countryside. Undoubtedly, the migration from the countryside of the best and most intelligent workers is an "obstacle" to the full development of rational agriculture; but it is equally indubitable that the farmers combat this obstacle by *developing technique*, e.g., by introducing machinery.

Kautsky investigates the following "difficulties": a) ground rent; b) right of inheritance; c) limitation of right of inheritance; entailment (*fideicommissum, Anerbenrecht*)[55]; d) the exploitation of the countryside by the town; e) depopulation of the countryside.

Ground rent is that part of surplus-value which remains after the average profit on invested capital is deducted. The monopoly of landed property enables the landowner to appropriate this surplus, and the price of land (= capitalised rent) *keeps* rent at the level it has once reached. Clearly, rent "hinders" the complete rationalisation of agriculture: under the tenant farmer system the incentive to improvements, etc., becomes weaker, and under the mortgage system the major part of the capital has to be invested, not in production, but in the purchase of land. In his objection Mr. Bulgakov points out, first, that there is "nothing terrible" in the growth of mortgage debts. He forgets, however, that Kautsky, not "in another sense," but precisely in this sense, has pointed to the necessary increase in mortgages even when agriculture is prospering (see above, First Article, II). Here, Kautsky does not raise the question as to whether an increase in mortgages is "terrible" or not, but asks what difficulties prevent capitalism from accomplishing its mission. Secondly, in Mr. Bulgakov's opinion, "it is hardly correct to regard increased rent only as an obstacle.... The rise in rent, the possibility of raising it, serves as an independent incentive to agriculture, stimulating progress of technique and every other form" of progress ("process" is obviously a misprint). Stimuli to progress in capitalist agriculture are: population growth, growth of competition, and growth of industry; rent, however, is a tribute exacted by the landowner from social development, from the growth of technique. It is, therefore, incorrect to state, that the rise in rent is an "*independent* incentive" to progress. Theoretically, it is possible for capitalist production to exist in the absence of private property in land, i.e., with the land nationalised (Kautsky, S. 207), when absolute rent would not exist at all, and differential rent would be appropriated by the state. This would not weaken the incentive to agronomic progress; on the contrary, it would greatly increase it.

"There can be nothing more erroneous than to think that it is in the interest of agriculture to force up (*in die Höhe treiben*) the prices of estates or artificially to keep them at a high level," says Kautsky. "This is in the interest of the present (*augenblicklichen*) landowners, of the mortgage banks and the real estate speculators, but not in the interest of agriculture, and least of all in the interest of its future, of the future generation of farmers" (S. 199). As to the price of land, it is capitalised rent.

The second difficulty confronting commercial agriculture is that it necessarily requires private property in land. This leads to the situation in which the land is either split up on passing to heirs (such parcellisation even

leading in *some places* to technical retrogression) or is burdened by mortgages (when the heir who receives the land
pays the co-heirs money capital which he obtains by a mortgage on the land). Mr. Bulgakov reproaches Kautsky for
"overlooking, in his exposition, the positive side" of the mobilisation of the land. This reproach is absolutely groundless; for in the historical part of his book (in particular
Chapter III of Part I, which deals with feudal agriculture
and the reasons for its supersession by capitalist agriculture), as well as in the practical part,* Kautsky clearly pointed
out to his readers the positive side and the historical necessity of private property in land, of the subjection of agriculture to competition, and, consequently, of the mobilisation of the land. The other reproach that Mr. Bulgakov
directs at Kautsky, namely, that he does not investigate the
problem of "the different degrees of growth of the population
in different places," is one that we simply cannot understand.
Did Mr. Bulgakov really expect to find studies in demography in Kautsky's book?

Without dwelling on the question of entailment, which,
after what has been said above, represents nothing new, we
shall proceed to examine the question of the exploitation of
the countryside by the town. Mr. Bulgakov's assertion that
Kautsky "does not contrapose the positive to the negative
sides and, primarily, the importance of the town as a market
for agricultural produce," is in direct contradiction to the
facts. Kautsky deals very definitely with the importance of
the town as a market for agriculture *on the very first page*
of the chapter which investigates "modern agriculture"
(*S.* 30, et seq.). It is precisely to "urban industry" (*S.* 292)
that Kautsky ascribes the principal role in the transformation of agriculture, in its rationalisation, etc.**

That is why we cannot possibly understand how Mr. Bulgakov could repeat in his article (page 32, *Nachalo*, No. 3)
these very ideas *as if in opposition to Kautsky*! This is a

---

* Kautsky emphatically expressed his opposition to every medieval restriction upon the mobilisation of the land, to entailment
(*fideicommissum*, *Anerbenrecht*), and to the preservation of the medieval peasant commune (*S.* 332), etc.
** Cf. also *S.* 214, where Kautsky discusses the role urban capital
plays in the rationalisation of agriculture.

particularly striking example of this stern critic's false exposition of the book he is subjecting to criticism. "It must not be forgotten," Mr. Bulgakov says to Kautsky admonishingly, that "part of the values [which flow to the towns] returns to the countryside." Anyone would think that Kautsky forgets this elementary truth. As a matter of fact Kautsky distinguishes between the flow of values (from the countryside to the town) with or without an equivalent return much more clearly than Mr. Bulgakov attempts to do. In the first place, Kautsky examines the "flow of commodity values from the country to the town without equivalent return (*Gegenleistung*)" (*S.* 210) (rent which is spent in the towns, taxes, interest on loans obtained in city banks) and justly regards this as the economic exploitation of the countryside by the town. Kautsky further discusses the question of the efflux of values with an equivalent return, i.e., the exchange of agricultural produce for manufactured goods. He says: "From the point of view of the law of value, this efflux does not signify the exploitation of agriculture*; actually, however, in the same way as the above-mentioned factors, it leads to its agronomic (*stofflichen*) exploitation, to the impoverishment of the land in nutritive substances" (*S.* 211).

As for the agronomic exploitation of the countryside by the town, here too Kautsky adheres to one of the fundamental propositions of the theory of Marx and Engels, i.e., that the antithesis between town and country destroys the necessary correspondence and interdependence between agriculture and industry, and that with the transition of capitalism to a higher form this antithesis must disappear.**

---

* Let the reader compare Kautsky's clear statement as quoted above with the following "critical" remark by Mr. Bulgakov: "If Kautsky regards the giving of grain to the non-agricultural population by direct grain producers as exploitation," etc. One cannot believe that a critic who has read Kautsky's book at all attentively could have written that "if"!

** It goes without saying that the opinion that it is necessary to abolish the antithesis between town and country in a society of associated producers does not in the least contradict the admission that the attraction of the population to industry from agriculture plays a historically progressive role. I had occasion to discuss this elsewhere (*Studies*, p. 81, footnote 69). (See present edition, Vol. 2, p. 229.—*Ed.*)

Mr. Bulgakov thinks that Kautsky's opinion on the agronomic exploitation of the country by the town is a "strange" one; that, "at all events, Kautsky has here stepped on the soil of absolute fantasy" (*sic*!!!). What surprises us is that Mr. Bulgakov ignores the fact that Kautsky's opinion, which he criticises, is identical with one of the fundamental ideas of Marx and Engels. The reader would be right in concluding that Mr. Bulgakov considers the idea of the abolition of the antithesis between town and country to be "absolute fantasy." If such indeed is the critic's opinion, then we emphatically disagree with him and go over to the side of "fantasy" (actually, not to the side of fantasy, of course, but to that of a more profound criticism of capitalism). The view that the idea of abolishing the antithesis between town and country is a fantasy is not new by any means. It is the ordinary view of the bourgeois economists. It has even been borrowed by several writers with a more profound outlook. For example, Dühring was of the opinion that antagonism between town and country "is inevitable by the very nature of things."

Further, Mr. Bulgakov is "astonished" (!) at the fact that Kautsky refers to the growing incidence of epidemics among plants and animals as one of the difficulties confronting commercial agriculture and capitalism. "What has this to do with capitalism...?" asks Mr. Bulgakov. "Could any higher social organisation abolish the necessity of improving the breeds of cattle?" We in our turn are astonished at Mr. Bulgakov's failure to understand Kautsky's perfectly clear idea. The old breeds of plants and animals created by natural selection are being superseded by "improved" breeds created by artificial selection. Plants and animals are becoming more susceptible and more demanding; with the present means of communication epidemics spread with astonishing rapidity. Meanwhile, farming remains individual, scattered, frequently small (peasant) farming, lacking knowledge and resources. Urban capitalism strives to provide all the resources of modern science for the development of the technique of agriculture, but it leaves the social position of the producers at the old miserable level; it does not systematically and methodically transplant urban culture to the rural districts. No higher social organisation will abolish the necessity of improving the breeds of cattle (and Kautsky, of course, did not think of saying anything so absurd); but the more technique develops, the more susceptible the breeds of cattle and plants* become, the more the present capitalist social organisation suffers from lack of social control and from the degraded state of the peasants and workers.

The last "difficulty" confronting commercial agriculture that Kautsky mentions is the "depopulation of the countryside," the absorption by the towns of the best, the most energetic and most intelligent labour forces. Mr. Bulgakov is of the opinion that in its general form this proposition "is at all events incorrect," that "the present development of the urban at the expense of the rural population in no sense expresses a law of development of capitalist agriculture," but the migration of the agricultural population of industrial, exporting countries overseas, to the colonies. I think that Mr. Bulgakov is mistaken. The growth of the urban (more generally: industrial) population *at the expense of* the rural population is not only a present-day phenomenon but a general phenomenon which expresses *precisely the law* of capitalism. The theoretical grounds of this law are, as I have pointed out elsewhere,** first, that the growth of social division of labour wrests from primitive agriculture an increasing number of branches of industry,*** and,

---

* That is why in the practical part of his book Kautsky recommends the sanitary inspection of cattle and of the conditions of their maintenance (S. 397).

** *The Development of Capitalism in Russia*, Chapter I, Section II, and Chapter VIII, Section II. (See present edition, Vol. 3.—*Ed.*)

*** Pointing to this circumstance, Mr. Bulgakov says that "the agricultural population may diminish *relatively* [his italics] even when agriculture is flourishing." Not only "may," but *necessarily must* in capitalist society.... "The relative diminution [of the agricultural population] merely (*sic!*) indicates here a growth of new branches of people's labour," concludes Mr. Bulgakov. That "merely" is very strange. New branches of industry do actually withdraw "the most energetic and most intelligent labour forces" from agriculture. Thus, this simple reason is sufficient to enable one to accept Kautsky's general thesis as being *fully correct*: the *relative* diminution of the rural population sufficiently confirms the correctness of the general thesis (that capitalism withdraws the most energetic and most intelligent labour forces from agriculture).

secondly, that the variable capital required to work a given
plot of land, on the whole, diminishes (cf. *Das Kapital*,
III, 2, S. 177; Russian translation, p. 526,[56] which I quote
in my book, *The Development of Capitalism*, pp. 4 and 444*).
We have indicated above that in certain cases and certain
periods we observed an increase in the variable capital required for the cultivation of a given plot of land; hut this
does not affect the correctness of the general law. Kautsky
of course, would not think of denying that not in every case
does the relative diminution of the agricultural population
become absolute diminution; that the degree of this absolute diminution is also determined by the growth of capitalist colonies. In relevant places in his book Kautsky
very clearly points to this growth of capitalist colonies
which flood Europe with cheap grain. ("The flight from the
land of the rural population (*Landflucht*) which leads to the
depopulation of the European countryside, constantly brings,
not only to the towns, but also to the colonies, fresh crowds
of robust country dwellers..." S. 242.) The phenomenon of
industry depriving agriculture of its strongest, most energetic, and most intelligent workers is general, not only in
industrial, but also in agricultural, countries; not only in
Western Europe, but also in America and in Russia. The
contradiction between the culture of the towns and the barbarism of the countryside which capitalism creates inevitably leads to this. The "argument" that "a decrease in the agricultural population side by side with a general increase
in the population is inconceivable without the importa-
tion of large quantities of grain" is, in Mr. Bulgakov's opinion, "obvious." But in my opinion this argument is not
only not obvious, but wrong. A decrease in the agricultural
population side by side with a general increase in the population (growth of the towns) is quite conceivable without
grain imports (the productivity of agricultural labour increases and this enables a smaller number of workers to
produce as much as and even more than was formerly produced). A general increase in the population parallel with a

---

* See present edition, Vol. 3, pp. 40, 561.—Ed.

decrease in the agricultural population and a decrease (or a disproportionate increase) in the quantity of agricultural products is also conceivable—"conceivable" because the nourishment of the people has deteriorated under capitalism.

Mr. Bulgakov asserts that the increase of the medium-sized peasant farms in Germany in the period 1882-95, a fact established by Kautsky, which he connected with the other fact that these farms suffer least from a shortage of labour, "is capable of shaking the whole structure" of Kautsky's argument. Let us examine Kautsky's statements more closely.

According to agricultural statistics, the largest increase in area in the period 1882-95 occurred in the farms of from 5 to 20 hectares. In 1882 these farms occupied 28.8 per cent of the total area of all farms and in 1895, 29.9 per cent. This increase in the total area of medium-sized peasant farms was accompanied by a decrease in the area of big peasant farms (20 to 100 hectares; 1882—31.1 per cent, 1895—30.3 per cent). "These figures," says Kautsky, "gladden the hearts of all good citizens who regard the peasantry as the strongest bulwark of the present system. 'And so, it does not move, this agriculture,' they exclaim in triumph; 'Marx's dogma does not apply to it.'" This increase in the medium-sized peasant farms is interpreted as the beginning of a new era of prosperity for peasant farming.

"But this prosperity is rooted in a bog," Kautsky replies to these good citizens. "It arises, not out of the *well-being* of the peasantry, but out of the *depression* of agriculture as a whole" (230). Shortly before this Kautsky said that, "notwithstanding all the technical progress which has been made, *in some places* [Kautsky's italics] there is a decline in agriculture; there can be no doubt of that" (228). This decline is leading, for example, to the revival of feudalism—to attempts to tie the workers to the land and impose certain duties upon them. Is it surprising that backward forms of agriculture should revive on the soil of this "depression"? That the peasantry, which in general is distinguished from workers employed in large-scale production by its lower level of requirements, greater ability to starve, and greater exertion while at work, can hold out longer during a

crisis?* "The agrarian crisis affects all agricultural classes
that produce commodities; it does not stop at the middle
peasant" (S. 231).

One would think that all these propositions of Kautsky
are so clear that it is impossible not to understand them.
Nevertheless, the critic has evidently failed to understand
them. Mr. Bulgakov does not come forward with an opinion:
he does not tell us how he explains this increase in the medium-

---

* Kautsky says elsewhere: "The small farmers hold out longer in
a hopeless position. We have every reason to doubt that this is an
advantage of small-scale production" (S. 134).

In passing, let us mention data fully confirming Kautsky's view
that are given by Koenig in his book, in which he describes in detail
the condition of English agriculture in a number of typical counties
(*Die Lage der englischen Landwirtschaft, etc.* [*The Condition of English
Agriculture, etc.*], Jena, 1896, von Dr. F. Koenig). In this book we
find *any amount* of evidence of overwork and under-consumption on
the part of the small farmers, as compared with hired labourers, but no
evidence of the opposite. We read, for instance, that the small farms
pay "because of immense (*ungeheuer*) diligence and frugality" (88);
the farm buildings of the small farmers are inferior (107); the small
landowners (*yeoman farmers* [these words are in English in the original.—*Ed.*]) are worse off than the tenant farmers (149); "their conditions
are very miserable (in Lincolnshire), their cottages being worse than
those of the labourers employed on the big farms, and some are in a
very bad state. The small landowners work harder and for longer hours
than ordinary labourers, but they earn less. They live more poorly
and eat less meat ... their sons and daughters work without pay and are
badly clothed" (157). "The small farmers work like slaves; in the summer they often work from 3 a.m. to 9 p.m." (a report of the Chamber
of Agriculture in Boston, S. 158). "Without a doubt," says a big farmer,
"the small man (*der kleine Mann*), who has little capital and on whose
farm all the work is done by members of his family, finds it easier to
cut down housekeeping expenses, while the big farmer must feed his
labourers equally well in bad years and good" (218). The small farmers
(in Ayrshire) "are extraordinarily (*ungeheuer*) diligent; their wives and
children do no less, and often more, work than the day labourers;
it is said that two of them will do as much work in a day as three hired
labourers" (231). "The life of the small tenant farmer, who must work
with his whole family, is the life of a slave" (253). "Taken as a whole ...
the small farmers have evidently withstood the crisis better than the
big farmers, but this does not imply that the small farm is more
profitable. The reason, in our opinion, is that the small man (*der kleine
Mann*) utilises the unpaid assistance of his family.... Usually ... the
whole family of the small farmer works on the farm.... The children
are fed and clothed, and only rarely do they get a definite daily wage"
(277-78), etc., etc.

sized peasant farms, but he ascribes to Kautsky the opinion that "the development of the capitalist mode of production is ruining agriculture." And Mr. Bulgakov exclaims angrily: "Kautsky's assertion that agriculture is being destroyed is wrong, arbitrary, unproved, and contradicts all the main facts of reality," etc., etc.

To this we can only say that Mr. Bulgakov *conveys Kautsky's ideas altogether incorrectly*. Kautsky does not state that the development of capitalism is ruining agriculture; he says the opposite. Only by being very inattentive in reading Kautsky's book can one deduce from his words on the depression (= crisis) in agriculture and on the technical retrogression to be observed *in some places* (*nota bene*) that he speaks of the "destruction," the "doom" of agriculture. In Chapter X, which deals especially with the question of overseas competition (i.e., the main reason for the agrarian crisis), Kautsky says: "The impending crisis, of course (*natürlich*), need not necessarily (*braucht nicht*) ruin the industry which it affects. It does so only in very rare cases. As a general rule, a crisis merely causes a change in the existing property relations in the capitalist sense" (273-74). This observation made in connection with the crisis in the agricultural industries clearly reveals Kautsky's general view of the significance of a crisis. In the same chapter Kautsky again expresses the view in relation to the whole of agriculture: "What has been said above does not give one the least right to speak about the doom of agriculture (*Man braucht deswegen noch lange nicht von einem Untergang der Landwirtschaft zu sprechen*), but where the modern mode of production has taken a firm hold its conservative character has disappeared for ever. The continuation of the old routine (*das Verharren beim Alten*) means certain ruin for the farmer; he must constantly watch the development of technique and continuously adapt his methods of production to the new conditions.... Even in the rural districts economic life, which hitherto has with strict uniformity moved in an eternal rut, has dropped into a state of constant revolutionisation, a state that is characteristic of the capitalist mode of production" (289).

Mr. Bulgakov "does not understand" how trends toward the development of productive forces in agriculture can be com-

bined with trends that increase the difficulties of commercial agriculture. What is there unintelligible in this? Capitalism in both agriculture and industry gives an enormous
impetus to the development of productive forces; but it is
precisely this development which, the more it proceeds,
causes the contradictions of capitalism to become more acute
and creates new "difficulties" for the system. Kautsky develops one of the fundamental ideas of Marx, who categorically emphasised the progressive historical role of agricultural capitalism (the rationalisation of agriculture, the separation of the land from the farmer, the emancipation of
the rural population from the relations of master and slave,
etc.), at the same time no less categorically pointing to the
impoverishment and oppression of the direct producers and
to the fact that capitalism is incompatible with the requirements of rational agriculture. It is very strange indeed that
Mr. Bulgakov, who admits that his "general social-philo-
sophic world outlook is the same as Kautsky's,"* should
fail to note that Kautsky here develops a fundamental idea
of Marx. The readers of *Nachalo* must inevitably remain in
perplexity over Mr. Bulgakov's attitude towards these fundamental ideas and wonder how, in view of the identity of
their general world outlook, he can say: *"De principiis non
est disputandum"*!!?** We permit ourselves not to believe
Mr. Bulgakov's statement; we consider that an argument
between him and other Marxists is possible precisely because
of the community of these *"principia."* In saying that capitalism rationalises agriculture and that industry provides
machinery for agriculture, etc., Mr. Bulgakov merely repeats one of these *"principia."* Only he should not have
said "quite the opposite" in this connection. Readers might
think that Kautsky holds a different opinion, whereas he
very emphatically and definitely develops these fundamental ideas of Marx in his book. He says: "It is precisely industry which has created the technical and scientific conditions for new, rational agriculture. It is precisely industry
which has revolutionised agriculture by means of machines

---

* As for the philosophic world outlook, we do not know whether
what Mr. Bulgakov says is true. Kautsky does not seem to be an
adherent of the critical philosophy, as Mr. Bulgakov is.
** In matters of principle there is no disputing.—*Ed.*

and artificial fertilisers, by means of the microscope and the chemical laboratory, giving rise in this way to the technical superiority of large-scale capitalist production over small-scale, peasant production" (*S.* 292). Thus, Kautsky does not fall into the contradiction in which we find Mr. Bulgakov bogged: on the one hand, Mr. Bulgakov admits that "capitalism [i.e., production carried on with the aid of wage-labour, i.e., not peasant, but large-scale production?] rationalises agriculture," while on the other, he argues that "it is not large-scale production which is the vehicle of this technical progress"!

II

Chapter X of Kautsky's book deals with the question of overseas competition and the industrialisation of agriculture. Mr. Bulgakov treats this chapter in a very offhand manner: "Nothing particularly new or original, more or less well-known main facts," etc., he says, leaving in the background the fundamental question of the conception of the agrarian crisis, its essence and significance. And yet this question is of enormous theoretical importance.

The conception of the agrarian crisis inevitably follows from the general conception of agrarian evolution which Marx presented and on which Kautsky enlarges in detail. Kautsky sees the essence of the agrarian crisis in the fact that, owing to the competition of countries which produce very cheap grain, agriculture in Europe has lost the opportunity of shifting to the masses of consumers the burdens imposed on it by the private ownership of land and capitalist commodity production. From now on agriculture in Europe *"must itself bear them* [these burdens], *and this is what the present agrarian crisis amounts to"* (*S.* 239, Kautsky's italics). Ground rent is the main burden. In Europe, ground rent has been raised by preceding historical development to an extremely high level (both differential and *absolute* rent) and is fixed in the price of land.* On the other hand, in

---

* For the process of inflating and fixing rent see the apt remarks of Parvus in *The World Market and the Agricultural Crisis.* Parvus shares Kautsky's main view on the crisis and on the agrarian question generally.

the colonies (America, Argentina, and others), insofar as they remain colonies, we see *free* land occupied by new settlers, either entirely gratis or for an insignificant price; moreover, the virginal fertility of this land reduces production costs to a minimum. Up to now, capitalist agriculture in Europe has quite naturally transferred the burden of excessively high rents to the consumer (in the form of high grain prices); now, however, the burden of these rents falls upon the farmers and the landowners themselves and ruins them.* Thus, the agrarian crisis has upset, and continues to upset, the prosperity which capitalist landed property and capitalist agriculture formerly enjoyed. Hitherto capitalist landed property has exacted an ever-increasing tribute from social development; and it fixed the level of this tribute in the price of land. Now it has to forego this tribute.** Capitalist agriculture has now been reduced to the state of instability that is characteristic of capitalist industry and is compelled to adapt itself to new market conditions. Like every crisis, the agrarian crisis is ruining a large number of farmers, is bringing about important changes in the established property relations, and *in some places* is leading to technical retrogression, to the revival of medieval relations and forms of economy. Taken as a whole, however, it is *accelerating* social evolution, ejecting patriarchal stagnation from its last refuge, and making necessary the further specialisation of agriculture (a principal factor of agricultural progress in capitalist society), the further application of machinery, etc. On the whole, as Kautsky shows by data

---

* Parvus, op. cit. p. 141, quoted in a review of Parvus' book in *Nachalo*, No. 3, p. 117. (See present volume, p. 66.—*Ed.*) We should add that the other "difficulties" of commercial agriculture confronting Europe affect the colonies to an incomparably smaller degree.

** Absolute rent is the result of monopoly. "Fortunately, there is a limit to the raising of absolute rent.... Until recent times it rose steadily in Europe in the same way as differential rent. But overseas competition has undermined this monopoly to a very considerable extent. We have no grounds for thinking that differential rent in Europe has suffered as a result of overseas competition, except for a few counties in England.... But absolute rent has dropped, and this has benefited (*zu gute gekommen*) primarily the working classes" (*S*. 80; cf. also *S*. 328).

for several countries, in Chapter IV of his book, *even* in Western Europe, instead of the stagnation in agriculture in the period 1880-90, we see technical progress. We say *even* in Western Europe, because in America, for example, this progress is still more marked.

In short, there are no grounds for regarding the agrarian crisis as an obstacle to capitalism and capitalist development.

REPLY TO Mr. P. NEZHDANOV

In issue No. 4 of *Zhizn*, Mr. P. Nezhdanov examined articles by me and other authors on the market theory. I intend to reply to only one of Mr. Nezhdanov's assertions—that in my article in *Nauchnoye Obozreniye*, issue No. 1 for this year, I "distorted my struggle against the theory of third persons." As far as the other questions are concerned, those raised by Mr. P. Nezhdanov in respect of the market theory and, in particular, of P. B. Struve's views, I shall confine myself to a reference to my article in reply to Struve ("Once More on the Theory of Realisation"; the delay in its publication in *Nauchnoye Obozreniye* was due to circumstances over which the author had no control).

Mr. P. Nezhdanov maintains that "capitalist production does not suffer from any contradiction between production and consumption." From this he concludes that Marx, in recognising this contradiction, "suffered from a serious internal contradiction" and that I am repeating Marx's error.

I believe Mr. Nezhdanov's opinion to be a mistaken one (or one based on a misunderstanding) and cannot see any contradiction in Marx's views.

Mr. P. Nezhdanov's assertion that there is no contradiction between production and consumption in capitalism is so strange that it is only to be explained by the very *special meaning* that he attaches to the concept "contradiction." Mr. P. Nezhdanov is of the opinion that "if there really were a contradiction between production and consumption that contradiction would provide a regular surplus-product" (p. 301; the same in the final theses, p. 316). This is an utterly

arbitrary and, in my opinion, utterly incorrect interpretation. In criticising my assertions on the contradiction between production and consumption in capitalist society, Mr.
P. Nezhdanov should (I think) have told the reader how I
understand that contradiction and should not have limited
himself to an exposition of his own views on the essence and
significance of that contradiction. The whole essence of the
question (which has given rise to Mr. P. Nezhdanov's polemic
against me) is that I understand the contradiction under
discussion quite differently from the way in which Mr. P.
Nezhdanov wishes to understand it. I did not say anywhere
that this contradiction should *regularly** produce a surplus-
product; I do not think so and such a view cannot be deduced
from Marx's words. The contradiction between production
and consumption that is inherent in capitalism is due to the
tremendous rate at which production is growing, to the
tendency to unlimited expansion which competition gives it,
while consumption (individual), if it grows at all, grows
very slightly; the proletarian condition of the masses of the
people makes a rapid growth of individual consumption
impossible. It seems to me that any one reading carefully
pages 20 and 30 of my *Studies* (the article on the Sismondists
cited by Mr. P. Nezhdanov) and page 40 of *Nauchnoye
Obozreniye* (1899, No. 1)** can convince himself that, from
the outset, I gave *only this meaning* to the contradiction
between production and consumption in capitalism. Indeed,
no other meaning can be ascribed to this contradiction by
one who adheres strictly to Marx's theory. The contradiction
between production and consumption that is inherent in
capitalism consists only in this, that the growth of the national
wealth proceeds side by side with the growth of the people's
poverty; that the productive forces of society increase
without a corresponding increase in consumption by the
people, without the employment of these productive forces
for the benefit of the working masses. The contradiction

---

* I stress *regularly* because the irregular production of a surplus-
product (crises) is inevitable in capitalist society as a result of the
disturbance in proportion between the various branches of industry.
But a certain state of consumption is one of the elements of proportion.
** See present edition, Vol. 2, pp. 155 and 167 and pp. 58-59 of
the present volume.—*Ed.*

under discussion, understood in this sense, is a fact that does not admit of any doubt and that is confirmed by the daily experience of millions of people, and it is the observation of this fact that leads the working men to the views that have found a full scientific expression in Marx's theory. This contradiction does not, by any means, lead inevitably to the regular production of a surplus-product (as Mr. Nezhdanov would like to think). We can quite well imagine (if we argue from a purely theoretical standpoint about an ideal capitalist society) the realisation of the entire product in a capitalist society without any surplus-product, *but we cannot imagine capitalism* without a disparity between production and consumption. This disparity is expressed (as Marx has demonstrated clearly in his Schemes) by the fact that the production of the means of production can and must outstrip the production of articles of consumption.

Mr. Nezhdanov, therefore, was completely mistaken in his deduction that the contradiction between production and consumption must regularly provide a surplus-product, and this mistake led to his unjustly accusing Marx of inconsistency. Marx, on the contrary, remains consistent when he shows:

1) that the product *can* be realised in a capitalist society (it goes without saying that this is true if proportionality between the various branches of industry is assumed); that it would be incorrect to introduce foreign trade or "third persons" to explain this realisation;

2) that the theories of the petty-bourgeois economists (*à la* Proudhon) on the impossibility of realising *surplus-value* are based on a complete misunderstanding of the very process of realisation in general;

3) that even with fully proportional, ideally smooth realisation we cannot imagine capitalism without a contradiction between production and consumption, without the tremendous growth of production being accompanied by an extremely slow growth (or even stagnation and worsening) of consumption by the people. Realisation is due more to means of production than to articles of consumption—this is obvious from Marx's Schemes; and from this, in turn, it follows inevitably that "the more productiveness develops, the more it finds itself at variance with the narrow basis on

which the conditions of consumption rest" (Marx).[57] It is obvious from all the passages in *Capital* devoted to the contradiction between production and consumption* that it is *only in this sense* that Marx understood the contradiction between production and consumption.

Incidentally, Mr. P. Nezhdanov is of the opinion that Mr. Tugan-Baranovsky also denies the contradiction between production and consumption in a capitalist society. I do not know whether this is true. Mr. Tugan-Baranovsky himself introduced into his book a scheme showing the possibility of the growth of production accompanied by a contraction of consumption (which, of course, is possible and actual under capitalism). How can one deny that we see here a contradiction between production and consumption, although there is no surplus-product?

In charging Marx (and me) with inconsistency, Mr. P. Nezhdanov also lost sight of the fact that he should have explained, as a basis for his viewpoint, how one should understand the "independence" of the production of means of production from the production of articles of consumption. According to Marx, this "independence" is limited to the following: a certain (and constantly growing) part of the product which consists of means of production is realised by exchanges within the given department, i.e., exchanges of means of production for means of production (or the use of the product obtained, *in natura*,** for fresh production); but in *the final analysis* the manufacture of means of production is necessarily bound up with that of articles of consumption, since the former are not manufactured for their own sake, but only because more and more means of production are demanded by the branches of industry manufacturing articles of consumption.*** The views of the petty-bourgeois economists, therefore, do not differ from those of Marx because the

---

* These passages are quoted in my article in *Nauchnoye Obozreniye*, 1899, No. 1 (see present volume, p. 56, et seq.—*Ed.*) and are repeated in the first chapter of *The Development of Capitalism in Russia*, pp. 18-19. (See present edition, Vol. 3, p. 56-57.—*Ed.*)

** In its natural form.—*Ed.*

*** *Das Kapital*, III, 1, 289.[58] Quoted by me in *Nauchnoye Obozreniye*, p. 40 (see present volume, p. 59.—*Ed.*), and in *The Development of Capitalism*, 17. (See present edition, Vol. 3, p. 55.—*Ed.*)

former recognised in general the connection between production and consumption in a capitalist society while the latter
denied in general that connection (which would be absurd).
The difference is that the petty-bourgeois economists considered this connection between production and consumption
to be *a direct one*, that they thought *production follows consumption*. Marx showed that this connection is *an indirect
one*, that it only makes itself felt *in the final analysis*, because
in capitalist society *consumption follows production*. But
the connection nevertheless exists, even if it is indirect;
consumption must, in the final analysis, follow production,
and, if the productive forces are driving towards an unlimited growth of production, while consumption is restricted by
the proletarian condition of the masses of the people, there
is undoubtedly a contradiction present. This contradiction
does not signify the impossibility of capitalism,* but it does
signify that its transformation to a higher form is a necessity:
the stronger this contradiction becomes, the more developed become the objective conditions for this transformation,
as well as the subjective conditions, i.e., the workers' consciousness of this contradiction.

The question now arises: what position could Mr. Nezhdanov adopt on the question of the "independence" of the means
of production as regards articles of consumption? One of
two: either he will completely deny any dependence between
them, will assert the possibility of realising means of production that are *in no way connected* with articles of consumption, that are not connected even in "the final analysis"
—in which case he will inevitably descend to the absurd, or
he will admit, following Marx, that in the final analysis
means of production are connected with articles of consumption, in which case he must admit the correctness of my understanding of Marx's theory.

In conclusion, let me take an example to illustrate these
abstract arguments with concrete data. It is known that in
any capitalist society exceptionally low wages (= the low

---

* *Studies*, p. 20 (see present edition, Vol. 2, p. 155.—*Ed*.); *Nauchnoye Obozreniye*, No. 1, p. 41 (see present volume, p. 60.—*Ed*.);
The Development of Capitalism, pp. 19-20. (See present edition, Vol. 3,
p. 58.—*Ed*.) If this contradiction were to lead to "a regular surplusproduct," it would signify precisely the impossibility of capitalism.

level of consumption by the masses of the people) often hinder the employment of machinery. What is more, it even happens that machines acquired by entrepreneurs are in disuse because the price of labour drops so low that manual labour becomes more profitable to the owner!* The existence of a contradiction between consumption and production, between the drive of capitalism to develop the productive forces to an unlimited extent and the limitation of this drive by the proletarian condition, the poverty and unemployment of the people, is, in this case, as clear as daylight. But it is no less clear that it is correct to draw one single conclusion from this contradiction—that the development of the productive forces themselves must, with irresistible force, lead to the replacement of capitalism by an economy of associated producers. It would, on the other hand, be utterly incorrect to draw from this contradiction the conclusion that capitalism must *regularly* provide a surplus-product, i.e., that capitalism cannot, in general, realise the product, and can, therefore, play no progressive historical role, and so on.

Written in May 1899

Published in December 1899
in the magazine *Zhizn*
Signed: *Vladimir Ilyin*

Published according to
the text in the magazine

---

* I bring an instance of this phenomenon in the sphere of Russian capitalist agriculture in *The Development of Capitalism in Russia*, page 165. (See present edition, Vol. 3, p. 234.—*Ed.*) Similar phenomena are not individual instances but are the usual and *inevitable* consequences of the basic features of capitalism.

A PROTEST BY RUSSIAN SOCIAL-DEMOCRATS [59]

Written at the end of August-
beginning of September 1899
First published abroad in
December 1899 as the separate
reprints from No. 4-5 of the
magazine *Rabochaya Dyelo* [60]

Published according to the
text in the magazine

РОССІЙСКАЯ СОЦІАЛЬДЕМОКРАТИЧЕСКАЯ РАБОЧАЯ ПАРТІЯ

Пролетаріи всѣхъ странъ, соединяйтесь!

Оттискъ изъ № 4-5 „Рабочаго Дѣла“.

ПРОТЕСТЪ

РОССІЙСКИХЪ СОЦІАЛЬДЕМОКРАТОВЪ

СЪ ПОСЛѢСЛОВІЕМЪ ОТЪ РЕДАКЦІИ „РАБОЧАГО ДѢЛА

Собраніе соціальдемократовъ одной мѣстности (Россіи), въ числѣ семнадцати человѣкъ, приняло ЕДИНОГЛАСНО слѣдующую резолюцію и постановило опубликовать ее и передать на обсужденіе всѣмъ товарищамъ.

Въ послѣднее время среди русскихъ соціальдемократовъ замѣчаются отступленія отъ тѣхъ основныхъ принциповъ русской соціальдемократіи, которые были провозглашены какъ основателями и передовыми борцами—членами Группы „Освобожденія Труда“,—такъ и соціальдемократическими изданіями русскихъ рабочихъ организацій 90-хъ годовъ. Ниже приводимое „credo“, долженствующее выражать основные взгляды нѣкоторыхъ („молодыхъ“) русскихъ соціальдемократовъ, представляетъ изъ себя попытку систематическаго и опредѣленнаго изложенія „новыхъ возрѣній“. — Вотъ это „credo“ въ полномъ видѣ.

„Существованіе цехового и мануфактурнаго періода на Западѣ наложило рѣзкій слѣдъ на всю послѣдующую исторію, въ особенности на исторію соціальдемократіи. Необходимость для буржуазіи завоевать свободныя формы, стремленіе освободиться отъ сковывающихъ производство цеховыхъ регламентацій, сдѣлали ее, буржуазію, революціоннымъ элементомъ; она повсюду на Западѣ начинаетъ съ liberté, fraternité, égalité (свобода, братство и равенство).

Facsimile of the first page of the reprint of "A Protest by Russian Social-Democrats" from No. 4-5 of *Rabocheye Dyelo*. 1899.

A MEETING OF SOCIAL-DEMOCRATS, SEVENTEEN IN NUMBER,
HELD AT A CERTAIN PLACE (IN RUSSIA), ADOPTED *UNANIMOUSLY*
THE FOLLOWING RESOLUTION AND RESOLVED TO PUBLISH IT AND
TO SUBMIT IT TO ALL COMRADES FOR THEIR CONSIDERATION

A tendency has been observed among Russian Social-Democrats recently to depart from the fundamental principles of Russian Social-Democracy that were proclaimed by its founders and foremost fighters, members of the Emancipation of Labour group[61] as well as by the Social-Democratic publications of the Russian workers' organisations of the nineties. The *Credo* reproduced below, which is presumed to express the fundamental views of certain ("young") Russian Social-Democrats, represents an attempt at a systematic and definite exposition of the "new views." The following is its full text:

"The guild and manufacture period in the West laid a sharp impress on all subsequent history and particularly on the history of Social-Democracy. The fact that the bourgeoisie had to fight for free forms, that it strove to release itself from the guild regulations fettering production, made the bourgeoisie a revolutionary element; everywhere in the West it began with *liberté, fraternité, égalité* (liberty, fraternity, equality), with the achievement of free political forms. By these gains, however, as Bismarck expressed it, it drew a bill on the future payable to its antipode—the working class. Hardly anywhere in the West did the working class, as a class, win the democratic institutions—it made use of them. Against this it may be argued that the working class took part in revolutions. A reference to history will refute this opinion, for, precisely in 1848, when the consolidation of Constitutions took place in the West, the working class represented the urban artisan element, the petty-bourgeois democracy; a factory proletariat hardly existed, while the proletariat employed in large-scale industry (the German weavers depicted by Hauptmann, the weavers of Lyons) represented a wild mass capable only of rioting, but not of advancing any political demands. It can be definitely stated that the Constitutions of 1848 were won by the bourgeoisie and the small urban artisans. On the other hand, the working class (artisans, manufactory workers, printers, weavers, watchmakers, etc.) have been accustomed since the Middle Ages to membership in organisations, mutual benefit societies, religious societies, etc. This spirit of organisation is still alive among the skilled workers in the West, sharply distinguishing them from the factory proletariat, which submits to organisation badly and slowly and is capable only of *lose-organisation* (temporary organisations) and not of permanent organisations with rules and regulations. It was these manufactory skilled workers that comprised the core of the Social-Democratic parties. Thus, we get the picture: on the one hand, the relative ease of political struggle and every possibility for it, on the other hand, the possibility for the systematic organisation of this struggle with the aid of the workers trained in the manufacturing period. It was on this basis that theoretical and practical Marxism grew up in the West. The starting-point was the parliamentary political struggle with the prospect—only superficially resembling Blanquism, but of totally different origin—of capturing power, on the one hand, and of a *Zusammenbruch* (collapse), on the other. Marxism was the theoretical expression of the prevailing practice: of the political struggle predominating over the economic. In Belgium, in France, and particularly in Germany, the workers organised the political struggle with incredible ease; but it was with enormous difficulty and tremendous friction that they organised the economic struggle. Even to this day the economic organisations as compared with the political organisations (leaving aside England) are extraordinarily weak and unstable, and everywhere *laissent à désirer quelque chose* (leave something to be desired). So long as the energy in the political struggle had not been completely exhausted, *Zusammenbruch* was an essential organisational *Schlagwort* (slogan) destined to play an extremely important historical role. The fundamental law that can be discerned by studying the working-class movement is that of the line of least resistance. In the West, this line was political activity, and Marxism, as formulated in the *Communist Manifesto*, was the best possible form the movement could assume. But when all energy in political activity had been exhausted, when the political movement had reached a point of intensity difficult and almost impossible to surpass (the slow increase in votes in the recent period, the apathy of the public at meetings the note of despondency in literature), this, in conjunction with the ineffectiveness of parliamentary action and the entry into the arena of the ignorant masses, of the unorganised and almost unorganisable factory proletariat, gave rise in the West to what is now called Bernsteinism,[62] the crisis of Marxism. It is difficult to imagine a more logical course than the period of development of the labour movement from the *Communist Manifesto* to Bernsteinism, and a careful study of this whole process can determine with astronomical exactitude the outcome of this "crisis." Here, of course, the issue is not the defeat or victory of Bernsteinism—that is of little interest; it is the radical change in practical activity that has been gradually taking place for a long time within the party.

"The change will not only be towards a more energetic prosecution of the economic struggle and consolidation of the economic organisations, but also, and most importantly, towards a change in the party's attitude to other opposition parties. Intolerant Marxism, negative Marxism, primitive Marxism (whose conception of the class division of society is too schematic) will give way to democratic Marxism, and the social position of the party within modern society must undergo a sharp change. The party *will recognise* society, its narrow corporative and, in the majority of cases, sectarian tasks will be widened to social tasks, and its striving to seize power will be transformed into a striving for change, a striving to reform present-day society on democratic lines adapted to the present state of affairs, with the object of protecting the rights (all rights) of the labouring classes in the most effective and fullest way. The concept 'politics' will be enlarged and will acquire a truly social meaning, and the practical demands of the moment will acquire greater weight and will be able to count on receiving greater attention than they have been getting up to now.

"It is not difficult to draw conclusions for Russia from this brief description of the course of development taken by the working-class movement in the West. In Russia, the line of least resistance will never tend towards political activity. The incredible political oppression will prompt much talk about it and cause attention to be concentrated precisely on this question, but it will never prompt practical action. While in the West the fact that the workers were drawn into political activity served to strengthen and crystallise their weak forces, in Russia, on the contrary, these weak forces are confronted with a wall of political oppression. Not only do they lack practical ways of struggle against this oppression, and hence, also for their own development, but they are systematically stifled and cannot give forth even weak shoots. If to this we add that the working class in our country has not inherited the spirit of organisation which distinguished the fighters in the West, we get a gloomy picture, one that is likely to drive into despondency the most optimistic Marxist who believes that an extra factory chimney stack will by the very fact of its existence bring great welfare. The economic struggle too is hard, infinitely hard, but it is possible to wage it, and it is in fact being waged by the masses themselves. By learning in this struggle to organise, and coming into constant conflict with the political regime in the course of it, the Russian worker will at last create what may be called a form of the labour movement, the organisation or organisations best conforming to Russian conditions. At the present, it can be said with certainty that the Russian working-class movement is still in the amoeba state and has not yet acquired any form. The strike movement, which goes on with any form of organisation, cannot yet be described as the crystallised form of the Russian movement, while the illegal organisations are not worth consideration even from the mere quantitative point of view (quite apart from the question of their usefulness under present conditions).

"Such is the situation. If to this we add the famine and the process of ruination of the countryside, which facilitate *Streikbrecher*-ism,* and, consequently, the even greater difficulty of raising the masses of the workers to a more tolerable cultural level, then ... well, what is there for the Russian Marxist to do?! The talk about an independent workers' political party merely results from the transplantation of alien aims and alien achievements to our soil. The Russian Marxist, so far, is a sad spectacle. His practical tasks at the present time are paltry, his theoretical knowledge, insofar as he utilises it *not as an instrument for research* but as a schema for activity, is worthless for the purpose of fulfilling even these paltry practical tasks. Moreover, these borrowed patterns are harmful from the practical point of view. Our Marxists, forgetting that the working class in the West entered political activity after that field had already been cleared, are much too contemptuous of the radical or liberal opposition activity of all other non-worker strata of society. The slightest attempt to concentrate attention on public manifestations of a liberal political character rouses the protest of the orthodox Marxists, who forget that a number of historical conditions prevent us from being Western Marxists and demand of us a different Marxism, suited to, and necessary in, Russian conditions. Obviously, the lack in every Russian citizen of political feeling and sense cannot be compensated by talk about politics or by appeals to a non-existent force. This political sense can only be acquired through education, i.e., through participation in that life (however un-Marxian it may be) which is offered by Russian conditions. 'Negation' is as harmful in Russia as it was appropriate (temporarily) in the West, because negation proceeding from something organised and possessing real power is one thing, while negation proceeding from an amorphous mass of scattered individuals is another.

"For the Russian Marxist there is only one course: participation in, i.e., assistance to, the economic struggle of the proletariat, and participation in liberal opposition activity. As a 'negator,' the Russian Marxist came on the scene very early, and this negation has weakened the share of his energy that should be turned in the direction of political radicalism. For the time being, this is not terrible; but if the class schema prevents the Russian intellectual from taking an active part in life and keeps him too far removed from opposition circles it will be a serious loss to all who are compelled to fight for legal forms separately from the working class, which has not yet put forward political aims. The political innocence concealed behind the cerebrations of the Russian Marxist intellectual on political topics may play mischief with him."

We do not know whether there are many Russian Social-Democrats who share these views. But there is no doubt that ideas of this kind have their adherents, and we there-

* Strike-breaking.—*Ed*.

fore feel obliged to protest categorically against such views and to warn all comrades against the menacing deflection of Russian Social-Democracy from the path it has already marked out—the formation of an independent political working-class party which is inseparable from the class struggle of the proletariat and which has for its immediate aim the winning of political freedom.

The above-quoted *Credo* represents, first, "a brief description of the course of development taken by the working-class movement in the West," and, secondly, "conclusions for Russia."

First of all, the authors of the *Credo* have an entirely false conception of the history of the West-European working-class movement. It is not true to say that the working class in the West did not take part in the struggle for political liberty and in political revolutions. The history of the Chartist movement and the revolutions of 1848 in France, (Germany, and Austria prove the opposite. It is absolutely untrue to say that "Marxism was the theoretical expression of the prevailing practice: of the political struggle predominating over the economic." On the contrary, "Marxism" appeared at a time when non-political socialism prevailed (Owenism, "Fourierism," "true socialism") and the *Communist Manifesto* took up the cudgels at once against non-political socialism. Even when Marxism came out fully armed with theory (*Capital*) and organised the celebrated International Working Men's Association,[63] the political struggle was by no means the prevailing practice (narrow trade-unionism in England, anarchism and Proudhonism in the Romance countries). In Germany the great historic service performed by Lassalle was the transformation of the working class from an appendage of the liberal bourgeoisie into an independent political party. Marxism linked up the economic and the political struggle of the working class into a single inseparable whole; and the effort of the authors of the *Credo* to separate these forms of struggle is one of their most clumsy and deplorable departures from Marxism.

Further, the authors of the *Credo* also have an entirely wrong conception of the present state of the West-European working-class movement and of the theory of Marxism, under the banner of which that movement is marching.

To talk about a "crisis of Marxism" is merely to repeat the nonsense of the bourgeois hacks who are doing all they can to exacerbate every disagreement among the socialists and turn it into a split in the socialist parties. The notorious Bernsteinism—in the sense in which it is commonly understood by the general public, and by the authors of the *Credo* in particular—is an attempt to narrow the theory of Marxism, to convert the revolutionary workers' party into a reformist party. As was to be expected, this attempt has been strongly condemned by the majority of the German Social-Democrats. Opportunist trends have repeatedly manifested themselves in the ranks of German Social-Democracy, and on every occasion they have been repudiated by the Party, which loyally guards the principles of revolutionary international Social-Democracy. We are convinced that every attempt to transplant opportunist views to Russia will encounter equally determined resistance on the part of the overwhelming majority of Russian Social-Democrats.

Similarly, there can be no suggestion of a "radical change in the practical activity" of the West-European workers' parties, in spite of what the authors of the *Credo* say: the tremendous importance of the economic struggle of the proletariat, and the necessity for such a struggle, were recognised by Marxism from the very outset. As early as the forties Marx and Engels conducted a polemic against the utopian socialists who denied the importance of this struggle.[64]

When the International Working Men's Association was formed about twenty years later, the question of the importance of trade unions and of the economic struggle was raised at its very first Congress, in Geneva, in 1866. The resolution adopted at that Congress spoke explicitly of the importance of the economic struggle and warned the socialists and the workers, on the one hand, against exaggerating its importance (which the English workers were inclined to do at that time) and, on the other, against underestimating its importance (which the French and the Germans, particularly the Lassalleans, were inclined to do). The resolution recognised that the trade unions were not only a natural, but also an essential phenomenon under capitalism and considered them an extremely important means for organising the working class in its daily struggle against capital and for the abolition of wage-labour. The resolution declared that the trade unions must not devote attention exclusively to the "immediate struggle against capital," must not remain aloof from the general political and social movement of the working class; they must not pursue "narrow" aims, but must strive for the general emancipation of the millions of oppressed workers. Since then the workers' parties in the various countries have discussed the question many times and, of course, will discuss it again and again—whether to devote more or less attention at any given moment to the economic or to the political struggle of the proletariat; but the general question, or the question in principle, today remains as it was presented by Marxism. The conviction that the class struggle must necessarily combine the political and the economic struggle into one integral whole has entered into the flesh and blood of international Social-Democracy. The experience of history has, furthermore, incontrovertibly proved that absence of freedom, or restriction of the political rights of the proletariat, always make it necessary to put the political struggle in the forefront.

Still less can there be any suggestion of a serious change in the attitude of the workers' party towards the other opposition parties. In this respect, too, Marxism has mapped out the correct line, which is equally remote from exaggerating the importance of politics, from conspiracy (Blanquism, etc.), and from decrying politics or reducing it to opportunist, reformist social tinkering (anarchism, utopian and petty-bourgeois socialism, state socialism, professorial socialism, etc.). The proletariat must strive to form independent political workers' parties, the main aim of which must be the capture of political power by the proletariat for the purpose of organising socialist society. The proletariat must not regard the other classes and parties as "one reactionary mass"[65]; on the contrary, it must take part in all political and social life, support the progressive classes and parties against the reactionary classes and parties, support every revolutionary movement against the existing system, champion the interests of every oppressed nationality or race, of every persecuted religion, of the disfranchised sex, etc. The arguments the *Credo* authors advance on this subject merely reveal a desire to obscure the class character of the struggle of the proletariat, weaken this struggle by a meaningless "recognition of society," and reduce revolutionary Marxism to a trivial reformist trend. We are convinced that the overwhelming majority of Russian Social-Democrats will resolutely reject this distortion of the fundamental principles of Social-Democracy. Their erroneous premises regarding the West-European working-class movement led the authors of the *Credo* to draw still more erroneous "conclusions for Russia."

The assertion that the Russian working class "has not yet put forward political aims" simply reveals ignorance of the Russian revolutionary movement. The North-Russian Workers' Union[66] formed in 1878 and the South-Russian Workers' Union[67] formed in 1875 put forward even then the demand for political liberty in their programmes. After the reaction of the eighties, the working class repeatedly put forward the same demand in the nineties. The assertion that "the talk about an independent workers' political party merely results from the transplantation of alien aims and alien achievements to our soil" reveals a complete failure to understand the historical role of the Russian working class and the most vital tasks of Russian Social-Democracy. Apparently, the programme of the authors of the *Credo* inclines to the idea that the working class, following "the line of least resistance," should confine itself to the economic struggle, while the "liberal opposition elements" fight, with the "participation" of the Marxists, for "legal forms." The application of such a programme would be tantamount to the political suicide of Russian Social-Democracy, it would greatly retard and debase the Russian working-class movement and the Russian revolutionary movement (for us the two concepts coincide). The mere fact that it was possible for a programme like this to appear shows how well grounded were the fears expressed by one of the foremost champions of Russian Social-Democracy, P. B. Axelrod, when, at the end of 1897, he wrote of the possibility of the following prospect:

"The working-class movement keeps to the narrow rut of purely economic conflicts between the workers and employers and, in itself taken as a whole, is not of a political character, while in the struggle for political freedom the advanced strata of the proletariat follow the revolutionary circles and groups of the so-called intelligentsia" (Axelrod, *Present Tasks and Tactics of the Russian Social-Democrats*, Geneva, 1898, p. 19).

Russian Social-Democrats must declare determined war upon the whole body of ideas expressed in the *Credo*, for these ideas lead straight to the realisation of this prospect. Russian Social-Democrats must bend every effort to translate into reality another prospect, outlined by P. B. Axelrod in the following words:

"The other prospect: Social-Democracy organises the Russian proletariat into an independent political party which fights for liberty, *partly side by side and in alliance with* the bourgeois revolutionary groups (if such should exist), and partly by recruiting directly into its ranks or securing the following of the most democratic-minded and revolutionary elements from among the intelligentsia" (*ibid.*, p. 20).

At the time P. B. Axelrod wrote the above lines the declarations made by Social-Democrats in Russia showed clearly that the overwhelming majority of them adhered to the same point of view. It is true that one St. Petersburg workers' paper, *Rabochaya Mysl*,[68] seemed to incline toward the ideas of the authors of the *Credo*. In a leading article setting forth its programme (No. 1, October 1897) it expressed, regrettably, the utterly erroneous idea, an idea running counter to Social-Democracy, that the "economic basis of the movement" may be "obscured by the effort to keep the political ideal constantly in mind." At the same time, however, another St. Petersburg workers' newspaper, *S. Peterburgsky Rabochy Listok*[69] (No. 2, September 1897), emphatically expressed the opinion that "the overthrow of the autocracy ... can be achieved only by a well-organised and numerically strong working-class party" and that "organised in a strong party" the workers will "emancipate themselves, and the whole of Russia, from all political and economic oppression." A third newspaper, *Rabochaya Gazeta*,[70] in its leading article in issue No. 2 (November 1897), wrote: "The fight against the autocratic government for political liberty is the immediate task of the Russian working-class movement." "The Russian working-class movement will increase its forces tenfold if it comes out as a single harmonious whole, with a common name and a well-knit organisation...." "The separate workers' circles should combine into one common party." "The Russian workers' party will be a Social-Democratic Party."

That precisely these views of *Rabochaya Gazeta* were fully shared by the vast majority of Russian Social-Democrats is seen, furthermore, from the fact that the Congress of Russian Social-Democrats[71] in the spring of 1898 formed the Russian Social-Democratic Labour Party, published its manifesto and recognised *Rabochaya Gazeta* as the official Party organ. Thus, the *Credo* authors are taking an enormous step backward from the stage of development which Russian Social-Democracy has already achieved and which it has recorded in the *Manifesto of the Russian Social-Democratic Labour Party*. Since the frenzied persecution by the Russian Government has led to the present situation in which the Party's activity has temporarily subsided and its official organ has ceased publication, it is the task of all Russian Social-Democrats to exert every effort for the utmost consolidation of the Party, to draw up a Party programme and revive its official organ. In view of the ideological vacillations evidenced by the fact that programmes like the above-examined *Credo* can appear, we think it particularly necessary to emphasise the following fundamental principles that were expounded in the *Manifesto* and that are of enormous importance to Russian Social-Democracy. First, Russian Social-Democracy "desires to be and to remain the class movement of the organised working masses." Hence it follows that the motto of Social-Democracy must be: aid to the workers, not only in their economic, but also in their political struggle; agitation, not only in connection with immediate economic needs, but also in connection with all manifestations of political oppression; propaganda, not only of the ideas of scientific socialism, but also of democratic ideas. Only the theory of revolutionary Marxism can be the banner of the class movement of the workers, and Russian Social-Democracy must concern itself with the further development and implementation of this theory and must safeguard it against the distortions and vulgarisations to which "fashionable theories" are so often subjected (and the successes of revolutionary Social-Democracy in Russia have already made Marxism a "fashionable" theory). While concentrating all their present efforts on activity among factory and mine workers, Social-Democrats must not forget that with the expansion of the movement home workers, handicraftsmen, agricultural labourers, and the millions of ruined and starving peasants must be drawn into the ranks of the labouring masses they organise.

Secondly: "On his strong shoulders the Russian worker must and will carry to a finish the cause of winning political liberty." Since its immediate task is the overthrow of the autocracy, Social-Democracy must act as the vanguard in the fight for democracy, and consequently, if for no other reason, must give every support to all democratic elements of the population of Russia and win them as allies. Only an independent working-class party can serve as a strong bulwark in the fight against the autocracy, and only in alliance with such a party, only by supporting it, can all the other fighters for political liberty play an effective part.

Thirdly and finally: "As a socialist movement and trend, the Russian Social-Democratic Party carries on the cause and the traditions of the whole preceding revolutionary movement in Russia; considering the winning of political liberty to be the most important of the immediate tasks of the Party as a whole, Social-Democracy marches towards the goal that was already clearly indicated by the glorious representatives of the old Narodnaya Volya.[72]" The traditions of the whole preceding revolutionary movement demand that the Social-Democrats shall at the present time concentrate all their efforts on organising the Party, on strengthening its internal discipline, and on developing the technique for illegal work. If the members of the old Narodnaya Volya managed to play an enormous role in the history of Russia, despite the fact that only narrow social strata supported the few heroes, and despite the fact that it was by no means a revolutionary theory which served as the banner of the movement, then Social-Democracy, relying on the class struggle of the proletariat, will be able to render itself invincible. "The Russian proletariat will throw off the yoke of autocracy in order to continue the struggle against capital and the bourgeoisie for the complete victory of socialism with still greater energy."

We invite all groups of Social-Democrats and all workers' circles in Russia to discuss the above-quoted *Credo* and our resolution, and to express a definite opinion on the question raised, in order that all differences may be removed and the work of organising and strengthening the Russian Social-Democratic Labour Party may be accelerated.

Groups and circles may send their resolutions to the Union of Russian Social-Democrats Abroad which, by Point 10 of the decision of the 1898 Congress of Russian Social-Democrats, is a part of the Russian Social-Democratic Party and its representative abroad.

REVIEW

S. N. Prokopovich. *The Working-Class Movement in the West*[73]

"...to turn to social science and to its alleged conclusion that the capitalist system of society is hastening inexorably to its doom by virtue of the contradictions developing within it. We find the relevant explanations in Kautsky's *Erfurt Programme*" (147). Before dealing with the content of the passage quoted by Mr. Prokopovich, we must take note of a peculiarity highly typical of him and similar reformers of theory. Why is it that our "critical investigator," in turning to "social science," looks for "explanations" in Kautsky's popular booklet and nowhere else? Does he really believe that the whole of "social science" is contained in that little booklet? He knows perfectly well that Kautsky is "a faithful custodian of the traditions of Marx" (I, 187) and that an exposition and a substantiation of the "conclusions" of a certain school of "social science" are to be found precisely in Marx's treatises on political economy; yet he acts as though such a thing were altogether unknown to him. What are we to think of an "investigator" who confines himself to attacks on "custodians" of a theory but who does not once, throughout his book, risk crossing swords openly and directly with the theory itself?

In the passage quoted by Mr. Prokopovich, Kautsky says that the technological revolution and the accumulation of capital are progressing with increasing rapidity, that the expansion of production is made necessary by the fundamental properties of capitalism and must be uninterrupted, while the expansion of the market "has for some time been proceed-

ing too slowly" and that "the time is apparently at hand
when the market for European industry will not only cease
its further expansion but will even begin to shrink. This
event can only mean the bankruptcy of the entire capitalist
society." Mr. Prokopovich "criticises" the "conclusions"
drawn by "social science" (*i.e.*, Kautsky's citation of one
of the laws of development evolved by Marx): "The basis
thus given for the inevitability of the collapse of capitalist
society allots the chief role to the contradiction between
'the constant drive to expand production and the ever slow-
er expansion of the market and, finally, its shrinkage.'
It is this contradiction, according to Kautsky, that must
bring about the collapse of the capitalist system of society.
But [listen well!] the expansion of production presumes the
'productive consumption' of part of the surplus-value—i.e.,
first its realisation and then its expenditure on machinery,
buildings, etc., for new production. In other words, the expansion of production is most closely connected with the
existence of a market for the commodities already produced;
the constant expansion of production with a market that is
relatively shrinking is, therefore, an impossibility" (148)..
And Mr. Prokopovich is so well satisfied with his excursion
into the sphere of "social science" that in the very next line
he speaks with condescending disdain of a "scientific"
(in inverted commas) substantiation of faith, etc. Such
jockeying with criticism would be outrageous, were it not for
the fact that it is, more than anything else, amusing. Our
good Mr. Prokopovich has heard a knell, but knows not from
what bell. Mr. Prokopovich has heard of the abstract theory
of realisation that has recently been heatedly discussed in
Russian literature in the course of which the role of "productive consumption" has been particularly stressed on account of
errors in Narodnik economics. Mr. Prokopovich has not properly understood this theory and imagines that it *denies*
(!) the existence in capitalism of those basic and elementary contradictions Kautsky speaks of. To listen to Mr. Prokopovich, we would have to believe that "productive consumption" could develop *quite independently* of individual
consumption (in which consumption by the masses plays
the dominant role), i.e., that capitalism does not contain within itself any contradiction between production and

Page 6 of the manuscript of Lenin's "Rewiev of S. N. Prokopovich'
Book." End of 1899

Reduced

consumption. This is simply absurd, and Marx and his Russian supporters* have clearly opposed such misconstruc-
tions. Not only does the bourgeois-apologetic theory into
which our "critical investigator" has wandered not follow
from the fact that "the expansion of production presumes
productive consumption," but, on the contrary, from it follows the contradiction between the tendency towards the unlimited growth of production and limited consumption that
is inherent precisely in capitalism and that must bring
about its collapse.

Apropos of what has been said, it is worth while mentioning the following interesting point. Mr. Prokopovich is
a fervent follower of Bernstein, whose magazine articles
he quotes and translates for several pages. In his well-know
book, *Die Voraussetzungen, etc.*,** Bernstein even recommends Mr. Prokopovich to the German public as his Russian
supporter, but he makes a reservation, the substance of which
is that Mr. Prokopovich is more Bernsteinian than Bernstein. And, a remarkable thing, Bernstein and his Russian
yesman both distort the theory of realisation, but *in diametrically opposite directions*, so that they *cancel each other out.*
Firstly, Bernstein regarded as a "contradiction" the fact
that Marx turned against Rodbertus' theory of crises and at
the same time declared that "the ultimate cause of all real
crises is the poverty and limited consumption of the masses."
Actually there is no contradiction here at all, as I have had
occasion to point out in other places (*Studies*, p. 30,*** *The
Development of Capitalism in Russia*, p. 19****). Secondly,
Bernstein argues in precisely the same manner as does Mr.
V. V. here in Russia, that the tremendous growth of the surplus-product must inevitably mean an increase in the number of well-to-do (or the greater prosperity of the workers),

---

* Cf. my article in *Nauchnoye Obozreniye* for August 1899, especially page 1572 (see pp. 74-93 of this volume, especially p. 84.—*Ed.*),
and *The Development of Capitalism in Russia*, p. 16, et seq. (See present edition, Vol. 3, p. 54, et seq.—*Ed.*)

** *The Premises, etc.—Ed.*

*** See present edition, Vol. 2, *A Characterisation of Economic
Romanticism*, pp. 167-68.—*Ed.*

**** See present edition, Vol. 3, p. 58.—*Ed.*

since the capitalists themselves and their servants (*sic!*)
cannot "consume" the entire surplus-product (*Die Voraussetzungen, etc., S.* 51-52). This naïve argument completely
ignores the role of productive consumption, *as Kautsky pointed out in his book against Bernstein* (Kautsky, *Gegen Bernstein*, II. *Abschnitt*,*—the paragraph on "the employment of
surplus-value"). And now there appears a Russian Bernsteinian, recommended by Bernstein, who says exactly the opposite, who lectures Kautsky on the role of "productive consumption" and then reduces Marx's discovery to the absurdity
that productive consumption can develop quite independently of individual consumption (!), that the realisation of surplus-value by its use for the production of means of
production does away with the dependence, in the final analysis, of production on consumption and, consequently, with
the contradiction between them! By this example the reader
may judge whether Mr. Prokopovich's "loss of a good half of
the theoretical premises" is due to the "investigations" or
whether our "critical investigator" is "at a loss" due to some
other cause.

A second example. Taking up three pages (25-27), our
author "investigated" the question of peasant associations
in Germany. He gave a list of the various kinds of associations and statistical data on their rapid growth (especially of dairy associations) and argued: "The artisan has been
almost deprived of his roots in the modern economic system,
whereas the peasant continues to stand firm [!] in it." How
very simple, isn't it really? The undernourishment of the
German peasants, their exhaustion from excessive labour,
the mass flight of people from the countryside to the towns—
all that must be mere invention. It suffices to point to the
rapid growth of associations (especially dairy associations
that result in depriving the peasants' children of milk
and lead to the peasants' greater dependence on capitalists)
in order to prove the "stability" of the peasantry. "The development of capitalist relations in the manufacturing industry ruins the artisan but improves the condition of the
peasant. It [the condition?] hinders the penetration of capitalism into agriculture." This is new! Until now it has been

---

* Kautsky, *Against Bernstein*, Section II.—*Ed.*

believed that it is the development of capitalism in the manufacturing industry that is the main force which gives rise to, and develops, capitalism in agriculture. But Mr. Prokopovich, like his German prototypes, could truly say of himself: *nous avons changé tout ca*—we have changed all that! But would that be true, gentlemen? Have you really changed *anything at all*, have you shown the error in even one of the basic postulates of the theory you have "torn to pieces" and replaced it by a truer postulate? Have you not, on the contrary, returned to the old prejudices?... "On the other hand, the development of the manufacturing industry ensures subsidiary earnings for the peasant."... A return to the doctrine of Messrs. V. V. & Co. on the subsidiary earnings of the peasantry! Mr. Prokopovich does not deem it worth mentioning the fact that in a large number of cases these "earnings" express the conversion of the peasant into a wage-labourer. He prefers to conclude his "investigation" with the high-sounding sentence: "The sap of life has not yet left the peasant class." It is true that Kautsky has shown, precisely in respect of Germany, that agricultural associations are a transition stage on the way *to capitalism*—but, you see, we already know how the terrible Mr. Prokopovich has crushed Kautsky!

We see this resurrection of Narodnik views (Narodnik views of the V. V. hue) not only in the above passage but in many other places in Mr. Prokopovich's "critical investigation." The reader probably knows the fame (a sorry fame) that Mr. V. V. earned for himself by his excessive narrowing and debasing of the theory known as "economic" materialism: this theory, as "adapted" by Mr. V. V., did not postulate that in the final analysis all factors are reduced to the development of the productive forces, but postulated that many extremely important (although in the final analysis secondary) factors could be neglected. Mr. Prokopovich offers us a very similar distortion when he attempts to expose Kautsky as one who does not understand the significance of "material forces" (144), in the course of which Mr. Prokopovich himself light-mindedly confuses "economic organisation" (145) with "economic force" (on 146 and especially 149). Unfortunately we cannot dwell to the needed extent on an analysis of this error of Mr. Prokopovich, but must refer the reader to the above-mentioned book by Kautsky

against Bernstein (*Abschnitt* III, Section *a*), where the
original versions of Mr. Prokopovich's rehashings are discussed at length. We also hope that the reader who peruses
Mr. Prokopovich's book attentively will see quite easily that
the theory torn to pieces by our "critical investigator"
(Mr. Prokopovich, incidentally, here, too, maintains a modest
silence about the views of the founders of the theory and
refrains from examining them, preferring to confine himself
to extracts from the speeches and articles of present-day
adherents of this theory)—that the theory is in no way to
blame for this disgraceful narrowing of "economic" materialism (cf., for example, statements by authoritative Belgian
spokesmen on pp. 74, 90, 92, 100 in the second part).

As far as the extracts quoted by Mr. Prokopovich are concerned, it should be said that he often seizes on individual
passages and gives the reader a distorted impression of views
and arguments that have not been expounded in Russian
literature. On account of this, Mr. Prokopovich's jockeying with criticism creates a most repulsive impression.
In some cases it would be worth the while of those who
read Mr. Prokopovich's book to refer even to a book by
Professor Herkner that has recently been translated into
Russian: *Wage-Labour in Western Europe* (St. Petersburg,
1899, published by the magazine *Obrazovaniye*). For instance,
in a note to page 24 (Part I) Mr. Prokopovich writes that
the Congress of 1892 "adopted a resolution sympathising
with the organisation of producers' associations" and follows
this up with a quotation which, first, does not fully support
the words of the author and, secondly, *breaks off* precisely at
the point where it speaks of the necessity "to conduct a particular struggle against the belief that associations are in a
position to bring any influence to bear on capitalist production relations, etc." (Herkner, Notes, pp. xi-xii, Note
6 to Chapter IX).

Mr. Prokopovich is just as successful in his crushing of
Kautsky on pages 56, 150, 156, 198, and in many other places
as he is in the case we have examined. Mr. Prokopovich's
assertions that Liebknecht, in the sixties, for a time renounced his ideals, betrayed them, etc. (111, 112), are in
no sense to be taken seriously. We have had occasion to see
how well-founded his judgements are, and the following

sentence (once again directed, not against the founder of the theory, but against its "custodian") will, for example, show us to what Pillars of Hercules the insolence and self-assurance of our "investigator" will take him: "We should be acting superficially, if we undertook to criticise this whole conception of the working-class movement from the standpoint of its conformity to the true course taken by the development of this movement—from the standpoint of its *scientific basis* [Mr. Prokopovich's italics]. There is not and cannot be (*sic!*) a grain of science in it" (156). This is what you call categorical criticism! All this Marxism, it isn't even worth criticising, and that's that! Obviously we have before us either a man who is destined to make a great revolution in the science "of which there cannot be even a grain" in the theory that is dominant in Germany, or ... or—how can it be put delicately?—or a man who, when "at a loss," repeats the phrases of others. Mr. Prokopovich prostrates himself with such fervour before this very latest of gods who has pronounced those words for the thousandth time that he has no pity on his own forehead. Bernstein, if you please, "has some shortcomings in his theoretical views" (198) that consist—can you imagine it?—in his belief in the necessity of a scientific theory that defines the aims of the men of action concerned. "Critical investigators" are not subject to this strange belief. "Science will become free," utters Mr. Prokopovich, "only when it is admitted that it must *serve* the aims of a party and not *define* them. It must be recognised that science cannot define the aims of a practical party" (197). Be it noted that Bernstein renounced precisely these views of his follower. "A principled programme inevitably leads to dogmatism and is only a hindrance in the way of the party's sound development.... Theoretical principles are all very well in propaganda but not in a programme" (157). "Programmes are unnecessary; they are harmful." "The individual himself may be a programme if he is sensitive to, and has a fine feeling for, the needs of the times."... The reader probably thinks that I am continuing to quote Mr. Prokopovich. But no, I am now quoting the newspaper *Novoye Vremya*,[74] which recently published articles on a programme that attracted a great deal of attention—not the programme of a party, of course, but of the new Minister for Internal Affairs....

The relationship of the freedom of unprincipledness—excuse me, "freedom of science"—preached by Mr. Prokopovich to the views of the majority of the West-European personalities of whom our valiant critic so valiantly writes, may be seen from the following quotations drawn from that same book by Mr. Prokopovich: "Of course, without a betrayal of principles..." (159). "Not in any way violating one's independence, loyalty to principle...." "I renounce compromise only in the case ... in which it leads to a renunciation of principles or even to the ignoring of principles..." (171). "Introducing no unprincipledness...", (174). "Not, of course, selling one's soul, in the present case, one's principles..." (176). "The principles are now firmly established..." (183). "A compass [is needed] that would rid us of the need to grope our way," against "short-sighted empiricism," against "a thoughtless attitude to principles" (195). "Primary importance attaches to principles, to the theoretical part..." (103, Part II), etc.

In conclusion, two more quotations: "If German Social-Democracy were the expression of socialism and not of the proletariat that is acting in defence of its own interests in present-day society, for the first time recognising its significance, then—since not all Germans are idealists—side by side with this party that pursues idealist aims we should see another, stronger party, a working-class party that represents the practical interests of that part of the German proletariat that is not idealist."... "If socialism were not to play the role of a mere symbol in that movement, a symbol distinguishing one definite organisation, if it were the motive idea, the principle that demands of party members a certain specific service—in that ease the socialist party would separate from the general labour party, and the mass of the proletariat, which strives for better living conditions under the existing system and cares little for the ideal future, would form an independent labour party." The reader will again probably think....

Written at the end 1899
First published in 1928
in *Lenin Miscellany VII*

Published according to
the manuscript

REVIEW

Karl Kautsky. *Bernstein und das sozialdemokratische Programm. Eine Antikritik**

...In the introduction Kautsky gives voice to some extremely valuable and apt ideas on the conditions that must be satisfied by serious and conscientious criticism if those undertaking it do not wish to confine themselves within the narrow bounds of soulless pedantry and scholasticism, if they do not wish to lose sight of the close and indestructible bonds that exist between the "theoretical reason" and the "practical reason"—not the practical reason of individuals, but of the masses of the population placed in specific conditions. Truth, of course, comes first, says Kautsky, and if Bernstein has become sincerely convinced of the error of his former views, it is his plain duty to give definite expression to his convictions. But the trouble with Bernstein is his lack of precisely this directness and definiteness. His pamphlet is amazingly "encyclopaedic" (as Antonio Labriola has remarked in a French magazine); it touches on a mass of problems, an agglomeration of questions, but *not on any one* of them does it provide an integral and precise exposition of the critic's new views. The critic merely expresses his doubts and abandons difficult and complicated questions without any independent analysis after having scarcely touched upon them. This brings about, Kautsky notes sarcastically, a strange phenomenon: Bernstein's followers understand his

---

* Karl Kautsky. *Bernstein and the Social-Democratic Programme. A Counter-Critique.—Ed.*

book in the most diverse ways, whereas his opponents all understand it in the same way. Bernstein's chief objection to his opponents is that they do not understand him, that they do not want to understand him. The whole series of newspaper and magazine articles that Bernstein has written in answer to his opponents has failed to explain his positive views.

Kautsky begins his Counter-Criticism with the question of method. He examines Bernstein's objections to the materialist conception of history and shows that Bernstein confuses the concept of "determinism" with that of "mechanism," that he confuses freedom of will with freedom of action, and without any grounds identifies historical necessity with the hopeless position of people under compulsion. The outworn accusation of fatalism, which Bernstein also repeats, is refuted by the very premises of Marx's theory of history. Not everything can be reduced to the development of the productive forces, says Bernstein. Other factors "must be taken into consideration."

Very well, answers Kautsky, that is something every investigator must do, irrespective of what conception of history guides him. Anyone who wants to make us reject Marx's method, the method that has so brilliantly justified itself and continues to justify itself in practice, must take one of two paths: either he must reject altogether the idea of objective laws, of the necessity of the historical process, and in so doing abandon all attempts at providing a scientific basis for sociology; or he must show how he can evolve the necessity of the historical process from other factors (ethical views, for example), he must show this by an analysis that will stand up to at least a remote comparison with Marx's analysis in *Capital*. Not only has Bernstein not made the slightest attempt to do this, but, confining himself to empty platitudes about "taking into consideration" other factors, he *has continued* to use the old materialist method in his book as though he did not declare it to be wanting! As Kautsky points out, Bernstein, at times, even applies this method with the most impermissible crudity and one-sidedness! Further on Bernstein's accusations are levelled against dialectics which, he alleges, lead to arbitrary constructions, etc., etc. Bernstein repeats these phrases (that have already managed to disgust also the Russian readers) without making the slightest attempt to show what is incorrect in dialectics, whether Hegel or Marx and Engels are guilty of methodological errors (and precisely what errors). The only means by which Bernstein tries to motivate and fortify his opinion is a reference to the "tendentiousness" of one of the concluding sections of *Capital* (on the historical tendency of capitalist accumulation). This charge has been worn threadbare: it was made by Eugen Dühring and Julius Wolf and many others in Germany, and it was made (we add on our part) by Mr. Y. Zhukovsky in the seventies and by Mr. N. Mikhailovsky in the nineties—by the very same Mr. Mikhailovsky who had once accused Mr. Y. Zhukovsky of acrobatics for making the selfsame charge. And what *proof* does Bernstein offer in confirmation of this worn-out nonsense? Only the following: Marx began his "investigation" with ready-made conclusions, since in 1867 *Capital* drew the same conclusion that Marx had drawn as early as the forties. Such "proof" is tantamount to fraud, answers Kautsky, because Marx based his conclusions on two investigations and not on one, as he points out very definitely in the introduction to *Zur Kritik* (see Russian translation: *A Critique of Some of the Propositions of Political Economy*[75]). Marx made his first investigation in the forties, after leaving the Editorial Board of the *Rheinische Zeitung*.[76] Marx left the newspaper because he had to treat of material interests and he realised that he was not sufficiently prepared for this. From the arena of public life, wrote Marx about himself, I withdrew into the study. And so (stresses Kautsky, hinting at Bernstein), Marx had doubts regarding the correctness of his judgement of material interests, regarding the correctness of the dominant views on this subject at that time, but he did not think his doubts to be important enough to write a whole book and inform the world about them. On the contrary, Marx set out to study in order to advance from doubtings of the old views to positive new ideas. He began to study French social theories and English political economy. He came into close contact with Engels, who was at that time making a detailed study of the actual state of the economy in England. The result of this joint work, this *first* inquiry, was the

well-known conclusions which the two writers expounded
very definitely towards the end of the forties.[77] Marx moved
to London in 1850, and the favourable conditions there for
research determined him "to begin afresh *from the very beginning* and to work through the new material critically" (*A
Critique of Some of the Propositions*, 1st edition, p. xi.[78]
Our italics). The fruit of this *second* inquiry, lasting many
long years, were the works: *Zur Kritik* (1859) and *Das
Kapital* (1867). The conclusion drawn in *Capital* coincides
with the former conclusion drawn in the forties because the
second inquiry confirmed the results of the first. "My views,
however they may be judged ... are the result of conscientious
investigation lasting many years," wrote Marx in 1859
(*ibid.*, p. xii).[79] Does this, asks Kautsky, resemble conclusions found ready-made long before the investigation?

From the question of dialectics Kautsky goes over to
the question of value. Bernstein says that Marx's theory
is unfinished, that it leaves many problems "that are by
no means fully explained." Kautsky does not think of refuting this: Marx's theory is not the last word in science, he
says. History brings new facts and new methods of investigation that require the further development of the theory.
If Bernstein had made an attempt to utilise new facts and
new methods of inquiry for the further development of
the theory, everybody would have been grateful to him.
But Bernstein does not dream of doing that; he confines
himself to cheap attacks on Marx's disciples and to extremely vague, purely eclectic remarks, such as: the Gossen-
Jevons-Böhm theory of marginal utility is no less just than
Marx's theory of labour-value. Both theories retain their
significance for different purposes, says Bernstein, because
Böhm-Bawerk has as much right, *a prior*, to abstract from
the property of commodities that they are produced by
labour, as Marx has to abstract from the property that they
are use-values. Kautsky points out that it is utterly absurd
to regard two opposite, mutually exclusive theories suitable
for different purposes (and, furthermore, Bernstein does
not say for what purposes either of the two theories is suitable). It is by no means a question as to which property of
commodities we are, *a priori* (*von Hause aus*), entitled to
abstract from; the question is how to explain the principal

phenomena of present-day society, based on the *exchange* of products, how to explain the value of commodities, the function of money, etc. Even if Marx's theory may leave a number of still unexplained problems, Bernstein's theory of value is a totally unexplained problem. Bernstein further quotes Buch, who constructed the concept of the "maximum density" of labour; but Bernstein does not give a complete exposition of Buch's views or make a definite statement of his own opinion on that question. Buch, it seems, gets entangled in contradictions by making value depend on wages and wages depend on value. Bernstein senses the eclecticism of his statements on value and tries to defend eclecticism in general. He calls it "the revolt of the sober intellect against the tendency inherent in every dogma to constrict thought within narrow confines." If Bernstein were to recall the history of thought, retorts Kautsky, he would see that the great rebels against the constriction of thought within narrow confines were never eclectics, that what has always characterised them has been the striving for the unity, for the integrity of ideas. The eclectic is too timid to dare revolt. If, indeed, I click my heels politely to Marx and at the same time click my heels politely to Böhm-Bawerk, that is still a long way from revolt! Let anyone name even one eclectic in the republic of thought, says Kautsky, who has proved worthy of the name of rebel!

Passing from the method to the results of its application, Kautsky deals with the so-called *Zusammenbruchstheorie*, the theory of collapse, of the sudden crash of West-European capitalism, a crash that Marx allegedly believed to be inevitable and connected with a gigantic economic crisis. Kautsky says and proves that Marx and Engels never propounded a special *Zusammenbruchstheorie*, that they did not connect a *Zusammenbruch* necessarily with an economic crisis. This is a distortion chargeable to their opponents who expound Marx's theory one-sidedly, tearing out of context odd passages from different writings in order thus triumphantly to refute the "one-sidedness" and "crudeness" of the theory. Actually Marx and Engels considered the transformation of West-European economic relations to be dependent on the maturity and strength of the classes brought to the fore by modern European history. Bernstein tries to assert that this is not the theory of Marx, but Kautsky's interpretation and extension of it. Kautsky, however, with precise quotations from Marx's writings of the forties and sixties, as well as by means of an analysis of the basic ideas of Marxism, has completely refuted this truly pettifogging trickery of the Bernstein who so blatantly accused Marx's disciples of "apologetics and pettifoggery." This part of Kautsky's book is particularly interesting, the more so, since some Russian writers (e.g., Mr. Bulgakov in the magazine *Nachalo*) have been in a hurry to repeat the distortion of Marx's theory which Bernstein offered in the guise of "criticism" (as does Mr. Prokopovich in his *Working-Class Movement in the West*, St. Petersburg, 1899).

Kautsky analyses the basic tendencies of contemporary economic development in particularly great detail in order to refute Bernstein's opinion that this development is not proceeding in the direction indicated by Marx. It stands to reason that we cannot present here a detailed exposition of the chapter "Large- and Small-Scale Production" and of other chapters of Kautsky's book which are devoted to a political-economic analysis and contain extensive numerical data, but shall have to confine ourselves to a brief mention of their contents. Kautsky emphasises the point that the question is one of the direction, by and large, of development and by no means of particularities and superficial manifestations, which *no* theory can take into account in all their great variety. (Marx reminds the reader of this simple but oft forgotten truth in the relevant chapters of *Capital*.) By a detailed analysis of the data provided by the German industrial censuses of 1882 and 1895 Kautsky shows that they are a brilliant confirmation of Marx's theory and have placed beyond all doubt the process of the concentration of capital and the elimination of small-scale production. In 1896 Bernstein (when he himself still belonged to the guild of apologists and pettifoggers, says Kautsky ironically) most emphatically recognised this fact, but now he is excessive in his exaggeration of the strength and importance of small-scale production. Thus, Bernstein estimates the number of enterprises employing fewer than 20 workers at several hundred thousand, "apparently adding in his pessimistic zeal an extra

nought to the figure," since there are only 49,000 such enterprises in Germany. Further, whom do the statistics not
place among the petty entrepreneurs—cabmen, messengers,
gravediggers, fruit hawkers, seamstresses (even though they
may work at home for a capitalist), etc., etc.! Here let us note
a remark of Kautsky's that is particularly important from
the theoretical standpoint—that petty commercial and industrial enterprises (such as those mentioned above) in
capitalist society are often merely one of the forms of relative over-population; ruined petty producers, workers
unable to find employment turn (sometimes temporarily)
into petty traders and hawkers, or rent out rooms or beds
(also "enterprises," which are registered by statistics equally with all other types of enterprise!), etc. The fact that
these employments are overcrowded does not by any means
indicate the viability of petty production but rather the
growth of poverty in capitalist society. Bernstein, however,
emphasises and exaggerates the importance of the petty
"industrial producers" when to do so seems to him to serve his
advantage (on the question of large- and small-scale production), but keeps silent about them when he finds it to his
disadvantage (on the question of the growth of poverty).

Bernstein repeats the argument, long known to the Russian public as well, that joint-stock companies "permit"
the fragmentation of capital and "make unnecessary" its
concentration, and he cites some figures (cf. *Zhizn*, No. 3
for 1899) on the number of small shares. Kautsky replies
that these figures prove exactly nothing, since small shares
in any companies might belong to big capitalists (as even
Bernstein must admit). Bernstein does not adduce any evidence, nor can he, to prove that joint-stock companies
increase the number of property-owners, for the joint-
stock companies actually serve to expropriate the gullible
men of small means for the benefit of big capitalists and
speculators. The growth in the number of shares merely
shows that wealth has a tendency to take on the form of
shares; but this growth tells us nothing about the distribution of wealth. In general, Bernstein's attitude to the
question of an increase in the number of wealthy people,
the number of property-owners, is an astonishingly thoughtless one, which has not prevented his bourgeois followers

from praising precisely this part of his book and announcing that it is based on "a tremendous amount of numerical data." And Bernstein proved himself skilful enough, says Kautsky ironically, to compress this tremendous amount of data into two pages! He confuses property-owners with capitalists, although no one has denied an increase in the number of the latter. In analysing income-tax data, he ignores their fiscal character, and their confusion of income from property with income in the form of salary, etc. He compares data for different times that have been collected by different methods (on Prussia, for example) and are, therefore, not comparable. He even goes so far as to borrow data on the growth of property-owners in England (printing these figures in heavy type, as his trump card) from an article in some sensational newspaper that was singing the praises of Queen Victoria's jubilee and whose handling of statistics was the *nec plus ultra* of light-mindedness! The source of this information is unknown and, indeed, such information cannot be obtained on the basis of data on the English income tax, since these do not permit one to determine the number of tax-payers and the total income of each tax-payer. Kautsky adduces data from Kolb's book on the English income tax from 1812 to 1847 and shows that they, in exactly the same way as Bernstein's newspaper data, indicate an (apparent) increase in the number of property-owners—and that, in a period of the most terrible increase in the most horrible poverty of the people in England! A detailed analysis of Bernstein's data led Kautsky to the conclusion that Bernstein had not quoted a single figure that actually proved a growth in the number of property-owners.

Bernstein tried to give this phenomenon a theoretical grounding: the capitalists, he said, cannot themselves consume the entire surplus-value that increases to such a colossal extent; this means that the number of property-owners that consume it must grow. It is not very difficult for Kautsky to refute this grotesque argument that totally ignores Marx's theory of realisation (expounded many times in Russian literature). It is particularly interesting that for his refutation Kautsky does not employ theoretical arguments alone, but offers concrete data attesting to the growth of luxury and lavish spending in the West-European countries; to the influence of rapidly changing fashions, which greatly intensify this process; to mass unemployment; to the tremendous increase in the "productive consumption" of surplus-value, i.e., the investment of capital in new enterprises, especially the investment of European capital in the railways and other enterprises of Russia, Asia, and Africa.

Bernstein declares that everyone has abandoned Marx's "theory of misery" or "theory of impoverishment." Kautsky demonstrates that this is again a distorted exaggeration on the part of the opponents of Marx, since Marx propounded no such theory. He spoke of the growth of poverty, degradation, etc., indicating at the same time the counteracting tendency and the real social forces that alone could give rise to this tendency. Marx's words on the growth of poverty are fully justified by reality: first, we actually see that capitalism has a tendency to engender and increase poverty, which acquires tremendous proportions when the above-mentioned counteracting tendency is absent. Secondly, poverty grows, not in the physical but in the social sense, i.e., in the sense of the disparity between the increasing level of consumption by the bourgeoisie and consumption by society as a whole, and the level of the living standards of the working people. Bernstein waxes ironical over such a conception of "poverty," saying that this is a Pickwickian conception. In reply Kautsky shows that people like Lassalle, Rodbertus, and Engels have made very definite statements to the effect that poverty must be understood in its social, as well as in its physical, sense. As you see—he parries Bernstein's irony—it is not such a bad company that gathers at the "Pickwick Club"! Thirdly and lastly, the passage on increasing impoverishment remains perfectly true in respect of the "border regions" of capitalism, the border regions being understood both in the geographical sense (countries in which capitalism is only beginning to penetrate and frequently not only gives rise to physical poverty but to the outright starvation of the masses) and in the political-economic sense (handicraft industries and, in general, those branches of economy in which backward methods of production are still retained).

The chapter on the "new middle estate" is likewise extremely interesting and, for us Russians, particularly instructive. If Bernstein had merely wanted to say that in place of the declining petty producers a new middle estate, the intelligentsia, is appearing, he would be perfectly correct, says Kautsky, pointing out that he himself noted the importance of this phenomenon several years before. In all spheres of people's labour, capitalism increases the number of *office and professional workers* with particular rapidity and makes a growing demand for intellectuals. The latter occupy a special position among the other classes, attaching themselves partly to the bourgeoisie by their connections, their outlooks, etc., and partly to the wage-workers as capitalism increasingly deprives the intellectual of his independent position, converts him into a hired worker and threatens to lower his living standard. The transitory, unstable, contradictory position of that stratum of society now under discussion is reflected in the particularly widespread diffusion in its midst of hybrid, eclectic views, a farrago of contrasting principles and ideas, an urge to rise verbally to the higher spheres and to conceal the conflicts between the historical groups of the population with phrases—all of which Marx lashed with his sarcasm half a century ago.

In the chapter on the theory of crises Kautsky shows that Marx did not at all postulate a "theory" of the ten-year cycle of industrial crises, but merely stated a fact. The change in this cycle in recent times has been noted by Engels himself. It is said that cartels of industrialists can counteract crises by limiting and regulating production. But America is a land of cartels; yet instead of a limitation we see there a tremendous growth of production. Further, the cartels limit production for the home market but expand it for the foreign market, selling their goods abroad at a loss and extracting monopoly prices from consumers in their own country. This system is inevitable under protectionism and there are no grounds for anticipating a change from protectionism to Free Trade. The cartels close small factories, concentrate and monopolise production, introduce improvements, and in this way greatly worsen the condition of the producers. Bernstein is of the opinion that the speculation which gives rise to crises weakens as the conditions on the world market change from unforeseeable to foreseeable and known conditions; but he forgets that it is the "unfore-seeable" conditions in the new countries that give a tremendous impetus to speculation in the old countries. Using statistical data, Kautsky shows the growth of speculation in precisely the last few years, as well as the growth in the symptoms indicating a crisis in the not very distant future.

With regard to the remaining part of Kautsky's book, we must mention his analysis of the muddle people get into through confusing (as does Mr. S. Prokopovich, op. cit.) the economic strength of certain groups with their economic organisations. We must mention Kautsky's statement to the effect that Bernstein ascribes to purely temporary conditions of a given historical situation the dignity of a general law—his refutation of Bernstein's incorrect views on the essence of democracy; and his explanation of Bernstein's statistical error, in comparing the number of industrial workers in Germany with the number of voters and overlooking the mere trifle that not all the workers in Germany (but only males over the age of 25) enjoy the franchise and that not all participate in the elections. We can only strongly recommend to the reader who is interested in the question of the significance of Bernstein's book and in the polemic around it to turn to the German literature and under no circumstances to believe the biased and one-sided reviews by the proponents of eclecticism that dominate in Russian literature. We have heard that part of Kautsky's book here under-review will probably be translated into Russian. This is-very desirable, but is no substitute for an acquaintanceship-with the original.

Written at the end 1899
First published in 1928
in *Lenin Miscellany VII*

Published according to
the manuscript

ARTICLES FOR "RABOCHAYA GAZETA"[80]

Written in the second half of 1899
First published in 1925
in *Lenin Miscellany III*

Published according
to manuscripts copied
by an unknown hand

LETTER TO THE EDITORIAL GROUP

Dear Comrades!

In response to your request I am sending three articles for the newspaper and deem it essential to say a few words about my collaboration in general and the relations between us in particular.

From your previous communication I gathered that you wanted to found a publishing firm and give me a series of Social-Democratic pamphlets to edit.

Now I see that matters are different, that you have set up your Editorial Board, which is beginning the publication of a newspaper and invites me to collaborate.

Needless to say, I agree willingly to this proposal as well, but I must state, in doing so, that I consider successful collaboration possible *only on the following terms*: 1) *regular* relations between the editors and the collaborator, *who shall be informed* of decisions on all manuscripts (accepted, rejected, changed) and of *all publications of your firm*; 2) my articles to be signed with a special pseudonym (if the one I sent you has been lost, choose another yourselves); 3) agreement between the editors and the collaborator on fundamental views concerning theoretical questions, concerning immediate practical tasks, and concerning the desired character of the newspaper (or series of pamphlets).

I hope the editors will agree to these terms and, in order to effect the earliest possible agreement between us, I will deal in brief with the questions arising out of the third condition.

I am informed that you find that "the old current is strong" and that there is no particular need for a polemic against Bernsteinism and its Russian echoers. I consider this view to he too optimistic. Bernstein's public announcement that the majority of the Russian Social-Democrats agree with him[81]; the split between the "young" Russian Social-Democrats abroad and the Emancipation of Labour group[82] which is the founder, the representative, and the most faithful custodian of the "old current"; the vain efforts of *Rabochaya Mysl* to say some new word, to revolt against the "extensive" political tasks, to raise petty matters and amateurish work to the heights of apotheosis, to wax vulgarly ironical over "revolutionary theories" (No. 7, "In Passing"); lastly, complete disorder in the legal Marxist literature and the frantic efforts on the part of the majority of its representatives to seize upon Bernsteinism, the "criticism" *à la mode*—all this, in my opinion, serves to show clearly that the re-establishment of the "old current" and its energetic defence is a matter of real urgency.

You will see from the articles what my views on the tasks of the paper and the plan of its publication are, and I should very much like to know the extent of our solidarity on this question (unfortunately the articles have been written in somewhat of a hurry: it is very important for me to know the deadline for their delivery).

I think it is *necessary to launch a direct polemic* against *Rabochaya Mysl*, but for this purpose I should like to receive *Nos. 1-2, 6, and those following 7*; also *Proletarskaya Borba.*[83] I need the last-named pamphlet also in order to review it in the paper.

As to length, you write that I am to impose no constraint on myself. I think that as long as there is a newspaper I shall give preference to newspaper articles and deal in them even with pamphlet themes, reserving for myself the right to work the articles up into pamphlets at a later date. The subjects with which I propose to deal in the immediate future are: 1) the Draft Programme (I'll send it soon)[84]; 2) questions of tactics and organisation that are to be discussed at the next congress of the Russian Social-Democratic Labour Party[85]; 3) a pamphlet on rules of conduct for workers and socialists at liberty, in prison, and in exile—modelled after the Polish pamphlet (on "rules of conduct"—if you can, I should like you to obtain it for me); 4) strikes (I—their significance, II—laws on strikes; III—a review of some of the strikes of recent years); 5) the pamphlet, *Woman and the Working-Class Cause*, and others.

I should like to know approximately what material the Editorial Board has in hand, so as to avoid repetition and the tackling of questions that have already been "exhausted."

I shall await an answer from the Editorial Board through the same channels. (*Apart from this way I have not had nor have I any other means of communicating with your group.*)

F. P. [86]

OUR PROGRAMME

International Social-Democracy is at present in a state of ideological wavering. Hitherto the doctrines of Marx and Engels were considered to be the firm foundation of revolutionary theory, but voices are now being raised everywhere to proclaim these doctrines inadequate and obsolete. Whoever declares himself to be a Social-Democrat and intends to publish a Social-Democratic organ must define precisely his attitude to a question that is preoccupying the attention of the German Social-Democrats and not of them alone.

We take our stand entirely on the Marxist theoretical position: Marxism was the first to transform socialism from a utopia into a science, to lay a firm foundation for this science, and to indicate the path that must be followed in further developing and elaborating it in all its parts. It disclosed the nature of modern capitalist economy by explaining how the hire of the labourer, the purchase of labour-power, conceals the enslavement of millions of propertyless people by a handful of capitalists, the owners of the land, factories, mines, and so forth. It showed that all modern capitalist development displays the tendency of large-scale production to eliminate petty production and creates conditions that make a socialist system of society possible and necessary. It taught us how to discern, beneath the pall of rooted customs, political intrigues, abstruse laws, and intricate doctrines—the *class struggle*, the struggle between the propertied classes in all their variety and the propertyless mass, the *proletariat*, which is at the head of all the propertyless. It made clear the real task of a revolutionary socialist party: not to draw up plans for refashioning society, not to preach to the capitalists and their hangers-on about improving the lot of the workers, not to hatch conspiracies, *but to organise the class struggle of the proletariat and to lead this struggle, the ultimate aim of which is the conquest of political power by the proletariat and the organisation of a socialist society.*

And we now ask: Has anything new been introduced into this theory by its loud-voiced "renovators" who are raising so much noise in our day and have grouped themselves around the German socialist Bernstein? *Absolutely nothing.* Not by a single step have they advanced the science which Marx and Engels enjoined us to develop; they have not taught the proletariat any new methods of struggle; they have only retreated, borrowing fragments of backward theories and preaching to the proletariat, not the theory of struggle, but the theory of concession—concession to the most vicious enemies of the proletariat, the governments and bourgeois parties who never tire of seeking new means of baiting the socialists. Plekhanov, one of the founders and leaders of Russian Social-Democracy, was entirely right in ruthlessly criticising Bernstein's latest "critique"[87]; the views of Bernstein have now been rejected by the representatives of the German workers as well (at the Hannover Congress).[88]

We anticipate a flood of accusations for these words; the shouts will rise that we want to convert the socialist party into an order of "true believers" that persecutes "heretics" for deviations from "dogma," for every independent opinion, and so forth. We know about all these fashionable and trenchant phrases. Only there is not a grain of truth or sense in them. There can be no strong socialist party without a revolutionary theory which unites all socialists, from which they draw all their convictions, and which they apply in their methods of struggle and means of action. To defend such a theory, which to the best of your knowledge you consider to be true, against unfounded attacks and attempts to corrupt it is not to imply that you are an enemy of *all* criticism. We do not regard Marx's theory as something completed and inviolable; on the contrary, we are convinced that it has only laid the foundation stone of the science which socialists *must* develop in all directions if they wish to keep pace with life. We think that an *independent* elaboration of Marx's theory is especially essential for Russian socialists; for this theory provides only general *guiding* principles, which, *in particular*, are applied in England differently than in France, in France differently than in Germany, and in Germany differently than in Russia. We shall therefore gladly afford space in our paper for articles on theoretical questions and we invite all comrades openly to discuss controversial points.

What are the main questions that arise in the application to Russia of the programme common to all Social-Democrats? We have stated that the essence of this programme is to organise the class struggle of the proletariat, and to lead this struggle, the ultimate aim of which is the conquest of political power by the proletariat and the establishment of a socialist society. The class struggle of the proletariat comprises the economic struggle (struggle against individual capitalists or against individual groups of capitalists for the improvement of the workers' condition) and the political struggle (struggle against the government for the broadening of the people's rights, i.e., for democracy, and for the broadening of the political power of the proletariat). Some Russian Social-Democrats (among them apparently those who direct *Rabochaya Mysl* regard the economic struggle as incomparably the more important and almost go so far as to relegate the political struggle to the more or less distant future. This standpoint is utterly false. All Social-Democrats are agreed that it is necessary to organise the economic struggle of the working class, that it is necessary to carry on agitation among the workers on this basis, i.e., to help the workers in their day-to-day struggle against the employers, to draw their attention to every form and every case of oppression and in this way to make clear to them the necessity for combination. But to forget the political struggle for the economic would mean to depart from the basic principle of international Social-Democracy, it would mean to forget what the entire history of the labour movement teaches us. The confirmed adherents of the bourgeoisie and of the government which serves it have even made repeated attempts to organise purely economic unions of workers and to divert them in this way from "politics," from socialism. It is quite possible that the Russian Government, too, may undertake something of the kind, as it has always endeavoured to throw some paltry sops or, rather, sham sops, to the people, only to turn their thoughts away from the fact that they are oppressed and without rights. No economic struggle can bring the workers any lasting improvement, or can even be conducted on a large scale, unless the workers have the right freely to organise meetings and unions, to have their own newspapers, and to send their representatives to the national assemblies, as do the workers in Germany and all other European countries (with the exception of Turkey and Russia). But in order to win these rights it is necessary to wage a *political struggle*. In Russia, not only the workers, but all citizens are deprived of political rights. Russia is an absolute and unlimited monarchy. The tsar alone promulgates laws, appoints officials and controls them. For this reason, *it seems* as though in Russia the tsar and the tsarist government are independent of all classes and accord equal treatment to all. But *in reality* all officials are chosen exclusively from the propertied class and all are subject to the influence of the big capitalists, who make the ministers dance to their tune and who achieve whatever they want. The Russian working class is burdened by a double yoke; it is robbed and plundered by the capitalists and the landlords, and to prevent it from fighting them, the police bind it hand and foot, gag it, and every attempt to defend the rights of the people is persecuted. Every strike against a capitalist results in the military and police being let loose on the workers. Every economic struggle necessarily becomes a political struggle, and Social-Democracy must indissolubly combine the one with the other into a *single class struggle of the proletariat*. The first and chief aim of such a struggle must be the conquest of political rights, *the conquest of political liberty*. If the workers of St. Petersburg alone, with a little help from the socialists, have rapidly succeeded in wringing a concession from the government—the adoption of the law on the reduction of the working day[89]—then the Russian working class as a whole, led by a single Russian Social-Democratic Labour Party, will be able, in persistent struggle, to win incomparably more important concessions.

The Russian working class is able to wage its economic
and political struggle alone, even if no other class comes
to its aid. But in the political struggle the workers do
not stand alone. The people's complete lack of rights and
the savage lawlessness of the bashi-bazouk officials rouse
the indignation of all honest educated people who cannot
reconcile themselves to the persecution of free thought
and free speech; they rouse the indignation of the persecuted
Poles, Finns, Jews, and Russian religious sects; they rouse
the indignation of the small merchants, manufacturers, and
peasants, who can nowhere find protection from the persecution of officials and police. All these groups of the population
are incapable, separately, of carrying on a persistent political struggle. But when the working class raises the banner
of this struggle, it will receive support from all sides. Russian
Social-Democracy will place itself at the head of all fighters for the rights of the people, of all fighters for democracy,
and it will prove invincible!

These are our fundamental views, and we shall develop
them systematically and from every aspect in our paper.
We are convinced that in this way we shall tread the path
which has been indicated by the Russian Social-Democratic
Labour Party in its published *Manifesto*.

OUR IMMEDIATE TASK

The Russian working-class movement is today going through a period of transition. The splendid beginning achieved by the Social-Democratic workers' organisations in the Western area, St. Petersburg, Moscow, Kiev, and other cities was consummated by the formation of the Russian Social-Democratic Labour Party (spring 1898). Russian Social-Democracy seems to have exhausted, for the time being, all its strength in making this tremendous step forward and has gone back to the former isolated functioning of separate local organisations. The Party has not ceased to exist, it has only withdrawn into itself in order to gather strength and put the unification of all Russian Social-Democrats on a sound footing. To effect this unification, to evolve a suitable form for it and to get rid completely of narrow local isolation—such is the immediate and most urgent task of the Russian Social-Democrats.

We are all agreed that our task is that of the organisation of the proletarian class struggle. But what is this class struggle? When the workers of a single factory or of a single branch of industry engage in struggle against their employer or employers, is this class struggle? No, this is only a weak embryo of it. The struggle of the workers becomes a class struggle only when all the foremost representatives of the entire working class of the whole country are conscious of themselves as a single working class and launch a struggle that is directed, not against individual employers, but against the *entire class* of capitalists and against the government that supports that class. Only when the individual worker realises that he is a member

of the entire working class, only when he recognises the
fact that his petty day-to-day struggle against individual
employers and individual government officials is a struggle
against the entire bourgeoisie and the entire government,
does his struggle become a class struggle. "Every class struggle is a political struggle"[90]—these famous words of Marx
are not to be understood to mean that any struggle of workers
against employers must *always be* a political struggle. They
must be understood to mean that the struggle of the workers
against the capitalists inevitably *becomes* a political struggle
insofar as it becomes a *class* struggle. It is the task of the
Social-Democrats, by organising the workers, by conducting
propaganda and agitation among them, to *turn* their spontaneous struggle against their oppressors into the struggle
of the whole class, into the struggle of a definite political
party for definite political and socialist ideals. This is something that cannot be achieved by local activity alone.

Local Social-Democratic activity has attained a fairly
high level in our country. The seeds of Social-Democratic
ideas have been broadcast throughout Russia; workers' leaflets—the earliest form of Social-Democratic literature—are
known to all Russian workers from St. Petersburg to Krasno-
yarsk, from the Caucasus to the Urals. All that is now lacking is the unification of all this local work into the work
of a single *party*. Our chief drawback, to the overcoming
of which we must devote all our energy, is the narrow "amateurish" character of local work. Because of this amateurish character many manifestations of the working-class movement in Russia remain purely local events and lose a great
deal of their significance as examples for the whole of Russian Social-Democracy, as a stage of the whole Russian
working-class movement. Because of this amateurishness,
the consciousness of their community of interests throughout
Russia is insufficiently inculcated in the workers, they do
not link up their struggle sufficiently with the idea of
Russian socialism and Russian democracy. Because of this
amateurishness the comrades' varying views on theoretical
and practical problems are not openly discussed in a central newspaper, they do not serve the purpose of elaborating
a common programme and devising common tactics for the
Party, they are lost in narrow study-circle life or they lead

to the inordinate exaggeration of local and chance peculiarities. Enough of our amateurishness! We have attained sufficient maturity to go over to *common action*, to the elaboration of a common Party programme, to the joint discussion of our Party tactics and organisation.

Russian Social-Democracy has done a great deal in criticising old revolutionary and socialist theories; it has
not limited itself to criticism and theorising alone; it has
shown that its programme is not hanging in the air but
is meeting the extensive spontaneous movement among the
people, that is, among the factory proletariat. It has now
to make the following, very difficult, but very important,
step—to elaborate an organisation of the movement adapted
to our conditions. Social-Democracy is not confined to
simple service to the working-class movement: it represents *"the combination of socialism and the working-class
movement"* (to use Karl Kautsky's definition which repeats
the basic ideas of the *Communist Manifesto*); the task of
Social-Democracy is to bring definite socialist ideals to
the spontaneous working-class movement, to connect this
movement with socialist convictions that should attain the
level of contemporary science, to connect it with the regular political struggle for democracy as a means of achiev-
ing socialism—in a word, to fuse this spontaneous movement
into one indestructible whole with the activity of the *revolutionary party*. The history of socialism and democracy
in Western Europe, the history of the Russian revolutionary
movement, the experience of our working-class movement—
such is the *material* we must master to elaborate a purposeful organisation and purposeful tactics for our Party.
"The analysis" of this material must, however, be done independently, since there are no ready-made models to be
found anywhere. On the one hand, the Russian working-class
movement exists under conditions that are quite different
from those of Western Europe. It would be most dangerous
to have any illusions on this score. On the other hand,
Russian Social-Democracy differs very substantially from
former revolutionary parties in Russia, so that the necessity of learning revolutionary technique and secret organisation from the old Russian masters (we do not in the least
hesitate to admit this necessity) does not in any way relieve

us of the duty of assessing them critically and elaborating
our own organisation independently.

In the presentation of such a task there are two main
questions that come to the fore with particular insistence:
1) How is the need for the complete liberty of local Social-
Democratic activity to be combined with the need for establishing a single—and, consequently, a centralist—party?
Social-Democracy draws its strength from the spontaneous
working-class movement that manifests itself differently
and at different times in the various industrial centres;
the activity of the local Social-Democratic organisations is
the *basis* of all Party activity. If, however, this is to be
the activity of isolated "amateurs," then it cannot, strictly
speaking, be called Social-Democratic, since it will not be
the organisation and leadership of the *class* struggle of the
proletariat. 2) How can we combine the striving of Social-
Democracy to become a revolutionary party that makes
the struggle for political liberty its chief purpose with the
determined refusal of Social-Democracy to organise political conspiracies, its emphatic refusal to "call the workers
to the barricades" (as correctly noted by P. B. Axelrod),
or, in general, to impose on the workers this or that "plan"
for an attack on the government, which has been thought
up by a company of revolutionaries?

Russian Social-Democracy has every right to believe that
it has provided the *theoretical* solution to these questions;
to dwell on this would mean to repeat what has been said in
the article, "Our Programme." It is now a matter of the
practical solution to these questions. This is not a solution
that can be made by a single person or a single group;
it can be provided only by the organised activity of Social-
Democracy as a whole. We believe that the most urgent
task of the moment consists in undertaking the solution of
these questions, for which purpose we must have as our immediate aim *the founding of a Party organ that will appear
regularly and be closely connected with all the local groups*.
We believe that *all* the activity of the Social-Democrats
should be directed to this end throughout the whole of the
forthcoming period. Without such an organ, local work
will remain narrowly "amateurish." The formation of the
Party—if the correct representation of that Party in a

certain newspaper is not organised—will to a considerable extent remain bare words. An economic struggle that is not united by a central organ cannot become the *class* struggle of the entire Russian proletariat. It is impossible to conduct a political struggle if the Party as a whole fails to make statements on all questions of policy and to give direction to the various manifestations of the struggle. The organisation and disciplining of the revolutionary forces and the development of revolutionary technique are impossible without the discussion of all these questions in a central organ, without the collective elaboration of certain *forms and rules for the conduct of affairs*, without the establishment—through the central organ—of every Party member's *responsibility* to the entire Party.

In speaking of the necessity to concentrate *all* Party forces—all literary forces, all organisational abilities, all material resources, etc.—on the foundation and correct conduct of the organ of the whole Party, we do not for a moment think of pushing other forms of activity into the background—e.g., local agitation, demonstrations, boycott, the persecution of spies, the bitter campaigns against individual representatives of the bourgeoisie and the government, protest strikes, etc., etc. On the contrary, we are convinced that all these forms of activity constitute the *basis* of the Party's activity, but, *without* their unification through an organ of the whole Party, these forms of revolutionary struggle *lose nine-tenths of their significance*; they do not lead to the creation of common Party experience, to the creation of Party traditions and continuity. The Party organ, far from competing with such activity, will exercise tremendous influence on its extension, consolidation, and systematisation.

The necessity to concentrate *all* forces on establishing a regularly appearing and regularly delivered organ arises out of the peculiar situation of Russian Social-Democracy as compared with that of Social-Democracy in other European countries and with that of the old Russian revolutionary parties. Apart from newspapers, the workers of Germany, France, etc., have numerous other means for the public manifestation of their activity, for organising the movement—parliamentary activity, election agitation, public meetings,

participation in local public bodies (rural and urban), the
open conduct of trade unions (professional, guild), etc.,
etc. *In place of all of that*, yes, *all* of that, we must be
served—until we have won political liberty—by a revolutionary newspaper, without which *no* broad organisation of
the entire working-class movement is possible. We do not
believe in conspiracies, we renounce individual revolutionary ventures to destroy the government; the words of Liebknecht, veteran of German Social-Democracy, serve as the
watchword of our activities: "*Studieren, propagandieren,
organisieren*"—Learn, propagandise, organise—and the piv-
ot of this activity can and must be only the *organ of the
Party*.

But is the regular and more or less stable establishment
of such an organ possible, and under what circumstances
is it possible? We shall deal with this matter next time.

AN URGENT QUESTION

In the previous article we said that our immediate task is to establish a Party organ, one that appears and can be delivered regularly, and we raised the question of whether and under what circumstances it is possible to achieve this aim. Let us examine the more important aspects of this question.

The main objection that may be raised is that the achievement of this purpose *first* requires the development of local group activity. We consider this fairly widespread opinion to be fallacious. We can and must immediately set about founding the Party organ—and, it follows, the Party itself—and putting them on a sound footing. The conditions essential to such a step already exist: local Party work is being carried on and obviously has struck deep roots; for the destructive police attacks that are growing more frequent lead to only short interruptions; fresh forces rapidly replace those that have fallen in battle. The Party has resources, for publishing and literary forces, not only abroad, but in Russia as well. The question, therefore, is whether the work *that is already being conducted* should be continued in "amateur" fashion or whether it should be organised into the work of one party and in such a way that it is reflected in its entirety in one common organ.

Here we come to the most urgent question of our movement, to its sore point—organisation. The improvement of revolutionary organisation and discipline, the perfection of our underground technique are an absolute necessity. We must openly admit that in this respect we are lagging behind the old Russian revolutionary parties and must bend all our efforts to overtake and surpass them. Without improved organisation there can be no progress of our working-class movement in general, and no establishment of an active party with a properly functioning organ, in particular. That is on the one hand. On the other, the existing Party organs (organs in the sense of institutions and groups, as well as newspapers) must pay greater attention to questions of organisation and exert an influence in this respect on local groups.

Local, amateurish work always leads to a great excess of personal connections, to study-circle methods, and we have grown out of the study-circle stage which has become too narrow for our present-day work and which leads to an over-expenditure of forces. Only fusion into a single party will enable us strictly to observe the principles of division of labour and economy of forces, which must be achieved in order to reduce the losses and build as reliable a bulwark as possible against the oppression of the autocratic government and against its frantic persecutions. Against us, against the tiny groups of socialists hidden in the expanses of the Russian "underground," there stands the, huge machine of a most powerful modern state that is exerting all its forces to crush socialism and democracy. We are convinced that we shall, in the end, smash that police state, because all the sound and developing sections of our society are in favour of democracy and socialism; but, in order to conduct a systematic struggle against the government, we must raise revolutionary organisation, discipline, and the technique of underground work to the highest degree of perfection. It is essential for individual Party members or separate groups of members to specialise in the different aspects of Party work—some in the duplication of literature, others in its transport across the frontier, a third category in its distribution inside Russia, a fourth in its distribution in the cities, a fifth in the arrangement of secret meeting places, a sixth in the collection of funds, a seventh in the delivery of correspondence and all information about the movement, an eighth in maintaining relations, etc., etc. We know that this sort of specialisation requires much greater self-restraint, much greater ability to concentrate on modest, unseen, everyday work, much greater real heroism than the usual work in study circles.

The Russian socialists and the Russian working class, however, have shown their heroic qualities and, in general, it would be a sin to complain of a shortage of people. There is to be observed among the working youth an impassioned, uncontrollable enthusiasm for the ideas of democracy and socialism, and helpers for the workers still continue to arrive from among the intellectuals, despite the fact that the prisons and places of exile are overcrowded. If the idea of the necessity for a stricter organisation is made widely known among all these recruits to the revolutionary cause, the plan for the organisation of a regularly published and delivered Party newspaper will cease to be a dream. Let us take one of the conditions for the success of this plan—that the newspaper be assured a regular supply of correspondence and other material from everywhere. Has not history shown that at all times when there has been a resurgence of our revolutionary movement such a purpose has proved possible of achievement even in respect of papers published abroad? If Social-Democrats working in various localities come to regard the Party newspaper as *their own* and consider the maintenance of regular contact with it, the discussion of their problems and the reflection of the whole movement in it to be their main task, it will be quite possible to ensure the supply to the paper of full information about the movement, provided methods of maintaining secrecy, not very complicated ones, are observed. The other aspect of the question, that of delivering the newspaper regularly to all parts of Russia, is much more difficult, more difficult than the similar task under previous forms of revolutionary movement in Russia when newspapers were not, to such an extent, intended for the masses of the people. The purpose of Social-Democratic newspapers, however, facilitates their distribution. The chief places to which the newspaper must be delivered regularly and in large numbers are the industrial centres, factory villages and towns, the factory districts of big cities, etc. In such centres the population is almost entirely working class; in actual fact the worker in such places is master of the situation and has hundreds of ways of outwitting the police; relations with neighbouring factory centres are

distinguished by their extraordinary activity. At the time
of the Exceptional Law against the Socialists (1878-90)[91]
the German political police did not function worse, but probably better, than the Russian police; nevertheless, the
German workers, thanks to their organisation and discipline,
were able to ensure the regular transport across the fron-
tiers of a weekly illegal newspaper and to deliver it to
the houses of all subscribers, so that even the ministers
could not refrain from admiring the Social-Democratic post
("the red mail"). We do not, of course, dream of such successes, but we can, if we bend our efforts towards it, ensure that our Party newspaper appears no less than twelve
times a year and is regularly delivered in all the main
centres of the movement to all groups of workers that can
be reached by socialism.

To return to the question of specialisation, we must
also point out that its insufficiency is due partially to
the dominance of "amateur" work and partially to the fact
that our Social-Democratic newspapers usually devote far
too little attention to questions of organisation.

Only the establishment of a common Party organ can give
the "worker in a given field" of revolutionary activity the
consciousness that he is marching with the "rank' and file,"
the consciousness that his work is directly essential to the
Party, that he is one of the links in the chain that will
form a noose to strangle the most evil enemy of the Russian
proletariat and of the whole Russian people—the Russian
autocratic government. Only strict adherence to this type
of specialisation can economise our forces; not only will
every aspect of revolutionary work be carried out by a
smaller number of people, but there will be an opportunity
to make a number of aspects of present-day activities *legal*
affairs. This *legalisation* of activity, its conduct within
the framework of the law, has long been advised for Russian socialists by *Vorwärts (Forward)*,[92] the chief organ
of the German Social-Democrats. At first sight one is
astonished at such advice, but in actual fact it merits
careful attention. Almost everyone who has worked in
a local study circle in some city will easily remember that
among the numerous and diverse affairs in which the circle
engaged some were, in themselves, legal (e.g., the gathering

of information on the workers' conditions; the study of legal
literature on many questions; consultation and reviewing of
certain types of foreign literature; maintenance of certain kinds of relations; aid to workers in obtaining a general education, in studying factory laws, etc.). Making
affairs of this sort the specific function of a special con-
tingent of people would reduce the strength of the revolutionary army "in the firing line" (without any reduction of its "fighting potential") and increase the strength
of the reserve, those who replace the "killed and wound-
ed." This will be possible only when both the active members and the reserve see their activities reflected in
the common organ of the Party and sense their connection
with it. Local meetings of workers and local groups will,
of course, always be necessary, no matter to what extent
we carry out our specialisation; but, on the one hand, the
number of mass revolutionary meetings (particularly dangerous from the standpoint of police action and often having
results far from commensurate with the danger involved)
will become considerably less and, on the other hand, the
selection of various aspects of revolutionary work as special
functions will provide greater opportunities to screen such
meetings behind legal forms of assembly: entertainments,
meetings of societies sanctioned by law, etc. Were not the
French workers under Napoleon III and the German workers
at the time of the Exceptional Law against the Socialists
able to devise all possible ways to cover up their political
and socialist meetings? Russian workers will be able to do
likewise.

Further: only by better organisation and the establishment of a common Party organ will it be possible to extend
and deepen the very content of Social-Democratic propaganda and agitation. We stand in great need of this. Local work
must almost inevitably lead to the exaggeration of local
particularities, to . . . .*
this is impossible without a central organ which will,
at the same time, be an advanced democratic organ. Only
then will our *urge* to convert Social-Democracy into a leading
fighter for democracy become *reality*. Only then, too, shall

* Part of the manuscript is not extant.—*Ed.*

we be able to work out definite political tactics. Social-Democracy has renounced the fallacious theory of the "one reactionary mass." It regards utilisation of the support of the progressive classes against the reactionary classes to be one of the most important political tasks. As long as the organisations and publications are local in character, this task can hardly be carried out at all: matters do not go farther than relations with individual "liberals" and the extraction of various "services" from them. Only a common Party organ, consistently implementing the principles of political struggle and holding high the banner of democracy will be able to win over to its side all militant democratic elements and use all Russia's progressive forces in the struggle for political freedom. Only then shall we be able to convert the workers' smouldering hatred of the police and the authorities into conscious hatred of the autocratic government and into determination to conduct a desperate struggle for the rights of the working class and of the entire Russian people! In modern Russia, a strictly organised revolutionary party built up on this foundation will prove the greatest political force!

In subsequent issues we shall publish the draft programme of the Russian Social-Democratic Labour Party and begin a more detailed discussion of the various organisational questions.

A DRAFT PROGRAMME
OF OUR PARTY[93]

Written at the end 1899

First published in 1924 in the first edition of V. I. Lenin's *Collected Works*, Vol. 1

Published according to the manuscript

The thing to begin with, most likely, is the question of whether there is really a pressing need for a programme of the Russian Social-Democrats. From comrades active in Russia we have heard the opinion expressed that at this particular moment there is no special need to draw up a programme; that the urgent question is one of developing and strengthening local organisations, of placing agitation and the delivery of literature on a more sound footing; that it would be better to postpone the elaboration of a programme until such time as when the movement stands on firmer ground; that a programme might, at the moment, turn out to be unfounded.

We do not share this opinion. It goes without saying that "every step of real movement is more important than a dozen programmes,"[94] as Karl Marx said. But neither Marx nor any other theoretician or practical worker in the Social-Democratic movement has ever denied the tremendous importance of a programme for the consolidation and consistent activity of a political party. The Russian Social-Democrats have just got over the period of the most bitter polemics with socialists of other trends and with non-socialists who were unwilling to understand Russian Social-Democracy; they have also got over the initial stages of the movement during which the work was carried on piecemeal by small local organisations. The need for unity, for the establishment of common literature, for the appearance of Russian workers' newspapers arises out of the real situation, and the foundation in the spring of 1898 of the Russian Social-Democratic Labour Party, which announced its intention of elaborating a Party programme in the near future, showed clearly that the demand for a programme grew out of the needs of the movement itself. At the present time the urgent question of our movement is no longer that of developing the former scattered "amateur" activities, but of uniting—of organisation. This is a step for which a programme is a necessity. The programme must formulate our basic views; precisely establish our immediate political tasks; point out the immediate demands that must show the area of agitational activity; give unity to the agitational work, expand and deepen it, thus raising it from fragmentary partial agitation for petty, isolated demands to the status of agitation for the sum total of Social-Democratic demands. Today, when Social-Democratic activity has aroused a fairly wide circle of socialist intellectuals and class-conscious workers, it is urgently necessary to strengthen connections between them by a programme and in this way give all of them a sound basis for further, more extensive, activity. Lastly, a programme is urgently necessary because Russian public opinion is very often most profoundly mistaken in respect of the real tasks and methods of action of the Russian Social-Democrats: these mistaken views in some cases grow naturally in the morass of political putrefaction that is our real life, in others they are artificially nurtured by the opponents of Social-Democracy. In any case, this is a fact that has to be taken into account. The working-class movement, merging with socialism and with the political struggle, must establish a party that will have to dispel all these misunderstandings, if it is to stand at the head of all the democratic elements in Russian society. The objection may be raised, further, that the present moment is inopportune for the elaboration of a programme because there are differences of opinion that give rise to polemics among the Social-Democrats themselves. I believe the contrary to be true—this is another argument *in favour* of the necessity for a programme. On the one hand, since the polemic has begun, it is to be hoped that in the discussion of the draft programme all views and all shades of views will be afforded expression, that the discussion will be comprehensive. The polemic indicates that the Russian Social-Democrats are showing a revived interest in extensive questions pertaining to the aims of our movement and to its immediate tasks and tactics; precisely such a revival is essential to a discussion of the draft programme. On the other hand, if the polemic is not to be fruitless, if it is not to degenerate into personal rivalry, if it is not to lead to a confusion of views, to a confounding of enemies and friends, it is absolutely essential that the question of the programme be introduced into the polemic. The polemic will be of benefit only if it makes clear in what the differences actually consist, *how profound they are*, whether they are differences of substance or differences on partial questions, whether or not these differences interfere with common work in the ranks of one and the same party. *Only* the introduction of the programme question into the polemic, only a definite statement by the two polemising parties on their *programmatic* views, can provide an answer to all these questions, questions that insistently demand an answer. The elaboration of a common programme for the Party should not, of course, put an end to all polemics; it will firmly establish those basic views on the character, the aims, and the tasks of our movement which must serve as the banner of a fighting party, a party that remains consolidated and united despite partial differences of opinion among its members on partial questions.

And now, to the matter.

When a programme of the Russian Social-Democrats is spoken of, all eyes naturally turn towards the members of the Emancipation of Labour group who founded Russian Social-Democracy and have done so much for its theoretical and practical development. Our older comrades were not slow in responding to the demands of the Russian Social-Democratic movement Almost at the very same time— in the spring of 1898—when preparations were being made for the congress of Russian Social-Democrats which laid the foundations for the Russian Social-Democratic Labour Party, P. B. Axelrod published his pamphlet, *Present Tasks and Tactics of the Russian Social-Democrats* (Geneva, 1898; the foreword being dated March 1898), and reprinted as an appendix to it "A Draft Programme of the Russian Social-Democrats," published by the Emancipation of Labour group as early as 1885.

We shall begin with a discussion of this draft. Despite the fact that it was published almost 15 years ago, it is our opinion that, by and large, it adequately serves it

purpose and is on the level of present-day Social-Democratic
theory. The draft designates precisely that class which alone,
in Russia as in other countries, is capable of being an independent fighter for socialism—the working class, the
"industrial proletariat"; it states the aim which this class
must set itself—"the conversion of all means and objects
of production into social property," "the abolition of commodity production" and "its replacement by a new system of social
production"—"the communist revolution"; it indicates the
"inevitable preliminary condition" for "the reconstruction
of social relations"—"the seizure of political power by the
working class"; it affirms the international solidarity of the
proletariat and the necessity for an "element of variety in
the programmes of the Social-Democrats of different states
in accordance with the social conditions in each of them
taken separately"; it points to the specific feature of Russia
"where the masses of working people suffer under the double
yoke of developing capitalism and moribund patriarchal
economy"; it shows the connection between the Russian revolutionary movement and the process of the creation (by the
forces of developing capitalism) of "a new class, the industrial proletariat—the most responsive, mobile, and developed";
it indicates the necessity for the formation of "a revolutionary working-class party" and specifies "its first political
task"—"the overthrow of absolutism"; it shows the "means
of political struggle" and formulates its basic demands.

All these elements are, in our opinion, absolutely essential to a programme of the Social-Democratic working-class
party; they all enunciate theses that have, until now, been
again and again confirmed both in the development of socialist theory and in the development of the working-class
movement of all countries, specifically, in the development
of Russian social thought and the Russian working-class
movement. In view of this, the Russian Social-Democrats
can and should, in our opinion, make the draft of the Emancipation of Labour group—a draft requiring editorial changes,
corrections, and additions only in respect of details—
the basis of the programme of the Russian Social-Democratic
working-class party.

Let us try to note which of these changes of detail we
deem advisable and in regard to which it would be desirable

to have an exchange of opinions among all Russian Social-Democrats and class-conscious workers.

In the first place, there must, of course, be some slight changes in the structural character of the programme; in 1885 it was the programme of a group of revolutionaries abroad who had proved able to define the only path of development for the movement that offered success, but who, at that time, still did not see before them anything like an extensive and independent working-class movement in Russia. In 1900 it has become a question of a programme for a working-class party founded by a large number of Russian Social-Democratic organisations. In addition to the editorial changes that are in consequence essential (and that need not be dealt with in detail, since they are self-evident), this difference makes it necessary to bring into the foreground and emphasise more strongly the process of economic development that is engendering the material and spiritual conditions for the Social-Democratic working-class movement, and the class struggle of the proletariat which the Social-Democratic Party sets itself the aim of organising. The cardinal point of the programme should be the characterisation of the basic features of the present-day economic system of Russia and its development (cf. in the programme of the Emancipation of Labour group: "Capitalism has achieved tremendous success in Russia since the abolition of serfdom. The old system of natural economy is giving way to commodity production..."). This should be followed by an outline of the fundamental tendency of capitalism—the splitting of the people into a bourgeoisie and a proletariat, the growth of "the mass of misery, oppression, slavery, degradation, exploitation."[95] These famous words of Marx are repeated in the second paragraph of the Erfurt Programme of the German Social-Democratic Party,[96] and the critics that are grouped about Bernstein have recently made particularly violent attacks precisely against this point, repeating the old objections raised by bourgeois liberals and social-politicians against the "theory of impoverishment." In our opinion the polemic that has raged round this question has demonstrated the *utter groundlessness* of such "criticism." Bernstein himself admitted that the above words of Marx were true as a characterisation of the *tendency* of

capitalism—a tendency that becomes a reality in the absence of the class struggle of the proletariat against it, in
the absence of labour protection laws achieved by the
working class. It is precisely in Russia today that we see
the above tendency manifesting its effect with tremendous force on the peasantry and the workers. Further, Kautsky has shown that these words on the growth of "the mass
of misery, etc.," are true in the sense, not only of character-
ising a tendency, but of indicating the growth of "social
poverty," i.e., the growth of the disparity between the
condition of the proletariat and the living standard of the
bourgeoisie—the standard of social consumption that continues to rise parallel with the gigantic growth in the productivity of labour. Lastly, these words are true also in
the sense that in "the border regions" of capitalism (i.e.,
those countries and those branches of the national economy
in which capitalism is only just emerging and clashing with
pre-capitalist conditions) the growth of poverty—not only
"social," but also the most horrible physical poverty, to
the extent of starvation and death from starvation—assumes
a mass scale. Everybody knows that this is ten times more
applicable to Russia than to any other European country.
And so, the words about the growth of "the mass of misery,
oppression, slavery, degradation, exploitation" must, in
our opinion, imperatively be included in our programme—
first, because they faithfully describe the basic and essential features of capitalism, they characterise precisely the
process that unrolls before our eyes and that is one of the
chief reasons for the emergence of the working-class movement and socialism in Russia; secondly, because these words
provide a fund of material for agitation, because they
summarise a whole series of phenomena that most oppress
the masses of the workers, but, at the same time, most
arouse their indignation (unemployment, low wages, undernourishment, famine, the Draconian discipline of capital,
prostitution, the growth in the number of domestics, etc.,
etc.); and, thirdly, because by this precise characterisation of the ruinous effect of capitalism and of the necessary, inevitable indignation of the workers we draw a line
between ourselves and the indecisive elements who ,"sympathise" with the proletariat and demand "reforms" for its

benefit, while trying to occupy the "golden mean" between the proletariat and the bourgeoisie, between the autocratic government and the revolutionaries. It is particularly necessary today to dissociate ourselves from such people, if we are to strive for a united and consolidated working-class party that conducts a determined and unswerving struggle for political liberty and socialism.

Here a few words are in order on our attitude to the Erfurt Programme. From what has been said above it is clear to everyone that we consider it necessary to make changes in the draft of the Emancipation of Labour group that will bring the programme of the Russian Social-Democrats closer to that of the German. We are not in the least afraid to say that we want to imitate the Erfurt Programme: there is nothing bad in imitating what is good, and precisely today, when we so often hear opportunist and equivocal criticism of that programme, we consider it our duty to speak openly in its favour. Imitating, however, must under no circumstances be simply copying. Imitation and borrowing are quite legitimate insofar as in Russia we see the same *basic* processes of the development of capitalism, the same *basic* tasks for the socialists and the working class; but they must not, under any circumstances, lead to our forgetting the *specific features* of Russia which must find *full expression* in the specific features of our programme. Running ahead somewhat, let us say here that among these specific features are, first, our political tasks and means of struggle; and, secondly, our struggle against all remnants of the patriarchal, pre-capitalist regime and the specific posing of the *peasant* question arising out of that struggle.

Having made this necessary reservation, let us continue. The statement on the growth of "the mass of misery" must be followed by a characterisation of the *class struggle* of the proletariat—a declaration of the aim of this struggle (the conversion of all means of production into social property and the replacement of capitalist production by socialist production), a declaration of the international character of the working-class movement, a declaration of the *political* character of the class struggle and its *immediate* objective (the winning of political liberty). It is particularly necessary to recognise the struggle against the autocracy for political

liberties as the first political task of the working-class
party; this task should, in our opinion, be explained by
an exposition of the class nature of the present-day Russian
autocracy and of the need to overthrow it, not only in
the interests of the working class, but also in the interests of
social development as a whole. Such a description is essential
both in regard to theory, because, from the standpoint of the
basic ideas of Marxism, the interests of social development
are higher than the interests of the proletariat—the interests
of the working-class movement as a whole are higher than the
interests of a separate section of the workers or of separate
phases of the movement; and in regard to practice, the eluci-
dation is essential because of the need to characterise the
focal point to which all the variety of Social-Democratic
activity—propaganda, agitation, and organisation—must be
directed and round which it must be concentrated. *In addition*, we think a special paragraph of the programme should be
devoted to the provision that the Social-Democratic working-
class party set itself the *aim* of supporting every revolutionary movement against the autocracy and the struggle
against all attempts on the part of the autocratic government
to corrupt and befog the political consciousness of the people
by means of bureaucratic guardianship and sham doles, by
means of that demagogic policy which our German comrades
have called the *"Peitsche und Zuckerbrot"* policy (whip and
biscuit policy). The biscuit = the doles to those who, for the
sake of partial and individual improvements in their material
conditions, renounce their political demands and remain
the humble slaves of police violence (hostels for students,
etc.) and for workers—one has only to recall the proclamations of Minister of Finance Witte at the time of the St.
Petersburg strikes in 1896 and 1897,[97] or the speeches in
defence of the workers delivered by representatives of the
Ministry of Internal Affairs at the commission on the promulgation of the law of June 2, 1897). The whip = the increased persecution of those who, despite the doles, remain
fighters for political liberty (the drafting of students into
the army[98]; the circular of August 12, 1897, on the trans-
portation of workers to Siberia; increased persecution of
Social-Democracy, etc.). The biscuit is to decoy the weak,
to bribe and corrupt them; the whip is to overawe and "rend-

er harmless" honest and class-conscious fighters for the-work-
ing-class cause and for the cause of the people. As long as
the autocracy exists (and we must now in drawing up our
programme take into account the existence of the autocracy,
since its collapse would inevitably call forth such huge
changes in political conditions that they would compel the
working-class party to make essential changes in the formulation of its immediate political tasks)—as long as the autocracy exists, we must expect a continued renewal and increase
of the government's demagogic measures. Consequently,
we must conduct against them a systematic struggle, exposing the falseness of the police benefactors of the people,
showing the connection between government reforms and the
struggle of the workers, teaching the proletariat to make use
of every reform to strengthen its fighting position and extend
and deepen the working-class movement. The point on the
support for *all* fighters against the autocracy is necessary
in the programme, because Russian Social-Democracy, indissolubly fused with the advanced elements of the Russian
working class, must raise the *general-democratic* banner,
in order to group about itself all sections and all elements
capable of fighting for political liberty or at least of supporting that fight in some way or another.

Such is our view on the demands that must be met by
the section of our programme dealing with *principles* and
on the basic postulates that must be expressed in it with
the maximum precision and clarity. In our opinion the following should be deleted from the draft programme of the
Emancipation of Labour group (from the part dealing with
principles): 1) statements on the form of peasant land tenure (we shall discuss the peasant question later); 2) statements on the causes of "instability," etc., of the intelligentsia; 3) the point on the "abolition of the present system
of political representation and its replacement by direct
people's legislation"; 4) the point on the "means of political
struggle." True, we do not see anything obsolete or erroneous in the last point, but, on the contrary, believe that
the means of struggle should be precisely those indicated
by the Emancipation of Labour group (agitation, revolutionary organisation, transition at "a suitable moment"
to determined attack, not rejecting, *in principle*, even ter-

ror); but we believe that the programme of *a working-class party* is no place for indications of the means of activity that were necessary in the programme of a group of revolutionaries abroad in 1885. The programme should leave the question of means open, allowing the choice of means to the militant organisations and to Party congresses that determine the *tactics* of the Party. Questions of tactics, however, can hardly be introduced into the programme (with the exception of the most important questions, questions of *principle*, such as our attitude to other fighters against the autocracy). Questions of tactics will be discussed by the Party newspaper as they arise and will be eventually decided at Party congresses. The same applies, in our opinion, to the question of terror. The Social-Democrats must imperatively undertake the discussion of this question—of course, from the standpoint of tactics and not of principle—because the growth of the movement leads of its own accord, spontaneously, to more frequent cases of the killing of spies and to greater, more impassioned indignation in the ranks of the workers and socialists who see ever greater numbers of their comrades being tortured to death in solitary confinement and at places of exile. In order to leave nothing unsaid, we will make the reservation that, in our own personal opinion, terror is *not* advisable as a means of struggle *at the present moment*, that the Party (*as a party*) must renounce it (until there occurs a change of circumstances that might lead to a change of tactics) and concentrate *all its energy* on organisation and the regular delivery of literature. This is not the place to speak in greater detail on the question.

As far as the issue of direct people's legislation is concerned, it seems to us that at the present moment it should not be included in the programme. The victory of socialism must not be connected, in principle, with the *substitution* of direct people's legislation for parliamentarism. This was proved, in our view, by the discussion on the Erfurt Programme and by Kautsky's book on people's legislation. Kautsky admits (on the basis of an historical and political analysis) that a certain benefit accrues from people's legislation under the following conditions: 1) the absence of an antithesis between town and village or the preponderance of the towns, 2) the existence of highly developed political parties; 3) "the absence of excessively centralised state power, independently opposed to people's legislation." In Russia we see *exactly the opposite* conditions, and the danger of "people's legislation" degenerating into an imperialist "plebiscite" would be particularly great in our country. If Kautsky could say, in 1893, speaking of Germany and Austria, that "for us, East-Europeans, direct people's legislation belongs to the sphere of the 'state of the future,'" what is there to be said of Russia? We, therefore, believe that at present, when the autocracy is dominant in Russia, we should limit ourselves to the demand for a "democratic constitution" and prefer the first two points of the practical part of the programme of the Emancipation of Labour group to the first two points of the practical part of the "Erfurt Programme."

Now let us look at the practical part of the programme. This part consists, in our opinion, of three sections, in substance if not in arrangement: 1) the demands for general democratic reforms; 2) the demands for measures of protection for the workers; and 3) the demands for measures in the Interests of the peasants. There is hardly any need to make substantial changes in the "draft programme" of the Emancipation of Labour group as regards the first section, which demands: 1) universal franchise; 2) salaries for deputies; 3) general, secular, free, and compulsory education, etc.; 4) inviolability of the person and domicile of citizens; 5) uncurtailed freedom of conscience, speech, assembly, etc. (here it should perhaps be added specifically: the right to strike); 6) freedom of movement and occupation (here it would probably be correct to add: "freedom of migration" and "the complete abolition of passports"); 7) full equality of all citizens, etc.; 8) replacement of the permanent army by the general arming of the people; 9) "the revision of our entire civil and criminal legislation, the abolition of social-estate divisions and of punishments incompatible with the dignity of man." Here it would be well to add: "complete equality of rights for men and women." To this section should be added the demand for fiscal reforms formulated in the programme of the Emancipation of Labour group as one of the demands to "be put forward by the working-class party, basing itself on these fundamental political rights"—"the abolition of the present system of taxation and the institution of a progressive income tax." Lastly, there should also be here a demand for "the election of civil servants by the people; for every citizen to be granted the right to prosecute in court any government official without first having to make a complaint to superiors."

In the second section of the practical demands we find in the programme of the Emancipation of Labour group a general demand for "the legislative regulation of relations between workers (urban and rural) and employers, and the organisation of a relevant inspectorate with workers' representation." We think that the *working-class party* should define the demands made on this point more thoroughly and in greater detail; the party should demand: 1) an eight-hour working day; 2) prohibition of night-work and prohibition of the employment of children under 14 years of age; 3) uninterrupted rest periods, for every worker, of no less than 36 hours a week; 4) extension of factory legislation and the Factory Inspectorate to all branches of industry and agriculture, to government factories, to artisan establishments, and to handicraftsmen working at home; election, by the workers, of assistant inspectors having the same rights as the inspectors; 5) establishment of factory and rural courts for all branches of industry and agriculture, with judges elected from the employers and-the workers in equal numbers; 6) unconditional prohibition everywhere of payment in kind; 7) legislation fixing the responsibility of factory owners for all accidents and maiming of workers, both industrial and agricultural; 8) legislation fixing payment of wages at least once a week in all cases of the hire of workers of all kinds; 9) repeal of all laws violating the equality of employers and employees (for example, the laws making factory and farm workers criminally responsible for leaving their work, the laws giving employers greater freedom to cancel hiring agreements than their employees, etc.). (It goes without saying that we are only outlining desirable demands without giving them the final formulation required for the draft.) This section of the programme must (in conjunction with the preceding section) provide the basic, guiding principles for agitation, without in any way, of course, hindering agitators in this or that locality, branch of production, factory, etc., from putting forward demands in a somewhat modified form, demands that are more concrete or more specific. In drawing up this section of the programme, we should strive, therefore, to avoid two extremes—on the one hand, we must not omit any one of the main, basic demands that hold great significance for the *entire* working class; on the other, we must not go into minute particulars with which it would hardly be rational to load the programme.

The demand for "state assistance for producers' associations" in the programme of the Emancipation of Labour group should, in our opinion, be completely eliminated. The experience of other countries, as well as theoretical considerations, and the specific features of Russian life (the tendency of the bourgeois liberals and the police government to flirt with "artels" and with "the patronage ... of people's industry," etc.)—all this should counsel against our putting forward this demand. (Fifteen years ago, of course, matters were quite different in many respects; *then* it was quite natural for Social-Democrats to include such a demand in their programme.)

There remains the third and last section of the practical part of the programme—the demands related to the peasant question. In the programme of the Emancipation of Labour group we find only one demand pertaining to this question—the demand for a "radical revision of our agrarian relations, i.e., a revision of the conditions of land redemption and the allotment of the land to the village communes; the granting of the right to refuse an allotment and to leave the village commune to those peasants who find it convenient to do so, etc."

It seems to me that the basic idea here expressed is perfectly correct and that the Social-Democratic working-class party should, in point of fact, include a relevant demand in its programme (I say "a relevant demand" because I think certain amendments are desirable).

I understand this problem in the following way. The peasant question in Russia differs substantially from the peasant question in the West, the *sole* difference being that in the West the question is almost exclusively one of a peasant in a capitalist, bourgeois society, whereas in Russia it is one of a peasant who suffers no less (if not more) from *pre-capitalist* institutions and relations, from the *survivals of serfdom*. The role of the peasantry as a class that provides fighters against the autocracy and against the survivals of serfdom is by now played out in the West, but not yet in Russia. In the West the industrial proletariat has long since become completely alienated from the countryside; this alien-ation has been made final by relevant legal institutions. In Russia "the industrial proletariat, both by its composition and by the conditions of its existence, is to a very great ex-tent still connected with the countryside" (P. B. Axelrod, op. cit., p. 11). True enough, the differentiation of the peasantry into a petty bourgeoisie and into wage-workers is proceeding with great power and astounding rapidity in Russia, but it is a process that has not yet come to an end, and what is most important—this process is still evolving within the framework of the old institutions of serfdom that fetter all the peasants with the heavy chains of collective liability and the tax-assessed community. The Russian Social-Demo-crat, therefore, even if he (like the writer of these lines) belongs to the determined opponents of the protection or support of small proprietorship or small agricultural economy in capitalist society, i.e., even if, on the agrarian question, he (like the writer of these lines) is on the side of those Marx-ists whom the bourgeois and opportunists of all stripes love to deride as "dogmatists" and "orthodox"—the Russian Social-Democrat can and must, without betraying his convictions in the slightest, but, rather, because of those convictions, insist that the working-class party should in-scribe on its banner *support* for the peasantry (*not by any means* as a class of small proprietors or small farmers), *insofar as the peasantry is capable of a revolutionary struggle against the survivals of serfdom in general and against the autocracy in particular*. Do not all of us Social-Democrats declare that we are ready to support even the big bourgeoisie *insofar as it is capable* of a *revolutionary* struggle against the above manifestations—how then can we refuse to support the petty-bourgeois class, many millions strong, that is gradual-ly, step by step, merging with the proletariat? If support for the liberal demands of the big bourgeoisie does not mean sup-port of the big bourgeoisie, then support for the democratic demands of the petty bourgeoisie certainly does not mean support of the petty bourgeoisie; on the contrary, it is precisely this development which political liberty will make possible in Russia that will, with particular force, lead to the destruction of small economy under the blows of capital. I do not think there will be any arguments among the Social-Democrats on this point. The question, therefore, is: 1) how to elaborate demands in such a way that they *do not degenerate* into support of small property-owners in a capitalist society? and 2) is our peasantry capable, at least in part, of a *revolutionary* struggle against the remnants of serfdom and against absolutism?

Let us begin with the second question. It is doubtful whether anyone will deny the existence of revolutionary elements among the Russian peasantry. In the post-Reform period, too, we know, there have been peasant revolts against the landlords, their stewards, and the government officials who support them. Well known are the agrarian killings, revolts, etc. Well known is the growing indignation of the peasantry (in whom even pitiful fragments of education have already begun to arouse a sense of human dignity) against the savage lawlessness of the gang of aristocratic wastrels that has been let loose against the peasantry under the title of Rural Superintendents.[99] Well known is the fact that famines of growing frequency involve millions of people who cannot remain passive spectators of such "food difficulties." Well known is the fact of the growth of religious sects and rationalism among the peasantry; political protests in religious guise are common to all nations at a certain stage of their development, and not to Russia alone. The existence of revolutionary elements among the peasantry, therefore, is not open to the slightest doubt. We do not in the least exaggerate the strength of these elements; we do not forget the political backwardness and ignorance of the peasants, nor in the least wipe out the difference between "the Russian revolt, senseless and ruthless," and the revolutionary struggle; we do not in the least forget the endless means which the government has at its disposal for the political deception and demoralisation of the peasantry. But from all this there follows only one thing, that it would be senseless to make the peasantry the *vehicle* of the revolutionary movement, that a party would be insane to *condition* the revolutionary character of its movement upon the revolutionary mood of the peasantry. There can be no thought of proposing anything of the sort to the Russian Social-Democrats. We say only that a working-class party cannot, without violating the basic tenets of Marxism and without committing a tremendous political mistake, *overlook* the revolutionary elements that exist among the peasantry and not afford those elements support. Whether or not the revolutionary elements among the Russian peasantry will be able to behave at least in the way the West-European peasants behaved at the time of the overthrow of the autocracy is a question to which history has not yet provided an answer. If they prove themselves incapable, the Social-Democrats will have lost nothing as far as their good name or their movement is concerned, since it will not be their fault if the peasantry does not respond (may not have the strength to respond) to their revolutionary appeal. The working-class movement is going its own way and will continue to do so, despite all the betrayals of the big bourgeoisie or the petty bourgeoisie. If the peasantry should prove itself capable—then that Social-Democracy which did not afford it support under these circumstances would for ever lose its good name and the right to be regarded as the leading fighter for democracy.

Returning to the first question presented above, we must say that the demand for a "radical revision of agrarian relations" seems unclear to us: it may have been sufficient fifteen years ago, but we can hardly be satisfied with it today when we must provide guidance for agitation and, at the same time, guard ourselves against the defenders of small economy, all too numerous in present-day Russian society, who have such "influential" supporters as Messrs. Pobedonostsev, Witte, and very many officials in the Ministry of Internal Affairs. We take the liberty of offering our comrades for discussion the following approximate formulation of the third section of the practical part of our programme:

"The Russian Social-Democratic working-class party, giving its support to every revolutionary movement against the present state and social system, declares that it will support the peasantry, insofar as it is capable of revolutionary struggle against the autocracy, as the class that suffers most from the Russian people's lack of rights and from the survivals of serfdom in Russian society.

"Proceeding from this principle, the Russian Social-Democratic working-class party demands:

"1) The abrogation of land redemption[100] and quit-rent payments and of all duties at present obligatory for the peasantry as a tax-paying social-estate.

"2) The return to the people of the sums of which the government and the landed proprietors have robbed the peasants in the form of redemption payments.

"3) The abolition of collective liability and of all laws that hamper the peasant in disposing of his land.

"4) The abolition of all remnants of the peasant's feudal dependence on the landlord, whether they are due to special laws and institutions (e.g., the position of the peasants and workers in the iron-foundry districts of the Urals) or to the fact that the land of the peasants and the landlords has not yet been demarcated (e.g., survivals of the law of easement in the Western territory),[101] or to the fact that the cutting-off of the peasant land by the landlords has left the peasants in what is in actual fact the hopeless position of former corvée peasants.

"5) That peasants be granted the right to demand, in court, the reduction of excessively high rents and to prosecute for usury landlords and, in general, all persons who take advantage of the necessitous condition of the peasants to conclude with them shackling agreements."

We shall have to deal in particular detail with the motives for such a proposal—not because this is the most important part of the programme, but because it is the most disputed and has a more remote connection with the generally established truths that are accepted by all Social-Democrats. The introductory proposition on (conditional) "support" for the peasantry seems to us to be necessary, because the proletariat cannot and must not, in general, take upon itself the defence of the interests of a class of small property-owners; it can support it only *to the extent to which* that class is revolutionary. And since it is

the autocracy that is today the embodiment of all that is
backward in Russia, all the survivals of serfdom, lack of
rights, and "patriarchal" oppression, it is essential to point
out that the working-class party supports the peasantry
only to the extent that the latter is capable of revolutionary struggle against the *autocracy*. Such a proposition is
apparently excluded by the following proposition in the
draft of the Emancipation of Labour group: "The main
bulwark of the autocracy resides precisely in the political
apathy and intellectual backwardness of the peasantry."
But this is not a contradiction of theory alone; it is a contradiction of reality, because the peasantry (like the class
of small property-owners in general) is distinguished by
the duality of its character. We do not wish to repeat well-
known political-economic arguments showing the internal
contradictions of the condition of the peasantry, but we
shall call to mind the following characterisation by Marx
of the French peasantry of the early fifties:

"The Bonaparte dynasty represents not the revolutionary, but the conservative peasant; not the peasant that
strikes out beyond the condition of his social existence,
the small holding, but rather the peasant who wants to
consolidate this holding, not the country folk who, linked
up with the towns, want to overthrow the old order through
their own energies, but on the contrary those who, in
stupefied seclusion within this old order, want to see themselves and their small holdings saved and favoured by
the ghost of the Empire. It represents not the enlightenment, but the superstition of the peasant; not his judgement, but his prejudice; not his future, but his past; not
his modern Cevennes, but his modern Vendée" (*Der 18.
Brumaire. S.* 99[102]). The working-class party needs precisely to support the peasantry which is striving to overthrow
"the old order," i.e., in Russia, first and foremost the
autocracy. The Russian Social-Democrats have always recognised the necessity to extract and absorb the revolutionary side of the Narodnik doctrine and trend. In the programme of the Emancipation of Labour group this is
expressed not only in the above-quoted demand for "a radical revision," etc., but also in the following words: "It
goes without saying, incidentally, that even today, people

who are in direct contact with the peasantry could, by
their activities among them, render important service to
the socialist movement in Russia. Far from repelling
such people, the Social-Democrats will make every effort
to come to an agreement with them on the basic principles and methods of their work." Fifteen years ago, when
the traditions of revolutionary Narodism were still alive,
such a declaration was sufficient; but today we must
ourselves begin to discuss "basic principles of work"
among the peasantry if we want the Social-Democratic
working-class party to become a vanguard fighter for
democracy.

But do not the demands we propose lead to the support,
not of the peasants themselves, but of their property, to the
consolidation of small economy, and do they correspond to
the entire course of capitalist development? Let us examine
these questions that are of the highest importance to the
Marxist.

There can scarcely be any differences of opinion among
Social-Democrats with regard to *the substance* of the first
and third demands. The second demand, by its essence,
will probably give rise to differences of opinion. The following considerations, to our view, speak in its favour:
1) it is a fact that the redemption payments represented
direct plunder of the peasants on the part of the landlords,
that the payments were not only for peasant land but for
serf-holding rights, and that the government gathered
more from the peasants than it paid to the landlords; 2) we
have no grounds for regarding this fact as something ended
and filed away in the archives of history, for the aristocratic exploiters themselves do not so regard the peasant
Reform when they lament over the "sacrifices" they made at
the time; 3) precisely today, when the starvation of millions
of peasants is becoming chronic, when the government
that wastes millions on gifts to the landlords and capitalists, and on an adventurist foreign policy, is haggling for
pennies off the grants to the starving—precisely today it is
appropriate and essential to recall what the rule of the
autocratic government that serves the interests of the
privileged classes has cost the people; 4) the Social-Democrats cannot remain indifferent spectators of peasant

hunger and the death of peasants from starvation; there
have never been two opinions among Russian Social-
Democrats as to the need for the most extensive help to the
starving, and hardly anyone will claim that serious help
is possible without revolutionary measures; 5) the expropriation of the royal demesne[103] and greater mobilisation of lands belonging to the aristocracy, i.e., that which
would result from the implementation of the proposed
demand, would bring only benefit to the entire social
development of Russia. *Against* the proposed demand we
shall probably be told, mostly, that it is "impracticable."
If such an objection is supported only by phrases against
"revolutionism" and "utopianism," we can say in advance
that such *opportunist phrases* do not frighten us in the least
and that we do not attach any significance to them. If,
however, the objection is supported by an analysis of the
economic and political conditions of our movement, we
fully admit the necessity for a more detailed discussion of
the question and the benefit accruing from a polemic in
regard to it. We would only mention that this demand does
not stand alone but forms part of the demand to support
the peasantry *to the extent* that the latter is revolutionary.
History will decide precisely how and with what strength
these elements in the peasantry will manifest themselves.
If we understand by the "practicability" of a demand its
general correspondence, not to the interests of social development, but to a specific state of economic and political conditions, it will be a totally fallacious criterion, as
Kautsky showed convincingly in his polemic with Rosa
Luxemburg when the latter spoke of the "impracticability"
(for the Polish working-class party) of the demand for
Polish independence. Kautsky, at that time, pointed out
as an example (if our memory serves us) the demand made
by the Erfurt Programme on the election of civil servants
by the people. The "practicability" of this demand is more
than doubtful in present-day Germany, but none of the
Social-Democrats proposed limiting the demands to the
narrow bounds of what is possible at a given moment or
under given conditions.

Further, as far as the fourth point is concerned, probably no one will object, in principle, to the necessity for

Social-Democrats to advance the demand for the abolition of all remnants of feudal dependence. What will need clarification will probably be only the formulation of that demand, as well as its extent, i.e., whether it should include, for example, measures for abolishing the *factual* corvée dependence of the peasants that was created by the cutting-off of peasant lands in 1861.[104] In our opinion this question should be decided in the affirmative. The tremendous significance of the actual survival of corvée (labour-service) economy has been fully established in literature, as has also the tremendous retardation of social development (and the development of capitalism) caused by this survival. The development of capitalism, of course, is leading up to, and will in the end result in, the elimination of these survivals "of their own accord, in a natural way." But, first, these survivals are extraordinarily tenacious, so that their rapid elimination is not to be expected; secondly—and mainly—the "natural way" means nothing other than the dying-out of the peasants who, *in point of fact* (due to labour-service, etc.), are tied to the soil and enslaved by the landlords. It stands to reason that under these circumstances the Social-Democrats cannot allow their programme to be silent on this question. It may be asked: How could this demand be implemented? We think it unnecessary to deal with this in the programme. The implementation of this demand (as of almost all others in this section, depending on the strength of the revolutionary elements among the peasantry) will, of course, necessitate a detailed examination of local conditions by local, elective, peasant committees as a counterweight to the Committees of Nobles[105] that accomplished their "legal" plunder in the sixties; the democratic demands of the programme adequately define the democratic institutions required for this purpose. This would be precisely the "radical revision of agrarian relations" of which the programme of the Emancipation of Labour group speaks. As we said above, we agree in principle with this point of the Emancipation of Labour group's draft and would only: 1) specify the conditions under which the proletariat can struggle for the class interests of the peasantry; 2) define the *character* of the revision—the abolition of the remnants of feudal dependence; 3) express the demands more precisely.

We foresee another objection: a re-examination of the question of cut-off lands, etc., should lead to the return of those lands to the peasantry. This is obvious. But will this not strengthen small property, small holdings. Can the Social-Democrats desire the replacement of the big capitalist economy, which is perhaps being conducted on the lands plundered from the peasantry, by small economy? This would, indeed, be a *reactionary* measure!

We answer: undoubtedly the substitution of small-scale for large-scale economy is reactionary, and we must not favour it. But the demand we are discussing is *conditioned* by the aim of "abolishing the remnants of feudal dependence"; consequently, it cannot lead to the fragmentation of big holdings; it applies only to old holdings that are, in essence, based purely on the corvée system; *in relation to them* a peasant holding, free of all medieval impediments (cf. point 3) *is progressive, not reactionary*. It is, of course, not easy to draw a line of demarcation here, but we do not believe that any one demand in our programme can be "easily" realised. Our role is to outline the basic principles and basic tasks; those who will be called upon to decide these problems in practice will know how to consider the details.

The purpose of last point is identical with that of the preceding: the struggle against all remnants of the *pre-capitalist mode of production* (so abundant in the Russian countryside). It will be remembered that the renting of land by peasants in Russia very often serves to conceal survivals of corvée relations. The idea for this last point was borrowed from Kautsky, who pointed out that, in relation to Ireland, even Gladstone's liberal administration had enacted a law in 1881 granting the courts the right to reduce excessively high rents, and included in the number of desirable demands: "The reduction of exorbitant rents by courts especially set up for this purpose" (*Reduzierung übermässiger Pachtzinsen durch dazu eingesetzte Gerichtshöfe*). This would be particularly useful in Russia (given the condition, of course, of the courts being democratically organised) in the sense that it would eliminate corvée relations. We think that to this we could also add the

demand for the extension of the laws on usury to cover enslaving agreements; in the Russian village, bondage is so
widespread, so heavily oppressive to the peasant in his
capacity as a worker, so exceedingly obstructive to social
progress, that the struggle against it is particularly necessary. And it would not be more difficult for a court to
establish the enslaving, usurious character of an agreement,
than to establish the excessive nature of rent.

In general, the demands we propose reduce themselves,
in our opinion, to two main objectives: 1) to abolish all
pre-capitalist, feudal institutions and relations in the
countryside (the complement to these demands being contained in the first section of the practical part of the programme); 2) to give the class struggle in the countryside a
more open and conscious character. We believe that precisely
these principles should serve as a guide for the Social-
Democratic "agrarian programme" in Russia. It is necessary to dissociate ourselves resolutely from the attempts,
so numerous in Russia, to *smooth down* the class struggle in
the countryside. The dominant liberal-Narodnik tendency
is distinguished precisely by this feature, but, in resolutely
rejecting it (as was done in the "Appendix to the Report
of the Russian Social-Democrats at the International Congress in London"), we should not forget that we must take
particular note of the revolutionary content of Narodism.
"To the extent that Narodism was revolutionary, i.e.,
came out against the social-estate, bureaucratic rule and
against the barbarous forms of exploitation and oppression of the people which the state supported, to that extent
Narodism had to be included, with relevant amendments,
as a component part of the programme of Russian
Social-Democracy" (Axelrod, *Present Tasks and Tactics*,
p. 7). Two basic forms of the class struggle are today
intertwined in the Russian countryside: 1) the struggle
of the peasantry against the privileged landed proprietors and against the remnants of serfdom; 2) the struggle of the emergent rural proletariat against the rural
bourgeoisie. For Social-Democrats the second struggle,
of course, is of greater importance; but they must also
indispensably support the first struggle *to the extent that
it does not contradict* the interests of social development.

It is no accident that the peasant question has always occupied and continues to occupy such a prominent place in Russian society and in the Russian revolutionary movement: this fact is a reflection of the great significance still retained by the first of the two forms of struggle.

In conclusion, there is one possible misunderstanding against which we should be on guard. We spoke of Social-Democracy's "revolutionary appeal" to the peasants. Does this not mean diffusion, is it not harmful to the essential concentration of forces for work among the industrial proletariat? Not in the least; the necessity for such a concentration is recognised by *all* Russian Social-Democrats; it figures in the draft of the Emancipation of Labour group (1885) and again in the pamphlet, *The Tasks of the Russian Social-Democrats* (1898). Consequently, there are absolutely no grounds at all to fear that the Social-Democrats will split their forces. A programme is not an instruction; a programme must embrace the *whole* movement, and in practice, of course, first one and then another aspect of the movement has to be brought into the foreground. No one will dispute the necessity to speak in the programme of rural, as well as industrial, workers, although in the present situation there is not a single Russian Social-Democrat who would think of calling upon the comrades to go to the village. The working-class movement, however, even apart from our efforts, will inevitably lead to the spread of democratic ideas in the countryside. "Agitation based on economic interests will inevitably lead Social-Democratic circles directly up against facts that show clearly the closest solidarity of interests between our industrial proletariat and the peasant masses" (Axelrod, *ibid.*, p. 13). For this reason an *"Agrarprogramm"* (*in the sense indicated*; strictly speaking, of course, it is not an "agrarian programme" at all) is an absolute necessity for Russian Social-Democrats. In our propaganda and agitation we constantly come upon peasant-workers, that is, factory-workers who retain their connections with the village, who have relatives or a family in the village and who travel back and forth. Questions of land redemption payments, collective liability, and rent are of vital interest even to large numbers of metropolitan workers (to say nothing of the workers in the Urals, for example, amongst whom Social-Democratic propaganda and agitation has begun to find its way). We should be remiss in performing our duty, if we did not take care to give precise guidance to Social-Democrats and class-conscious workers who go to the village. Nor should we forget the rural intelligentsia, elementary school teachers, for instance. The latter are so humiliated, materially and spiritually, they observe so closely and know from their own experience the lack of rights and the oppression of the people, that there can be no doubt at all of the sympathetic reception among them of Social-Democratic ideas (given the further growth of the movement).

These then, in our opinion, should be the component parts of a programme of the Russian Social-Democratic working-class party: 1) a statement on the basic character of the economic development of Russia; 2) a statement on the inevitable result of capitalism: the growth of poverty and the increasing indignation of the workers; 3) a statement on the class struggle of the proletariat as the basis of our movement; 4) a statement on the final aims of the Social-Democratic working-class movement—on its striving to win political power for the accomplishment of these aims—and on the international character of the movement; 5) a statement on the essentially political nature of the class struggle; 6) a statement to the effect that the Russian absolutism, which conditions the lack of rights and the oppression of the people and patronises the exploiters, is the chief hindrance to the working-class movement, and that the winning of political liberty, essential in the interests of the entire social development, is, therefore, the most urgent political task of the Party; 7) a statement to the effect that the Party will support all parties and sections of the population that struggle against the autocracy and will combat the demagogic intrigues of our government; 8) the enumeration of the basic democratic demands; then, 9) demands for the benefit of the working class; and 10) demands for the benefit of the peasantry, with an explanation of the general character of these demands.

We are fully conscious of the difficulty of providing a completely satisfactory formulation of the programme without a number of conferences with comrades; but we consider it essential to set about this task, believing (for the reasons indicated above) that postponement is impermissible. We hope to receive the aid of all the theoreticians of the Party (headed by the members of the Emancipation of Labour group), as well as of all socialists doing practical work in Russia (not only of Social-Democrats: it would be very desirable to hear the opinion of socialists of other groups and we would not refuse to publish their opinion), and the aid of all class-conscious workers.

A RETROGRADE TREND IN RUSSIAN
SOCIAL-DEMOCRACY

The Editorial Board of *Rabochaya Mysl* has published a *Separate Supplement to "Rabochaya Mysl"* (September 1899), for the purpose of "dispelling the mass of misunderstanding and indefiniteness that exists with regard to the trend of *Rabochaya Mysl* (such as our 'renunciation of politics')." (From the Editorial Board.) We are very glad that *Rabochaya Mysl* is at last raising programmatic questions which, until now, it sought to ignore, but we emphatically protest against the statement that the "trend of *Rabochaya Mysl* is that of progressive Russian workers" (as the Editorial Board declares in the cited text). In fact, if the Editorial Board of *Rabochaya Mysl* wants to follow the path indicated (so far only *indicated*) in that publication, this means that it has falsely understood the programme elaborated by the founders of Russian Social-Democracy, a programme that has to-date had the adherence of all Russian Social-Democrats working in Russia; it means that it is taking a *step backwards* with respect to the level of theoretical and practical development already attained by Russian Social-Democracy.

The *Rabochaya Mysl* trend is expounded in the leading article of the *Separate Supplement* entitled "Our Reality" (signed: *R. M.*), which article we must now analyse in the greatest detail.

From the very beginning of the article we see that *R. M.* gives a *false* description of "our reality" in general, and of our working-class movement in particular, that he reveals an extremely narrow conception of the working-class movement and a desire to close his eyes to the higher forms of that movement which have evolved under the leadership of the Russian Social-Democrats. "Our working-class movement," says R. M., indeed, at the outset of the article, "contains the germs of the most diverse forms of organisation" ranging from strike associations to legal societies (permitted by law).

"And is that all?" asks the reader, in perplexity. Surely R. M. must have noticed some *higher*, more advanced forms of organisation in the working-class movement in Russia! Apparently he is unwilling to notice them because, on the next page, he repeats his assertion in a still more emphatic manner: "The tasks of the movement at the present moment, the real working-class cause of the Russian workers," he says, "reduce themselves to the workers' amelioration of their condition *by all possible means*," and yet the *only* means enumerated are strike organisations and legal societies! Thus, the Russian working-class movement *reduces itself*, it would seem, to strikes and legal societies! But this is an absolute *untruth*! As far back as twenty years ago, the Russian working-class movement founded a much broader organisation put forward much more extensive aims (of which in detail below). The Russian working-class movement founded such organisations as the St. Petersburg[106] and Kiev[107] Leagues of Struggle, the Jewish Workers' League,[108] and others. R. M. does indeed say that the Jewish working-class movement has a "specific political character" and is an exception. But this, again, is an untruth; for if the Jewish Workers' League were something "specific," it *would not have amalgamated* with a number of Russian organisations to form the Russian Social-Democratic Labour Party. The foundation of this Party is the biggest step taken by the Russian working-class movement *in its fusion* with the Russian revolutionary movement. This step shows clearly that the Russian working-class movement *does not reduce itself* to strikes and legal societies. How could it have happened that the Russian socialists writing in *Rabochaya Mysl* are unwilling to recognise this step and to grasp its significance?

It happened because R. M. does not understand the relation of the Russian working-class movement to socialism and to the revolutionary movement in Russia, because he does not understand the political aims of the Russian working class. "The most characteristic index of the trend of our movement," writes *R. M.*, "is, of course, the demands put forward by the workers." We ask: why are the demands of the *Social-Democrats* and Social-Democratic organisations not included among the indices of *our movement*? On what grounds does *R. M.* separate the demands of the workers from the demands of the Russian Social-Democrats? *R. M.* makes this division throughout his article in the same way as the editors of *Rabochaya Mysl* make it, in general, in every issue of their paper. In order to explain this error of *Rabochaya Mysl* we must clarify the general question of the relation of *socialism* to *the working-class movement*. At first socialism and the working-class movement existed separately in all the European countries. The workers struggled against the capitalists, they organised strikes and unions, while the socialists stood aside from the working-class movement, formulated doctrines criticising the contemporary capitalist, bourgeois system of society and demanding its replacement by another system, the higher, socialist system. The separation of the working-class movement and socialism gave rise to weakness and underdevelopment in each: the theories of the socialists, unfused with the workers' struggle, remained nothing more than utopias, good wishes that had no effect on real life; the working-class movement remained petty, fragmented, and did not acquire political significance, was not enlightened by the advanced science of its time. For this reason we see in all European countries a constantly growing urge to *fuse* socialism with the working-class movement in a single *Social-Democratic* movement. When this fusion takes place the class struggle of the workers becomes *the conscious struggle of the proletariat* to emancipate itself from exploitation by the propertied classes, it is evolved into a higher form of the socialist workers' movement— *the independent working-class Social-Democratic party*. By directing socialism towards a fusion with the working-class movement, Karl Marx and Frederick Engels did their greatest service: they created a revolutionary theory that explained the necessity for this fusion and gave socialists the task of organising the class struggle of the proletariat.

Precisely this is what happened in Russia. In Russia, too, socialism has been in existence for a long time, for many decades, *standing aside* from the struggle of the workers against the capitalists, aside from the workers' strikes, etc. On the one hand, the socialists did not understand Marx's theory, they thought it inapplicable to Russia; on the other, the Russian working-class movement remained in a purely embryonic form. When the South-Russian Workers' Union was founded in 1875 and the North-Russian Workers' Union in 1878, those workers' organisations did not take the road chosen by the Russian socialists; they demanded political rights for the people, they wanted to wage a struggle for those rights, but at that time the Russian socialists mistakenly considered the political struggle a deviation from socialism. However, the Russian socialists did not hold to their undeveloped, fallacious theory. They went forward, accepted Marx's teaching, and evolved a theory of workers' socialism applicable to Russia— the theory of the Russian Social-Democrats. The foundation of Russian Social-Democracy was the great service rendered by the Emancipation of Labour group, Plekhanov, Axelrod, and their friends.* Since the foundation of Russian Social-Democracy (1883) the Russian working-class movement—in each of its broader manifestations—has been drawing closer to the Russian Social-Democrats in an effort to merge with them. The founding of the Russian Social-Democratic Labour Party (in the spring of 1898) marked the biggest step forward towards this fusion. At the present time the *principal* task for all Russian socialists and all class-conscious Russian workers is to strengthen this fusion, consolidate and organise the Social-Democratic Labour Party. He who does not wish to recognise this fusion, he who tries to draw some sort of artificial line of demarcation between the working-class movement and Social-Democracy in Russia renders no service

---

* The fusion of Russian socialism with the Russian working-class movement has been analysed historically in a pamphlet by one of our comrades, *The Red Flag in Russia, A Brief History of the Russian Working-Class Movement*. The pamphlet will shortly be off the press.[109]

but does *harm* to workers' socialism and the working-class movement in Russia.

To continue. "As far as extensive demands, political demands, are concerned," writes *R. M.*, "it is only in those of the St. Petersburg weavers ... in 1897 that we see the first and still weakly conscious case of our workers putting forward such broad political demands." We must again say that this is *beyond all doubt untrue*. In publishing such utterances, Editorial Board of *Rabochaya Mysl* displays, first, a forgetfulness of the history of the Russian revolutionary and working-class movement that is unpardonable in a Social-Democrat, and, secondly, an unpardonably narrow conception of the workers' cause. The Russian workers put forward extensive political demands in the May, 1898, leaflet of the St. Petersburg League of Struggle and in the newspapers *S. Peterburgsky Rabochy Listok* and *Rabochaya Gazeta*, the latter having been recognised, in 1898, by leading Russian Social-Democratic organisations as the official organ of the Russian Social-Democratic Labour Party. *Rabochaya Mysl*, by ignoring these facts, is moving backwards and fully justifies the opinion that it is not representative of advanced workers, but of the lower, undeveloped strata of the proletariat (*R. M.* himself says in his article that this has already been pointed out to *Rabochaya Mysl*). The lower strata of the proletariat do not know the history of the Russian revolutionary movement, nor does *R. M.* know it. The lower strata of the proletariat do not understand the relationship between the working-class movement and Social-Democracy, nor does *R. M.* understand that relationship. Why was it that in the nineties the Russian workers did not form their special organisations separate and apart from the socialists as they had done in the seventies? Why did they not put forward their own political demands separate and apart from the socialists? *R. M.* apparently understands this to mean that "the Russian workers are still little prepared for this" (p. 5 of his article), but this explanation is only further proof that he has the right to speak only on behalf of the lower strata of the proletariat. The lower strata of the workers, during the movement of the nineties, were not conscious of its political character. Nevertheless,

everyone knows (and *R. M.* himself speaks of it) that the
working-class movement of the nineties acquired an extensive political significance. This was due to the fact that the
advanced workers, as always and everywhere, determined
the character of the movement, and they were followed by
the working masses because they showed their readiness and
their ability to serve the cause of the working class, because
they proved able to win the full confidence of the masses.
Those advanced workers were Social-Democrats; many of
them even took a personal part in the disputes between the
Narodnaya Volya adherents and the Social-Democrats that
typified the transition of the Russian revolutionary movement from peasant and conspiratorial socialism to working-class socialism. It can, therefore, be understood why
these advanced workers have not alienated themselves from
the socialists and revolutionaries in a separate organisation. Such an alienation had a meaning and was necessary
at the time when socialism alienated itself from the working-class movement. Such alienation would have been
impossible and meaningless once the advanced workers
had seen before them working-class socialism and the *Social-Democratic* organisations. The *fusion* of the advanced
workers and the Social-Democratic organisations was altogether natural and inevitable. It was the result of the great
historical fact that in the nineties two profound social
movements converged in Russia: one, a spontaneous movement, a popular movement within the working class, the
other, the movement of social thought in the direction of
the theory of Marx and Engels, towards the theory of Social-Democracy.

From the following it can be seen how extremely narrow
is *Rabochaya Mysl*'s conception of the political struggle.
Speaking of the breadth of political demands, *R. M.* states:
"For the workers to conduct such a political struggle consciously and independently, it is essential that it be waged by
the working-class organisations themselves, that the workers' political demands should find support in the workers' consciousness of their common political requirements
and the interests of the moment [note well!], that they
should be the demands of the workers' [craft] organisations
themselves, that they should really be drawn up by them

jointly and also put forward jointly by those working-class organisations on their own initiative...." It is further explained that the immediate common political demands of the workers are, for the time being (!!), still the ten-hour working day and the restoration of holidays abolished by the law of June 2, 1897.

And after this the editors of *Rabochaya Mysl* are still surprised that they are accused of renouncing politics! Indeed, is not this reduction of politics to the struggle of craft unions for individual reforms the renunciation of politics? Is this not the rejection of the basic tenet of world Social-Democracy that the Social-Democrats must strive to organise the class struggle of the proletariat into independent political working-class parties that fight for democracy *as a means* for the proletariat to win political power and organise a socialist society? With a strangely unbounded thoughtlessness our latest distorters of Social-Democracy cast overboard everything dear to the Social-Democrats, everything that gives us the right to regard the working-class movement as a world-historical movement. It matters little to them that the long experience of European socialism and European democracy teaches the lesson that it is essential to strive for the formation of independent working-class political parties. It matters little to them that in the course of a long and arduous historical path the Russian revolutionary movement has evolved the union of socialism and the working-class movement, the union of the great social and political ideals and the class struggle of the proletariat. It matters little to them that the advanced Russian workers have laid the foundation of the Russian Social-Democratic Labour Party. Down with all that! Let us liberate ourselves from a too extensive ideological equipment and from a too difficult and exacting historical experience—and let "there remain for the time being" only craft unions (the possibility of organising which in Russia has not yet been proved at all, if we leave legal societies out of the reckoning), let these craft unions, "on their own initiative," elaborate demands, the demands of the "moment," demands for tiny, petty reforms!! What is this, if not the preachment of a retrograde trend? What, indeed, if not propaganda for the destruction of socialism!

And please note that *Rabochaya Mysl* does not merely outline the idea that local organisations should elaborate their own local forms of struggle and specific motives for agitation, methods of agitation, etc.—nobody would object to this idea. Russian Social-Democrats have never laid claim to anything hampering the independence of the workers in this respect. But *Rabochaya Mysl* wants *to push aside* the great political aims of the Russian proletariat altogether and "for the time being" confine itself "exclusively" to "the interests of the moment." Until now the Russian Social-Democrats have always wanted to make use of every demand of the moment and, by agitating for that demand, to organise the proletariat for the struggle against the autocracy as the immediate objective. Now *Rabochaya Mysl* wants *to limit* the struggle of the proletariat to a petty struggle for petty demands. *R. M.*, knowing very well that he is retreating from the views of the entire Russian Social-Democracy, makes the following reply to those who accuse *Rabochaya Mysl*: It is said that the overthrow of tsarism is the immediate objective of the Russian working-class movement. But of which working-class movement, asks *R. M.*, "*the strike movement? the mutual benefit societies? the workers' circles?*" (page 5 of the article). To this we reply: Speak for yourself alone, for your group, for the lower strata of the proletariat of a given locality which it represents, but do not presume to speak on behalf of the advanced Russian workers! The representatives of the lower strata of the proletariat often do not realise that the struggle for the overthrow of the autocracy can only be conducted by a revolutionary party. Nor does *R. M.* know this. The advanced workers, however, do. The less advanced representatives of the proletariat often do not know that the Russian working-class movement is not limited to the strike struggle, to mutual benefit societies and workers' circles; that the Russian working-class movement has long been striving to organise itself into a revolutionary party and has demonstrated this striving by action. *R. M.* does not know this, either. But the advanced Russian workers know it.

R. M. tries to represent his complete misunderstanding of Social-Democracy as a sort of specific understanding

of "our reality." Let us look more closely at his ideas on
this subject.

"As far as the concept of the autocracy itself is concerned,"
writes *R. M.*, "...we shall not deal with that at length,
assuming that all to whom we speak have the most precise
and clear conception of such things." We shall soon see
that *R. M.* himself has an extremely imprecise and unclear
conception of such things; but first let us mention one other
circumstance. Are there workers among those to whom *R. M.*
is speaking? Of course, there are. And if so, where are they
to get a precise and clear conception of the autocracy?
Obviously this requires the broadest and most systematic
propaganda of the ideas of political liberty in general;
agitation is required to connect every individual manifestation of police violence and of oppression by officialdom
with a "precise conception" (in the minds of the workers)
of the autocracy. This, it would seem, is elementary. But if
it is, then can purely local propaganda and agitation against
the autocracy be successful? Is it not absolutely essential
to *organise* such propaganda and agitation throughout
Russia into a single planned activity, i.e., into the activity of a single party? Why then does *R. M.* not indicate
that the task of organising systematic propaganda and
agitation against the autocracy is one of the immediate
objectives of the Russian working-class movement? Only
because he has the most *im*precise and *un*clear conception
of the tasks of the Russian working-class movement and of
Russian Social-Democracy.

R. M. proceeds to explain that the autocracy is a tremendous "personal power" (a bureaucracy drilled like
soldiers) and a tremendous "economic power" (financial
resources). We shall not dwell on the "*im*precise" aspects
of his explanation (and there is much that is "*im*-
precise" here), but shall pass over directly to the main
point:

"And so," *R. M.* asks of Russian Social-Democracy, "is
it not the overthrow of this personal power and the seizure
of this economic power that the Russian workers are at
this very moment advised to project as the first and immediate task of their present (embryonic) organisations? (we
shall not even mention the revolutionaries, who say that

this task must be undertaken by the circles of advanced workers)."

In amazement we rub our eyes and read this monstrous passage over two or three times. Surely we must be mistaken! But no, we are not. *R. M. actually does not know what is meant by the overthrow of the autocracy.* Hard to believe as this is, it is a fact. But after the confusion of ideas that *R. M.* has displayed, is it hard to believe after all?

R. M. confuses the seizure of power by revolutionaries with the overthrow of the autocracy by revolutionaries.

Old Russian revolutionaries (of the Narodnaya Volya) strove for the seizure of power by a revolutionary party. They thought that by the seizure of power the "party would overthrow the personal power" of the autocracy, i.e., appoint its agents in place of the government officials, "seize economic power," i.e., all the financial means of the state and carry out the social revolution. The Narodnaya Volya members (the old ones) actually did strive to "overthrow the personal power and seize the economic power" of the autocracy, to employ *R. M.*'s clumsy expression. The Russian Social-Democrats have decidedly set themselves against this revolutionary theory. Plekhanov subjected it to trenchant criticism in his essays, *Socialism and the Political Struggle* (1883) and *Our Differences* (1885), pointing out the task of the Russian revolutionaries—the foundation of a revolutionary working-class party whose immediate aim should be the overthrow of the autocracy. What is meant by the overthrow of the autocracy? To explain this to *R. M.* we must answer the question: what is the autocracy? The autocracy (absolutism, unlimited monarchy) is a form of rule under which all supreme power is wielded wholly and indivisibly by an absolute monarch, the tsar. The tsar issues laws, appoints officials, collects and disburses the national revenues *without any participation by the people in legislation or in control over the administration.* The autocracy, therefore, means the absolute power of government officials and the police and the absence of rights for the people. The entire people suffers from this absence of rights, but the propertied classes (especially the rich landed proprietors and capitalists) exercise a powerful influence over the bureaucracy. The working class suffers doubly: both from the lack of rights to which the entire Russian people is subjected and from the oppression of the workers by the capitalists, who compel the government to serve their interests.

What is meant by the overthrow of the autocracy? It implies the tsar's renunciation of absolute power; the granting to the people of the right to elect their own representatives for legislation, for supervision over the actions of the government officials, for supervision over the collection and disbursement of state revenues. This type of government in which the people participate in legislation and administration is called the *constitutional* form of government (constitution = law on the participation of people's representatives in legislation and the administration of the state). Thus, the overthrow of the autocracy means the replacement of the autocratic form of government by the constitutional form of government. For the overthrow of the autocracy, therefore, no "overthrow of personal power or seizure of economic power" is necessary, but it is necessary to compel the tsarist government to renounce its unlimited power and convene a Zemsky Sobor* of representatives of the people for the elaboration of a constitution ("to win a democratic constitution" [people's constitution, drawn up in the interests of the people], as it is put in the draft programme of the Russian Social-Democrats published in 1885 by the Emancipation of Labour group).

Why must the overthrow of the autocracy be the first task of the Russian working class? Because under the autocracy the working class is not able to develop its struggle extensively, to gain for itself any stable positions in either the economic or political fields, to establish sound mass organisations and unfurl the banner of the social revolution before the masses of the working people and teach them to struggle for it. The decisive struggle of the entire working classs against the bourgeois class is possible only under conditions of political liberty, and the final aim of that struggle is for the proletariat to win political power and organise a socialist society. The conquest of

---

* A central representative assembly.—*Ed.*

political power by an organised proletariat that has gone
through a lengthy schooling in struggle will really be "the
overthrow of the personal power and the seizure of the economic power" of the bourgeois government; but the Russian
Social-Democrats have never put forward *this* seizure of
power as the immediate task of the Russian workers. Russian Social-Democrats have always maintained that only
under conditions of political liberty, when there is an extensive mass struggle, can the Russian working class develop organisations for the final victory of socialism.

But how can the Russian working class overthrow the
autocracy? The editors of *Rabochaya Mysl* make mock even
of the Emancipation of Labour group which founded Russian Social-Democracy and stated in its programme that
"the struggle against the autocracy is obligatory even for
those workers' circles that now constitute the germs of the
future Russian working-class party." It seems ridiculous to
Rabochaya Mysl (see No. 7 and the article under review):
the overthrow of the autocracy—by workers' circles! In
reply, we say to the editors of *Rabochaya Mysl*: Whom are
you mocking? It is yourselves you are mocking! The editors
of *Rabochaya Mysl* complain that the Russian Social-Democrats *are not comradely* in their polemic with them. Let
the readers judge on whose side the polemic is uncom-
radely: on the side of the old Russian Social-Democrats
who have set forth their views clearly and who say outright which views of the "young" they consider mistaken
and why; or on the side of the "young" who *do not name*
their opponents but jab from behind cover, first at "the
author of a German book on Chernyshevsky" (Plekhanov,
whom, moreover, they groundlessly confuse with certain
legal writers), then at the Emancipation of Labour group,
citing *with distortions* passages from its programme without
putting forward anything like a definite programme of their
own. Yes, we recognise the duty of comradeship, the duty to
support all comrades, the duty to tolerate the opinions of
comrades *but as far as we are concerned, the duty of comradeship derives from our duty to Russian and international
Social-Democracy, and not vice versa*. We recognise our
comradely obligations to *Rabochaya Mysl*, not because its
editors are our comrades; we consider the editors of *Rabo-*

chaya Mysl our comrades only because and to the extent
that they work in the ranks of Russian (and, consequently,
of international) Social-Democracy. Therefore, if we are
certain that the "comrades" are moving backwards, away
from the Social-Democratic programme, that the "comrades" are hemming in and distorting the aims of the
working-class movement, we consider it our *duty* to give expression to our convictions with a complete certainty that
leaves nothing unsaid!

We have just stated that the editors of *Rabochaya Mysl*
distort the views of the Emancipation of Labour group.
Let the reader judge for himself. "We are prepared not to
understand those of our comrades," writes *R. M.*, "who
consider their programme for 'the emancipation of labour'
a simple answer to the question: 'Where are we to get the
forces for the struggle against the autocracy?'" (elsewhere:
"Our revolutionaries regard the workers' movement as the
best means of overthrowing the autocracy"). Open the draft
programme of the Russian Social-Democrats published by
the Emancipation of Labour group in 1885 and reprinted by
P. B. Axelrod in his booklet, *Present Tasks and Tactics
of Russian Social Democracy* (Geneva, 1898), and you will
see that the programme *is based on* the emancipation of
labour from the oppression of capital, the transfer of all
means of production to social ownership, the seizure of
political power by the working class, and the founding of
a revolutionary *working-class* party. It is clear that *R. M.*
distorts that programme and is *unwilling* to understand it.
He has seized upon P. B. Axelrod's words at the beginning of
his booklet wherein it is stated that the programme of the
Emancipation of Labour group "was an answer" to the
question: Where are we to get the forces for the struggle
against absolutism? It is, however, *an historical fact* that
the programme of the Emancipation of Labour group was
the answer to the question posed by the Russian revolutionaries and by the Russian revolutionary movement as a
whole. However, because the programme answered that
question, does it mean that the working-class movement
was only the means to an end for the Emancipation of
Labour group? Such a *"misunderstanding"* on the part
of *R. M.* merely shows that he is unacquainted with the

generally-known facts of the activities of the Emancipation
of Labour group.

To continue. How can the "overthrow of the autocracy"
be a task for workers' circles? *R. M.* does not understand.
Open the programme of the Emancipation of Labour group:
"Russian Social-Democrats consider that for the workers'
circles the chief means of political struggle against the autocracy," we read, "is agitation amongst the working class
and the further spreading of socialist ideas and revolutionary organisations amongst the workers. These organisations, closely bound together in an integral whole and not
content with individual clashes with the government, will
lose no time in going over, at a suitable moment, to a general, decisive offensive against the government." These were
precisely the tactics followed by the Russian organisations
that established the Russian Social-Democratic Labour
Party in the spring of 1898. And they proved that such
organisations are a powerful political force in Russia. If
these organisations form one single party and carry on widespread agitation against the autocratic government, using
for this purpose all elements of the liberal opposition, the
objective of winning political liberty will undoubtedly be one
that can be attained by such a party. If the editors of *Rabochaya Mysl* are "prepared not to understand" this, we are
"prepared" to advise them: learn, gentlemen, for these things
are not in themselves very difficult to understand.

Let us, however, get back to *R. M.*, whom we left arguing
about the struggle against the autocracy. *R. M.*'s own views
on this subject illustrate still more clearly the new, retrograde, trend of *Rabochaya Mysl*.

"The end of the autocracy is clear," writes *R. M.* "...The
struggle against the autocracy is one of the conditions for
the sound development of all vital social elements." From
this the reader will probably think that the struggle against
the autocracy is essential to the working class. But wait.
R. M. has his own logic and his own terminology. By the
word "struggle," through the addition of the word "social"
(struggle), he understands something very specific. *R. M.*
describes the *legal opposition* of many sections of the Russian population to the government, and he draws the conclusion: "Indeed, the struggles for Zemstvo and urban

public self-government, for public schools, and for public aid to the starving population, etc., constitute a struggle against the autocracy." "The necessity to wage a social struggle against the bureaucratic autocracy is obvious to all class-conscious, progressive sections and groups of the population. More than this. This social struggle, which through some strange misunderstanding has not attracted the favourable attention of many Russian revolutionary writers, is, as we have seen, being conducted by Russian society; nor did it begin yesterday." "The real question is how these separate social strata ... are to conduct this [note this!] struggle against the autocracy with the maximum success. ... The main question for us is to know how our workers should conduct this social [!] struggle against the autocracy."...

These arguments of *R. M.* are again cluttered with an unbelievable amount of confusion and errors.

First, *R. M.* confuses *legal opposition* with the struggle against the autocracy, with the struggle to overthrow the autocracy. This confusion, unpardonable in a socialist, results from his employing the expression "struggle against the autocracy" without an explanation: this expression may mean (with a reservation) struggle *against* the autocracy, but also struggle against individual measures of the autocracy within the framework of that same autocratic system.

Secondly, by regarding legal opposition as the social struggle against the autocracy and affirming that our workers should wage "this social struggle," *R. M.* virtually says that our workers should carry on legal opposition, not a revolutionary struggle, against the autocracy; in other words, he sinks into a hideous debasement of Social-Democracy, which he confuses with the most commonplace and beggarly Russian liberalism.

Thirdly, *R. M.* declares a *flagrant untruth* regarding Russian Social-Democratic writers (true, he prefers making his reproaches in "all comradeship," without naming names; but if it is not Social-Democrats whom he has in mind, his words have no sense), when he states that they do not pay attention to legal opposition. On the contrary, the Emancipation of Labour group, and P. B. Axelrod in particular, as well as the *Manifesto of the Russian Social-*

Democratic Labour Party and the pamphlet, *The Tasks of the
Russian Social-Democrats* (published by the Russian
Social-Democratic Labour Party and designated by
Axelrod as a *commentary* to the *Manifesto*)—all, not only
paid attention to legal opposition, but even elucidated
with precision its relation to Social-Democracy.

Let us clarify the issue. What sort of "struggle against
the autocracy" is being conducted by our Zemstvos, by our
liberal societies in general, and by the liberal press? Are
they carrying on a struggle against the autocracy, for the
overthrow of the autocracy? *No, they never have engaged
and still do not engage in such a struggle.* This is a struggle
that is waged only by the revolutionaries, who frequently
come from the liberal society and rely on its sympathy.
But waging a revolutionary struggle is in no sense the same
thing as sympathising with the revolutionaries and supporting them; the struggle against the autocracy is in no
sense the same thing as legal opposition to the autocracy.
The Russian liberals express their dissatisfaction with the
autocracy only in the form *sanctioned* by the autocracy
itself, i.e., the form that the autocracy does not consider
dangerous to the autocracy. The grandest showing of liberal opposition has been nothing more than the *petitions*
of the liberals to the tsarist government to draw the people
into the administration. And each time the liberals patiently
accepted the brutal police rejections of their petitions;
they put up with the lawless and savage repressions with
which the government of gendarmes repaid even legal attempts to make known their opinion. Simply to present
the liberal opposition as a social struggle against the
autocracy is a pure *distortion* of the issue, because the Russian liberals have *never* organised a revolutionary party to
struggle for the overthrow of the autocracy, although they
could have found and can still find for this purpose both the
material means and representatives of Russian liberalism
abroad. *R. M.* not only distorts the issue, but he drags in the
name of the great Russian socialist N. G. Chernyshevsky. "The
workers' allies in this struggle," says *R. M.*, "are all the
advanced strata of Russian society, who are defending their
social interests and institutions, who have a clear conception of the common good, who 'never forget' [*R. M.* quotes

Chernyshevsky] that there is 'a great difference as to whether changes are brought about by an independent decision of the government or *by the formal demand of society.*'" If this comment is applied to all representatives of the "social struggle" in the way *R. M.* understands it, i.e., to all Russian liberals, then it is a *falsification pure and simple.* The Russian liberals have never presented any formal demands to the government, and precisely for this reason the Russian liberals have never played and now certainly cannot play an *independent* revolutionary role. Not "all the advanced strata of society" can be allies of the working class and Social-Democracy, but only revolutionary parties founded by members of that society. In general, the liberals can and should serve merely *as one of the sources* of additional forces and means for the revolutionary working-class party (as P. B. Axelrod so clearly stated in the above-mentioned pamphlet). N. G. Chernyshevsky ridiculed "the progressive strata of Russian society" for the very fact that they did not understand the necessity for formal demands to the government and indifferently watched revolutionaries from their own midst perish under the blows of the autocratic government. In this case *R. M.*'s quotations from Chernyshevsky are as senseless as his quotations from the same author, torn piecemeal out of context, in the second article of the *Separate Supplement,* which are meant to show that Chernyshevsky was not a utopian and that Russian Social-Democrats do not appreciate the full significance of the "great Russian socialist." In his book on Chernyshevsky (articles in the collection *Sotsial-Demokrat,*[110] issued as a separate volume in German) Plekhanov fully appreciated the significance of Chernyshevsky and explained his attitude to the theory of Marx and Engels. The editors of *Rabochaya Mysl* have merely revealed their own inability to give anything like a connected and comprehensive assessment of Chernyshevsky, of his strong and weak sides.

"The real question" for Russian Social-Democracy is by no means that of determining how the liberals are to conduct the "social struggle" (by "social struggle" *R. M.,* as we have seen, means legal opposition), but how to organise a revolutionary working-class party devoted to the struggle for the overthrow of the autocracy, a party that could gain the backing of *all* opposition elements in Russia, a party that could *utilise* all manifestations of opposition in its revolutionary struggle. It is precisely a revolutionary working-class party that is needed for this purpose, because in Russia only the working class can be a determined and consistent fighter for democracy, because without the vigorous influence of such a party the liberal elements "could remain a sluggish, inactive, dormant force" (P. B. Axelrod, op. cit., p. 23). In saying that our "more advanced strata" are conducting "a real [!!] social struggle against the autocracy" (p. 12 of *R. M.*'s article), that "the main question for us is how our workers should conduct *this social struggle* against the autocracy"—in saying such things, *R. M.* is, in fact, retreating completely from Social-Democracy. We can only offer serious advice to the editors of *Rabochaya Mysl* to ponder well the question of where they want to go and where their real place is: among the revolutionaries, who carry the banner of the social revolution to the working classes and want to organise them into a political revolutionary party, or among the liberals, who are conducting their own "social struggle" (i.e., the legal opposition)? There is nothing at all socialist in the theory of the "independent social activity" of the workers; in the theory of "social mutual aid" and of the craft unions that "so far" confine themselves to the 10-hour working day; in the theory of the "social struggle" of the Zemstvos, liberal societies, and others against the autocracy—there is nothing in this theory that the liberals would not accept! Indeed, the entire programme of *Rabochaya Mysl* (to the extent that one can call it a programme) tends, in essence, to leave the Russian workers undeveloped and split, and to make them the *tail-end of the liberals*!

Some of *R. M.*'s phrases are particularly strange. "The whole trouble is merely that our revolutionary intelligentsia," he proclaims, "mercilessly persecuted by the political police, mistake the struggle against the political police for the political struggle against the autocracy." What sense can there be in such a statement? The political police are called political because they persecute enemies of the autocracy and those who struggle against the autocracy. For this reason, *Rabochaya Mysl*, so long as its metamorphosis into a liberal is not completed, fights against the political police as do all Russian revolutionaries and socialists and all class-conscious workers. From the fact that the political police mercilessly persecute socialists and workers, that the autocracy maintains a "well-ordered organisation," "competent and resourceful statesmen" (p. 7 of *R. M.*'s article), only two conclusions are to be drawn: the cowardly and wretched liberal will pass judgement that our people in general and our workers in particular are still ill-prepared for the struggle and that all hopes must be placed in the "struggle" of the Zemstvos, the liberal press, etc., since this is the "real struggle against the autocracy" and not only a struggle against the political police. The socialist and every class-conscious worker will conclude that the working-class party must bend all its efforts to the formation of a "well-ordered organisation," to the training of "competent and resourceful revolutionaries" from among the advanced workers and socialists, people who will raise the working-class party to the high level of the loading fighter for democracy and who will be able to win over to its side all opposition elements.

The editors of *Rabochaya Mysl* do not realise that they are standing on an inclined plane down which they will roll to the first of these two conclusions!

Or, again: "What amazes us further in these programmes [i.e., in the programmes of the Social-Democrats]," writes *R. M.*, "is that they incessantly give first place to the advantages of workers' activities in a parliament [non-existent in Russia], while completely ignoring ... the importance of workers' participation" in the employers' legislative assemblies, on factory boards, and in municipal self-government (p. .15). If the advantages of parliament are not brought into the forefront, how will the workers learn about political rights and political liberty? If we keep silent on these questions—as does *Rabochaya Mysl*—does this not mean perpetuating the political ignorance of the lower strata of the workers? As to workers' participation in municipal self-government, no Social-Democrat has ever denied anywhere the advantages and the importance of the activities of *socialist* workers in municipal self-government;

but it is ridiculous to speak of this in Russia, where no open manifestation of socialism is possible and where firing the workers with enthusiasm for municipal self-government (even were this possible) would actually mean distracting advanced workers from the socialist working-class cause towards liberalism.

"The attitude of the advanced strata of the workers towards this [autocratic] government," says *R. M.*, "is as understandable as their attitude towards the factory owners." The common-sense view of this, therefore, is that the advanced strata of the workers are no less class-conscious Social-Democrats than the socialists from among the intelligentsia, so that *Rabochaya Mysl*'s attempt to separate the one from the other is absurd and harmful. The Russian working class, accordingly, has produced the elements necessary for the formation of an independent working-class political party. But the editors of *Rabochaya Mysl* draw from the fact of the political consciousness of the advanced strata of the workers the conclusion ... that it is necessary to hold these advanced elements back, so as to keep them marking time! "Which struggle is it most desirable for the workers to wage?" asks *R. M.*, and he answers: Desirable is the struggle that is possible, and possible is the struggle which the workers are "waging at the given moment"!!! It would be difficult to express more glaringly the senseless and unprincipled opportunism with which the editors of *Rabochaya Mysl*, allured by fashionable "Bernsteinism," have become infected! What is possible is desirable, and what we have at the given moment is possible! It is as though a man setting out on a long and difficult road on which numerous obstacles and numerous enemies await him were told in answer to his question "Where shall I go?": "It is desirable to go where it is possible to go, and it is possible to go where you are going at the given moment"! This is the sheerest nihilism, not revolutionary, however, but opportunist nihilism, manifested either by anarchists or bourgeois liberals! By "calling upon" the Russian workers to engage in a "partial" and "political" struggle (with political struggle understood, not as the struggle against the autocracy, but only as "the struggle to improve the condition of all workers"), *R. M.* is actually calling upon the Russian working-class movement and Russian Social-Democracy to take *a step backward*, he is actually calling upon the workers to separate from the Social-Democrats and thus throw overboard everything that has been acquired by European and Russian experience! The workers have no need for socialists in their struggle to improve their condition, if that is their only struggle. In all countries there are workers who wage the struggle for the improvement of their condition, but know nothing of socialism or are even hostile to it.

"In conclusion," writes *R. M.*, "a few words on our conception of working-class socialism." After what has been said above the reader will have no difficulty in imagining the sort of "conception" it is. It is simply a copy of Bernstein's "fashionable" book. Our "young" Social-Democrats substitute the "independent social and political activity of the workers" for the class struggle of the proletariat. If we recall how *R. M.* understands *social* "struggle" and "politics," it will be clear that this is a direct return to the "formula" of certain Russian legal writers. Instead of indicating precisely the aim (and essence) of socialism—the transfer of the land, factories, etc., in general, of all the means of production, to the ownership of the whole of society and the replacement of the capitalist mode of production by production according to a common plan in the interests of all members of society—instead of all this, *R. M.* indicates first of all the development of craft unions and consumers' co-operatives, and says only in passing that socialism leads to the complete socialisation of all the means of production. On the other hand, he prints in the heaviest type: "Socialism is merely a further and higher development of the modern community"—a phrase borrowed from Bernstein, which not only does not explain but even obscures the significance and substance of socialism. All the liberals and the entire bourgeoisie undoubtedly favour the "development of the modern community," so that they will all rejoice at *R. M.*'s declaration. Nevertheless, the bourgeois are the *enemies* of socialism. The point is that "the modern community" has many varied aspects, and of those who employ this general expression, some have one aspect in view, others another. And so, instead of

explaining the concept of the class struggle and socialism
to the workers, *R. M.* offers them only nebulous and mis-
leading phrases. Lastly, instead of indicating the means
modern socialism advances for the achievement of
socialism—the winning of political power by the organised proletariat—instead of this, *R. M.* speaks only of
placing production under their (the workers') social management or under the management of democratised social
power, democratised "by their [the workers'] active participation on boards examining all kinds of factory affairs,
in courts of arbitration, in all possible assemblies, commis-
sions, and conferences for the elaboration of labour laws;
by the workers' participation in public self-government,
and, lastly, in the country's general representative institution." In this way the editors of *Rabochaya Mysl* include
in working-class socialism only that which is to be obtained
along the *peaceful* path and exclude the revolutionary path.
This narrowing-down of socialism and its reduction to
common bourgeois liberalism represents again a tremendous
step backwards as compared with the views of all Russian
Social-Democrats and of the overwhelming majority of
European Social-Democrats. The working class would, of
course, prefer to take power *peacefully* (we have already
stated that this seizure of power can be carried out only by
the organised working class which has passed through the
school of the class struggle), but to *renounce* the revolutionary
seizure of power would be *madness* on the part of the proletariat, both from the theoretical and the practical-political
points of view; it would mean nothing but a disgraceful
retreat in face of the bourgeoisie and all other propertied
classes. It is very probable—even most probable—that
the bourgeoisie will not make peaceful concessions to the
proletariat and at the decisive moment will resort to violence for the defence of its privileges. In that case, no other
way will be left to the proletariat for the achievement of
its aim but that of revolution. This is the reason the programme of "working-class socialism" speaks of the winning
of political power in general *without defining* the method,
for the choice of method depends on a future which we cannot precisely determine. But, we repeat, to limit the activities of the proletariat under any circumstances to peaceful

"democratisation" alone is arbitrarily to narrow and vulgarise the concept of working-class socialism.

We shall not analyse the other articles in the *Separate Supplement* in such great detail. We have spoken of the article on the tenth anniversary of Chernyshevsky's death. As to the pro-Bernsteinian propaganda of the *Rabochaya Mysl* Editorial Board, which the enemies of socialism throughout the world, especially the bourgeois liberals, have seized on, and against which the vast majority of the German Social-Democrats and class-conscious German workers spoke out so decisively (at their Hannover Congress)—as to Bernsteinism, this is not the place to speak of it in detail. We are interested in our *Russian* Bernsteinism, and we have shown the limitless confusion of ideas, the absence of anything like independent views, the tremendous step backwards as compared with the views of Russian Social-Democracy which "our" Bernsteinism represents. As far as German Bernsteinism is concerned, we would rather leave it to the Germans themselves to handle. We would remark only that Russian Bernsteinism is infinitely lower than the German. Bernstein, despite his errors, despite his obvious striving to retrogress both theoretically and politically, still has sufficient intelligence and sufficient conscientiousness *not to propose changes* in the programme of German Social-Democracy without himself having arrived at any new theory or programme; in the final and decisive moment, he declared his acceptance of Bebel's resolution, a resolution that announced solemnly to the world that German Social-Democracy would stand by its old programme and its old tactics. And our Russian Bernsteinians? Without having done a hundredth of what Bernstein has done, they even go so far as to refuse to recognise the fact that all Russian Social-Democratic organisations laid the foundations of the Russian Social-Democratic Labour Party in 1898, published its *Manifesto*, and announced *Rabochaya Gazeta* to be its official organ, and that these publications stand by the "old" programme of the Russian Social-Democrats in its entirety. Our Bernsteinians do not seem to be aware of the fact that, if they have rejected the old views and adopted new ones it is their moral duty—to Russian Social-Democracy and

to the Russian socialists and workers who devoted all their
efforts to the preparations for, and the founding of, the Russian Social-Democratic Labour Party and who in their majority now all Russian prisons—that it is the duty of those who
profess the new views, not to confine themselves to jabbing
from holes and corners at "our revolutionaries" in general,
but to announce directly and publicly with whom and with
what they are in disagreement, what new views and what
new programme they advance in place of the old.

There is still one other question left for us to examine,
probably the most important one, namely, how such a retrograde trend in Russian Social-Democracy is *to be explained*.
In our opinion it is not to be explained solely by the
personal qualities of the *Rabochaya Mysl* editors or by the
influence of the fashionable Bernsteinism alone. We hold
that it is to be explained mainly by the peculiarities in the
historical development of Russian Social-Democracy, which
gave rise to—and *had temporarily* to give rise to—a narrow understanding of working-class socialism.

In the eighties and at the beginning of the nineties, when
Social-Democrats initiated their practical work in Russia,
they were confronted firstly with-the Narodnaya Volya,
which charged them with departing from the political struggle
that had been inherited from the Russian revolutionary
movement, and with which the Social-Democrats carried on
a persistent polemic. Secondly, they were confronted with
the Russian liberal circles, which were also dissatisfied
with the turn taken by the revolutionary movement—from
the Narodnaya Volya trend to Social-Democracy. The two-
fold polemic centred round the question of politics. In
their struggle against the narrow conceptions of the Narodnaya Volya adherents, who reduced politics to conspiracy-
making, the Social-Democrats could be led to, and did at
times, declare themselves against politics in general (in
view of the then prevailing narrow conception of politics).
On the other hand, the Social-Democrats often heard, in
the liberal and radical *salons* of bourgeois "society," regrets
that the revolutionaries had abandoned terror; people who
were mortally afraid for their own skins and at a decisive
moment failed to give support to the heroes who struck
blows at the autocracy, these people hypocritically accused

the Social-Democrats of political indifferentism and yearned
for the rebirth of a party that would pull the chestnuts
out of the fire for them. Naturally, the Social-Democrats
conceived a hatred for such people and their phrases, and
they turned to the more mundane but more serious work of
propaganda among the factory proletariat. At first it was
inevitable that this work should have a narrow character
and should be embodied in the narrow declarations of some
Social-Democrats. This narrowness, however, did not fright-
en those Social-Democrats who had not in the least forgotten the broad historical aims of the Russian working-class
movement. What matters it if the *words* of the Social-Democrats sometimes have a narrow meaning when *their deeds*
cover a broad field. They do not give themselves up to useless conspiracies, they do not hob-nob with the Balalai-
kins[111] of bourgeois liberalism, but they go to that class
which alone is the real revolutionary class and assist in the
development of its forces! They believed that this narrowness would disappear of its own accord with each step that
broadened Social-Democratic propaganda. And this, to a
considerable degree, is what has happened. From propaganda
they began to go over to widespread agitation. Widespread
agitation, naturally, brought to the forefront a growing
number of class-conscious advanced workers; revolutionary
organisations began to take form (the St. Petersburg, Kiev,
and other Leagues of Struggle, the Jewish Workers' Union).
These organisations naturally tended to merge and, eventually, they succeeded: they united and laid the foundations of the Russian Social-Democratic Labour Party.
It would seem that the old narrowness would then have
been left without any basis and that it would be completely
cast aside. But things turned out differently: the spread of
their agitation brought the Social-Democrats into contact
with the lower, less developed strata of the proletariat;
to attract these strata it was necessary for the agitator to be
able to adapt himself to the lowest level of understanding, he was taught to put the "demands and interests of
the given moment" in the foreground and to push back the
broad ideals of socialism and the political struggle. The
fragmentary, amateur nature of Social-Democratic work,
the extremely weak connections between the study circles in

the different cities, between the Russian Social-Democrats and their comrades abroad who possessed a profounder knowledge and a richer revolutionary experience, as well as a wider political horizon, naturally led to a gross exaggeration of this (*absolutely essential*) aspect of Social-Democratic activity, which could bring some individuals to lose sight of the other aspects, especially since with every reverse the most developed workers and intellectuals were wrenched from the ranks of the struggling army, so that sound revolutionary traditions and continuity could not as yet be evolved. It is in this extreme exaggeration of one aspect of Social-Democratic work that we see the chief cause of the sad retreat from the ideals of Russian Social-Democracy. Add to this enthusiasm over a fashionable book, ignorance of the history of the Russian revolutionary movement, and a childish claim to originality, and you have all the elements that go to make up "the retrograde trend in Russian Social-Democracy."

We shall, therefore, have to deal in greater detail with the question of the relation of the advanced strata of the proletariat to the less advanced, and the significance of Social-Democratic work among these two sections.

The history of the working-class movement in all countries shows that the better-situated strata of the working class respond to the ideas of socialism more rapidly and more easily. From among these come, in the main, the advanced workers that every working-class movement brings to the fore, those who can win the confidence of the labouring masses, who devote themselves entirely to the education and organisation of the proletariat, who accept socialism consciously, and who even elaborate independent socialist theories. Every viable working-class movement has brought to the fore such working-class leaders, its own Proudhons, Vaillants, Weitlings, and Bebels. And our Russian working-class movement promises not to lag behind the European movement in this respect. At a time when educated society is losing interest in honest, illegal literature, an impassioned desire for knowledge and for socialism is growing among the workers, real heroes are coming to the fore from amongst the workers, who, despite their wretched living conditions, despite the stultifying penal servitude of factory labour, possess so much character and will-power that they study, study, study, and turn themselves into conscious Social-Democrats—"the working-class intelligentsia." This "working-class intelligentsia" already exists in Russia, and we must make every effort to ensure that its ranks are regularly reinforced, that its lofty mental requirements are met and that leaders of the Russian Social-Democratic Labour Party come from its ranks. The newspaper that wants to become the organ of all Russian Social-Democrats must, therefore, be at the level of the advanced workers; not only must it not lower its level artificially, but, on the contrary, it must raise it constantly, it must follow up all the tactical, political, and theoretical problems of world Social-Democracy. Only then will the demands of the working-class intelligentsia be met, and it itself will take the cause of the Russian workers and, *consequently*, the cause of the Russian revolution, into its own hands.

After the numerically small stratum of advanced workers comes the broad stratum of average workers. These workers, too, strive ardently for socialism, participate in workers' study circles, read socialist newspapers and books, participate in agitation, and differ from the preceding stratum only in that they cannot become fully independent leaders of the Social-Democratic working-class movement. The average worker will not understand some of the articles in a newspaper that aims to be the organ of the Party, he will not be able to get a full grasp of an intricate theoretical or practical problem. This does not at all mean that the newspaper must lower itself to the level of the mass of its readers. The newspaper, on the contrary, must raise their level and help promote advanced workers from the middle stratum of workers. Such workers, absorbed by *local* practical work and interested mainly in the events of the working-class movement and the immediate problems of agitation, should connect their every act with thoughts of the entire Russian working-class movement, its historical task, and the ultimate goal of socialism, so that the newspaper, the mass of whose readers are average workers, must connect socialism and the political struggle with every local and narrow question.

Lastly, behind the stratum of average workers comes the mass that constitutes the lower strata of the proletariat. It is quite possible that a socialist newspaper will be completely or well-nigh incomprehensible to them (even in Western Europe the number of Social-Democratic voters is much larger than the number of readers of Social-Democratic newspapers), but it would be absurd to conclude from this that the newspaper of the Social-Democrats should adapt itself to the lowest possible level of the workers. The only thing that follows from this is that different forms of agitation and propaganda must be brought to bear on these strata—pamphlets written in more popular language, oral agitation, and chiefly—leaflets on local events. The Social-Democrats should not confine themselves even to this; it is quite possible that the first steps towards arousing the consciousness of the lower strata of the workers will have to take the form of legal educational activities. It is very important for the *Party* to make use of this activity, guide it in the direction in which it is most needed, send out legal workers to plough up virgin fields that can later be planted by Social-Democratic agitators. Agitation among the lower strata of the workers should, of course, provide the widest field for the personal qualities of the agitator and the peculiarities of the locality, the trade concerned, etc. "Tactics and agitation must not be confused," says Kautsky in his book against Bernstein. "Agitational methods must be adapted to individual and local conditions. Every agitator must be allowed to select those methods of agitation that he has at his disposal. One agitator may create the greatest impression by his enthusiasm, another by his biting sarcasm, a third by his ability to adduce a large number of instances, etc. While being adapted to the agitator, agitation must also be adapted to the public. The agitator must speak so that he will be understood; he must take as a starting-point something well known to his listeners. All this is self-evident and is not merely applicable to agitation conducted among the peasantry. One has to talk to cabmen differently than to sailors, and to sailors differently than to printers. *Agitation* must be *individualised*, but our *tactics*, our political *activity* must be *uniform*" (*S*. 2-3). These words from a leading representative of

Social-Democratic theory contain a superb assessment of agitation as part of the general activity of the party. These words show how unfounded are the fears of those who think that the formation of a revolutionary party conducting a political struggle will interfere with agitation, will push it into the background and curtail the freedom of the agitators. On the contrary, only an organised party can carry out widespread agitation, provide the necessary guidance (and material) for agitators on all economic and political questions, make use of every local agitational success for the instruction of all Russian workers, and send agitators to those places and into that *milieu* where they can work with the greatest success. It is only in an organised party that people possessing the capacities for work as agitators will be able to dedicate themselves wholly to this task—to the advantage both of agitation and of the other aspects of Social-Democratic work. From this it can be seen that whoever forgets political agitation and propaganda on account of the economic struggle, whoever forgets the necessity of organising the working-class movement into the struggle of a political party, will, aside from everything else, deprive himself of even an opportunity of successfully and steadily attracting the lower strata of the proletariat to the working-class cause.

However, such an exaggeration of one side of our activities to the detriment of the others, even the urge to throw overboard the other aspects, is fraught with still graver consequences for the Russian working-class movement. The lower strata of the proletariat may even become demoralised by such calumnies as that the founders of Russian Social-Democracy only want to use the workers to overthrow the autocracy, by invitations to confine themselves to the restoration of holidays and to craft unions, with no concern for the final aims of socialism and the immediate tasks of the political struggle. Such workers may (and will) always be ensnared by the bait of any sops offered by the government or the bourgeoisie. The lower strata of the proletariat, the very undeveloped workers, might, under the influence of the preaching of *Rabochaya Mysl*, fall victim to the bourgeois and profoundly reactionary idea that the worker cannot and should not interest himself in anything but increased wages and the restoration of holidays ("the interests of the moment"); that the working people can and should conduct the workers' struggle by their own efforts alone, by their own "private initiative," and not attempt to combine it with socialism; that they should not strive to turn the working-class movement into the essential, advanced cause of all mankind. We repeat, the most undeveloped workers might be demoralised by such an idea, but we are confident that the advanced Russian workers, those who guide the workers' study circles and all Social-Democratic activity, those who today fill our prisons and places of exile—from Archangel Gubernia to Eastern Siberia—that those workers will reject such a theory with indignation. To reduce the entire movement to the interests of the moment means to speculate on the backward condition of the workers, means to cater to their worst inclinations. It means artificially to break the link between the working-class movement and socialism, between the fully defined political strivings of the advanced workers and the spontaneous manifestations of protest on the part of the masses. Hence, the attempt of *Rabochaya Mysl* to introduce a special trend merits particular attention and calls for a vigorous protest. As long as *Rabochaya Mysl*, adapting itself, apparently, to the lower strata of the proletariat, assiduously avoided the question of the ultimate goal of socialism and the political struggle, with no declaration of its special trend, many Social-Democrats only shook their heads, hoping that with the development and extension of their work the members of the *Rabochaya Mysl* group would come to rid themselves of their narrowness. However, when people who, until now, have performed the useful work of a preparatory class clutch at fashionable opportunist theories and begin to deafen the ears of Europe with announcements about intending to put the whole of Russian Social-Democracy into the preparatory class for many years (if not for ever), when, in other words, people who have, until now, been labouring usefully over a barrel of honey begin "in full view of the public" to pour ladles of tar into it, then it is time for us to set ourselves decisively against this retrograde trend!

Russian Social-Democracy, both through its founders, the members of the Emancipation of Labour group, and through the Russian Social-Democratic organisations that founded the Russian Social-Democratic Labour Party, has always recognised the following two principles: 1) The essence of Social-Democracy is the organisation of the class struggle of the proletariat for the purpose of winning political power, of transferring all means of production to society as a whole, and of replacing capitalist by socialist economy; 2) the task of Russian Social-Democracy is to organise the Russian revolutionary working-class party which has as its immediate aim the overthrow of the autocracy and the winning of political liberty. Whoever departs from these basic principles (formulated precisely in the programme of the Emancipation of Labour group and expressed in the *Manifesto of the Russian Social-Democratic Labour Party*) departs from Social-Democracy.

Written at the end of 1899

First published in 1924
in the magazine *Proletarskaya
Revolyutsiya* (*Proletarian Revolution*),
No. 8-9

Published according to
a manuscript copied
by an unknown hand
and looked over by Lenin

APROPOS OF THE *PROFESSION DE FOI**

Although the *Profession de foi*, composed by the Kiev Committee, is only a rough draft, for the elaboration and polishing of which, according to the Committee, there was an insufficiency of time, it nevertheless allows one to obtain quite a clear idea of the views of the Kiev Committee. These views must certainly call forth an emphatic protest from those Russian Social-Democrats who abide by the viewpoint of the old principles of Social-Democracy proclaimed in Russia by the Emancipation of Labour group, enunciated repeatedly in the publications of the R.S.D.L.P. and reaffirmed in its manifesto. There is no doubt that the views of the Kiev Committee *reflect* the very considerable influence of the new trend of the "young Russian Social-Democrats," which, when developed to the extreme, has merged with Bernsteinism and yielded such products as the famous *Separate Supplement to "Rabochaya Mysl"* (September 1899) and the no less famous *Credo*.

It cannot be said that the *Profession de foi* has gone all the way towards this opportunist and reactionary trend, but it has taken such serious steps in that direction and denotes such confusion in the basic ideas of Social-Democracy, such a vacillation in revolutionary thinking, that we consider it our duty to give warning to the comrades in Kiev and to analyse in detail their deviation from principles long established both in international and in Russian Social-Democracy.

---

* Profession of faith, a programme, the exposition of a world outlook.—*Ed.*

The very first sentence of the *Profession de foi* gives rise to the most serious bewilderment: "While admitting that the struggle for the political rights of the proletariat is the immediate general task of the working-class movement in Russia, the Kiev Committee nevertheless does not believe it possible at the present time to turn to the mass of the workers and call on them to take political action, in other words, it does not believe it possible to carry on *political* agitation, because the Russian workers have not, in the mass, attained the maturity for political struggle." We shall not discuss the formulation of this passage; of importance to us only are the ideas contained in it and reiterated (note this) in many other places in the *Profession de foi*, ideas of such a nature that they simply leave us wondering: Can those who wrote this really be Social-Democrats?

"The Russian workers have not, in the mass, attained the maturity for political struggle"! If this is true, it is tantamount to a death sentence for Social-Democracy as a whole; for it means that the Russian workers have not, in the mass, reached the maturity necessary for Social-Democracy. In actual fact, there is not and never has been a Social-Democracy anywhere in the world that is not inseparably and indivisibly bound up with the political struggle. Social-Democracy without the political struggle is a river without water, it is a howling contradiction, it is either something in the nature of a return to the utopian socialism of our forefathers who despised "politics," or to anarchism, or to trade-unionism.

The first *profession de foi* of world socialism, the *Communist Manifesto*, established a truth that has since become an elementary verity—that every class struggle is a political struggle, that the working-class movement only then grows out of its embryonic state, its infancy, and becomes a *class* movement when it makes the transition to the political struggle. The first *profession de foi* of Russian socialism, Plekhanov's booklet, *Socialism and the Political Struggle*, which appeared in 1883, reaffirmed this elementary truth in its application to Russia and showed precisely how and why the Russian revolutionary movement must bring about a fusion of socialism and the political struggle, a fusion of the spontaneous movement of the masses of workers and the revolutionary movement, a fusion of the class struggle and the political struggle. By adopting the standpoint of socialism and the class struggle and simultaneously rejecting the possibility of "calling at the present moment on the masses to take political action," the Kiev Committee is, in essence, departing completely from the principles of Social-Democracy, and the desire to remain true to these principles has led the Committee into a number of glaring contradictions.

Indeed, how can one speak of the "political education" of the workers, if one does not recognise the possibility of conducting political agitation and political struggle? Surely there is no need to prove to Social-Democrats that there can be no political education except through political struggle and political action. Surely it cannot be imagined that any sort of study circles or books, etc., can politically educate the masses of workers if they are kept away from political activity and political struggle. Surely Russian Social-Democracy does not have to go back to the viewpoint of the serf-owners who declared that it was first necessary to educate the peasants and then to emancipate them, or to the viewpoint of those ink-slingers who grovel before the government and say that the people must first be educated and then granted political rights. How can one undertake to bring the workers to recognition of the need to struggle for political rights and at the same time not believe in the possibility of calling on them to take political action, in the possibility of conducting political agitation? Arouse the consciousness of the need for political struggle and at the same time not call for political struggle?! What falderal is this? What does it mean? This kind of tangle is not the result of something left unsaid or of the unfinished nature of a rough draft; it is the natural, inevitable result of the dualism and equivocation that permeate all the views of the Kiev Committee. The Committee wants, on the one hand, to remain true to the basic principles long established in international and Russian Social-Democracy and, on the other, is infatuated with the fashionable Bernsteinian catchwords, "necessity," "gradualness" (end of Section I of the Kiev Committee's *Profession de foi*), "the directly economic character of the

movement," the impossibility of political agitation and
struggle, the necessity of adhering to the solid ground of
real demands and needs (as though the struggle for political
liberty is not called forth by the most real demand and
need!); in a word, it is infatuated with the fashionable
catchwords out of which such writings *à la mode* as
the *Credo* and the *Separate Supplement to "Rabochaya
Mysl"* are spun. Let us examine in its essence the thesis
in which all the weak aspects of the *Profession de foi*
now under discussion are focused, the thesis that it is
"impossible at the present time to turn to the mass of the
workers with the call to take political action"; that it is
impossible, in other words, to conduct political agitation,
because the Russian workers have not yet attained the maturity for political struggle. This last assertion is, fortunately, untrue (we say "fortunately," for were it true, it
would inevitably lead Russian Marxists and Russian Social-Democrats into the quagmire of trade-unionist and bourgeois-liberal vulgarisation into which the authors of *Credo*,
Rabochaya Mysl, and their numerous hangers-on in our
legal literature are trying to push them). The Russian
workers have, in the mass, not only attained maturity for
political struggle, but they have on many occasions demonstrated it by engaging in acts of political struggle, often
even spontaneously.

Is not the mass distribution of manifestos in which the
government is condemned and castigated really an act of
political struggle? Have not the Russian workers in the mass
"used their own means" to deal with the police and the
soldiery when these became excessively arrogant; have
they not liberated arrested comrades by force? Have they
not in many places fought in real street battles against
troops and police? Have not the Russian workers in the
mass, for more than twenty years, sent the best, most developed, most honest, and most courageous of their comrades into the revolutionary circles and organisations? But
for the sake of a fashionable doctrine of bourgeois vulgarisation we, representatives of the revolutionary Social-
Democratic Party, are supposed to forget all that and admit
the impossibility of calling on the working masses to take political action! The objection will probably be raised that the

cited instances are more often spontaneous outbursts rather
than political struggles. To which we answer: Were not our
strikes mere spontaneous outbursts until the revolutionary
circles of socialists undertook extensive agitation and summoned the working masses to the class struggle, to the conscious struggle against their oppressors? Call one find in history a single case of a popular movement, of a class movement, that did not begin with spontaneous, unorganised
outbursts, that would have assumed an organised form and
created political parties without the conscious intervention
of enlightened representatives of the given class? If the
working-class urge, spontaneous and indomitable, to
engage in political struggle has so far taken mainly the
form of unorganised outbursts, only *Moskovskiye Vedomosti*[112] and *Grazhdanin*[113] can draw from this the conclusion that the Russian workers have not yet, in the mass,
attained the maturity for political agitation. A socialist,
on the contrary, will draw from it the conclusion that the
time has long been ripe for political agitation, for the
broadest possible appeal to the working masses to engage in
political action and political struggle. If we do not make this
appeal, we fail in our duty and, in actual fact, cease to be
Social-Democrats, since economic and trade-union organisations without political struggle have always and everywhere
been advocated by zealous champions of the bourgeoisie.
For this reason the persistent ignoring of the political struggle and the political tasks of the Russian working class, such
as we see, for instance, in *Rabochaya Mysl*, cannot be called
anything but criminal and disgraceful. This hushing-up is
tantamount to demoralising the political consciousness of the
workers, who see and feel political oppression, who revolt
spontaneously against it, but who meet with indifference
on the part of their socialist leaders or even with polemics
against the ideas of political struggle. When we are told
that the ideas of political liberty must be brought "gradually" to the masses, what can we call this but indifference
and extreme narrowness? One might think that hitherto
we have been too hasty in bringing these ideas to the
masses, so that we need to curb and moderate ourselves!!!
Or, when we are told that "a political clarification of the
condition of the working class" is necessary only "to the

extent that there is reason for it in each individual case," as though "reasons" for political agitation are not furnished by a multitude of the most widespread, day-to-day facts of working-class life!

The effort to limit political agitation to the existence of reasons in each individual case is either senseless or it reflects a desire to take a step backwards in the direction of *Credo* and *Rabochaya Mysl*, a desire to narrow the scope of our already far-too-narrow propaganda and agitation. The objection will also probably be raised that the working-class *masses* are not yet able to understand the idea of the political struggle, an idea that is comprehensible only to certain, more developed workers. To this objection, which we hear so frequently from "young" Russian Social-Democrats, our answer is that, firstly, Social-Democracy has everywhere and always been, and *cannot but be* the representative of the class-conscious, and not of the non-class-conscious, workers and that there cannot be anything more dangerous and more criminal than the demagogic speculation on the underdevelopment of the workers. If the criterion of activity were that which is immediately, directly, and to the greatest degree accessible to the broadest masses, we should have to preach anti-Semitism or to agitate, let us say, on the basis of an appeal to Father Johann of Kronstadt.[114]

It is the task of Social-Democracy to develop the political consciousness of the masses and not to drag along at the tail-end of the masses that have no political rights; secondly, and this is most important, it is untrue that the masses will not understand the idea of political struggle. Even the most backward worker will understand the idea, provided, of course, the agitator or propagandist is able to approach him in such a way as to communicate the idea to him, to explain it in understandable language on the basis of facts the worker knows from everyday experience. But this condition is just as indispensable for clarifying the economic struggle: in this field, too, the backward worker from the lower or middle strata of the masses will not be able to assimilate the general idea of economic struggle; it is an idea that can be absorbed by a few educated workers whom the masses will follow, guided by their instincts and their direct, immediate interests.

This is likewise true of the political sphere; of course, only the developed worker will comprehend the general idea of the political struggle, and the masses will follow him because they have a very good sense of their lack of political rights (as the Kiev Committee's *Profession de foi* admits in one place), and because their most immediate, everyday interests regularly bring them into contact with every kind of manifestation of political oppression. In no political or social movement, in no country has there ever been, or could there ever have been, any other relation between the mass of the given class or people and its numerically few educated representatives than the following: everywhere and at all times the leaders of a certain class have always been its advanced, most cultivated representatives. Nor can there be any other situation in the Russian working-class movement. The ignoring of the interests and requirements of this advanced section of the workers, and the desire *to descend* to the level of understanding of the lower strata (instead of constantly *raising* the level of the workers' class-consciousness) must, therefore, necessarily have a profoundly harmful effect and prepare the ground for the infiltration of all sorts of non-socialist and non-revolutionary ideas into the workers' midst.

To conclude the analysis of the Kiev Committee's views on the political struggle [I add the following]. The Committee, in a manner that is highly strange and, at the same time, highly typical of the entire *Profession de foi*, not considering it possible at the present time to call on the masses of the workers to take political action, recognises the desirability of organising *partial* demonstrations for purely agitational purposes (and not for the purpose of bringing pressure upon the government) on issues that are comprehensible to the broad masses Socialists calling on the workers *not* to bring pressure to bear on the government!!! That is about the limit. ...Only it is beyond our ken how demonstrations that do *not* bring pressure to bear on the government are possible. Should we perhaps recommend to the workers that they demonstrate within the four walls of their hovels and lock the doors before they begin? Or per-

haps they should demonstrate by making the gesture of the
fig with their hands in their pockets? That would probably
not bring such harmful and ruinous "pressure upon the
government"! And we also despair of understanding what is
meant by a "partial demonstration." Does it, perhaps, mean
of one trade, on issues of that trade alone (again: what has
this to do with socialism?), or, perhaps, on partial political
issues and not against the entire political system, the autocracy in its entirety? But if this is so, are these not purely
and simply the ideas of *Credo* and of the sheerest opportunism, ideas that extremely lower and obscure the political
consciousness and the political tasks of the working class?
If this is so, hadn't we better repeat the "winged phrase" of
a "young" metropolitan Social-Democrat: "It is premature
to discredit the autocracy among the workers"?...

The *Profession de foi* displays an extreme narrowness of
views not only in regard to the question of "politics." "At
the present time," we read, "agitational influence brought to
bear on the masses can only take the form of, firstly, assistance in the economic struggle of the proletariat. The Committee, therefore, takes advantage of every clash between the
workers and the employers, or every important fact of abuse
on the part of the employers, to address a manifesto to the
workers explaining to them their situation and calling on
them to protest; it takes a leading part in strikes, formulates the workers' demands, shows the best way to win the
demands, and by all these means develops class-consciousness in the workers." That is all; nothing more is told
us on the economic struggle. And this is a *profession de
foi*! Read these passages over again carefully: Again we
have here the language of the *Credo* and the ideas of the
Credo (which illustrates once more the abysmal blundering
of the *Rabocheye Dyelo* editors who stubbornly desire to
conceal the views of the "young economists" and to see in
them nothing but the deviations of individuals).

For the socialist, the economic struggle serves as a basis
for the organisation of the workers into a revolutionary
party, for the strengthening and development of their class
struggle against the whole capitalist system. If the economic struggle is taken as something complete in itself there
will be nothing socialist in it; the experience of all European

countries shows us many examples, not only of socialist, but also of anti-socialist trade unions.

It is the task of the bourgeois politician "to assist the economic struggle of the proletariat"; the task of the socialist is to bring the economic struggle to further the socialist movement and the successes of the revolutionary working-class party. The task of the socialist is to further the indissoluble fusion of the economic and the political struggle into the single class struggle of the socialist working-class masses. The diffuse expressions of the Kiev Committee's *Profession de foi*, therefore, open wide the doors to Bernsteinian ideas and legalise an impermissibly narrow attitude to the economic struggle.

Agitational activity among the masses must be of the broadest nature, both economic and political, on all possible issues and in regard to all manifestations of oppression whatever their form. We must utilise this agitation to attract growing numbers of workers into the ranks of the revolutionary Social-Democratic party, to encourage the political struggle in all conceivable manifestations, to organise this struggle and transform it from its spontaneous forms into the struggle of a single political party. Agitation, therefore, must serve as *a means* of widely expanding the political protest and the more organised forms of political struggle. Today our agitation is too hemmed in; the range of questions it touches upon is too limited. It is our duty therefore not to legitimise this narrowness but to try to liberate ourselves from it, to deepen and expand our agitational work.

In the *Profession de foi* now under discussion this narrowness leads, not only to the theoretical errors above analysed, but to the narrowing of the practical tasks. This narrowing can be seen in the desire "to make the investigation of the workers' conditions at local factories and works, through questionnaires and other means, the immediate pressing task." We, of course, can have nothing against questionnaires in general, Since they constitute an essential accessory to agitation, but to occupy ourselves with investigations means to expend unproductively revolutionary forces that are sparse enough as it is.

In fact, much can be gathered from our legal inquiries. We must make it our immediate and urgent task to

extend agitation and propaganda (especially on the political level), all the more so, since the very good habit, now
becoming widespread among our workers, of sending reports
of their own to the socialist newspapers guarantees an
abundance of material.

A still greater narrowing is to be seen in the fact that
on the question of funds only "trade-union strike" funds
are recognised as desirable, while not a word is said to
the effect that these funds must become integrated in
the Social-Democratic Party to be used for the political
struggle.

To limit our secret funds to purely economic activity
is a desire natural to the authors of the *Credo*; but it is
incomprehensible in the *Profession de foi* of a committee
of the Russian Social-Democratic Labour Party.

On the question of legal societies the *Profession de foi*
is no less narrow, displaying the same effort to make concessions to the notorious Bernsteinism. For a committee of
the Social-Democratic Party to assist in the founding
of funds means again to scatter forces and to wipe out the
distinction between purely cultural activity and revolutionary work; a revolutionary party can and must make
use of legal societies for the strengthening and consolidation of *its own* work, as centres of agitation, as a convenient
cover for establishing connections, etc., etc.—but only
for this. To expend socialist forces on rendering assistance to
the founding of societies is in the highest degree irrational;
it is incorrect to accord these societies an independent significance and it is simply ridiculous to believe that legal
societies can be "fully independent of the participation and
pressure of the employers."

Lastly, the narrowness and specific character of the Kiev
Committee's views are reflected in its organisational plans.
It is true we agree fully with the Kiev Committee that this
is not the time to announce the re-establishment of the
Party and to elect a new Central Committee; but we view as
utterly erroneous the opinion concerning the "directly
economic character of the movement," the opinion that
the Russian proletariat "is not prepared for political agitation." It would also be an error to wait until "local groups
grow stronger, increase their membership, and strengthen

their connections with the working-class *milieu*"—such reinforcement often leads to immediate collapse.

On the contrary, we must immediately set about the work of unification and begin it with literary unity, with the establishment of a common Russian newspaper that must make an effort to prepare for the re-establishment of the Party by serving as an organ for the whole of Russia; by gathering correspondence and news items from the circles in all localities; by providing space for the discussion of disputed questions; by extending the scope of our agitation and propaganda; by devoting special attention to organisational questions, to tactical and technical methods of conducting the work; by satisfying all the demands of the most developed workers, and by constantly raising the level of the lower strata of the proletariat (attracted by workers' correspondence, etc.) to an ever greater conscious participation in the socialist movement and in the political struggle.

Only in this way, we are convinced, can real conditions be provided for the unification and re-establishment of the Party, and only a direct and frank polemic against narrow "economism" and the growing spread of Bernsteinian ideas can ensure the correct development of the Russian working-class movement and Russian Social-Democracy.

Written at the end 1899
First published in 1928
in *Lenin Miscellany VII*

Published according to
a manuscript copied
by an unknown hand

FACTORY COURTS

Factory courts is the name given to courts consisting of elected representatives of workers and employers (factory owners in the case of industry) that examine cases and disputes arising in connection with the terms of hire, with the fixing of rates of pay for ordinary work and overtime, with the discharge of workers in violation of rules, with payments for damage to material, with unfair imposition of fines, etc., etc. Courts of this kind exist in the majority of the West-European countries, but not in Russia, and we propose to examine what advantages they bring the workers and why the institution of factory courts is desirable in addition to the ordinary courts, where cases are heard by a sole judge appointed by the government or elected by the propertied classes, with no elected representatives of the employers and the workers.

The first advantage of the factory court is that it is much more accessible to the workers. To present a petition to an ordinary court, one has to submit it in writing (which often requires the employment of a solicitor); stamp duty has to be paid; there are long waiting periods; the plaintiff has to appear in court, which takes him and the witnesses away from their work; then comes a further period of waiting until the case goes to a higher court to be retried after an appeal by dissatisfied litigants. Is it any wonder that workers do not willingly resort to the ordinary courts? Factory courts, on the contrary, consist of employers and workers elected as judges. It is not at all difficult for a worker to make a verbal complaint to one of his fellow workers whom he has himself elected. Sessions of factory courts are usually held on holidays or, in general, at times when the workers are free and do not have to interrupt their work. Cases are handled much more expeditiously by factory courts.

The second advantage that the workers gain from factory courts is that the judges have a far better understanding of factory affairs and, furthermore, are not outside officials but local people who have a knowledge of the workers' living conditions and local industrial conditions; half of them are workers, who will always be just to a worker and will not regard him as a drunkard, an insolent and ignorant fellow (as he is regarded by the majority of official judges, who come from the bourgeois class, the class of property owners, and who almost always retain their connections with bourgeois society, with the factory owners, directors, and engineers, but are separated from the workers as by a Chinese Wall). Official judges are mostly concerned that matters should go smoothly on paper; as long as things look all right on paper, the government official does not worry about anything else—he is merely concerned with receiving his salary and pleasing those in higher authority. This accounts for the disgusting amount of red tape, protracted litigation, and pettifoggery—something has been incorrectly recorded, something did not get properly entered in the court record, and the case is lost, however just it may have been. When the judges are elected from among the employers and from among the workers, they have no need to pile up red tape, because they are not working for a salary and are not dependent on parasitic government officials. They are not concerned with getting a still better post, but with settling disputes that prevent the factory owners from continuing production uninterruptedly and workers from continuing their work in peace and with less fear of chicaneries and unjust vexations on the part of the employers. Furthermore, one has to know factory life well and from personal experience in order to be able to settle disputes between employers and workers. The official judge glances at the worker's pay-book, reads the rules, and refuses to listen to anything else—you have broken the rules, he says, so you bear the responsibility, and the rest does not concern me. But judges elected from among the employers and from among the workers do not merely look at papers but at what happens in real life. It sometimes happens that a rule remains unchanged on paper, while in practice things proceed differently. Very often the official judge, even if he wants to, even if he examines cases with the greatest attention, cannot understand the point at issue, because he does not know the customs, he does not know the methods of fixing rates, he does not know the methods by which a master often cheats the worker without infringing the rules and the rates (as by transferring the worker to another job, by giving him different material, etc.). Elected judges who themselves work or who manage factory affairs have an immediate understanding of such issues, they can easily understand what exactly the worker wants, they are not concerned merely with observing the rules but with ensuring that the worker cannot be cheated by the bypassing of the rules, with ensuring that there can be no pretexts for deception and arbitrariness. There was a recent report in the newspapers that hat-makers had almost been convicted of theft, on a complaint from the employers, for making use of the waste trimmings from hats. Fortunately honest barristers were found who gathered information to prove that this was the custom in the industry and that the workers, far from being thieves, had not violated a single regulation. The ordinary, simple worker who earns very small wages can hardly ever get to a good barrister, and for this reason, as every worker knows, official judges often pass cruel, senselessly cruel, sentences in cases affecting workers. Absolute justice is never to be expected from official judges: we have said above that these judges belong to the bourgeois class and are prejudiced in advance to give credence to whatever the factory owner says and to disbelieve the words of the worker. The judge consults the law: a master and servant contract (one man hires himself out for wages to do something for another or to serve him). As far as he is concerned, it is all the same whether an engineer, a doctor, a factory director, or an unskilled labourer hires himself out to the factory owner; the judge thinks (by the dictates of his bureaucratic soul and his bourgeois stupidity) that the unskilled labourer should know his rights and be able, as well as a director, engineer, or doctor, to make stipulations in his contract for everything needed.

But the judges in a factory court (half of the panel) are elected from among the workers, who know very well that a new worker, or a young worker, often feels in the factory or in the office as though he were in a dark forest and has not even the ghost of an idea that he is concluding a "free contract" and that he can "foresee" terms in that contract that are to his advantage. Let us take the following instance: a worker wants to register a complaint against unjust rejection of work or against fines. It is useless for him even to think of complaining to a judge or to a factory inspector, both of whom are government officials. An official will keep insisting on one thing: the *law* gives the factory owner the right to fine workers and to reject bad work, so that it is for the factory owner to decide whether the work is bad and whether blame rests with the worker. That is why workers so rarely seek recourse to the courts: they put up with abuses, put up with them until finally they strike when their cup of patience runs over. With judges elected from their midst, the workers would find it incomparably easier to secure equity and protection in such cases and in regard to all petty factory disputes and insults. The wealthy official judge does not regard such petty matters as worthy of his attention (like having hot water for tea, or an extra cleaning of a machine, or similar items); but to the worker these things are by no means petty. Only the workers themselves can judge what a huge amount of gross ill-treatment, of insults, and of humiliation can be caused by what at first sight appear trifling, innocuous, inoffensive rules and regulations in the factory.

The third advantage workers stand to gain from factory courts is that in and through them workers learn to know the laws. As a rule the workers (in their mass) do not know and cannot get to know the laws, although government officials and official judges often punish them for not knowing the laws. When an official confronts a worker with the law and the worker pleads ignorance of its very existence, the official (or the judge) either laughs at him or rebukes him with the statement: "Ignorance of the law is no excuse," as basic Russian legislation puts it. Any official and judge, therefore, *assumes* that every worker knows the laws. But this assumption is a bourgeois lie, a lie invented by proper-

tied people and by capitalists against the propertyless, the
same sort of lie as the assumption that a worker concludes
a "free contract" with the master. In actual fact, the worker
who starts in at the factory at a tender age, when he has
learned no more than to read and write (and very, very many
have not even been able to learn to read and write!), has never had time to learn anything about laws, has had nobody
to learn from, and, no doubt, has had no reason to learn—
because if bourgeois officials apply the laws without asking
him, the laws will not be of much benefit to the worker!
The bourgeois classes that accuse the workers of ignorance
of the laws have done absolutely nothing to help them acquire
the knowledge, so that it is not so much the workers themselves who are to blame for their ignorance of the law as
their exploiters (=those who plunder them), who own all
the property, live by the labour of others and want to be
the only ones to take advantage of education and knowledge.
There is no school and there are no books that will give
the workers a knowledge of the laws, because only very few
workers can read books—very, very few among the millions of working people oppressed by capital. For the same
reason there are very few who attend school, and even those
who have had some schooling can, in most cases, only read,
write, and count; this is too little for the understanding of
a branch of knowledge as complicated and difficult as are
the Russian laws. The workers will gain a knowledge of
the laws only when they have to apply them themselves
and hear and see justice done according to those laws.
Workers could learn to know the laws better if, for instance,
they were appointed to juries (with the factory owners
required to pay them their regular wages for the days spent
in court); but bourgeois society is so constructed that only
people from the propertied classes may serve as jurymen
(and also peasants who have been schooled in "social service," i.e., in the lower ranks of the police); the propertyless,
the proletarians, must submit to a court that is not theirs,
while they themselves have no right to judge! When factory courts are set up, the workers elect their own comrades
as judges and the elections take place at regular intervals;
in this way those elected from among the workers acquaint
themselves with the laws by applying them in practice,

that is, they not only read the laws as they are written in a book (for that does not by any means ensure a knowledge of the laws), but see for themselves in practice what particular laws are applicable to what cases and what their effect on the workers is. It is much easier for other workers, apart from the elected judges, to acquaint themselves with the laws through factory courts, because it is easy for a worker to speak to a judge elected from among his mates and obtain from him any necessary information. Workers will visit a factory court more often than a court conducted by civil servants, because it is more accessible; they will listen to cases in which their relatives and friends are participating and in this way acquaint themselves with the laws. For a working man to understand in whose interests the laws are drawn up and in whose interests those who apply them act, it is important that he should become acquainted with the laws in practice and not merely from books. Once the worker is acquainted with the laws he will see quite clearly that the interests are those of the propertied class, the men of property, the capitalists, the bourgeoisie and that the working class will never win a sound and radical improvement in its conditions, so long as it does not win the right to elect its representatives to participate in the formulation of laws and in supervision over their fulfilment.

Furthermore (fourthly), a good aspect of factory courts is that they teach the workers to take an independent part in public, state affairs (because the court is a state institution and the activity of the court is a part of state activity), they teach the workers to elect the most intelligent and honest of their comrades, those who firmly support the workers' cause, to post where their activities can be seen by the whole working class, where workers' representatives can declare the needs and demands of all the workers. It is to the interest of the capitalist class, of the entire bourgeoisie, to keep the workers ignorant and isolated, to remove as quickly as possible those among them who are more intelligent and who make use of their intellect and knowledge, not to become traitors to their class and to fawn on the foremen, masters, and police, but to help other workers acquire greater knowledge and to learn to stand up jointly for the working-class cause. But in order that such advanced representatives,

of whom that cause has great need, should come to be known
by all workers and win their trust, it is important that all
should witness their activities, that all should know whether they are capable of expressing and upholding the real
needs and desires of the workers. If the workers could elect
such people as judges, the best of them would be known to
all, they would gain wider trust, and the proletarian cause
would win by it greatly. If we look at our landowners, industrialists, and merchants, we see that they are not content with the fact that each of them is able to go to a governor or to a minister and present his requests; they also make
sure of having their representatives in the courts (the courts
with representatives from the social-estates) and that these
participate directly in the administration (e.g., Marshals
of the Nobility,[115] school inspectors, etc., are elected by
the nobility; members of factory affairs boards,[116] of stock-
exchange and fair committees are elected by the merchants,
etc.). The working class in Russia is without any rights at
all; workers are regarded as draught animals that have to
toil for others and hold their tongues, that never dare to
state their needs and desires. If the workers were to elect
their comrades to factory courts constantly, they would
have at least some possibility of participating in public
affairs and of stating, not only the opinions of individual workers—of Pyotr, Sidor, or Ivan—but also of
stating the opinions and demands of all the workers. In that
case the workers would not be so mistrustful of the courts
as they are of those conducted by government officials; they
would see their comrades there, those who would intercede
for them.

Further (fifthly), the factory courts are of benefit to the
workers because they would give greater publicity to factory affairs and to all incidents in factory life. We see today
that the factory owners and the government are doing everything in their power to conceal what is happening in the
factory world from the general public; it is forbidden to
publish anything about strikes, the reports of factory inspectors on the condition of the workers are no longer being
printed, an effort is being made to have all abuses passed
in silence and get matters settled as quickly as possible
"in camera," by government officials, and all workers'

meetings are prohibited. It is not surprising that the mass of the workers frequently has very little knowledge of what is going on in other factories or even in other departments of the same factory. Factory courts, to which workers could frequently appeal, which would be held in public, i.e., in the presence of a working-class public, in non-working hours, would benefit the workers by helping to make known all abuses and would thus facilitate their struggle against various factory outrages and accustom them to think, not only of the regime at their own factory, but of the regime at all factories, of the conditions of all workers.*

Finally, there is one other benefit accruing from factory courts that must be mentioned: they get factory owners, directors, and foremen into the habit of treating workers decently, of treating them as equal citizens and not as slaves. Every worker knows that factory owners and foremen all too often permit themselves to treat workers in a disgracefully insulting manner, to rail at them, etc. It is difficult for a worker to complain against this attitude; it can be rebuffed only when the workers are sufficiently developed and are able to give support to their comrade. The factory owners and foremen say that our workers are very ignorant and coarse, for which reason they have to be treated roughly. There are still many survivals, actually, of serfdom among our workers, there is little education and much uncouthness—this cannot be denied. But who is mostly to blame for this? It is precisely the factory owners, foremen, and government officials who are to blame, they, whose attitude to the workers is that of feudal lords towards serfs,

---

* It must, of course, be remembered that factory courts can be only one of the ways and means of publicity, and not even the chief means. The life in factories, the conditions of the workers and their struggle can be brought to public knowledge in a real and comprehensive manner only by a free working-class press and by free meetings of the people to discuss all state affairs. Similarly, workers' representation at factory courts is only one of the means of representation and is far from being the chief means. The real representation of the workers' needs and interests is possible only through a national representative assembly (a parliament) that would promulgate laws and supervise their execution. Below we shall deal with the question as to whether factory courts are possible under the conditions now obtaining in Russia.

they, who do not want to consider the worker as an equal. If workers make a request or ask a question civilly, they are everywhere met with rudeness, with oaths and threats. Is it not obvious that when factory owners blame the workers for their rudeness under these circumstances they are placing the blame on the wrong shoulders? Factory courts would speedily wean our exploiters of their insulting manner: there would be worker judges in the court side by side with the factory owners, and they would discuss cases and vote together. The factory-owner judges would have to regard the worker judges as their equals and not as their hired servants. The contestants and witnesses in court would come from the factory owners and the workers, and the former would get their training in addressing workers civilly. This is very important to the workers, in view of the fact that at present discussions of this sort are extremely rare: the factory owner refuses to recognise delegates elected by the workers, so that the latter have only one way open to them—to strike, a difficult and often a very burdensome way. Further, if there were also workers among the judges, workers would be able to appeal freely to the court against rough treatment. Worker judges would always be on their side, and if a factory owner or a master ware summoned to court for insulting behaviour, he would lose all desire to display his arrogance and insolence.

Factory courts consisting of representatives of masters and workers in equal numbers, therefore, would have great significance for the workers and would bring them many benefits. They would be more accessible to the workers than the ordinary courts, there would be less pettifoggery and red tape, the judges would have a better knowledge of the factory conditions, and would judge more fairly; they would acquaint the workers with the laws, they would teach the workers to elect their representatives and to participate in state affairs, they would give greater publicity to factory life and to the working-class movement, and they would accustom the factory owners to treat the workers decently, to have polite dealings with them as equals with equals. It is no matter for wonder, therefore, that the workers in all European countries demand the establishment of factory courts, that they demand that these courts should be set up, not only for factory workers (which the Germans and the French already have), but also for workers engaged in home-work for capitalists (for handicraftsmen), as well as for agricultural labourers. No officials appointed by the government (*no judges and no factory inspectors*) can *ever* replace institutions in which the *workers themselves participate*: after what has been said above, this requires no further explanation. Every worker, furthermore, knows from his own experience what he has to expect from government officials; if he is told that government officials can be concerned with the workers' welfare equally with people elected from among the workers themselves, he knows it to be a lie and a deception. Deception of this sort is of great advantage to the government that wants the workers to remain the ignorant, rightless, and inarticulate slaves of the capitalists, and for this reason one often hears these lying assertions from government officials or from writers who defend the interests of the factory owners and the government.

The need for factory courts and the benefits they could bring the workers are so obvious that they were long ago recognised *even by Russian government officials*. True, it was so long ago that many have forgotten it! It was at the time when our peasants were liberated from serf dependence (in 1861, over 38 years ago). About that time the Russian Government decided also to replace the laws governing artisans and factory workers with new ones; it was all too obvious then that the old laws for workers could not remain when the peasants had been liberated, since many of the workers had been serfs when the old laws were drawn up. And so the government appointed a commission of several officials to study the factory laws of France and Germany (and of other countries) and to draft a bill to change the Russian laws for artisans and factory workers. The commission included some very important people. Nevertheless, they got down to the task and printed five tomes in which they outlined foreign laws and proposed a new law for Russia. This new law, proposed by the commission, *was to institute factory courts with the judges elected from among the factory owners and the workers in equal numbers*. The draft was printed in 1865, that is, thirty-four years ago. But what, the

worker will ask, happened to this draft law? Why did not
the government, which had itself instructed the officials
to draft a law on the necessary changes, introduce factory
courts in Russia?

Our government dealt with the commission's draft in
the same manner in which it deals with any draft laws that
are in any way of benefit to the people and to the workers.
The officials were rewarded for their labours for the good
of the tsar and the fatherland; they were given decorations
to hang from ribbons round their necks and accorded higher
ranks and more lucrative posts. And the draft law they had
prepared was quietly "pigeon-holed," as they say in offices.
And so this draft law is still stacked away in its pigeon-hole.
The government has even stopped thinking of according
the workers the right to elect comrades from their midst
to factory courts.

It cannot, however, be said that the government has not
once thought about the workers since that time. True, it
has not thought of them of its own free will, but only when
forced to do so by menacing workers' unrest and strikes;
nevertheless, it has thought of them. It has published
laws prohibiting child labour in factories, prohibiting
night-work for women in certain industries, reducing the
working day, and appointing factory inspectors. Despite
all the pettifoggery employed in drafting them, despite the
numerous loopholes left open for the factory owners to vio-
late and get round them, these laws have still been of some
benefit. Why, then, does the government prefer introducing
new laws and new officials—factory inspectors—instead of
introducing factory courts, provided for by a law that has
been fully elaborated? The reason for this is very obvious
and the workers must fully understand it, for this example
will make clear the entire policy of the Russian Government with respect to the working class.

The government has appointed new officials instead of
factory courts, because factory courts would raise the
level of the workers' class-consciousness; make them more
conscious of their rights, of their human and civic dignity;
teach them to think independently about state affairs and
about the interests of the entire working class; teach them
to elect their more developed comrades to represent them,

and in this way undermine, if only in part, the undivided
authority assumed by government officials. This is what
the government fears more than anything else. It is even
prepared to dispense a few hand-outs to the workers (only
mites, of course, and only with one hand that does the giving ceremonially in full view of the public, so that it may
pose as a benefactor, while taking them away slyly and gradually with the other hand! The workers now know this
trick, having had a sample of it in the factory law of June 2,
1897!)—it is prepared to dole out crumbs as long as the autocratic power of the bureaucracy is left untouched and there
is no awakening of the workers' class-consciousness, no development of their independence. The government can easily
avoid this terrible danger by appointing new officials, since
officials are the humble servants of the government. It is
no trouble to forbid officials (factory inspectors, for instance)
to publish their reports, it is no trouble to forbid them
to talk to the workers regarding their rights and regarding
the abuses of the masters, it is no trouble to turn them into
factory police sergeants and to order them to report to the
police all dissatisfaction and unrest on the part of the
workers.

Therefore, so long as the present political system remains
in Russia—i.e., denial of rights to the people, lawless
actions on the part of government officials and the police, who are not answerable to the people—the workers
cannot expect the introduction of factory courts which can
be of benefit to them. The government understands full
well that factory courts would very speedily cause the workers to go over to more radical demands. Having elected
their representatives to the factory courts, the workers would
soon realise the insufficiency of this step, because the factory
owners and landlords who exploit them send their representatives to very many state institutions at a much higher
level; the workers would certainly demand a general all-
people's representation. Having once secured court publicity for factory affairs and the workers' needs, they would soon
see that this is not enough, because in our day real publicity can be obtained only through newspapers and popular
meetings, so that the workers would demand freedom of
assembly, freedom of speech, and freedom of the press.

This is why the government has buried the draft law to introduce factory courts in Russia!

On the other hand, let us assume for a moment that the government were deliberately, with deception of the workers in mind, to introduce factory courts today and to retain the present political system intact. Would this be of any benefit to the workers? It would bring them no benefits at all: the workers would not even elect to these courts the most class-conscious and most loyal of their comrades, those who are most devoted to the cause of the working class, knowing that in Russia for every straightforward and honest word a man may be seized simply by order of the police and thrown into prison or transported to Siberia without trial!

It follows, therefore, that the demand for factory courts with judges elected from among the workers is only one small part of a wider and more radical demand: the demand for political rights for the people, i.e., the right to participate in the administration of the state and the right to make known the needs of the people openly, not only in the press, but also at popular meetings.

Written at the end of 1899

First published in 1924
in the magazine *Proletarskaya
Revolyutsiya*, No. 8-9

Published according to
a manuscript copied
by an unknown hand

ON STRIKES[117]

In recent years, workers' strikes have become extremely frequent in Russia. There is no longer a single industrial gubernia in which there have not occurred several strikes. And in the big cities strikes never cease. It is understandable, therefore, that class-conscious workers and socialists should more and more frequently concern themselves with the question of the significance of strikes, of methods of conducting them, and of the tasks of socialists participating in them.

We wish to attempt to outline some of our ideas on these questions. In our first article we plan to deal generally with the significance of strikes in the working-class movement; in the second we shall deal with anti-strike laws in Russia; and in the third, with the way strikes were and are conducted in Russia and with the attitude that class-conscious workers should adopt to them.

I

In the first place we must seek an explanation for the outbreak and spread of strikes. Everyone who calls to mind strikes from personal experience, from reports of others, or from the newspapers will see immediately that strikes break out and spread wherever big factories arise and grow in number. It would scarcely be possible to find a single one among the bigger factories employing hundreds (at times even thousands) of workers in which strikes have not occurred. When there were only a few big factories in Russia there were few strikes; but ever since big factories have been

multiplying rapidly in both the old industrial districts and in
new towns and villages, strikes have become more frequent.

Why is it that large-scale factory production always leads
to strikes? It is because capitalism must necessarily lead to
a struggle of the workers against the employers, and when
production is on a large scale the struggle of necessity takes
on the form of strikes.

Let us explain this.

Capitalism is the name given to that social system under
which the land, factories, implements, etc., belong to a
small number of landed proprietors and capitalists, while
the mass of the people possesses no property, or very little
property, and is compelled to hire itself out as workers. The
landowners and factory owners hire workers and make them
produce wares of this or that kind which they sell on the
market. The factory owners, furthermore, pay the workers
only such a wage as provides a bare subsistence for them
and their families, while everything the worker produces
over and above this amount goes into the factory owner's
pocket, as his profit. Under capitalist economy, therefore,
the people in their mass are the hired workers of others,
they do not work for themselves but work for employers for
wages. It is understandable that the employers always try
to reduce wages; the less they give the workers, the greater
their profit. The workers try to get the highest possible wage
in order to provide their families with sufficient and whole-
some food, to live in good homes, and to dress as other people do and not like beggars. A constant struggle is, therefore, going on between employers and workers over wages;
the employer is free to hire whatever worker he thinks fit
and, therefore, seeks the cheapest. The worker is free to
hire himself out to an employer of his choice, so that he seeks
the dearest, the one that will pay him the most. Whether
the worker works in the country or in town, whether he
hires himself out to a landlord, a rich peasant, a contractor,
or a factory owner, he always bargains with the employer,
fights with him over the wages.

But is it possible for a single worker to wage a struggle
by himself? The number of working people is increasing:
peasants are being ruined and flee from the countryside to
the town or the factory. The landlords and factory owners

are introducing machines that rob the workers of their jobs.
In the cities there are increasing numbers of unemployed
and in the villages there are more and more beggars; those
who are hungry drive wages down lower and lower. It becomes impossible for the worker to fight against the employer
by himself. If the worker demands good wages or tries not to
consent to a wage cut, the employer tells him to get out,
that there are plenty of hungry people at the gates who would
be glad to work for low wages.

When the people are ruined to such an extent that there
is always a large number of unemployed in the towns and
villages, when the factory owners amass huge fortunes and
the small proprietors are squeezed out by the millionaires,
the individual worker becomes *absolutely powerless* in face
of the capitalist. It then becomes possible for the capitalist
to crush the worker completely, to drive him to his death at
slave labour and, indeed, not him alone, but his wife and
children with him. If we take, for instance, those occupations
in which the workers have not yet been able to win the protection of the law and in which they cannot offer resistance
to the capitalists, we see an inordinately long working day,
sometimes as long as 17-19 hours; we see children of 5 or 6
years of age overstraining themselves at work; we see a generation of permanently hungry workers who are gradually
dying from starvation. Example: the workers who toil in
their own homes for capitalists; besides, any worker can bring
to mind a host of other examples! Even under slavery or
serfdom there was never any oppression of the working
people as terrible as that under capitalism when the workers
cannot put up a resistance or cannot win the protection of
laws that restrict the arbitrary actions of the employers.

And so, in order to stave off their reduction to such ex-
tremities, the workers begin a desperate struggle. As they
see that each of them, individually, is completely powerless
and that the oppression of capital threatens to crush him,
the workers begin to revolt jointly against their employers.
Workers' strikes begin. At first the workers often fail to
realise what they are trying to achieve, lacking consciousness of the *wherefore* of their action; they simply smash the
machines and destroy the factories. They merely want to
display their wrath to the factory owners; they are trying

out their joint strength in order to get out of an unbearable situation, without yet understanding why their position is so hopeless and what they should strive for.

In all countries the wrath of the workers first took the form of isolated revolts—the police and factory owners in Russia call them "mutinies." In all countries these isolated revolts gave rise to more or less peaceful strikes, on the one hand, and to the all-sided struggle of the working class for its emancipation, on the other.

What significance have strikes (or stoppages) for the struggle of the working class? To answer this question, we must first have a fuller view of strikes. The wages of a worker are determined, as we have seen, by an agreement between the employer and the worker, and if, under these circumstances, the individual worker is completely powerless, it is obvious that workers must fight jointly for their demands, they are compelled to organise strikes either to prevent the employers from reducing wages or to obtain higher wages. It is a fact that in every country with a capitalist system there are strikes of workers. Everywhere, in all the European countries and in America, the workers feel themselves powerless when they are disunited; they can only offer resistance to the employers jointly, either by striking or threatening to strike. As capitalism develops, as big factories are more rapidly opened, as the petty capitalists are more and more ousted by the big capitalists, the more urgent becomes the need for the joint resistance of the workers, because unemployment increases, competition sharpens between the capitalists who strive to produce their wares at the cheapest (to do which they have to pay the workers as little as possible), and the fluctuations of industry become more accentuated and crises* more acute. When industry prospers, the factory owners make big profits but do not think of sharing them with the

---

* We shall deal elsewhere in greater detail with crises in industry and their significance to the workers. Here we shall merely note that during recent years in Russia industrial affairs have been going well, industry has been "prospering," but that now (at the end of 1899) there are already clear signs that this "prosperity" will end in a crisis: difficulties in marketing goods, bankruptcies of factory owners, the ruin of petty proprietors, and terrible calamities for the workers (unemployment, reduced wages, etc.).

workers; but when a crisis breaks out, the factory owners
try to push the losses on to the workers. The necessity for
strikes in capitalist society has been recognised to such an
extent by everybody in the European countries that the law
in those countries does not forbid the organisation of
strikes; only in Russia barbarous laws against strikes
still remain in force (we shall speak on another occasion of
these laws and their application).

However, strikes, which arise out of the very nature
of capitalist society, signify the beginning of the working-
class struggle against that system of society. When the
rich capitalists are confronted by individual, propertyless
workers, this signifies the utter enslavement of the workers.
But when those propertyless workers unite, the situation
changes. There is no wealth that can be of benefit to the capitalists if they cannot find workers willing to apply their labour-power to the instruments and materials belonging to
the capitalists and produce new wealth. As long as workers
have to deal with capitalists on an individual basis they
remain veritable slaves who must work continuously to
profit another in order to obtain a crust of bread, who must
for ever remain docile and inarticulate hired servants. But
when the workers state their demands jointly and refuse to
submit to the money-bags, they cease to be slaves, they become human beings, they begin to demand that their labour
should not only serve to enrich a handful of idlers, but should
also enable those who work to live like human beings. The
slaves begin to put forward the demand to become masters,
not to work and live as the landlords and capitalists want them
to, but as the working people themselves want to. Strikes,
therefore, always instil fear into the capitalists, because
they begin to undermine their supremacy. "All wheels stand
still, if your mighty arm wills it," a German workers' song
says of the working class. And so it is in reality: the factories, the landlords' land, the machines, the railways, etc.,
etc., are all like wheels in a giant machine—the machine
that extracts various products, processes them, and delivers
them to their destination. The whole of this machine is set
in motion by *the worker* who tills the soil, extracts ores,
makes commodities in the factories, builds houses, workshops, and railways. When the workers refuse to work, the

entire machine threatens to stop. Every strike reminds the capitalists that it is the workers and not they who are the real masters—the workers who are more and more loudly proclaiming their rights. Every strike reminds the workers that their position is not hopeless, that they are not alone. See what a tremendous effect strikes have both on the strikers themselves and on the workers at neighbouring or nearby factories or at factories in the same industry. In normal, peaceful times the worker does his job without a murmur, does not contradict the employer, and does not discuss his condition. In times of strikes he states his demands in a loud voice, he reminds the employers of all their abuses, he claims his rights, he does not think of himself and his wages alone, he thinks of all his workmates who have downed tools together with him and who stand up for the workers' cause, fearing no privations. Every strike means many privations for the working people, terrible privations that can be compared only to the calamities of war—hungry families, loss of wages, often arrests, banishment from the towns where they have their homes and their employment. Despite all these sufferings, the workers despise those who desert their fellow workers and make deals with the employers. Despite all these sufferings, brought on by strikes, the workers of neighbouring factories gain renewed courage when they see that their comrades have engaged themselves in struggle. "People who endure so much to bend one single bourgeois will be able to break the power of the whole bourgeoisie,"[118] said one great teacher of socialism, Engels, speaking of the strikes of the English workers. It is often enough for one factory to strike, for strikes to begin immediately in a large number of factories. What a great moral influence strikes have, how they affect workers who see that their comrades have ceased to be slaves and, if only for the time being, have become people on an equal footing with the rich! Every strike brings thoughts of socialism very forcibly to the worker's mind, thoughts of the struggle of the entire working class for emancipation from the oppression of capital. It has often happened that before a big strike the workers of a certain factory or a certain branch of industry or of a certain town knew hardly anything and scarcely ever thought about socialism, but after the strike, study circles and associations become much more widespread among them and more and more workers become socialists.

A strike teaches workers to understand what the strength of the employers and what the strength of the workers consists in; it teaches them not to think of their own employer alone and not of their own immediate workmates alone but of all the employers, the whole class of capitalists and the whole class of workers. When a factory owner who has amassed millions from the toil of several generations of workers refuses to grant a modest increase in wages or even tries to reduce wages to a still lower level and, if the workers offer resistance, throws thousands of hungry families out into the street, it becomes quite clear to the workers that the capitalist class as a whole is the enemy of the whole working class and that the workers can depend only on themselves and their united action. It often happens that a factory owner does his best to deceive the workers, to pose as a benefactor, and conceal his exploitation of the workers by some petty sops or lying promises. A strike always demolishes this deception at one blow by showing the workers that their "benefactor" is a wolf in sheep's clothing.

A strike, moreover, opens the eyes of the workers to the nature, not only of the capitalists, but of the government and the laws as well. Just as the factory owners try to pose as benefactors of the workers, the government officials and their lackeys try to assure the workers that the tsar and the tsarist government are equally solicitous of both the factory owners and the workers, as justice requires. The worker does not know the laws, he has no contact with government officials, especially with those in the higher posts, and, as a consequence, often believes all this. Then comes a strike. The public prosecutor, the factory inspector, the police, and frequently troops, appear at the factory. The workers learn that they have violated the law: the employers are permitted by law to assemble and openly discuss ways of reducing workers' wages, but workers are declared criminals if they come to a joint agreement! Workers are driven out of their homes; the police close the shops from which the workers might obtain food on credit, an effort is made to incite the soldiers against the workers even when the workers conduct themselves quietly and peacefully. Soldiers are even ordered to fire on the workers and when they kill unarmed workers by shooting the fleeing crowd in the back, the tsar himself sends the troops an expression of his gratitude (in this way the tsar thanked the troops who had killed striking workers in Yaroslavl in 1895). It becomes clear to every worker that the tsarist government is his worst enemy, since it defends the capitalists and binds the workers hand and foot. The workers begin to understand that laws are made in the interests of the rich alone; that government officials protect those interests; that the working people are gagged and not allowed to make known their needs; that the working class must win for itself the right to strike, the right to publish workers' newspapers, the right to participate in a national assembly that enacts laws and supervises their fulfilment. The government itself knows full well that strikes open the eyes of the workers and for this reason it has such a fear of strikes and does everything to stop them as quickly as possible. One German Minister of the Interior, one who was notorious for the persistent persecution of socialists and class-conscious workers, not without reason, stated before the people's representatives: "Behind every strike lurks the hydra [monster] of revolution."[119] Every strike strengthens and develops in the workers the understanding that the government is their enemy and that the working class must prepare itself to struggle against the government for the people's rights.

Strikes, therefore, teach the workers to unite; they show them that they can struggle against the capitalists only when they are united; strikes teach the workers to think of the struggle of the whole working class against the whole class of factory owners and against the arbitrary, police government. This is the reason that socialists call strikes "a school of war," a school in which the workers learn to make war on their enemies for the liberation of the whole people, of all who labour, from the yoke of government officials and from the yoke of capital.

"A school of war" is, however, not war itself. When strikes are widespread among the workers, some of the workers (including some socialists) begin to believe that the working class can confine itself to strikes, strike funds, or strike associations alone; that by strikes alone the working class can achieve a considerable improvement in its conditions or even its emancipation. When they see what power there is in a united working class and even in small strikes, some think that the working class has only to organise a general strike throughout the whole country for the workers to get everything they want from the capitalists and the government. This idea was also expressed by the workers of other countries when the working-class movement was in its early stages and the workers were still very inexperienced. *It is a mistaken idea.* Strikes are *one* of the ways in which the working class struggles for its emancipation, but they are not the only way; and if the workers do not turn their attention to other means of conducting the struggle, they will slow down the growth and the successes of the working class. It is true that funds are needed to maintain the workers during strikes, if strikes are to be successful. Such workers' funds (usually funds of workers in separate branches of industry, separate trades or workshops) are maintained in all countries; but here in Russia this is especially difficult, because the police keep track of them, seize the money, and arrest the workers. The workers, of course, are able to hide from the police; naturally, the organisation of such funds is valuable, and we do not want to advise workers against setting them up. But it must not be supposed that workers' funds, when prohibited by law, will attract large numbers of contributors, and so long as the membership in such organisations is small, workers' funds will not prove of great use. Furthermore, even in those countries where workers' unions exist openly and have huge funds at their disposal, the working class can still not confine itself to strikes as a means of struggle. All that is necessary is a hitch in the affairs of industry (a crisis; such as the one that is approaching in Russia today) and the factory owners will even deliberately cause strikes, because it is to their advantage to cease work for a time and to deplete the workers' funds. The workers, therefore, cannot, under any circumstances, confine themselves to strike actions and strike associations. Secondly, strikes can only be successful where workers are sufficiently class-conscious, where they are able to select an opportune moment for striking, where they know how to put forward their demands, and where they have connections with socialists and are able to procure leaflets and pamphlets through them. There are still very few such workers in Russia, and every effort must be exerted to increase their number in order to make the working-class cause known to the masses of workers and to acquaint them with socialism and the working-class struggle. This is a task that the socialists and class-conscious workers must undertake jointly by organising a socialist working-class party for this purpose. Thirdly, strikes, as we have seen, show the workers that the government is their enemy and that a struggle against the government must be carried on. Actually, it is strikes that have gradually taught the working class of all countries to struggle against the governments for workers' rights and for the rights of the people as a whole. As we have said, only a socialist workers' party can carry on this struggle by spreading among the workers a true conception of the government and of the working-class cause. On another occasion we shall discuss specifically how strikes are conducted in Russia and how class-conscious workers should avail themselves of them. Here we must point out that strikes are, as we said above, "a school of war" and not the war itself, that strikes are only one means of struggle, only one aspect of the working-class movement. From individual strikes the workers can and must go over, as indeed they are actually doing in all countries, to a struggle of the entire working class for the emancipation of all who labour. When all class-conscious workers become socialists, i.e., when they strive for this emancipation, when they unite throughout the whole country in order to spread socialism among the workers, in order to teach the workers all the means of struggle against their enemies, when they build up a socialist workers' party that struggles for the emancipation of the people as a whole from government oppression and for the emancipation of all working people from the yoke of capital—only then will the working class become an integral part of that great movement of the workers of all countries that unites all workers and raises the red banner inscribed with the words: "Workers of all countries, unite!"

Written at the end of 1899
First published in 1924
in the magazine *Proletarskaya
Revolyutsiya*, No. 8-9

Published according to
a manuscript copied
by an unknown hand

DRAFT OF A DECLARATION OF THE EDITORIAL BOARD OF *ISKRA*[120] AND *ZARYA*[121]

In undertaking the publication of two Social-Democratic organs—a scientific and political magazine and an all-Russian working-class newspaper—we consider it necessary to say a few words concerning our programme, the objects for which we are striving, and the understanding we have of our tasks.

We are passing through an extremely important period in the history of the Russian working-class movement and Russian Social-Democracy. All evidence goes to show that our movement has reached a critical stage. It has spread so widely and has brought forth so many strong shoots in the most diverse parts of Russia that it is now striving with unrestrained vigour to consolidate itself, assume a higher form, and develop a definite shape and organisation. Indeed, the past few years have been marked by an astonishingly rapid spread of Social-Democratic ideas among our intelligentsia; and meeting this trend in social ideas is the spontaneous, completely independent movement of the industrial proletariat, which is beginning to unite and struggle against its oppressors and is manifesting an eager striving for socialism. Study circles of workers and Social-Democratic intellectuals are springing up everywhere, local agitation leaflets are beginning to appear, the demand for Social-Democratic literature is increasing and is far outstripping the supply, and intensified government persecution is powerless to restrain the movement.

The prisons and places of exile are filled to overflowing. Hardly a month goes by without our hearing of socialists "caught in dragnets" in all parts of Russia, of the capture of underground couriers, of the arrest of agitators, and the confiscation of literature and printing-presses; but the movement goes on and is growing, it is spreading to ever wider regions, it is penetrating more and more deeply into the working class and is attracting public attention to an ever-increasing degree. The entire economic development of Russia and the history of social thought and of the revolutionary movement in Russia serve as a guarantee that the Social-Democratic working-class movement will grow and surmount all the obstacles that confront it.

The principal feature of our movement, which has become particularly marked in recent times, is its state of disunity and its amateur character, if one may so express it. Local study circles spring up and function in almost complete isolation from circles in other districts and—what is particularly important—from circles that have functioned and now function simultaneously in the same districts. Traditions are not established and continuity is not maintained; local publications fully reflect this disunity and the lack of contact with what Russian Social-Democracy has already achieved. The present period, therefore, seems to us to be critical precisely for the reason that the movement is outgrowing this amateur stage and this disunity, is insistently demanding a transition to a higher, more united, better and more organised form, which we consider it our duty to promote. It goes without saying that at a certain stage of the movement, at its inception, this disunity is entirely inevitable; the absence of continuity is natural in view of the astonishingly rapid and universal growth of the movement after a long period of revolutionary calm. Undoubtedly, too, there will always be diversity in local conditions; there will always be differences in the conditions of the working class in one district as compared with those in another; and, lastly, there will always be the particular aspect in the points of view among the active local workers; this very diversity is evidence of the virility of the movement and of its sound growth. All this is true; yet disunity and lack of organisation are not a necessary consequence of this diversity. The maintenance of continuity and the unity of the movement do not by any means exclude diversity, but,

on the contrary, create for it a much broader arena and a
freer field of action. In the present period of the movement,
however, disunity is beginning to show a definitely harmful
effects and is threatening to divert the movement to a false
path: narrow practicalism, detached from the theoretical clarification of the movement as a whole, may destroy the contact between socialism and the revolutionary movement
in Russia, on the one hand, and the spontaneous working-
class movement, on the other. That this danger is not merely
imaginary is proved by such literary productions as the
Credo—which has already called forth legitimate protest and
condemnation—and the *Separate Supplement to "Rabochaya
Mysl"* (September 1899). That supplement has brought out
most markedly the trend that permeates the whole of *Rabochaya Mysl*; in it a particular trend in Russian Social-
Democracy has begun to manifest itself, a trend that may
cause real harm and that must be combated. And the Russian
legal publications, with their parody of Marxism capable
only of corrupting public consciousness, still further intensify the confusion and anarchy which have enabled the celebrated Bernstein (celebrated for his bankruptcy) to publish
before the whole world the untruth that the majority of
the Social-Democrats active in Russia support him.

It is still premature to judge how deep the cleavage is,
and how far the formation of a special trend is probable
(at the moment we are not in the least inclined to answer
these questions in the affirmative and we have not yet lost
hope of our being able to work *together*), but it would be
more harmful to close our eyes to the gravity of the situation than to exaggerate the cleavage, and we heartily welcome the resumption of literary activity on the part of the
Emancipation of Labour group, and the struggle it has begun
against the attempts to distort and vulgarise Social-Democracy.[122]

The following practical conclusion is to be drawn from
the foregoing: we Russian Social-Democrats must unite and
direct all our efforts towards the formation of a single,
strong party, which must struggle under the banner of
a revolutionary Social-Democratic programme, which must
maintain the continuity of the movement and systematically support its organisation. This conclusion is not

a new one. The Russian Social-Democrats reached it two years ago when the representatives of the largest Social-Democratic organisations in Russia gathered at a congress in the spring of 1898, formed the Russian Social-Democratic Labour Party, published the *Manifesto* of the Party, and recognised *Rabochaya Gazeta* as the official Party organ. Regarding ourselves as members of the Russian Social-Democratic Labour Party, we agree entirely with the fundamental ideas contained in the *Manifesto* and attach extreme importance to it as the open and public declaration of the aims towards which our Party should strive. Consequently, we, as members of the Party, present the question of our immediate and direct tasks as follows: What plan of activity must we adopt to revive the Party on the firmest possible basis? Some comrades (even some groups and organisations) are of the opinion that in order to achieve this we must resume the practice of electing the central Party body and instruct it to resume the publication of the Party organ.[123] We consider such a plan to be a false one or, at all events, a hazardous one. To establish and consolidate the Party means to establish and consolidate unity among all Russian Social-Democrats; such unity cannot be decreed, it cannot be brought about by a decision, say, of a meeting of representatives; it must be worked for. In the first place, it is necessary to develop a common Party literature—common, not only in the sense that it must serve the whole of the Russian movement rather than separate districts, that it must discuss the questions of the movement as a whole and assist the class-conscious proletarians in their struggle instead of dealing merely with local questions, but common also in the sense that it must unite all the available literary forces, that it must express all shades of opinion and views prevailing among Russian Social-Democrats, not as isolated workers, but as comrades united in the ranks of a single organisation by a common programme and a common struggle. Secondly, we must work to achieve an organisation especially for the purpose of establishing and maintaining contact among all the centres of the movement, of supplying complete and timely information about the movement, and of delivering our newspapers and periodicals regularly to all parts of Russia. Only when such an organisation has been founded,

only when a Russian socialist post has been established, will
the Party possess a sound foundation, only then will it become a real fact and, therefore, a mighty political force. We
intend to devote our efforts to the first half of this task, i.e.,
to creating a common literature, since we regard this as
the pressing demand of the movement today, and a necessary preliminary measure towards the resumption of Party
activity.

The character of our task naturally determines the programme for conducting our publications. They must devote
considerable space to theoretical questions, i.e., to the
general theory of Social-Democracy and its application
to Russian conditions. The urgent need to promote a wide
discussion of these questions at the present time in particular is beyond all doubt and requires no further explanation after what has been said above. It goes without
saying that questions of general theory are inseparably
connected with the need to supply information about
the history and the present state of the working-class
movement in the West. Furthermore, we propose systematically to discuss all political questions—the Social-Democratic Labour Party must respond to all questions that
arise in all spheres of our daily life, to all questions of home
and foreign politics, and we must see to it that every Social-
Democrat and every class-conscious worker has definite
views on all important questions. Unless this condition is
fulfilled, it will be impossible to carry on wide and systematic
propaganda and agitation. The discussion of questions
of theory and policy will be connected with the drafting of
a Party programme, the necessity for which was recognised
at the congress in 1898. In the near future we intend to
publish a draft programme; a comprehensive discussion of
it should provide sufficient material for the forthcoming
congress that will have to adopt a programme.[124] A further
vital task, in our opinion, is the discussion of questions
of organisation and practical methods of conducting our
work. The lack of continuity and the disunity, to which
reference has been made above, have a particularly harmful
effect upon the present state of Party discipline, organisation, and the technique of secrecy. It must be publicly and frankly owned that in this respect we Social-Demo-

crats lag behind the old workers in the Russian revolutionary movement and behind other organisations functioning in Russia, and we must exert all our efforts to come abreast of the tasks. The attraction of large numbers of working-class and intellectual young people to the movement, the increasing failures and the cunningness of governmental persecution make the propaganda of the principles and methods of Party organisation, discipline, and the technique of secrecy an urgent necessity.

Such propaganda, if supported by all the various groups and by all the more experienced comrades, can and must result in the training of young socialists and workers as able leaders of the revolutionary movement, capable of overcoming all obstacles placed in the way of our work by the tyranny of the autocratic police state and capable of serving all the requirements of the working masses, who are spontaneously striving towards socialism and political struggle. Finally, one of the principal tasks arising out of the above-mentioned issues must be the analysis of this spontaneous movement (among the working masses, as well as among our intelligentsia). We must try to understand the social movement of the intelligentsia which marked the late nineties in Russia and combined various, and sometimes conflicting, tendencies. We must carefully study the conditions of the working class in all spheres of economic life, study the forms and conditions of the workers' awakening, and of the struggles now setting in, in order that we may unite the Russian working-class movement and Marxist socialism, which has already begun to take root in Russian soil, into one integral whole, in order that we may combine the Russian revolutionary movement with the spontaneous upsurge of the masses of the people. Only when this contact has been established can a Social-Democratic working-class party be formed in Russia; for Social-Democracy does not exist merely to serve the spontaneous working-class movement (as some of our present-day "practical-workers" are sometimes inclined to think), but to combine socialism with the working-class movement. And it is only this combination that will enable the Russian proletariat to fulfil its immediate political task—to liberate Russia from the tyranny of the autocracy.

The distribution of these themes and questions between the magazine and the newspaper will be determined exclusively by differences in the size and character of the two publications—the magazine should serve mainly for propaganda, the newspaper mainly for agitation. But all aspects of the movement should be reflected in both the magazine and the newspaper, and we wish particularly to emphasise our opposition to the view that a workers' newspaper should devote its pages exclusively to matters that immediately and directly concern the spontaneous working-class movement, and leave everything pertaining to the theory of socialism, science, politics, questions of Party organisation, etc., to a periodical for the intelligentsia. On the contrary, it is necessary to combine all the concrete facts and manifestations of the working-class movement with the indicated questions; the light of theory must be cast upon every separate fact; propaganda on questions of politics and Party organisation must be carried on among the broad masses of the working class; and these questions must be dealt with in the work of agitation. The type of agitation which has hitherto prevailed almost without exception—agitation by means of locally published leaflets—is now inadequate; it is narrow, it deals only with local and mainly economic questions. We must try to create a higher form of agitation by means of the newspaper, which must contain a regular record of workers' grievances, workers' strikes, and other forms of proletarian struggle, as well as all manifestations of political tyranny in the whole of Russia; which must draw definite conclusions from each of these manifestations in accordance with the ultimate aim of socialism and the political tasks of the Russian proletariat. "Extend the bounds and broaden the content of our propagandist, agitational, and organisational activity"—this statement by P. B. Axelrod must serve as a slogan defining the activities of Russian Social-Democrats in the immediate future, and we adopt this slogan in the programme of our publications.

Here the question naturally arises: if the proposed publications are to serve the purpose of uniting all Russian Social-Democrats and mustering them into a single party, they must reflect all shades of opinion, all local specific features, and all the various practical methods. How can

we combine the varying points of view with the maintenance
of a uniform editorial policy for these publications? Should
these publications be merely a jumble of various views,
or should they have an independent and quite definite
tendency?

We hold to the second view and hope that an organ having
a definite tendency will prove quite suitable (as we shall show
below), both for the purpose of expressing various viewpoints,
and for comradely polemics between contributors. Our views
are in complete accord with the fundamental ideas of Marxism (as expressed in the *Communist Manifesto*, and in the
programmes of Social-Democrats in Western Europe); we
stand for the consistent development of these ideas in the
spirit of Marx and Engels and emphatically reject the equiv-
ocating and opportunist corrections *à la* Bernstein which
have now become so fashionable. As we see it, the task of
Social-Democracy is to organise the class struggle of the
proletariat, to promote that struggle, to point out its essential ultimate aim, and to analyse the conditions that determine the methods by which this struggle should be conducted. "The emancipation of the working classes must be
conquered by the working classes themselves.[125] But while
we do not separate Social-Democracy from the working-class
movement, we must not forget that the task of the former is
to represent the interests of this movement in all countries
as a whole, that it must not blindly worship any particular
phase of the movement at any particular time or place. We
think that it is the duty of Social-Democracy to support
every revolutionary movement against the existing political and social system, and we regard its aim to be the conquest of political power by the working class, the expropriation of the expropriators, and the establishment of a
socialist society. We strongly repudiate every attempt to
weaken or tone down the revolutionary character of Social-
Democracy, which is the party of social revolution, ruthlessly hostile to all classes standing for the present social
system. We believe the historical task of Russian Social-
Democracy is, in particular, to overthrow the autocracy:
Russian Social-Democracy is destined to become the vanguard fighter in the ranks of Russian democracy; it is destined to achieve the aim which the whole social development

of Russia sets before it and which it has inherited from the
glorious fighters in the Russian revolutionary movement.
Only by inseparably connecting the economic and political
struggles, only by spreading political propaganda and agitation among wider and wider strata of the working class,
can Social-Democracy fulfil its mission.

From this point of view (outlined here only in its general
features, since it has been dealt with in greater detail and
more thoroughly substantiated on many occasions by the
Emancipation of Labour group, in the *Manifesto* of the
Russian Social-Democratic Labour Party and in the "commentary" to the latter—the pamphlet, *The Tasks of the Russian Social-Democrats**—and in *The Working-Class Cause in
Russia* [a basis of the programme of Russian Social-
Democracy]), we shall deal with all theoretical and practical questions; and we shall try to connect all manifestations of the working-class movement and of democratic
protest in Russia with these ideas.

Although we carry out our literary work from the standpoint of a definite tendency, we do not in the least intend to
present all our views on partial questions as those of all
Russian Social-Democrats; we do not deny that differences
exist, nor shall we attempt to conceal or obliterate them. On
the contrary, we desire our publications to become organs for
the *discussion* of all questions by all Russian Social-Democrats of the most diverse shades of opinion. We do not
reject polemics between comrades, but, on the contrary, are
prepared to give them considerable space in our columns.
Open polemics, conducted in full view of all Russian Social-
Democrats and class-conscious workers, are necessary and
desirable in order to clarify the depth of existing differences, in order to afford discussion of disputed questions
from all angles, in order to combat the extremes into which
representatives of various views, various localities, or various "specialities" of the revolutionary movement inevitably
fall. Indeed, we regard one of the drawbacks of the present-
day movement to be the absence of open polemics between
avowedly differing views, the effort to conceal differences
on fundamental questions.

---

* See present edition, Vol. 2, p. 323.—*Ed*.

Moreover, while recognising the Russian working class and Russian Social-Democracy as the vanguard in the struggle for democracy and for political liberty, we think it necessary to strive to make our publications *general-democratic* organs, not in the sense that we would for a single moment agree to forget the class antagonism between the proletariat and other classes, nor in the sense that we would consent to the slightest toning-down of the class struggle, but in the sense that we would bring forward and discuss *all* democratic questions, not confining ourselves merely to narrowly proletarian questions; in the sense that we would bring forward and discuss all instances and manifestations of political oppression, show the connection between the working-class movement and the political struggle in all its forms, attract all honest fighters against the autocracy, regardless of their views or the class they belong to, and induce them to support the working class as the only revolutionary force irrevocably hostile to absolutism. Consequently, although we appeal primarily to the Russian socialists and class-conscious workers, we do not appeal to them alone. We also call upon all who are oppressed by the present political system in Russia, on all who strive for the emancipation of the Russian people from their political slavery to support the publications which will be devoted to organising the working-class movement into a revolutionary political party; we place the columns of our publications at their disposal in order that they may expose all the abominations and crimes of the Russian autocracy. We make this appeal in the conviction that the banner of the political struggle raised by Russian Social-Democracy can and will become the banner of the whole people.

The tasks we set ourselves are extremely broad and all-embracing, and we would not have dared to take them up, were we not absolutely convinced from the whole of our past experience that these are the most urgent tasks of the whole movement, were we not assured of the sympathy and of promises of generous and constant support on the part of: 1. several organisations of the Russian Social-Democratic Labour Party and of separate groups of Russian Social-Democrats working in various towns; 2. the Emancipation of Labour group, which founded Russian Social-Democracy and has always been in the lead of its theoreticians and literary representatives; 3. a number of persons who are unaffiliated with any organisation, but who sympathise with the Social-Democratic working-class movement, and have proved of no little service to it. We will exert every effort to carry out properly the part of the general revolutionary work which we have selected, and will do our best to bring every Russian comrade to regard our publications as his own, to which all groups would communicate every kind of information concerning the movement, in which they would express their views, indicate their needs for political literature, relate their experiences, and voice their opinions concerning Social-Democratic editions; in a word, the medium through which they would thereby share whatever contribution they make to the movement and whatever they draw from it. Only in this way will it be possible to establish a genuinely all-Russian Social-Democratic organ. Russian Social-Democracy is already finding itself constricted in the underground conditions in which the various groups and isolated study circles carry on their work. It is time to come out on the road of open advocacy of socialism, on the road of open political struggle. The establishment of an all-Russian organ of Social-Democracy must be *the first step* on *this road*.

Written in the spring of 1900   Published according to
First published in 1925   a manuscript copied
in *Lenin Miscellany IV*   by an unknown hand

First page of the manuscript of Lenin's "How the 'Spark' Was Nearly Extinguished." 1900

Reduced

HOW THE "SPARK"
WAS NEARLY EXTINGUISHED*

I first went to Zurich. I arrived alone without having seen Arsenyev (Potresov). P. B. Axelrod met me in Zurich with open arms and I spent two days in a heart-to-heart talk with him. The conversation was as between friends who had not seen each other for a long time; we spoke about anything and everything, in no particular order, and not at all in the manner of a business discussion. Indeed, in regard to practical matters, there is not much that Axelrod *mitsprechen kann,*** but it was quite evident that he gravitated towards G. V. Plekhanov, from the manner in which he insisted on setting up the printing-press for the magazine in Geneva. Generally speaking, Axelrod was very "flattering" (excuse the expression), he said that our enterprise meant *everything* to them, that it meant their revival, that "we" would now be able to counteract Plekhanov's extremism. I took particular note of the last remark, and the entire subsequent "history" has proved that those were words of especial significance.

I went to Geneva. Arsenyev warned me to be particularly cautious with Plekhanov, who was terribly wrought up over the split[126] and very suspicious. My conversation with him did indeed show that he really was suspicious, distrustful, and *rechthaberisch* to the *nec plus ultra.**** I tried to observe caution and avoided all "sore" points, but the constant restraint that I had to place on myself could not but greatly

---

* A play of words on the title of the newspaper *Iskra* meaning "spark."—*Ed.*
** Can contribute.—*Ed.*
*** Holding himself to be right to the nth degree.—*Ed.*

affect my mood. From time to time little "frictions" arose in the form of sharp retorts on the part of Plekhanov to any remark that might even in the least degree cool down or soothe the passions that had been aroused (by the split). There was also "friction" over questions concerning the tactics of the magazine, Plekhanov throughout displaying complete intolerance, an inability or an unwillingness to understand other people's arguments, and, to employ the correct term, insincerity. We declared that we must make *every possible* allowance for Struve, that *we ourselves* bore some guilt for his development, since we, *including Plekhanov*, had failed to protest when protest was necessary (1895, 1897). Plekhanov absolutely refused to admit even the slightest guilt, employing transparently worthless arguments by which he *dodged* the issue without clarifying it. This diplomacy in the course of comradely conversations between future co-editors was extremely unpleasant. Why the self-deception with the pretence that he, Plekhanov, had in 1895 been "ordered [??] not to shoot" (at Struve) and that he was accustomed to doing as he was ordered (really!)?[127] Why the self-deception with the assertion that in 1897 (when Struve wrote in *Novoye Slovo* that his object was to refute one of the fundamental theses of Marxism) he had not opposed it, because he never could (and never would) conceive of polemics between collaborators[128] in one and the same magazine? This insincerity was extremely irritating, the more so by the fact that in the discussion Plekhanov sought to make it appear that we did not desire to carry on a ruthless fight against Struve, that we desired to "reconcile everything," etc. A heated discussion arose over the question of polemics in general in columns of the magazine. Plekhanov was opposed and refused to listen to our arguments. He displayed a hatred towards "the Union-Abroad people" that bordered on the indecent (suspecting them of espionage, accusing them of being swindlers and rogues, and asserting that he would not hesitate to "shoot" such "traitors," etc.). The remotest suggestion that he went to extremes (for example, my allusion to the publication of private letters[129] and to the imprudence of such a procedure) roused him to a high pitch of excitement and manifest irritability. It became evident that he and we were becoming increasingly disgruntled.

But with him it expressed itself, among other things, in the following: We had a draft prepared of an editorial declaration ("In the Name of the Editorial Board"),* in which we explained the aims and the programme of the publications. This was written in an "opportunist" spirit (from Plekhanov's point of view)—polemics between members of the staff were to be permitted, the tone was modest, allowance was made for the possibility of a peaceful ending of the controversy with the "economists," etc. The declaration laid stress on our belonging to the Party and on our desire to work for its unification. Plekhanov had read this declaration together with Arsenyev and Zasulich before my arrival; he had read it and raised no objection to the content. He had merely expressed a desire to improve the style, to elevate the tone, without changing the trend of the ideas. A. N. Potresov had left the declaration with him for this purpose. When I arrived, Plekhanov did not say a word to me about the matter, but when I visited him a few days later, he returned the declaration to me with an air of—Here you are, in the presence of witnesses, I return it to you intact; you see I have not lost it. I inquired why he had not made the suggested changes. He replied evasively that it could be done later, that it would not take long and was not worth doing at the time. I took the declaration, made the changes myself (it was a rough draft outlined when I was still in Russia), and read it a second time to Plekhanov (in the presence of Vera Zasulich), this time asking him *point-blank* to take the thing and correct it. Again he resorted to evasions and turned the job over to Vera Zasulich who was sitting beside him (an altogether strange suggestion, since we had never requested her to work on the statement, besides which, she could not have made the corrections, i.e., have "elevated" the tone and given the declaration the character of a manifesto).

Thus matters went on until the conference (the conference of the entire Emancipation of Labour group: Plekhanov, Axelrod, and Zasulich, and we two, our third man being absent[130]). Finally Axelrod arrived and the conference began. On the question of our attitude towards the Jewish Union (the Bund), Plekhanov displayed extreme intolerance and

---

* See p. 320 of this volume—*Ed.*

openly declared it to be an organisation of exploiters who exploit the Russians and not a Social-Democratic organisation.
He said that our aim was to eject this Bund from the Party,
that the Jews are all chauvinists and nationalists, that a Russian party should be Russian and should not render itself into
"captivity" to the "brood of vipers," etc. None of our objections to these indecent speeches had any result and
Plekhanov stuck to his ideas to the full, saying that we simply
did not know enough about the Jews, that we had no real
experience in dealing with Jews. No resolution on this
question was adopted. We read the "declaration" together at
the conference. Plekhanov's behaviour was very odd. He
remained silent, he suggested no changes, he did not take a
stand against the idea in the declaration that polemics be
permitted, and in general seemed to withdraw, precisely to
withdraw. He did not wish to participate, and only casually
threw in a venomous, malicious remark to the effect that he
(meaning they, i.e., the Emancipation of Labour group of
which he is dictator), of course, would have written a
different sort of declaration. This remark, uttered in passing,
after a sentence in connection with a different matter, struck
me as being particularly repellent; a conference of co-editors
is in session and one of them (who has been *twice* asked to
submit his own draft or to suggest changes to ours) suggests no
emendations, but sarcastically observes that he, of course,
would not have written so (in so timid, modest, and oppor-
tunistic a manner, he wished to say). This showed clearly
enough that normal relations did not exist between him and
us. Subsequently—let me pass over the less important issues
of the conference—the question of our attitude towards
Bobo[131] and M. I. Tugan-Baranovsky came up. We were in
favour of a *conditional* invitation (we were inevitably driven
to this by the bitterness Plekhanov displayed; we wanted him
to see that we desired a different attitude. His incredible
bitterness drove one instinctively, as it were, to protest and
to defend his opponents. Zasulich aptly remarked that
Plekhanov always argued in a manner that aroused his
readers' sympathy for his opponent). Very coldly and drily
Plekhanov declared that he completely disagreed, and he
demonstratively remained silent throughout the whole of our
fairly protracted conversation with Axelrod and Zasulich.

who were not disinclined to agree with us. The whole morning
passed in what might be called a very tense atmosphere. It
became clear beyond doubt that Plekhanov was presenting an
ultimatum to us—to choose between him and those "rogues."
Seeing that things were coming to such a pass, Arsenyev and I
agreed to give way and at the very opening of the evening
session declared that "on the insistence of Plekhanov" we had
withdrawn our proposal. This declaration met with silence
(as if it were a matter of course that we could do nothing else
but give way!). This "ultimatum atmosphere" (as Arsenyev
later described it) greatly irritated us—Plekhanov's desire to
have unlimited power was obvious. A little before that, in a
private conversation about Bobo (when Plekhanov, Arsenyev,
Zasulich, and I were taking an evening walk in the woods),
Plekhanov, after a heated discussion, said, laying his hand on
my shoulders, "But, gentlemen, I am not putting any conditions; we shall discuss all this together at the conference and
together we will decide." I was touched by this at the time.
But at the conference the very opposite happened; Plekhanov
stood aside from the comradely discussion, maintained an
angry silence, and by his silence obviously *put conditions.*"
To me it seemed to be a sharp display of insincerity (although
I did not at the moment formulate my impressions so
clearly), while Arsenyev declared outright: "I will never
forgive him this concession!" Saturday came. I do not
remember exactly what we spoke about that day; but in the
evening, when we were all walking together, a fresh conflict
flared up. Plekhanov proposed that a certain person (as yet
unpublished in our literature, but in whom he claims to see
philosophical talent; the person is unknown to me, except for
a blind worship of Plekhanov) be assigned the writing of an
article on a philosophical subject. Plekhanov went on to say:
"I shall advise the person to begin the article with a remark
against Kautsky somewhat as follows—a fine fellow, indeed!
has already become a 'critic' and publishes philosophic
articles by 'critics' in *Neue Zeit*,[132] but does not give full
scope to 'Marxists' [read: Plekhanov]." Arsenyev, on hearing
the proposal for a sharp attack upon Kautsky (who had
been invited to contribute to the magazine), became indignant and heatedly opposed it on the grounds that it was
uncalled for. Plekhanov became puffed up and irate, I

seconded Arsenyev, Axelrod and Zasulich remained silent. Half an hour later, Plekhanov departed (we had accompanied him to the steamer), in the final moments he had sat in silence, his brow black as a cloud. As soon as he left us, we felt as though a weight had been lifted from us all, and the discussion proceeded in a "friendly spirit." The next day, Sunday (today is September 2, Sunday. It happened *only* a week ago!!! But to me it seems like a year! How remote the thing has become!), we arranged to meet, not in our cottage, but at Plekhanov's. We came to the place, Arsenyev arriving first, I later. Plekhanov had sent Axelrod and Zasulich to inform Arsenyev that he declined to be co-editor, desiring to be just a contributor. Axelrod left, and Zasulich, quite put out and confused, murmured to Arsenyev: "Georg is displeased, he declines...." I entered. The door was opened for me by Plekhanov, who offered me his hand with a rather queer smile and then walked out. I stepped into the room and found Zasulich and Arsenyev sitting there, their faces wearing a strange expression. "Well, ladies and gentlemen," said I, "how goes it?" Plekhanov entered and invited us into his room. There he stated that it would be better if he were a contributor, an ordinary contributor, for otherwise there would be continual friction, that evidently his views on things differed from ours, that he understood and respected our, Party, point of view, but could not share it. Better, therefore, that we be the editors and he a contributor. We were amazed to hear this, positively amazed, and began to argue against the idea. Thereupon Plekhanov said: "Well, if we are to be together, how shall we vote; how many votes are there?" "Six." "Six is not a practical number." "Well, let Georg have two votes," suggested Zasulich, "otherwise he will always be alone—two votes on questions of tactics." We agreed to that. Upon that Plekhanov took the reins of management in his hands and with the air of editor-in-chief began apportioning departments among those present and assigning articles to this one and that in a tone that brooked no objection. We sat there as if we had been ducked; mechanically we agreed to everything, unable as yet to comprehend what had taken place. We realised that we had been made fools of; that our remarks were becoming more and more halting; that Plekhanov "waved them aside" (not refuting

them but waving them aside) more and more easily and
carelessly; that "the new system" was *de facto* tantamount to
his complete domination; and that Plekhanov understood
this perfectly, not hesitating to domineer over us without
ceremony. We realised that we had been fooled and utterly
defeated, but were as yet unable to get a full grasp of our
position. Yet no sooner did we find ourselves alone, no
sooner had we left the steamer and were on our way to the
cottage, than the lid flew off and we broke out in a wild
and furious tirade against Plekhanov.

But before relating the substance of this tirade and what
it led to, I shall go back a bit. Why did the idea of Plekhanov's complete domination (quite apart from the *form* it
assumed) rouse us to such indignation? Previously we had
thought that we would be the editors, and they—close collaborators. I had proposed (back in Russia) that the matter
be formally submitted in this manner, but Arsenyev had
objected to a formal proposition and suggested that we go
about it "in a friendly way" (which would achieve the same
result), to which I agreed. But both of us were in accord on
the point that we were to be the editors, because the "old
ones" were extremely intolerant, in addition to the fact
that they would not be able to perform painstakingly the
drudgery of editorial work. These were the only considerations that guided us, for we were quite ready to accept their
ideological guidance. The conversations I had had in Geneva
with those of Plekhanov's younger comrades and adherents
closest to him (members of the *Sotsial-Demokrat* group,[133]
long-standing adherents of Plekhanov, active Party workers,
not working men, but simple, industrious people entirely
devoted to Plekhanov)—these conversations strengthened
my conviction (and Arsenyev's) that this was exactly how
we should arrange the matter. Those adherents had told us
without equivocation that it was desirable to have the editorial office in Germany, *where we would be more independent
of Plekhanov*, and that to allow the old ones to have practical
control of the editorial work would bring about terrible delays,
if not the collapse of the entire enterprise. For the very same
reasons, Arsenyev was *unconditionally* in favour of Germany.

I broke off my description of how the "Spark" was nearly
extinguished at the point where we were returning home on

the evening of Sunday, August 26 (New Style). As soon
as we found ourselves alone, after leaving the steamer, we
broke out into a flood of angry expressions. Our pent-up
feelings got the better of us; the charged atmosphere burst
into a storm. Up and down our little village we paced far
into the night; it was quite dark, there was a rumbling of
thunder, and constant flashes of lightning rent the air.
We walked along, bursting with indignation. I remember
that Arsenyev began by declaring that as far as he was concerned his personal relations with Plekhanov were broken
off once and for all, never to be restored. He would maintain
business relations with him, but as for personal relations—
fertig.* Plekhanov's behaviour had been insulting to such a
degree that one could not help suspecting him of harbouring
"unclean" thoughts about us (i.e., that he regarded us as
Streber**). He trampled us underfoot, etc. I fully supported
these charges. My "infatuation" with Plekhanov disappeared
as if by magic, and I felt offended and embittered to an unbelievable degree. Never, never in my life, had I regarded any
other man with such sincere respect and veneration, never
had I stood before any man so "humbly" and never before
had I been so brutally "kicked." That's what it was, we had
actually been kicked. We had been scared like little children, scared by the grown-ups threatening to leave us to ourselves, and when we funked (the shame of it!) we were
brushed aside with an incredible unceremoniousness. We now
realised very clearly that Plekhanov had simply laid a
trap for us that morning when he declined to act as a co-editor; it had been a deliberate chess move, a snare for guileless
"pigeons." There could be no doubt whatever about that,
for, had Plekhanov sincerely feared to act as a co-editor because he would be a stumbling-block and might rouse useless
friction between us, he would not a moment later have revealed (and brutally revealed) the fact that his *co*-editorship
was absolutely the equivalent of his *sole* editorship. And
since a man with whom we desired to co-operate closely and
establish most intimate relations, resorted to chess moves in
dealing with comrades, there could be no doubt that this man

---

* Finished.—*Ed*.
** Careerists.—*Ed*.

was bad, yes, bad, inspired by petty motives of personal vanity and conceit—an insincere man. This discovery—and it was indeed a discovery—struck us like a thunderbolt; for up to that moment both of us had stood in admiration of Plekhanov, and, as we do with a loved one, we had forgiven him everything; we had closed our eyes to all his shortcomings; we had tried hard to persuade ourselves that those shortcomings were really non-existent, that they were petty things that bothered only people who had no proper regard for principles. Yet we ourselves had been taught practically that those "petty" shortcomings were capable of repelling the most devoted friends, that no appreciation of his theoretical correctness could make us forget his *repelling* traits. Our indignation knew no bounds. Our ideal had been destroyed; gloatingly we trampled it underfoot like a dethroned god. There was no end to the charges we hurled against him. It cannot go on like this, we decided. We do not wish, we will not, we *cannot* work together with him under such conditions. Good-bye, magazine! We will throw every thing up and return to Russia, where we will start all over again, right from the very beginning, and confine ourselves to the newspaper. We refuse to be pawns in the hands of that man; he does not understand, and cannot maintain comradely relations. We did not dare undertake the editorship *ourselves*; besides, it would be positively repulsive to do so now, for it would appear as though we really coveted the editor's post, that we really were *Streber*, careerists, and that we, too, were inspired by motives of vanity, though in a smaller way.... It is difficult to describe adequately what our feelings were that night—such mixed, heavy, confused feelings. It was a real drama; the complete abandonment of the thing which for years we had tended like a favourite child, and with which we had inseparably linked the whole of our life's work. And all because we had formerly been infatuated with Plekhanov. Had we not been so infatuated, had we regarded him more dispassionately, more level-headedly, had we studied him more objectively, our conduct towards him would have been different and we would not have suffered such disaster in the literal sense of the word, we would not have received such a "moral ducking," as Arsenyev correctly expressed it. We had received the most bitter lesson of our lives, a

painfully bitter, painfully brutal lesson. Young comrades
"court" an elder comrade out of the great love they bear for
him—and suddenly he injects into this love an atmosphere
of intrigue, compelling them to feel, not as younger brothers, but as fools to be led by the nose, as pawns to be moved
about at will, and, still worse, as clumsy *Streber* who
must be thoroughly frightened and quashed! An enamoured
youth receives from the object of his love a bitter lesson—
to regard all persons "without sentiment," to keep a stone
in one's sling. Many more words of an equally bitter nature
did we utter that night. The suddenness of the disaster naturally caused us to magnify it, but, in the main, the bitter
words we uttered were true. Blinded by our love, we had actually behaved like *slaves*, and it is humiliating to be a
slave. Our sense of having been wronged was magnified a hun-
dredfold by the fact that "he" himself had opened our eyes to
our humiliation....

Finally, we returned to our respective rooms to go to bed,
firmly determined to express our indignation to Plekhanov
on the following day, to give up the magazine and go away,
retain only the newspaper, and publish the material for
the magazine in pamphlet form. The cause would not suffer
by this, we thought, and we would avoid having intimate
dealings with "that man."

Next morning I woke up earlier than usual. I was awakened by footsteps on the stairs and the voice of Axelrod who
was knocking at Arsenyev's door. I heard Arsenyev call out
in reply and open the door—I heard all this and wondered
whether he would have pluck enough to come out with
everything immediately. Better to speak out at once, indeed
better, than to drag the thing out! I washed and dressed
and went to Arsenyev's room, where I found him at his
toilet. Axelrod was sitting in the armchair, his face wearing
a somewhat strained expression. "Listen, Comrade X," said
Arsenyev turning to me, "I have told Axelrod of our decision
to go back to Russia, and of our conviction that things cannot be run like this." I fully concurred with this, of course,
and supported Arsenyev's statement. We related everything
to Axelrod, quite frankly, so much so that Arsenyev even
spoke of our suspicion that Plekhanov regarded us as *Streber*.
Axelrod half-sympathised with us generally, shook his head

sadly, and appeared to be greatly perturbed, confused, put out. But hearing this last remark, he began to protest and to shout that our accusation was unfounded; that Plekhanov had many shortcomings, but not this one; that in this matter it was not he who was unjust to us, but we who were unjust to him; that until then he had been prepared to say to Plekhanov, "See what a mess you have made, now clear it up yourself, I wash my hands of the matter," but he could no longer say this, seeing that we were also unjust. His assurances made little impression upon us, as may be imagined, and poor Axelrod looked pitiful when he finally realised that we were firm in our decision.

We went out together to warn Vera Zasulich. It was to be expected that she would take the news of the "break" (for it did certainly look like a break) very badly. "I fear," Arsenyev had said to me the previous evening, "I do seriously fear that she will commit suicide...."

I shall never forget the mood in which we three went out that morning "It's like going to a funeral," I thought to myself. And indeed we walked as in a funeral procession— silent, with downcast eyes, oppressed to the extreme by the absurdness, the preposterousness, and the senselessness of our loss. As though a curse had descended upon us! Everything had been proceeding smoothly after so many misfortunes and failures, when suddenly, a whirlwind—and the end, the whole thing shattered again. I could hardly bring myself to believe it (as one cannot bring oneself to believe the death of a near one)—could it be I, the fervent worshipper of Plekhanov, who was now filled with bitter thoughts about him, who was walking along with clenched teeth and a devilish chill at the heart, intending to hurl cold and bitter words at him and almost to announce the "breaking-off of our relations"? Was this but a hideous dream, or was it reality?

The impression clung to us even during our conversation with Zasulich; She did not display any strong emotion, but she was obviously deeply depressed and she asked us, almost implored us, could we not go back on our decision, could we not try—perhaps it was not so terrible, after all, and it would be possible to set things to rights once we were at work; during the work the repellent features of his character would not be so apparent.... It was extremely painful to listen to the sincere pleadings of this woman, weak before Plekhanov, but absolutely sincere and passionately loyal to the cause, who bore the yoke of Plekhanovism with the "heroism of a slave" (Arsenyev's expression). It was, indeed, so painful that at times I thought I would burst into tears.... Words of pity, despair, etc., easily move one to tears at a funeral....

We left Axelrod and Zasulich. We lunched, dispatched letters to Germany saying that we were coming and that they were *to stop the machine* we had even sent a telegram about the matter (*prior* to our conversation with Plekhanov!!), and neither of us doubted for a moment that we had done right.

After lunch, at the appointed hour, we again went to the house of Axelrod and Zasulich, where Plekhanov was due to be by now. As we approached, the three of them came out to meet us. We greeted each other in silence. Plekhanov tried to start an extraneous conversation (we had asked Axelrod and Zasulich to warn him of our intention, so that he would know all about it), we returned to the room and sat down. Arsenyev began to speak—drily, briefly, and with restraint. He said that we despaired of the possibility of carrying on with relations *such* as they had developed on the previous evening; that we had decided to return to Russia to consult the comrades there, since we no longer dared to decide the matter ourselves, and that for the time being we would have to abandon the idea of publishing the magazine. Plekhanov was very calm and restrained, and apparently had complete command of himself; he did not show a trace of the nervousness betrayed by Axelrod and Zasulich (he had been in bigger battles than this! we thought to ourselves, gazing at him in fury). He inquired what it was all about. "We are in an atmosphere of ultimatums," replied Arsenyev, and he expounded the idea at greater length. "Were you afraid that after the first issue I would go on strike before we got out the second?" asked Plekhanov aggressively. He thought we would not dare to say a thing like that. But I too was calm and cool, as I replied: "Is that very much different from what Arsenyev said? Isn't that what he said?" Plekhanov seemed to bristle under the words. He had not expected such a dry tone and direct accusation.

"Well, if you have decided to leave, what is there to discuss?" he said. "I have nothing to say, my position is a very curious one. All you do is talk of impressions and nothing else. You have the impression that I am a bad man. I cannot help that."

"We may be to blame," I said, desiring to turn the conversation away from this "impossible" subject, "for having rushed across in this headlong manner without first sounding the ford."

"Not at all," replied Plekhanov. "To speak quite frankly, you are to blame (perhaps Arsenyev's state of nervousness may have had something to do with it) for attaching too much importance to impressions to which no importance whatever should have been attached." After a moment's silence we said that we could confine ourselves to publishing pamphlets for the time being. Plekhanov angrily retorted: "I haven't thought about pamphlets and am not thinking of them. *Don't count on me.* I shall not sit idle with my arms folded if you go away. I may take up some other enterprise before you return."

Nothing so much lowered Plekhanov in my eyes as this statement when later I recalled it and turned it over in my mind. This was such a crude threat and such a badly calculated attempt to intimidate us, that it simply "finished" Plekhanov as far as we were concerned and exposed his "policy" towards us: give them a good scare and that will suffice....

But we did not pay *the slighest attention* to his threat. I simply pressed my lips tight in silence: very well, if this is how you would have it, then *à la guerre comme à la guerre**; but you must be a fool if you cannot see that we have changed, that we have undergone a transformation overnight.

Perceiving that his threats were ineffective, Plekhanov tried another manoeuvre—for what else can it be called, when a few moments later he stated that the break with us would spell for him complete abandonment of political activity, that he would give up political work and devote himself to science, to purely scientific literature, for if he could not

---

* If it's war, then the way of war!—*Ed.*

work with us, it meant that he would not be able to work with anybody.... Having found threats to be unavailing, he tried flattery! But coming as that did *after* threats, it could only produce a feeling of revulsion.... The conversation was very brief and nothing came of it. Seeing this, Plekhanov switched the conversation to Russian atrocities in China, but he was almost the only one who spoke and very soon we parted company.

Our conversation with Axelrod and Zasulich after Plekhanov's departure was neither interesting nor important; Axelrod wriggled and tried to prove that Plekhanov was also crushed and that the sin would be on our heads if we left in this manner, etc., etc. In a tête-à-tête with Arsenyev, Zasulich confessed that "Georg" was always like that. She confessed to her "slavish heroism," but admitted that it would "teach him a lesson" if we went away.

We spent the rest of the evening in a state of idleness and depression.

On the next day, Tuesday, August 28 (New Style), we were due to leave for Geneva, and from there to proceed to Germany. Early in the morning, I was awakened by Arsenyev (a late riser usually). I was surprised. He said that he had slept badly and that he had thought of a last possible scheme by which the matter could somehow be adjusted so that a serious *Party* enterprise might not be ruined by spoiled *personal* relations. We would publish a *collection*, since we had the material ready and had established contact with the printing-house. We would publish this collection under the present undefined editorial relations and see what happened; from this it would be just as easy to pass on to the publication of a magazine as to the publication of pamphlets. If Plekhanov remained stubborn, then, to the devil with him, we would know that we had done all we could.... And thus it was decided.

We went out to inform Axelrod and Zasulich and met them on the way; they were coming to see us. They, of course, readily agreed and Axelrod undertook the task of negotiating with Plekhanov and of obtaining his consent.

We arrived at Geneva and had our *last interview* with Plekhanov. He adopted a tone which might have suggested that all that had happened was a sad misunderstanding due to nervousness. He inquired sympathetically after Arsenyev's health, and nearly embraced him—the latter almost gave a jump. Plekhanov agreed to the publication of a collection. We said that in regard to the editorial arrangements, three variations were possible: 1) we to be the editors, and he a contributor; 2) all of us to be the editors; 3) he to be the editor, and we contributors; that we would discuss all three alternatives in Russia, draw up a plan, and bring it back with us. Plekhanov declared that he absolutely rejected the third variant, that he insisted emphatically that *this* arrangement be definitely excluded, and that he *agreed* to the *first two*. We therefore decided that for the time being, *until we submitted* our proposal for the new editorial regime, the old system was to remain in force (the six of us to act as co-editors, with Plekhanov apportioned two votes).

Plekhanov then expressed the desire to know precisely what it was that we were dissatisfied with. I remarked that perhaps it would be better to pay more attention to the future rather than to the past. But he insisted that the question be gone into and clarified. A conversation started in which only Plekhanov and I took part, Arsenyev and Axelrod remaining silent. The conversation was carried on rather calmly, even very calmly. Plekhanov said he had noticed that Arsenyev was irritated by his refusal concerning Struve; I remarked that he, on the contrary, had laid down conditions to us, notwithstanding his statement, previously made during our conversation in the woods, that he would impose no conditions. Plekhanov defended himself, saying that he had been silent, not because he was laying down conditions, but because the question was clear as far as he was concerned. I urged the necessity for permitting polemics and the necessity for voting among ourselves. Plekhanov agreed to the latter, but added that voting, of course, was permissible on partial questions, but impossible on fundamental questions. I objected by saying that it would not always be easy to distinguish between fundamental and partial questions, and that it was precisely in drawing such distinctions that the co-editors would have to take a vote. Plekhanov was stubborn. He said that this was a matter of conscience, that the distinction between fundamental and partial questions was perfectly clear, and that there would

be no occasion for taking a vote. And so we got stuck in this
dispute as to whether voting should be permitted among
the editors on the question of defining what were fundamental and what were partial questions, and we could make no
progress. Plekhanov displayed all his dexterity, the brilliance
of his examples, smiles, jests, and citations, which compelled us to laugh in spite of ourselves; but he evaded the
question without definitely saying "no." I became convinced
that he positively could not concede the point; that he could
not abandon his "individualism" and his "ultimatums,"
since he would never agree to take a vote on such questions
but would present ultimatums.

That evening I departed without again meeting any of
the members of the Emancipation of Labour group. We had
agreed among ourselves not to relate what had passed to any
one except our most intimate friends. We decided to keep
up appearances and not give our opponents cause for triumph.
Outwardly it was as though nothing had happened; the apparatus must continue to work as it had worked till then, but
within a chord had broken, and instead of splendid personal relations, dry, business-like relations prevailed, with a
constant reckoning according to the principle: *si vis pacem,
para bellum.**

It will be of interest, however, to mention a conversation
I had that same evening with an intimate friend and adherent
of Plekhanov, a member of the *Sotsial-Demokrat* group.
I mentioned no word to him about what had occurred; I told
him that we had arranged to publish a magazine, that the
articles had been decided on—it was time to set to work.
I discussed with him the practical ways of arranging the
work. He gave stress to the opinion that the old ones were
absolutely incapable of doing editorial work. I discussed
with him the "three variations" and asked him directly which
in his opinion was the best. Without hesitation, he answered—the first (we to be the editors, they the contributors),
but in all probability, he thought, the magazine would be
Plekhanov's and the newspaper ours.

As the affair became more and more remote, we began to
think of it more calmly, and became convinced that it was

---

* If you desire peace, prepare for war.—*Ed*.

entirely unreasonable to give up the enterprise, that we had for the time being no ground for fearing to undertake the editorship (of the *collection*), but that indeed it was necessary for us to undertake it, for there was absolutely no other way of making the apparatus work properly, and of preventing the project from being ruined by the disruptive "propensities" of Plekhanov.

By the time we arrived at N.,[134] on September 4 or 5, we had drawn up the plan of the *formal* relations between us (I had begun to write it *en route*, on the train). That plan made us the editors and them the contributors, with the right to vote on all editorial questions. It was decided to discuss this plan with Yegor (Martov), and then to submit it to them.

Hopes were *beginning to rise* that the "Spark" would be rekindled.

Written at the beginning
of September 1900

First published in 1924
in *Lenin Miscellany I*

Published according to
the manuscript

DRAFT AGREEMENT

1. In view of the solidarity in fundamental conceptions and the identity of practical aims of the *Sotsial-Demokrat* group abroad and the Russian group that publishes the collection *Zarya* and the newspaper *Iskra*, these two organisations conclude an alliance.

2. The two groups will afford each other all-round support: firstly, in regard to literature. The Emancipation of Labour group will collaborate closely in editing the collection *Zarya* and the newspaper *Iskra**; secondly, in delivering and distributing literature, in expanding and consolidating revolutionary connections, and in obtaining material resources.

3. The *Sotsial-Demokrat* group and special *Iskra* agents will be the foreign representatives of the *Iskra* group.

4. Letters and packages from abroad addressed to the *Iskra* group will be forwarded to the address of the *Sotsial-Demokrat* group. In the event of any member of the *Iskra* group being abroad, all correspondence will be transmitted to him. If at any given moment there is no member of the *Iskra* group abroad, the *Sotsial-Demokrat* group and *Iskra* agents will take the duties upon themselves.

Written early
in September 1900

First published in 1940
in the magazine *Proletarskaya
Revolyutsiya*, No. 3

Published according to
the manuscript

---

* The terms of this collaboration are laid down in a special agreement.[135]

DECLARATION OF THE EDITORIAL BOARD OF *ISKRA*

IN THE NAME OF THE EDITORIAL BOARD

In undertaking the publication of a political newspaper, *Iskra*, we consider it necessary to say a few words concerning the objects for which we are striving and the understanding we have of our tasks.

We are passing through an extremely important period in the history of the Russian working-class movement and Russian Social-Democracy. The past few years have been marked by an astonishingly rapid spread of Social-Democratic ideas among our intelligentsia, and meeting this trend in social ideas is an independent movement of the industrial proletariat, which is beginning to unite and struggle against its oppressors, and to strive eagerly towards socialism. Study circles of workers and Social-Democratic intellectuals are springing up everywhere, local agitation leaflets are being widely distributed, the demand for Social-Democratic literature is increasing and is far outstripping the supply, and intensified government persecution is powerless to restrain the movement. The prisons and places of exile are filled to overflowing. Hardly a month goes by without our hearing of socialists "caught in dragnets" in all parts of Russia, of the capture of underground couriers, of the confiscation of literature and printing-presses. But the movement is growing, it is spreading to ever wider regions, it is penetrating more and more deeply into the working class and is attracting public attention to an ever-increasing degree. The entire economic development of Russia and the history of social thought and of the revolutionary movement in Russia serve as a guarantee that the Social-Democratic working-class movement will grow and will, in the end, surmount all the obstacles that confront it.

On the other hand, the principal feature of our movement, which has become particularly marked in recent times, is its state of disunity and its amateur character, if one may so express it. Local study circles spring up and function independently of one another and—what is particularly important—of circles that have functioned and still function in the same districts. Traditions are not established and continuity is not maintained; local publications fully reflect this disunity and the lack of contact with what Russian Social-Democracy has already achieved.

Such a state of disunity is not in keeping with the demands posed by the movement in its present strength and breadth, and creates, in our opinion, a critical moment in its development. The need for consolidation and for a definite form and organisation is felt with irresistible force in the movement itself; yet among Social-Democrats active in the practical field this need for a transition to a higher form of the movement is not everywhere realised. On the contrary, among wide circles an ideological wavering is to be seen, an infatuation with the fashionable "criticism of Marxism" and with "Bernsteinism," the spread of the views of the so-called "economist" trend, and what is inseparably connected with it—an effort to keep the movement at its lower level, to push into the background the task of forming a revolutionary party that heads the struggle of the entire people. *It is a fact* that such an ideological wavering is to be observed among Russian Social-Democrats; that narrow practicalism, detached from the theoretical clarification of the movement as a whole, threatens to divert the movement to a false path. No one who has direct knowledge of the state of affairs in the majority of our organisations has any doubt whatever on that score. Moreover, literary productions exist which confirm this. It is sufficient to mention the *Credo*, which has already called forth legitimate protest; the *Separate Supplement to "Rabochaya Mysl"* (September 1899), which brought out so markedly the trend that permeates the *whole* of *Rabochaya Mysl*; and, finally, the manifesto of the St. Petersburg Self-Emancipation of the Working Class group,[136] also drawn up in the spirit of "economism." And *completely untrue* are the assertions of *Rabocheye Dyelo* to the effect that the *Credo* merely represents the opinions of individuals, that the trend represented by *Rabochaya Mysl* expresses merely the confusion of mind and the tactlessness of its editors, and not a special tendency in the progress of the Russian working-class movement.

Simultaneously with this, the works of authors whom the reading public has hitherto, with more or less reason, regarded as prominent representatives of "legal" Marxism are increasingly revealing a change of views in a direction approximating that of bourgeois apologetics. As a result of all this, we have the confusion and anarchy which has enabled the ex-Marxist, or, more precisely, the ex-socialist, Bernstein, in recounting his successes, to declare, unchallenged, in the press that the majority of Social-Democrats active in Russia are his followers.

We do not desire to exaggerate the gravity of the situation, but it would be immeasurably more harmful to close our eyes to it. For this reason we heartily welcome the decision of the Emancipation of Labour group to resume its literary activity and begin a systematic struggle against the attempts to distort and vulgarise Social-Democracy.

The following practical conclusion is to be drawn from the foregoing: we Russian Social-Democrats must unite and direct all our efforts towards the formation of a strong party which must struggle under the single banner of revolutionary Social-Democracy. This is precisely the task laid down by the congress in 1898 at which the Russian Social-Democratic Labour Party was formed, and which published its *Manifesto*.

We regard ourselves as members of this Party; we agree entirely with the fundamental ideas contained in the *Manifesto* and attach extreme importance to it as a public declaration of its aims. Consequently, we, as members of the Party, present the question of our immediate and direct tasks as follows: What plan of activity must we adopt to revive the Party on the firmest possible basis?

The reply usually made to this question is that it is necessary to elect anew a central Party body and instruct it to

resume the publication of the Party organ. But, in the period of confusion through which we are now passing, such a
simple method is hardly expedient.

To establish and consolidate the Party means to establish and consolidate unity among all Russian Social-Democrats, and, for the reasons indicated above, such unity cannot be decreed, it cannot be brought about by a decision,
say, of a meeting of representatives; it must be worked
for. In the first place, it is necessary to work for solid ideological unity which should eliminate discordance and confusion that—let us be frank!—reign among Russian Social-
Democrats at the present time. This ideological unity must
be consolidated by a Party programme. Secondly, we must
work to achieve an organisation especially for the purpose
of establishing and maintaining contact among all the
centres of the movement, of supplying complete and timely
information about the movement, and of delivering our
newspapers and periodicals regularly to all parts of Russia.
Only when such an organisation has been founded, only when
a Russian socialist post has been established, will the Party
possess a sound foundation and become a real fact, and, therefore, a mighty political force. We intend to devote our efforts
to the first half of this task, i.e., to creating a common literature, consistent in principle and capable of ideologically
uniting revolutionary Social-Democracy, since we regard
this as the pressing demand of the movement today and a
necessary preliminary measure towards the resumption of
Party activity.

As we have said, the ideological unity of Russian Social-
Democrats has still to be created, and to this end it is, in
our opinion, necessary to have an open and all-embracing
discussion of the fundamental questions of principle and
tactics raised by the present-day "economists," Bernsteinians, and "critics." Before we can unite, and in order that
we may unite, we must first of all draw firm and definite
lines of demarcation. Otherwise, our unity will be purely
fictitious, it will conceal the prevailing confusion and hinder its radical elimination. It is understandable, therefore,
that we do not intend to make our publication a mere store-
house of various views. On the contrary, we shall conduct it
in the spirit of a strictly defined tendency. This tendency can

be expressed by the word Marxism, and there is hardly need
to add that we stand for the consistent development of the
ideas of Marx and Engels and emphatically reject the equivo-
cating, vague, and opportunist "corrections" for which Eduard
Bernstein, P. Struve, and many others have set the fashion.
But although we shall discuss all questions from our own
definite point of view, we shall give space in our columns
to polemics between comrades. Open polemics, conducted
in full view of all Russian Social-Democrats and class-conscious workers, are necessary and desirable in order to clarify the depth of existing differences, in order to afford discussion of disputed questions from all angles, in order to
combat the extremes into which representatives, not only
of various views, but even of various localities, or various
"specialities" of the revolutionary movement, inevitably
fall. Indeed, as noted above, we regard one of the drawbacks
of the present-day movement to be the absence of open
polemics between avowedly differing views, the effort to
conceal differences on fundamental questions.

We shall not enumerate in detail all questions and points
of subject-matter included in the programme of our publication, for this programme derives automatically from the
general conception of what a political newspaper, published under present conditions, should be.

We will exert our efforts to bring every Russian comrade
to regard our publication as his own, to which all groups
would communicate every kind of information concerning
the movement, in which they would relate their experiences,
express their views, indicate their needs for political literature, and voice their opinions concerning Social-Democratic
editions: in a word, they would thereby share whatever contribution they make to the movement and whatever they
draw from it. Only in this way will it be possible to establish
a genuinely all-Russian Social-Democratic organ. Only such
a publication will be capable of leading the movement on to
the high road of political struggle. "Extend the bounds and
broaden the content of our propagandist, agitational, and
organisational activity"—these words of P. B. Axelrod must
serve as a slogan defining the activities of Russian Social-
Democrats in the immediate future, and we adopt this
slogan in the programme of our publication.

We appeal not only to socialists and class-conscious workers, we also call upon all who are oppressed by the present political system; we place the columns of our publications at their disposal in order that they may expose all the abominations of the Russian autocracy.

Those who regard Social-Democracy as an organisation serving exclusively the spontaneous struggle of the proletariat may be content with merely local agitation and working-class literature "pure and simple." We do not understand Social-Democracy in this way; we regard it as a revolutionary party, inseparably connected with the working-class movement and directed against absolutism. Only when organised in such a party will the proletariat—the most revolutionary class in Russia today—be in a position to fulfil the historical task that confronts it—to unite under its banner all the democratic elements in the country and to crown the tenacious struggle in which so many generations have fallen with the final triumph over the hated regime.

* * *

The size of the newspaper will range from one to two printed signatures.

In view of the conditions under which the Russian underground press has to work, there will be no regular date of publication.

We have been promised contributions by a number of prominent representatives of international Social-Democracy, the close co-operation of the Emancipation of Labour group (G. V. Plekhanov, P. B. Axelrod, and V. I. Zasulich), and the support of several organisations of the Russian Social-Democratic Labour Party, as well as of separate groups of Russian Social-Democrats.

Written in September 1900
Published in 1900 by *Iskra*
as a separate leaflet

Published according to
the text of the leaflet, 1900

PREFACE TO THE PAMPHLET
MAY DAYS IN KHARKOV

The present pamphlet contains a description of the celebrated May Day demonstrations in Kharkov in 1900; it was drawn up by the Kharkov Committee of the Russian Social-Democratic Labour Party on the basis of descriptions sent in by the workers themselves. It was sent to us as a newspaper report, but we consider it necessary to publish it as a separate pamphlet because of its size, as well as because in this way it will be possible to secure wider distribution. In another six months, the Russian workers will celebrate the First of May of the first year of the new century, and it is time we set to work organising the celebrations in as large a number of centres as possible, and on a scale as imposing as possible. They must be imposing, not only in the numbers of participants, but in the organised character and the class-consciousness the participants will display, in their determination to launch a resolute struggle for the political liberation of the Russian people and, consequently, for a free opportunity for the class development of the proletariat and its open struggle for socialism. It is time to prepare for the forthcoming May Day celebrations, and one of the most important preparation measures must consist in learning what the Social-Democratic movement in Russia has already achieved, in examining the shortcomings of our movement in general and of the May Day movement in particular, in devising means to eliminate these shortcomings and achieve better results.

May Day in Kharkov showed what a great political demonstration a working-class festival can become and

what we lack to make these celebrations a really great
all-Russian manifestation of the class-conscious proletariat. What made the May Day celebrations in Kharkov an event of outstanding importance? The large-scale
participation of the workers in the strike, the huge mass
meetings in the streets, the unfurling of red flags, the presentation of demands put forth in proclamations and the
revolutionary character of these demands: the eight-hour
day and political liberty. The legend that the Russian workers have not yet matured for the political struggle, that
their principal concern should be the purely economic
struggle, which they should only little by little and very
slowly supplement with partial political agitation for partial political reforms and not for the struggle against the
entire political system of Russia—that legend has been totally refuted by the Kharkov May Day celebrations. But
here we want to draw attention to another aspect of the matter. Although the May Day celebrations in Kharkov have
once more demonstrated the political capacities of the Russian workers, they have, at the same time, revealed what we
lack for the full development of these capacities.

The Kharkov Social-Democrats tried to prepare for the
May Day celebrations by distributing pamphlets and leaflets
in advance, and the workers drew up a plan for the general
demonstration and for the speeches to be delivered in Kon-
naya Square. Why did the plan not succeed? The Kharkov
comrades say because the "general staff" of the class-conscious
socialist workers did not distribute its forces evenly, there
having been many in one factory, and in another few; and,
further, because the workers' plan "was known to the authorities," who, of course, took all steps to split the workers.
The conclusion to be drawn is obvious: we lack *organisation*. The masses of the workers were roused and ready to follow the socialist leaders; but the "general staff" failed to
organise a strong nucleus able to distribute properly all the
available forces of class-conscious workers and so ensure the
necessary secrecy that the drawn-up plans of action should
remain unknown, not only to the authorities, but to all individuals outside the organisation. This organisation must be
a *revolutionary* organisation. It must be composed of men
and women who clearly understand the tasks of the Social-

Россійская Соціалдемократическая Рабочая Партія.

МАЙСКІЕ ДНИ ВЪ ХАРЬКОВѢ

Изданіе „ИСКРЫ"

Типографія „Искры". Январь 1901.

Facsimile of the cover of the pamphlet,
May Days in Kharkov. 1901

Democratic working-class movement and who have resolved to engage in a determined struggle against the present political system. It must combine within itself the socialist knowledge and revolutionary experience acquired from many decades of activity by the Russian revolutionary intelligentsia with the knowledge of working-class life and conditions and the ability to agitate among the masses and lead them which is characteristic of the advanced workers. It should be our primary concern not to set up an artificial partition between the intellectual and the worker, not to form a "purely workers'" organisation, but to strive, above all, to achieve the above-stated combination. We permit ourselves in this connection to quote the following words of G. Plekhanov:

"A necessary condition for this activity [agitation] is the consolidation of the already existing revolutionary forces. Propaganda in the study circles can be conducted by men and women who have no mutual contact whatever with one another and who do not even suspect one another's existence; it goes without saying that the lack of organisation always affects propaganda, too, but it does not make it impossible. However, in a period of great social turmoil, when the political atmosphere is charged with electricity, when now here and now there, from the most varied and unforeseen causes, outbreaks occur with increasing frequency, heralding the approaching revolutionary storm—in a word, when it is necessary either to agitate or remain in the rear, at such a time *only organised* revolutionary forces can seriously influence the progress of events. The individual then becomes powerless; the revolutionary cause can then be carried forward only on the shoulders of units of a higher order—by *revolutionary organisations*" (G. Plekhanov, *The Tasks of the Socialists in the Fight Against the Famine*, p. 83).

Precisely such a period is approaching in the history of the Russian working-class movement, a period of turmoil and of outbreaks precipitated by the most varied causes, and if we do not wish to remain "in the rear," we must direct all our efforts towards establishing an all-Russian organisation capable of guiding all the separate outbreaks and ensuring in this way that the approaching storm (to which the Kharkov worker also refers at the end of the pamphlet) is not an elemental outburst, but a conscious movement of the proletariat standing at the head of the entire people in revolt against the autocratic government.

In addition to manifesting the insufficient unity and preparedness of our revolutionary organisations, the Kharkov May Day celebrations also furnish another and no less important practical indication. "The May Day festival and demonstration," we read in the pamphlet, "were unexpectedly interconnected with various practical demands presented without relevant preparation and, consequently, in general doomed to failure." Let us take, for example, the demands put forward by the railway-workshop employees. Of the fourteen demands, eleven have to do with minor improvements, which can quite easily be achieved even under the present political system—wage increases, reduction of hours, removal of abuses. Included among these demands, as though identical with them, are the following three: 4) introduction of an eight-hour day, 7) guarantee against victimisation of workers after the May First events, and 10) establishment of a joint committee of workers and employers for settling disputes between the two parties. The first of these demands (point 4) is a general demand advanced by the world proletariat; the fact that this demand was put forward seems to indicate that the advanced workers of Kharkov realise their solidarity with the world socialist working-class movement. But precisely for this reason it should not have been included among minor demands like better treatment by foremen, or a ten per cent increase in wages. Demands for wage increases and better treatment can (and should) be presented by the workers to their employers in each separate trade; these are trade demands, put forward by separate categories of workers. The demand for an eight-hour day, however, is the demand of the whole proletariat, presented, not to individual employers, but to the state authorities as the representative of the entire present-day social and political system, to the capitalist class as a whole, the owners of all the means of production. The demand for an eight-hour day has assumed special significance. It is a declaration of solidarity with the international socialist movement. We need to make the workers understand this difference, so that they do not reduce the demand for the eight-hour day to the level of demands like free railway tickets, or the dismissal of a watchman. Throughout the year the workers, first in one place and then in another, continuously present a variety of partial demands to their employers and fight for their achievement. In assisting the workers in this struggle, socialists must always explain its connection with the proletarian struggle for emancipation in all countries. And the First of May must be the day on which the workers solemnly declare that they realise this connection and resolutely join in the struggle.

Let us take the tenth demand which calls for the establishment of a committee for the settlement of disputes. Such a committee composed of representatives of the workers and the employers could, of course, be very useful, but only if the elections were absolutely free and the elected representatives enjoyed complete independence. What purpose would such a committee serve, if the workers, who wage a struggle against the election of creatures of the management or who strongly attack the management and expose its tyranny, end by being discharged? Such workers would not only be discharged, they would be arrested. Consequently, for such a committee to be of service to the workers, the delegates must, first, be absolutely independent of the factory management; this can be achieved only when there are free labour unions embracing many factories, unions that have their own resources and are prepared to protect their delegates. Such a committee can be useful only if many factories, if possible all the factories in the given trade, are organised. Secondly, it is necessary to secure guarantees of the inviolability of the person of the workers, i.e., that they will not be arrested arbitrarily by the police or the gendarmerie. This demand to guarantee the workers against victimisation was put forward (point 7). But from whom can the workers demand guarantees of the inviolability of the person and freedom of association (which, as we have seen, is a necessary condition for the success of the committees)? Only from the state authorities, because the absence of a guarantee of inviolability of the person and freedom of association is due to the fundamental laws of the Russian state. More than that, it is due to the very form of government in Russia. The form of government in Russia is that of an absolute monarchy. The tsar is an autocrat, he alone decrees the laws and appoints all the higher officials without any participation of the people, without participation of the people's representatives. Under such a state system there can be no inviolability of the person; citizens' associations, and particularly working-class associations, cannot be free. For that reason, it is senseless to demand guarantees of the inviolability of the person (and freedom of association) from an autocratic government; for such a demand is synonymous with demanding political rights for the people, and an autocratic government is termed autocratic precisely because it implies negation of political rights for the people. It will be possible to obtain a guarantee of the inviolability of the person (and freedom of association) only when *representatives of the people* take part in legislation and in the entire administration of the state. So long as a body of people's representatives does not exist, the autocratic government, upon making certain petty concessions to the workers, will always take away with one hand what it gives with the other. The May Day celebrations in Kharkov were another vivid proof that this is so—the governor conceded to the demands of the working masses and released those who had been arrested, but within a day or two, on orders from St. Petersburg, scores of workers were again rounded up. The gubernia and factory officials' "guarantee" immunity to delegates, while the gendarmes seize them and fling them into prison in solitary confinement or banish them from the city! Of what use are such guarantees to the people?

Hence, the workers must demand from the tsar the convocation of an assembly of the representatives of the people, the convocation of a Zemsky Sobor. The manifesto distributed in Kharkov on the eve of the First of May this year raised this demand, and we have seen that a section of the advanced workers fully appreciated its significance. We must make sure that *all* advanced workers understand clearly the necessity for this demand and spread it, not only among the masses of the workers, but among all strata of the people who come into contact with the workers and who eagerly desire to know what the socialists and the "urban" workers are fighting for. This year when a factory inspector asked a group of workers precisely what they wanted, only one voice shouted, "A constitution!"; and this voice sounded so isolated that the correspondent reported somewhat mockingly: "One proletarian *blurted out*...." Another correspondent put it, "Under the circumstances," this reply was "semi-comical" (see *Labour Movement in Kharkov*, Report of the Kharkov Committee of the Russian Social-Democratic Labour Party, published by *Rabocheye Dyelo*, Geneva, September 1900, p. 14). As a matter of fact, there was nothing comical in the reply at all. What may have seemed comical was the incongruity between the demand of this lone voice for a change in the whole state system and the demands for a half-hour reduction in the working day and for payment of wages during working hours. There is, however, an indubitable connection between these demands and the demand for a constitution; and if we can get the masses to understand this connection (and we undoubtedly will), then the cry "A constitution!" will not be an isolated one, but will come from the throats of thousands and hundreds of thousands, when it will no longer be comical, but menacing. It is related that a certain person driving through the streets of Kharkov during the May Day celebrations asked the cabby what the workers wanted, and he replied: "They want an eight-hour day and their own newspaper." That cabby understood that the workers were no longer satisfied with mere doles, but that they wanted to be free men, that they wanted to be able to express their needs freely and openly and to fight for them. But that reply did not yet reveal the consciousness that the workers are fighting for the liberty of the whole people and for their right to take part in the administration of the state. When the demand that the tsar convene an assembly of people's representatives is repeated with full consciousness and indomitable determination by the working masses in all industrial cities and factory districts in Russia; when the workers have reached the stage at which the entire urban population, and all the rural people who come into the towns, understand what the socialists want and what the workers are fighting for, then the great day of the people's liberation from police tyranny will not be far off!

Written early in November 1900   Published according to
    Published in January 1901   the text of the pamphlet
in a pamphlet issued by *Iskra*

THE URGENT TASKS OF OUR MOVEMENT

Russian Social-Democracy has repeatedly declared the immediate political task of a Russian working-class party to be the overthrow of the autocracy, the achievement of political liberty. This was enunciated over fifteen years ago by the representatives of Russian Social-Democracy—the members of the Emancipation of Labour group. It was affirmed two and a half years ago by the representatives of the Russian Social-Democratic organisations that, in the spring of 1898, founded the Russian Social-Democratic Labour Party. Despite these repeated declarations, however, the question of the political tasks of Social-Democracy in Russia is prominent again today. Many representatives of our movement express doubt as to the correctness of the above-mentioned solution of the question. It is claimed that the economic struggle is of predominant importance; the political tasks of the proletariat are pushed into the background, narrowed down, and restricted, and it is even said that to speak of forming an independent working-class party in Russia is merely to repeat somebody else's words, that the workers should carry on only the economic struggle and leave politics to the intelligentsia in alliance with the liberals. The latest profession of the new faith (the notorious *Credo*) amounts to a declaration that the Russian proletariat has not yet come of age and to a complete rejection of the Social-Democratic programme. *Rabochaya Mysl* (particularly in its *Separate Supplement*) takes practically the same attitude. Russian Social-Democracy is passing through a period of vacillation and doubt bordering on self-negation. On the one hand, the working-class movement is being sundered from socialism, the workers are being helped to carry on the economic struggle, but nothing, or next to nothing, is done to explain to them the socialist aims and the political tasks of the movement as a whole. On the other hand, socialism is being sundered from the labour movement; Russian socialists are again beginning to talk more and more about the struggle against the government having to be carried on entirely by the intelligentsia because the workers confine themselves to the economic struggle.

In our opinion the ground has been prepared for this sad state of affairs by three circumstances. First, in their early activity, Russian Social-Democrats restricted themselves merely to work in propaganda circles. When we took up agitation among the masses we were not always able to restrain ourselves from going to the other extreme. Secondly, in our early activity we often had to struggle for our right to existence against the Narodnaya Volya adherents, who understood by "politics" an activity isolated from the working-class movement and who reduced politics purely to conspiratorial struggle. In rejecting this sort of politics, the Social-Democrats went to the extreme of pushing politics entirely into the background. Thirdly, working in the isolation of small local workers' circles, the Social-Democrats did not devote sufficient attention to the necessity of organising a revolutionary party which would combine all the activities of the local groups and make it possible to organise the revolutionary work on correct lines. The predominance of isolated work is naturally connected with the predominance of the economic struggle.

These circumstances resulted in concentration on one side of the movement only. The "economist" trend (that is, if we can speak of it as a "trend") has attempted to elevate this narrowness to the rank of a special theory and has tried to utilise for this purpose the fashionable Bernsteinism and the fashionable "criticism of Marxism," which peddles old bourgeois ideas under a new label. These attempts alone have given rise to the danger of a weakening of connection between the Russian working-class movement and Russian Social-Democracy, the vanguard in the struggle for political liberty. The most urgent task of our movement is to strengthen this connection.

Social-Democracy is the combination of the working-class movement and socialism. Its task is not to serve the working-class movement passively at each of its separate stages, but to represent the interests of the movement as a whole, to point out to this movement its ultimate aim and its political tasks, and to safeguard its political and ideological independence. Isolated from Social-Democracy, the working-class movement becomes petty and inevitably becomes bourgeois. In waging only the economic struggle, the working class loses its political independence; it becomes the tail of other parties and betrays the great principle: "The emancipation of the working classes must be conquered by, the working classes themselves."[137] In every country there has been a period in which the working-class movement existed apart from socialism, each going its own way; and in every country this isolation has weakened both socialism and the working-class movement. Only the fusion of socialism with the working-class movement has in all countries created a durable basis for both. But in every country this combination of socialism and the working-class movement was evolved historically, in unique ways, in accordance with the prevailing conditions of time and place. In Russia, the necessity for combining socialism and the working-class movement was in theory long ago proclaimed, but it is only now being carried into practice. It is a very difficult process and there is, therefore, nothing surprising in the fact that it is accompanied by vacillations and doubts.

What lesson can be learned from the past?

The entire history of Russian socialism has led to the condition in which the most urgent task is the struggle against the autocratic government and the achievement of political liberty. Our socialist movement concentrated itself, so to speak, upon the struggle against the autocracy. On the other hand, history has shown that the isolation of socialist thought from the vanguard of the working classes is greater in Russia than in other countries, and that if this state of affairs continues, the revolutionary movement in Russia is doomed to impotence. From this condition emerges the task which the Russian Social-Democracy is

called upon to fulfil—to imbue the masses of the proletariat with the ideas of socialism and political consciousness,
and to organise a revolutionary party inseparably connected
with the spontaneous working-class movement. Russian
Social-Democracy has done much in this direction, but much
more still remains to be done. With the growth of the movement, the field of activity for Social-Democrats becomes
wider; the work becomes more varied, and an increasing number of activists in the movement will concentrate their efforts
upon the fulfilment of various special tasks which the
daily needs of propaganda and agitation bring to the fore.
This phenomenon is quite natural and is inevitable, but
it causes us to be particularly concerned with preventing
these special activities and methods of struggle from becoming ends in themselves and with preventing preparatory work from being regarded as the main and sole
activity.

Our principal and fundamental task is to facilitate the
political development and the political organisation of
the working class. Those who push this task into the background, who refuse to subordinate to it all the special
tasks and particular methods of struggle, are following
a false path and causing serious harm to the movement.
And it is being pushed into the background, firstly, by
those who call upon revolutionaries to employ only the
forces of isolated conspiratorial circles cut off from the working-class movement in the struggle against the government.
It is being pushed into the background, secondly, by those
who restrict the content and scope of political propaganda,
agitation, and organisation; who think it fit and proper
to treat the workers to "politics" only at exceptional moments in their lives, only on festive occasions; who too
solicitously substitute demands for partial concessions
from the autocracy for the political struggle against the
autocracy; and who do not go to sufficient lengths to ensure
that these demands for partial concessions are raised to
the status of a systematic, implacable struggle of a revolutionary, working-class party against the autocracy.

"Organise!" *Rabochaya Mysl* keeps repeating to the workers in all keys, and all the adherents of the "economist"
trend echo the cry. We, of course, wholly endorse this

appeal, but we will not fail to add: organise, but not only in mutual benefit societies, strike funds, and workers' circles; organise also in a political party; organise for the determined struggle against the autocratic government and against the whole of capitalist society. Without such organisation the proletariat will never rise to the class-conscious struggle; without such organisation the working-class movement is doomed to impotency. With the aid of nothing but funds and study circles and mutual benefit societies the working class will never be able to fulfil its great historical mission—to emancipate itself and the whole of the Russian people from political and economic slavery. Not a single class in history has achieved power without producing its political leaders, its prominent representatives able to organise a movement and lead it. And the Russian working class has already shown that it can produce such men and women. The struggle which has developed so widely during the past five or six years has revealed the great potential revolutionary power of the working class; it has shown that the most ruthless government persecution does not diminish, but, on the contrary, increases the number of workers who strive towards socialism, towards political consciousness, and towards the political struggle. The congress which our comrades held in 1898 correctly defined our tasks and did not merely repeat other people's words, did not merely express the enthusiasm of "intellectuals.".... We must set to work resolutely to fulfil these tasks, placing the question of the Party's programme, organisation, and tactics on the order of the day. We have already set forth our views on the fundamental postulates of our programme, and, of course, this is not the place to develop them in detail. We propose to devote a series of articles in forthcoming issues to questions of organisation, which are among the most burning problems confronting us. In this respect we lag considerably behind the old workers in the Russian revolutionary movement. We must frankly admit this defect and exert all our efforts to devise methods of greater secrecy in our work, to propagate systematically the proper methods of work, the proper methods of deluding the gendarmes and of evading the snares of the police. We must train people who will devote the whole of their lives, not only their spare evenings, to the revolution; we must build up an organisation large enough to permit the introduction of a strict division of labour in the various forms of our work. Finally, with regard to questions of tactics, we shall confine ourselves to the following: Social-Democracy does not tie its hands, it does not restrict its activities to some one preconceived plan or method of political struggle; it recognises all methods of struggle, provided they correspond to the forces at the disposal of the Party and facilitate the achievement of the best results possible under the given conditions. If we have a strongly organised party, a single strike may turn into a political demonstration, into a political victory over the government. If we have a strongly organised party, a revolt in a single locality may grow into a victorious revolution. We must bear in mind that the struggles with the government for partial demands and the gain of certain concessions are merely light skirmishes with the enemy, encounters between outposts, whereas the decisive battle is still to come. Before us, in all its strength, towers the enemy fortress which is raining shot and shell upon us, mowing down our best fighters. We must capture this fortress, and we will capture it, if we unite all the forces of the awakening proletariat with all the forces of the Russian revolutionaries into one party which will attract all that is vital and honest in Russia. Only then will the great prophecy of the Russian worker-revolutionary, Pyotr Alexeyev, be fulfilled: "The muscular arm of the working millions will be lifted, and the yoke of despotism, guarded by the soldiers' bayonets, will be smashed to atoms!"[138]

Written in early November 1900
Published in December 1900
in *Iskra*, No. 1

Published according to
the *Iskra* text

THE WAR IN CHINA

Russia is bringing her war with China to a close: a number of military districts have been mobilised, hundreds of millions of rubles have been spent, tens of thousands of troops have been dispatched to China, a number of battles have been fought and a number of victories won—true, not so much over regular enemy troops, as over Chinese insurgents and, particularly, over the unarmed Chinese populace, who were drowned or killed, with no holding back from the slaughter of women and children, not to speak of the looting of palaces, homes, and shops. The Russian Government, together with the press that kowtows to it, is celebrating a victory and rejoicing over the fresh exploits of the gallant soldiery, rejoicing at the victory of European culture over Chinese barbarism and over the fresh successes of Russia's "civilising mission" in the Far East.

But the voices of the class-conscious workers, of the advanced representatives of the many millions of the working people, are not heard amid this rejoicing. And yet, it is the working people who bear the brunt of the victorious new campaigns, it is working people who are sent to the other end of the world, from whom increased taxes are extorted to cover the millions expended. Let us, therefore, see: What attitude should the socialists adopt towards this war? In whose interests is it being fought? What is the real nature of the policy now being pursued by the Russian Government?

Our government asserts first of all that it is not waging war against China; that it is merely suppressing a rebellion, pacifying rebels; that it is helping the lawful government of China to re-establish law and order. True, war has not been declared, but this does not change the situation a bit, because war is being waged nonetheless. What made the Chinese attack Europeans, what caused the rebellion which the British, French, Germans, Russians, Japanese, etc., are so zealously crushing? "The hostility of the yellow race towards the white race," "the Chinese hatred for European culture and civilisation"— answer the supporters of the war. Yes! It is true the Chinese hate the Europeans, but which Europeans do they hate, and why? The Chinese do not hate the European peoples, they have never had any quarrel with them—they hate the European capitalists and the European governments obedient to them. How can the Chinese not hate those who have come to China solely for the sake of gain; who have utilised their vaunted civilisation solely for the purpose of deception, plunder, and violence; who have waged wars against China in order to win the right to trade in opium with which to drug the people (the war of England and France with China in 1856); and who hypocritically carried their policy of plunder under the guise of spreading Christianity? The bourgeois governments of Europe have long been conducting this policy of plunder with respect to China, and now they have been joined by the autocratic Russian Government. This policy of plunder is usually called a colonial policy. Every country in which capitalist industry develops rapidly has very soon to seek colonies, i.e., countries in which industry is weakly developed, in which a more or less patriarchal way of life still prevails, and which can serve as a market for manufactured goods and a source of high profits. For the sake of the profit of a handful of capitalists, the bourgeois governments have waged endless wars, have sent regiments to die in unhealthy tropical countries, have squandered millions of money extracted from the people, and have driven the peoples in the colonies to desperate revolts or to death from starvation. We need only recall the rebellion of the native peoples against the British in India[139] and the famine that prevailed there, or think of the war the English are now waging against the Boers.

And now the European capitalists have placed their rapacious paws upon China, and almost the first to do so was the Russian Government, which now so loudly proclaims its "disinterestedness." It "disinterestedly" took Port Arthur away from China and began to build a railway to Manchuria under the protection of Russian troops. One after another the European governments began feverishly to loot, or, as they put it, to "rent," Chinese territory, giving good grounds for the talk of the partition of China. If we are to call things by their right names, we must say that the European governments (the Russian Government among the very first) have already started to partition China. However, they have not begun this partitioning openly, but stealthily, like thieves. They began to rob China as ghouls rob corpses, and when the seeming corpse attempted to resist, they flung themselves upon it like savage beasts, burning down whole villages, shooting, bayonetting, and drowning in the Amur River unarmed inhabitants, their wives, and their children. And all these Christian exploits are accompanied by howls against the Chinese barbarians who dared to raise their hands against the civilised Europeans. The occupation of Niuchuang and the moving of Russian troops into Manchuria are temporary measures, declares the autocratic Russian Government in its circular note of August 12, 1900 addressed to the Powers; these measures "are called forth exclusively by the necessity to repel the aggressive operations of Chinese rebels"; they "cannot in the least be regarded as evidence of any selfish plans, which are totally alien to the policy of the Imperial Government."

Poor Imperial Government! So Christianly unselfish, and yet so unjustly maligned! Several years ago it unselfishly seized Port Arthur, and now it is unselfishly seizing Manchuria; it has unselfishly flooded the frontier provinces of China with hordes of contractors, engineers, and officers, who, by their conduct, have roused to indignation even the Chinese, known for their docility. The Chinese workers employed in the construction of the Chinese railway had to exist on a wage of ten kopeks a day—is this not unselfish on Russia's part?

How is our government's senseless policy in China to be explained? Who benefits by it? The benefit goes to a handful of capitalist magnates who carry on trade with China, to a handful of factory owners who manufacture goods for the Asian market, to a handful of contractors who are now piling up huge profits on urgent war orders (factories producing war equipment, supplies for the troops, etc., are now operating at full capacity and are engaging hundreds of new workers). This policy is of benefit to a handful of nobles who occupy high posts in the civil and military services. They need adventurous policies, for these provide them with opportunities for promotion, for making a career and gaining fame by their "exploits." In the interests of this handful of capitalists and bureaucratic scoundrels, our government unhesitatingly sacrifices the interests of the entire people. And in this case, as always, the autocratic tsarist government has proved itself to be a government of irresponsible bureaucrats servilely cringing before the capitalist magnates and nobles.

What benefits do the Russian working class and the labouring people generally obtain from the conquests in China? Thousands of ruined families, whose breadwinners have been sent to the war; an enormous increase in the national debt and the national expenditure; mounting taxation; greater power for the capitalists, the exploiters of the workers; worse conditions for the workers; still greater mortality among the peasantry; famine in Siberia—this is what the Chinese war promises and is already bringing. The entire Russian press, all the newspapers and periodicals are kept in a state of bondage; they dare not print anything without permission of the government officials. This is the reason for the lack of precise information as to what the Chinese war is costing the people; but there is no doubt that it requires the expenditure of *many hundreds of millions of rubles*. It has come to our knowledge that the government, by an unpublished decree, handed out the tidy sum of a hundred and fifty million rubles for the purpose of waging the war. In addition to this, current expenditures on the war absorb *one million rubles* every three or four days, and these terrific sums are

being squandered by a government which, haggling over
every kopek, has steadily cut down grants to the famine-
stricken peasantry; which can find no money for the people's
education; which, like any kulak, sweats the workers in
the government factories, sweats the lower employees in
the post offices, etc.!

Minister of Finance Witte declared that on January 1, 1900, there were two hundred and fifty million
rubles available in the treasury. Now this money is gone,
it has been spent on the war. The government is seeking
loans, is increasing taxation, is refusing necessary expenditures because of the lack of money, and is putting a stop to
the building of railways. The tsarist government is threatened with bankruptcy, and yet it is plunging into a policy
of conquest—a policy which not only demands the expenditure of enormous sums of money, but threatens to plunge
us into still more dangerous wars. The European states
that have flung themselves upon China are already beginning to quarrel over the division of the booty, and no one
can say how this quarrel will end.

But the policy of the tsarist government in China is
not only a mockery of the interests of the people—its
aim is to corrupt the political consciousness of the masses.
Governments that maintain themselves in power only
by means of the bayonet, that have constantly to restrain or suppress the indignation of the people, have
long realised the truism that popular discontent can
never be removed and that it is necessary to divert the
discontent from the government to some other object.
For example, hostility is being stirred up against the Jews;
the gutter press carries on Jew-baiting campaigns, as if the
Jewish workers do not suffer in exactly the same way as
the Russian workers from the oppression of capital and the
police government. At the present time, the press is conducting a campaign against the Chinese; it is howling about
the savage yellow race and its hostility towards civilisation, about Russia's tasks of enlightenment, about the enthusiasm with which the Russian soldiers go into battle,
etc., etc. Journalists who crawl on their bellies before the
government and the money-bags are straining every nerve
to rouse the hatred of the people against China. But the

Chinese people have at no time and in no way oppressed the Russian people. The Chinese people suffer from the same evils as those from which the Russian people suffer—they suffer from an Asiatic government that squeezes taxes from the starving peasantry and that suppresses every aspiration towards liberty by military force; they suffer from the oppression of capital, which has penetrated into the Middle Kingdom.

The Russian working class is beginning to move out of the state of political oppression and ignorance in which the masses of the people are still submerged. Hence, the duty of all class-conscious workers is to rise with all their might against those who are stirring up national hatred and diverting the attention of the working people from their real enemies. The policy of the tsarist government in China is a criminal policy which is impoverishing, corrupting, and oppressing the people more than ever. The tsarist government not only keeps our people in slavery but sends them to pacify other peoples who rebel against their slavery (as was the case in 1849 when Russian troops suppressed the revolution in Hungary). It not only helps the Russian capitalists to exploit the Russian workers, whose hands it ties to hold them back from combining and defending themselves, but it also sends soldiers to plunder other peoples in the interests of a handful of rich men and nobles. There is only one way in which the new burden the war is thrusting upon the working people can be removed, and that is the convening of an assembly of representatives of the people, which would put an end to the autocracy of the government and compel it to have regard for interests other than those solely of a gang of courtiers.

Iskra, No. 1, December 1900

Published according to
the *Iskra* text

THE SPLIT IN THE UNION OF RUSSIAN SOCIAL-DEMOCRATS ABROAD

In the spring of this year, there took place in Switzerland a conference of the members of the Union of Russian Social-Democrats Abroad which resulted in a split. The minority, led by the Emancipation of Labour Group, which had founded the Union Abroad and which until the autumn of 1898 had edited the Union publications, formed a separate organisation under the name of the Russian Revolutionary Organisation *Sotsial-Demokrat*. The majority, including the Editorial Board of *Rabocheye Dyelo*, continues to call itself the Union. The congress of Russian Social-Democrats in the spring of 1898, which formed the Russian Social-Democratic Labour Party, recognised the Union as the representative of our Party abroad. How must we regard the question of representation now that the Union has split? We shall not go into detail concerning the causes of the split; we shall observe merely that the widespread and serious accusation that Plekhanov has seized the Union's printing-press is not true. In reality, the manager of the printing-press had refused to turn it over entirely to only one part of the split Union, and the two parties soon divided the printing establishment between them. The most important thing, from our point of view, is the fact that *Rabocheye Dyelo* was in the wrong in this controversy; it erroneously denied the existence of an "economist" trend; it advocated the wrong tactics of ignoring the extremism of this trend and of refraining from combating it openly.

For this reason, while not denying the service which *Rabocheye Dyelo* has rendered in publishing literature and organising its distribution, we refuse to recognise either section of the split organisation as the representative of our Party abroad. This question must remain open until our next Party congress. The official representatives of Russian Social-Democracy abroad at the present time are the Russian members of the permanent international Committee set up in Paris by the International Socialist Congress in the autumn of this year.[140] Russia has two representatives on this Committee: G. V. Plekhanov and B. Krichevsky (one of the editors of *Rabocheye Dyelo*). Until the two groups of Russian Social-Democracy become reconciled or come to an agreement, we intend to conduct all our business pertaining to the representation of Russia with G. V. Plekhanov. Finally, we must express our opinion on the question of whom we desire to see as the Russian secretary of the permanent international Committee. At the present time, when under the cloak of the "criticism of Marxism," attempts are being made to corrupt Social-Democracy by bourgeois ideology and by a meek and mild policy towards an enemy armed to the teeth (the bourgeois governments), it is especially necessary to have at this responsible post a man able to stand against the tide and to speak with influence against ideological wavering. For this reason, as well as for those stated above, we cast our vote for G. V. Plekhanov.

Written not later
than December 8, 1900
Published in December 1900
in *Iskra*, No. 1

Published according to
the *Iskra* text

NOTE OF DECEMBER 29, 1900

29. XII. 1900. Sunday, 2 a. m.

I should like to set down my impressions of today's talks with the "twin." It was a remarkable meeting, "historic" in a way (Arsenyev, Velika, the twin+wife[141]+myself)—at least it was historic as far as my life is concerned; it summed up, if not a whole epoch, at least a page in a life history, and it determined my conduct and my life's path for a long time to come.

As the case was first stated by Arsenyev, I understood that the twin was coming over to us and wished to take the first steps, but the very opposite turned out to be the case. In all probability this strange error originated from the fact that Arsenyev keenly desired what the twin was "tempting" us with, viz., political material, correspondence, etc. "The wish is father to the thought," and Arsenyev believed in the possibility of what the twin was tempting him with; he wished to believe in the sincerity of the twin and in the possibility of a decent *modus vivendi* with him.

This very meeting utterly and irrevocably destroyed such a belief. The twin revealed himself in a totally new light, as a "politician" of the purest water, a politician in the worst sense of the word, an old fox, and a brazen huckster. He arrived *completely convinced of our impotence*, as Arsenyev himself described the results of our negotiations, and this formulation was entirely correct. Convinced of our impotence, the twin arrived for the purpose of laying down conditions of *surrender*, which he did in an exceedingly clever manner, without uttering a single impolite word,

yet without being able to conceal the coarse haggling nature of the common liberal that lay hidden beneath the
dapper, cultured exterior of this latest "critic."

In reply to my question (with which the business part
of the evening began) as to why he did not agree to work
simply as a contributor, the twin stated firmly that it was
psychologically impossible for him to work for a magazine
in which he would be "taken to task" (his precise words),
and that surely we did not think that we could abuse him
and he would "write political articles" (his very words!)
for us; that he could co-operate only on terms of complete
equality (i.e., evidently, equality between the critics and
the orthodox); that since the Declaration,* his comrade and
friend[142] has refused even to meet Arsenyev; that his,
the twin's, attitude was determined not so much by the
Declaration, in fact not at all by the Declaration, as
by the fact that at first he had desired to confine himself to the role of "benevolent helpmate," but that now he
did not intend so to limit himself but wanted also to be
an editor (he said it almost in these words!!). The twin
did not blurt this out all in one breath, the negotiations
concerning his collaboration dragged on for quite a long
time (too long in the opinion of Arsenyev and Velika),
but the negotiations made it quite clear to me that no
business could be done with this gentleman.

He then began to insist on his proposal: Why not establish a third political periodical on an equal basis with
the others? This would be to our and his advantage (the
newspaper would get material, we would "make" something out of the resources provided for it). He proposed
that on the cover we should have nothing Social-Democratic, nothing to indicate our firm, and that we were obliged (not formally but morally) to contribute to this organ
all our material of a general political nature.

Everything became clear, and I said openly that the publication of a third periodical was out of the question,
and that the whole matter reduced itself to the question
as to whether Social-Democracy must carry on the political
struggle or whether the liberals should carry it on as an

---

* See p. 351 of the present volume.—*Ed.*

independent and self-contained movement (I expressed myself more clearly and definitely, more precisely). The twin understood and angrily retorted that after I had expressed myself with *anerkennenswerter Klarheit** (literally!) there was nothing more to be said and all that we might discuss was the placing of orders—orders for the collections, but that would be a sort of third magazine (I put in). "Well, then place an order for just the one *available* pamphlet," replied the twin. "Which one?" I asked. "Why do you want to know?" retorted the wife insolently. "If you agree in principle, we shall decide, but if not, why do you want to know?" I inquired about the conditions of the printing. "Published by X, and nothing more; there must be no mention of your firm, nothing except the *Verlag*.** There must be no connection with your firm"—declared the twin. I argued also against that, demanding that mention be made of our firm. Arsenyev began to argue against me, and the conversation was cut off.

Finally, we decided to postpone the decision. Arsenyev and Velika had another heated discussion with the twin, demanded an explanation *from him*, argued with him. I remained silent for the most part and laughed (so that the twin could see it quite clearly) and the conversation soon came to an end.

First published in 1924
in *Lenin Miscellany I*

Published according to
the manuscript

---

* Commendable clarity.—*Ed*.
** Publishers.—*Ed*.

CASUAL NOTES

Written in January 1901

Published in April 1901
in the magazine *Zarya*, No. 1
Signed: *T. K.*

Published according to
the text in the magazine

№ 1

Апрѣль
1901-го г.

Die
Morgenrothe
Heft 1
April 1901

ЗАРЯ

Соціаль-демократическій
паучно-политическій журналъ.
Издается при ближайшемъ
участіи Г. В. Плеханова, В. И.
Засуличъ и П. Б. Аксельрода.

Цѣна 2 руб.

Stuttgart
J. H. W. Dietz Nachf. (G. m. b. H.)
1901

Facsimile of the cover of the first issue
of the magazine *Zarya.*
April 1901

I. BEAT—BUT NOT TO DEATH!

On January 23, in Nizhni-Novgorod, the Moscow High Court of Justice, in a special session, *with the participation of representatives of the social-estates*, tried the case of the murder of the peasant Timofei Vasilyevich Vozdukhov, who had been taken to the police-station "to sober up" and there beaten up by four policemen, Shelemetyev, Shulpin, Shibayev, and Olkhovin, and by acting Station Sergeant Panov, so that he died in the hospital the next day.

Such is the simple tale of this case, which throws a glaring light upon what usually and always goes on in our police-stations.

As far as can be gathered from the extremely brief newspaper reports, what appears to have happened is the following. On April 20, Vozdukhov drove up to the Governor's house in a cab. The superintendent of the Governor's house came out to him; in giving evidence at the trial the superintendent stated that Vozdukhov, hatless, had been drinking but was not drunk, and that he, Vozdukhov, complained to him about a certain steamboat booking office having refused to sell him a ticket (?). The superintendent ordered Shelemetyev, the policeman on duty, to take him to the police-station. Vozdukhov was sufficiently sober to be able to speak quietly with Shelemetyev and on arriving at the police-station quite distinctly told Sergeant Panov his name and occupation. Notwithstanding all this, Shelemetyev, no doubt with the knowledge of Panov, who had just questioned Vozdukhov, *"pushed"* the latter, not into the common cell, in which there were a number of other drunkards, but into the adjoining "*soldiers' lock-up.*" As he pushed him, his sword got caught on the latch of the door and it cut his hand slightly; imagining that Vozdukhov was holding the sword, he rushed at him to strike him, shouting that his hand had been cut. He struck Vozdukhov with all his might in the face, in the chest, in the side; he struck him so hard that Vozdukhov fell, striking his forehead on the door and begging for mercy. "Why are you beating me?" he implored, according to the statement of a witness, Semakhin, who was in the neighbouring cell at the time. "It was not my fault. Forgive me, for Christ's sake!" According to the evidence of this witness, it was not Vozdukhov who was drunk, but sooner Shelemetyev. Shelemetyev's colleagues, Shulpin and Shibayev, who had been continuously drinking in the police-station since the first day of Easter week (April 20 was Tuesday, the third day of Easter week), learned that Shelemetyev was "teaching" (the expression used in the indictment!) Vozdukhov a lesson. They went into the soldiers' lock-up accompanied by Olkhovin, who was on a visit from another station, and attacked Vozdukhov with their fists and feet. Police Sergeant Panov came on the scene and struck Vozdukhov on the head with a book, and then with his fists. "Oh! they beat and beat him so hard that my belly ached for pity," said a woman witness, who was under arrest there at the time. When the "lesson" was over, the sergeant very coolly ordered Shibayev to wipe the blood from the victim's face—it would not look so bad then; the chief might see it—and then to fling him into the common cell. "Brothers!" cried Vozdukhov to the other detainees, "see how the police have beaten me. Be my witnesses, I'll lodge a complaint." But he never lived to lodge the complaint. The following morning, he was found in a state of unconsciousness and sent to the hospital where he died within eight hours without coming to himself again. A post-mortem revealed ten broken ribs, bruises all over his body, and haemorrhage of the brain.

The court sentenced Shelemetyev, Shulpin, and Shibayev to four years' penal servitude, and Olkhovin and Panov *to one month's detention*, finding them guilty only of "insulting behaviour."...

With this sentence we shall commence our examination of the case. Those sentenced to penal servitude were charged according to Articles 346 and 1490, Part II, of the Penal Code. The first of these articles provides that an official inflicting wounds or injuries in the exercise of his duties is liable to the maximum penalty reserved "for the perpetration of such a crime." Article 1490, Part II, provides for a penalty of from eight to ten years' penal servitude for inflicting torture resulting in death. Instead of inflicting the *maximum penalty*, the court, consisting of representatives of the social-estates and crown judges, *reduced* the sentence *by two degrees* (sixth degree, eight to ten years of penal servitude; seventh degree, four to six years, i.e., it made the maximum reduction of sentence permitted by the law in cases of extenuating circumstances, and, moreover, imposed the *minimum* penalty of that low degree. In a word, the court did all it could to let the culprits off as lightly as possible; in fact, it did more than it could, because it evaded the law concerning the "maximum penalty." Of course, we do not wish to assert that "supreme justice" demanded precisely ten and not four years' penal servitude; the essential point is that the murderers were declared to be murderers and that they were sentenced to penal servitude. But we cannot refrain from noting a tendency characteristic of the court of crown judges and representatives of the estates; when they try a police official, they are ready to display the greatest clemency, but when they sit in judgement over an act committed against the police, as is well known, they display inexorable severity.*

---

* In passing, we shall adduce another fact indicating the punishments imposed by our courts for various crimes. A few days after the Vozdukhov murder trial, the Moscow District Military Tribunal tried a private in the local artillery brigade for stealing fifty pairs of trousers and a few pairs of boots, while on guard duty in the storeroom. The sentence was four years' *penal servitude*. A human life entrusted to the police is equal in value to fifty pairs of trousers and a few pairs of boots entrusted to a sentry. In this peculiar "equation" the whole of our police state system is reflected as the sun is reflected in a drop of water. The individual against state power is nothing. Discipline within the state power is everything ... pardon me, "everything" only for the small fry. A petty thief is sentenced to penal servitude, but the big thieves, the magnates, cabinet ministers, bank directors, build-

With a police sergeant before it, how could the court refuse him clemency? He had met Vozdukhov as he was brought in and apparently had ordered him to be placed, not in a common cell, but first, in order to teach him a lesson, in the soldiers' lock-up. He took part in the assault, using his fists and a book (no doubt a copy of the Penal Laws); he gave orders to have all traces of the crime removed (to wipe away the blood). On the night of April 20 he reported to the inspector, Mukhanov, upon his return, "everything in order at the station in his charge" (his exact words!)—but he had nothing to do with the murderers, he was only guilty of an insulting act, just insulting behaviour, punishable by detention. Quite naturally, this gentleman, Mr. Panov, innocent of murder, is still in the police service occupying the post of a village police sergeant. Mr. Panov has merely transferred his useful directing activities in "teaching lessons" to the common people from the town to the country. Now, reader, tell us in all conscience, can Sergeant Panov understand the sentence of the court to mean anything else than advice in the future to remove the traces of a crime more thoroughly, to "teach" in such a manner as to leave no trace? You did right in ordering the blood to be wiped from the face of the dying man, but you allowed him to die. That, pal, was careless. In the future be more careful and never forget the first and last commandment of the Russian Derzhimorda[143]: "Beat—but not to death!"

From the ordinary human point of view, the sentence Panov drew was a mockery of justice. It reveals a cringing, servile spirit, an attempt to throw the whole blame upon the minor police officers and to shield their immediate chief with whose knowledge, approval, and participation this brutal crime was committed. From the juridical point of view, the sentence is an example of the casuistry resorted to by bureaucratic judges who are themselves not far re-

---

ers of railways, engineers, contractors, etc., who plunder the Treasury of property valued at tens and hundreds of thousands of rubles are punished only on very rare occasions, and at the worst are banished to remote provinces where they may live at ease on their loot (the bank thieves in Western Siberia), and from where it is easy to escape across the frontier (Colonel of Gendarmes Méranville de Saint-Clair).

moved from police sergeants. Speech was given to man to conceal his thoughts, say the diplomats. Our jurists may say that the law is given to distort the concepts of guilt and responsibility. Indeed, what refined juridical art is required to be able to reduce complicity in torture to simple insulting behaviour! Panov was guilty of an offence equal in gravity to that perhaps committed by a factory hand who possibly on the morning of April 20 mischievously struck Vozdukhov's cap off his head! In fact, milder than that: it was not an offence but merely an "infringement." Even participation in a brawl (let alone the brutal assault upon a helpless man), if it results in a fatality, is liable to a severer punishment than that meted out to the police sergeant. Legal chicanery took advantage of the fact that the law provides for various degrees of punishment for inflicting injuries in the exercise of official duties and allows the court the discretion to pronounce sentences ranging from two months' imprisonment to permanent banishment to Siberia, according to the circumstances of the case. Of course, it is quite a rational rule not to bind a judge to strictly formal definitions, but to allow him certain latitude. Our professors of criminal law have often praised Russian legislation for this and have emphasised its liberal character. However, in praising our law, they lose sight of one trifle, namely, that, for rational laws to be applied, it is necessary to have judges who are not reduced to the role of mere officials, that it is necessary to have representatives of the public in the court, and for public opinion to play its part in the examination of cases. Secondly, the assistant public prosecutor came to the aid of the court by *withdrawing* the charge against Panov (and Olkhovin) of torture and cruelty and pleading only for a sentence for insulting behaviour. In his plea, the assistant prosecutor called expert evidence to prove that the blows inflicted by Panov were neither numerous nor painful. As you see, the juridical sophistry is not very ingenious: since Panov did less beating than the others, it *may* be argued that his punches were not *very* painful, and since they were not very painful, it *may* be argued that his offence was not "torture and cruelty"; and since it was not torture and cruelty, then it was merely insulting behaviour. All this works out to

everybody's satisfaction, and Mr. Panov remains in the
ranks of the guardians of law and order....*

We have just referred to the participation of representatives of the public in court trials, and to the part that
should be played by public opinion. The case in point is
an excellent illustration. In the first place, why was this
case tried, not by a jury, but by a court of crown judges
and representatives of the estates? Because the government of Alexander III, having declared ruthless war upon
every public aspiration towards liberty and independence,
very soon found that trial by jury was dangerous. The
reactionary press declared trial by jury to be "trial by the
street," and launched against it a campaign which, be it
said in passing, continues to this day. The government
adopted a reactionary programme. Having crushed the revolutionary movement of the seventies, it insolently declared
to the representatives of the people that it regarded them
as the "street," the mob, which must not interfere in the

---

* In Russia, instead of exposing the outrage in all its horror
before the court and the public, they prefer to hush up the case in
court and do nothing more than send out circular letters and orders
full of pompous but meaningless phrases. For instance, a few days ago
the Orel Chief of Police issued an order which, confirming previous
orders, instructs the local police inspectors to impress upon subordinates, personally and through their assistants, that they must refrain
from roughness and violence in handling drunkards in the streets and
when taking them to the police-station to sober up. The order further
specifies that police officers must explain to their subordinates that it
is the duty of the police to protect drunkards who cannot be left alone
without obvious danger to themselves; that subordinate police officers,
whom the law has placed in the position of first protectors and guardians of citizens, must, therefore, in taking drunkards into custody, not
only refrain from treating them roughly and inhumanly, but must do
all they can to protect them until they have become sober. The order
warns subordinate police officials that only by such conscientious
and lawful exercise of their duties will they earn the confidence and
respect of the population, and that if, on the contrary, police officials
treat drunkards harshly and cruelly, or resort to violent conduct incompatible with the duty of a police officer, who should serve as a
model of respectability and good morals, they will be punished with
all the vigour of the law and any subordinate police officer guilty
of such conduct will be rigorously prosecuted. A capital idea for a
cartoon in a satirical journal—a police sergeant, acquitted of the charge
of murder, reading an order that he must serve as a model of respectability and good morals!

work of legislation, let alone interfere in the administration of the state, and which must be driven from the sanctuary where Russian citizens are tried and punished according to the Panov method. In 1887 a law was passed removing crimes committed by and against officials from the jurisdiction of courts sitting with a jury and transferring them to courts of crown judges and representatives of the estates. It is well known that these representatives of the estates, merged into a single collegium with the bureaucratic judges, are mute super-numeraries playing the miserable role of witnesses ready to say yes to everything the officials of the Department of Justice decide. This is one of a long series of laws adopted during the latest reactionary period of Russian history and having one single tendency in common: to re-establish a "sound authority." Under the pressure of circumstances, the government in the latter half of the nineteenth century was compelled to come into contact with the "street"; but the character of the street changed with astonishing rapidity and the ignorant inhabitants gave place to citizens who were beginning to understand their rights and who were capable even of producing the champions of their rights. Realising this, the government drew back in horror, and is now making convulsive efforts to surround itself by a Chinese Wall, to immure itself in a fortress into which no manifestations of independent public action can penetrate.... But I have strayed somewhat from my subject.

Thanks to the reactionary law, the street was deprived of the right to try representatives of the government. Officials have been tried by officials. This has affected, not only the sentence passed by the court, but also the character of the preliminary investigation and the trial. Trial by the street is valuable because it breathes a living spirit into the bureaucratic formalism which pervades our government institutions. The street is interested, not only, and not so much, in the definition of the given offence (insulting behaviour, assault, torture), or in the category of punishment to be imposed; it is interested in exposing thoroughly and bringing to public light the significance and all the social and political threads of the crime, in order to draw lessons in public morals and practical

politics from the trial. The street does not want to see
in the court "an official institution," in which functionaries apply to given cases the corresponding articles of
the Penal Code, but a public institution which exposes the
ulcers of the present system, which provides material for
criticising it and, consequently, for improving it. Im-
pelled by its practical knowledge of public affairs and by
the growth of political consciousness, the street is discovering the truth for which our official, professorial juris-
prudence, weighed down by its scholastic shackles, is grop-
ing with such difficulty and timidity—namely, that in
the fight against crime the reform of social and political
institutions is much more important than the imposition
of punishment. For this reason the reactionary publicists
and the reactionary government hate, and cannot help hat-
ing, trial by the street. For this reason the curtailments
put on the competency of jury courts and the restrictions
on publicity run like a scarlet thread throughout the whole
of the post-Reform history of Russia; indeed, the reactionary character of the "post-Reform" epoch was exposed
immediately after the law of 1864, reforming our "judica-
ture," came into force.* The absence of "trial by the
street" was markedly felt in this particular case. Who
in the court that tried this case could have been interested
in its social aspect, and who would have sought to
bring it out prominently? The public prosecutor? The
official who is closely connected with the police, who
shares responsibility for the detention of prisoners and
the manner in which they are treated, who, in certain
cases, is actually the chief of police? We have seen that
the assistant prosecutor even withdrew the charge of torture against Panov. The civil plaintiff—in the event that
Vozdukhova, the widow of the murdered man and a witness

---

* In their polemics in the legal press against the reactionaries,
the liberal advocates of trial by jury often categorically deny its political significance and endeavour to show that they favour participation
of public representatives in the courts for reasons other than political.
This may partly be explained by the lack of ability on the part of
our jurists to think politically to a logical conclusion, notwithstanding
their specialisation in "political" science. But, chiefly, it is to be explained by the necessity to speak in Aesopean language, by the impossibility openly to declare their sympathies for a constitution.

at the trial, had put in a civil claim against the murderers? But how was this simple woman to know that it was permissible to bring a civil claim for damages before a criminal court? But even had she known it, would she have been able to retain a lawyer? And even had she been able to do so, could a lawyer have been found who was willing to call public attention to the state of affairs brought to light by this murder? And even if such a lawyer had been found, would his "civic zeal" have been supported by such "delegates" of the public as the representatives of the social-estates? Picture to yourself a rural district elder— I have in mind a provincial court—embarrassed in his rustic clothes, not knowing what to do with his rough, peasant hands, awkwardly trying to conceal his feet encased in greased top-boots, gazing with awe upon His Excellency, the president of the court, who is seated on the same bench with him. Or imagine a city mayor, a fat merchant, breathing heavily in his unaccustomed livery, with his chain of office round his neck, trying to ape his neighbour, a Marshal of the Nobility, a gentleman in a nobleman's uniform, who looks sleek and well tended, with aristocratic manners. By his side are judges, men who have gone through the hard grind of the school of bureaucracy, genuine functionaries who have grown grey in the service and are filled with a consciousness of the importance of the duty they have to fulfil—to try representatives of the authorities whom the street is not worthy to try. Would not this scene dampen the ardour of the most eloquent lawyer? Would it not remind him of the ancient aphorism: "neither cast ye your pearls before..."?

And so it happened that the case was rushed through at express speed, as if all concerned were eager to get it off their hands as quickly as possible,* as if they feared to rake too thoroughly in the muck; one may get accustomed to living near a cesspool and not notice the foul odours emanating from it, but as soon as an attempt is made to cleanse it,

---

* No one, however, thought of bringing the case to trial quickly. Despite the fact that the case was remarkably clear and simple, it was not tried until January 23, 1901, although the crime had been committed on April 20, 1899. A *speedy*, just, and merciful trial!

the stench assails the nostrils, not only of the inhabitants of the particular street, but also of those of the neighbouring streets.

Just think of the number of questions that naturally arise and that no one has taken the trouble to clear up! Why did Vozdukhov go to the Governor? The indictment—the document which embodied the effort of the prosecuting authorities to disclose the crime—not only failed to reply to this question, but deliberately obscured it with the statement that Vozdukhov "was detained in a state of intoxication in the courtyard of the Governor's house by policeman Shelemetyev." It even gives ground for the assumption that Vozdukhov was brawling—and where do you think? In the courtyard of the Governor's house! In actuality, Vozdukhov *drove up to the Governor's house in a cab in order to lodge a complaint*—this fact was established. What did he go to complain about? Ptitsyn, the superintendent of the Governor's house, stated that Vozdukhov had complained about the refusal of a steamship booking office to sell him a ticket (?). The witness Mukhanov, formerly inspector of the station in which Vozdukhov was assaulted (and now governor of the provincial prison in Vladimir), stated that he had heard from Vozdukhov's wife that she and her husband had been drinking and that *in Nizhni they had been beaten up in the river police-station and in the Rozhdestvensky police-station, and that Vozdukhov had gone to the Governor to complain about this*. Notwithstanding the fact that the witnesses obviously contradicted each other, the court did not make the slightest attempt to clear up the matter. On the contrary, one has every reason to conclude that the court *did not wish* to clear up the matter. Vozdukhov's wife gave evidence at the trial, but no one took the trouble to ask her whether she and her husband had really been assaulted in several Nizhni police-stations, under what circumstances they had been arrested, in what premises they had been assaulted, and by whom, whether her husband had really wished to complain to the Governor, and whether he had mentioned his intention to any one else. Most likely the witness Ptitsyn, an official in the Governor's office, was not inclined to accept complaints from Vozdukhov—who was not drunk? but whom, nevertheless, it was necessary to make sober!—against the police and ordered the *intoxicated* police-man Shelemetyev to take the complainant to the police-station to be sobered up. But this interesting witness was not cross-examined. The cabby, Krainov, who had driven Vozdukhov to the Governor's house and subsequently to the police-station, was not questioned as to whether Vozdukhov had told him why he was going to the Governor, as to what he had said to Ptitsyn, and whether anybody else had heard the conversation. The court was satisfied merely to hear the brief written affidavit of Krainov (who did not appear in court) which testified that Vozdukhov had not been drunk, but only slightly intoxicated, and the assistant prosecutor had not even taken the trouble to subpoena this important witness. If we bear in mind that Vozdukhov, a sergeant in the army reserve and consequently a man of experience who must have known something about law and order, had said even after the last fatal blows, "I am going to lodge a complaint," it appears more than likely that he went to the Governor to lodge a complaint against the police, that Ptitsyn lied to shield the police and that the servile judges and the servile prosecutor did not wish to bring this delicate story to light.

Further, why was Vozdukhov beaten? Again the indictment presents the case in a manner *most* favourable ... to the accused. The "motive for the torture," it is alleged, was the cutting of Shelemetyev's hand when he pushed Vozdukhov into the soldiers' lock-up. The question arises, why was Vozdukhov, who spoke calmly both with Shelemetyev and with Panov, pushed (assuming that it was really necessary to *push* him!), not into the common cell, but first into the soldiers' lock-up? He had been brought to the station to be sobered up—there were already a number of drunkards in the common cell, and later on Vozdukhov was put into the common cell; why, then, did Shelemetyev, after "introducing" him to Panov, push him into the *soldiers' lock-up*? Evidently for the purpose of beating him. In the common cell there were a number of people, whereas in the soldiers' lock-up Vozdukhov would be alone, and Shelemetyev could call to his aid his comrades and Mr. Panov, who was "in charge" of Police-Station No. 1 at the time. Consequently, the torture was inflicted, not for some chance reason, but deliberately and with forethought. We can assume one of two things—either that all who are taken to the police-station for sobering up (even when they behave themselves decently and quietly) are first put into the soldiers' lock-up to be "taught a lesson," or that Vozdukhov was put in there *precisely for the reason that he had gone to the Governor to lodge a complaint against the police.* The newspaper reports of the trial are so brief that one hesitates to express oneself categorically in favour of the second hypothesis (which is not at all improbable); but the preliminary investigation and the court examination could have cleared this point up beyond any doubt. It stands to reason that the court did not pay any attention whatever to this. I say "it stands to reason," because the indifference of the court reflects not only bureaucratic formalism, but the simple point of view of the Russian man in the street. "What is there to make a fuss about? A drunken muzhik was killed in a police-station! Worse things than that happen!" And the man in the street begins to relate scores of incomparably more revolting cases, in which the culprits have gone scot-free. The remarks of the man in the street are absolutely just; nevertheless, his attitude is absolutely wrong and by his arguments he merely reveals his extreme, philistine short-sightedness. Are not incomparably more revolting cases of police tyranny possible in our country only because this tyranny is the common, everyday practice in every police-station? And is not our indignation impotent against these exceptional cases because we, with customary indifference, tolerate the "normal" cases; because our indifference remains unperturbed, even when a customary practice like an assault upon a drunken (or allegedly drunken) "muzhik" in a police-station rouses the protest of this very muzhik (who ought to be accustomed to this sort of thing), of this very muzhik, who paid with his life for his most impertinent attempt to submit a humble petition to the Governor?

There is another reason why we must not ignore this all too common case. It has long been held that the preventive significance of punishment is not in its severity, but in its inevitableness. What is important is not that a crime shall be severely punished, but that *not a single* crime shall pass undiscovered. From this aspect, too, the present case is of interest. Illegal and savage assault is committed in police-stations in the Russian Empire—it may be said without exaggeration—daily and hourly,* and only rare and very exceptional cases are brought up in court. This is not in the least surprising, since the criminals are the very police who in Russia are charged with the duty of disclosing crime. These circumstances compel us to devote all the greater, if unusual, attention to those cases in which the courts are constrained to raise the curtain that conceals such habitual facts.

Note, for example, how the police perpetrate their assault. Five or six of them together set upon their victim with brutal cruelty, many of them are drunk, all are armed with swords. But not one of them ever strikes the victim with his sword. They are men of experience and they know how to beat a man up. A sword blow leaves a mark of guilt, but try and prove that bruises made by fists were in-

---

* These lines were already written when the press brought another confirmation of the correctness of this assertion. At the other end of Russia, in Odessa—a city enjoying the status of a capital—a magistrate acquitted a certain M. Klinkov who had been charged by Station Sergeant Sadukov with disorderly conduct while under arrest in the police-station. At the trial, the accused and his four witnesses testified to the following: Sadukov arrested M. Klinkov, who was in a state of drunkenness, and took him to the police-station. When he became sober, Klinkov demanded to be released, upon which a policeman grabbed him by the collar and began to punch him. Three other policemen arrived on the scene, and the four of them fell upon him, striking him in the face, on the head, the chest and the sides. Under the rain of blows and covered with blood, Klinkov fell to the floor, whereupon the policemen assaulted him with even greater fury. According to the evidence of Klinkov and his witnesses, this torture was inflicted at the instigation and with the encouragement of Sadukov. As a result of the blows he received, Klinkov lost consciousness. On reviving, he was released from the police-station. Immediately on his release he went to be examined by a physician. The magistrate advised Klinkov to lodge a complaint with the prosecutor against Sadukov and the policemen, to which Klinkov replied that he had already done so and that he would bring twenty witnesses.

One need not be a prophet to foretell that M. Klinkov will fail to get the policemen brought to trial and punished for torture. They did not actually beat him to death; but if, contrary to expectation, they are prosecuted, they are sure to get off lightly.

flicted by the police! "Arrested during a brawl in which he was beaten up,"—and your case isn't worth a straw. Even in the present instance, when the man, as it happened, was beaten to death ("the devil tempted him to die, a hefty muzhik like that! Who would have thought it!"), the prosecution was obliged to bring witnesses to testify that "Vozdukhov was absolutely sound in health before he was taken to the police-station." Apparently, the murderers, who maintained throughout the trial that they had not beaten the man, stated that they had brought him to the station in a battered condition. It is an extremely difficult matter to get witnesses to give evidence in a case like this. By a happy chance, the window between the common cell and the soldiers' lock-up was not completely curtained off. True, instead of glass the panes consisted of sheets of tin with holes punched through, and on the side of the soldiers' lock-up these holes were covered up by a leather curtain. By poking a finger through a hole, one could raise the curtain and see what was going on in the soldiers' lock-up. Only through this circumstance was it possible at the trial to obtain a picture of the scene of the "lesson." But such negligence as improperly curtained windows could exist only in the past century. In the twentieth century, the little window between the common cell and soldiers' lock-up in the Kremlin district Police-Station No. 1 in Nizhni-Novgorod is no doubt blocked up.... And since there are no witnesses, woe betide the poor fellow who finds himself in the soldiers' lock-up!

In no country in the world is there such a multitude of laws as in Russia. We have laws for everything. There are special regulations governing detention in custody, which specifically state that detention is legally permissible only in special premises, subject to special supervision. As you see, the law is observed. In the police-station, there is a special "common cell." But *before* a man is put into the common cell, it is "customary" to "shove" him into the soldiers' lock-up. Although the role of the soldiers' lock-up as a real torture chamber was perfectly clear throughout the trial, the judicial authorities did not even think of paying the matter the slightest attention. Surely, the prosecuting attorney cannot be expected to expose the excesses of our brutal police and to take measures against them!

We have referred to the question of witnesses in a case of this kind. At best, such witnesses can only be persons in the hands of the police. Only under the most exceptional circumstances would it be possible for an outsider to witness a police "lesson" given in a police-station. But it is possible for the police to influence the witnesses that are in their hands. And this is what happened in the present case. The witness Frolov, who at the time of the murder was in the common cell, stated during the preliminary investigation that Vozdukhov had been assaulted by the policemen and the sergeant; later he withdrew his testimony against Sergeant Panov; at the trial, however, he stated that none of the policemen had struck Vozdukhov, that he had been persuaded to give evidence against the police by Semakhin and Barinov (two other men in the common cell who were the principal witnesses for the prosecution), and that the police had not persuaded or prompted him to say this. The witnesses Fadeyev and Antonova stated that no one had laid a finger on Vozdukhov in the soldiers' lock-up, that everything had been quiet there and no quarrelling had taken place.

As is to be seen, quite the usual thing happened. And the judicial authorities behaved with customary indifference. There is a law that provides severe penalties for perjury. A prosecution instituted against the two perjurers would throw further light on the outrages the police perpetrate against those who have the misfortune to fall into their hands and are almost completely defenceless (hundreds of thousands of the "common" people meet with such misfortune every day). But all that the court is concerned about is applying this or that article of the Penal Code; it is not in the least concerned about that defencelessness. This detail in the trial, like all the others, showed clearly how strong and all-entangling is the net, how persistent the canker, which can only be removed by abolishing the whole system of police tyranny and denial of the people's rights.

About thirty-five years ago, F. M. Reshetnikov, a well-known Russian writer, met with an unpleasant adventure.

One evening he went to the Assembly of Nobles in St. Petersburg under the mistaken impression that a concert was to be given there. The policeman at the door barred his way and shouted at him: "What's the shoving? Who are you?" "A factory hand," roughly replied Reshetnikov, stung to anger by this affront. What followed this reply, as related by Gleb Uspensky, was that Reshetnikov spent the night in the police-station, from which he emerged bruised and battered, bereft of his money and his ring. "I report this matter to Your Excellency," wrote Reshetnikov in a petition to the St. Petersburg Chief of Police. "I seek no compensation. May I only humbly trouble you with the request that the police officers and their subordinates *shall not beat the people*.... As it is, the people have only sufferings in store for them."[144]

The modest request which a Russian writer was bold enough to make to the chief of police of the capital so long ago has not yet been fulfilled and it *cannot be fulfilled* so long as the present political system lasts. At the present time, however, every honest man who is tormented by the contemplation of this brutality and violence turns toward the great new movement among the people that is mustering its forces in order to wipe all brutality from the face of the land of Russia and to achieve mankind's finest ideals. During recent decades, hatred for the police has grown immensely and has become deep-rooted in the hearts of the masses of the common people. The development of urban life, the growth of industry, the spread of literacy, have all served to imbue even the uneducated masses with aspirations for a better life and a consciousness of their human dignity; the police, however, have remained as tyrannical and brutal as ever. To their bestiality we now see added a greater subtlety in the detection and persecution of the new, most dangerous enemy, i.e., everything that brings to the masses of the people a ray of consciousness of their rights and confidence in their strength. Fertilised by this consciousness and this confidence, popular hatred will find vent, not in savage vengeance, but in the struggle for liberty.

II. WHY ACCELERATE THE VICISSITUDE OF THE TIMES?

The Assembly of Nobles of Orel Gubernia has adopted an interesting project, but more interesting is the debate which it occasioned.

The issue is the following. The gubernia Marshal of the Nobility, M. A. Stakhovich, proposed in his report the conclusion of a contract with the Finance Department, under which the Orel nobles would be appointed to the posts of excise-collectors. With the introduction of the liquor monopoly forty collectors are to be appointed to gather the moneys from the government liquor shops. Their remuneration will amount to 2,180 rubles per annum (900 rubles salary, 600 rubles travelling expenses, and 680 rubles for hiring a guard). The nobles thought it would be a good thing to get these posts, and for this purpose it was suggested that they form a guild and enter into a contract with the Treasury. Instead of the required deposit (from 3,000 to 5,000 rubles), they suggested that at first 300 rubles per annum be deducted from the pay of each collector, which sums could serve to establish a nobles' guaranty fund to be deposited with the liquor department.

The proposal—certainly a practical one—proves that our higher estate possesses a highly developed flair for grabbing slices of the state pie wherever possible. But it is precisely this business acumen that seemed to many of the high-born landlords to be excessive, disreputable, and unworthy of nobility. A heated discussion flared up on the question, in the course of which three distinct points of view came to light.

The first is the practical point of view. A man must live, the nobility is in straitened circumstances ... here is an opportunity to earn money ... surely they cannot refuse to help the poor nobles. Besides, the collectors could help to encourage sobriety among the people. The second is the point of view of the romantics. To trade in liquor, to be in a position only slightly above that of a bartender, subordinate to common store managers, "very often persons of the lower orders"!?... and there followed a hot stream of words about the high calling of the nobility. We intend to deal with these speeches, but first let us men-

tion the third point of view—that of the statesmen. On
the one hand, there is no denying that the thing seems somewhat discreditable, but, on the other, it must be admitted
that it is lucrative. But we can make money and at the same
time preserve our virtue. The chief excise officer may
even hand out appointments without deposits, and all the
forty nobles may obtain posts at the request of the gubernia
Marshal of the Nobility without forming a guild or entering
into contracts, otherwise "the Minister of Internal Affairs
may refuse to endorse the decision in order to safeguard
the proper functioning of the existing state system." In
all probability, this wise opinion would have prevailed,
had not the Marshal of the Nobility made two important
statements: first, that the contract had already been submitted to the Council of the Ministry of Finance, which had
recognised its feasibility and approved it in principle;
and, secondly, that "it was impossible to obtain such posts
merely at the request of the gubernia Marshal of the Nobility." The report was approved.

Poor romantics! They suffered defeat. But how eloquent-
ly they had pleaded!

"Hitherto the nobility has provided people for leading
positions only. The report suggests the formation of some
sort of guild. Is this compatible with the past, the present, and the future of the nobility? According to the law,
if a bartender embezzles funds, the nobleman will have to
step behind the bar. Death is preferable to such a position!"

Good Lord! How noble man is! Death is preferable to
selling vodka! To trade in corn is quite a noble occupation, particularly in years of bad harvest, when high
profits can be made out of the starvation of the people. A
still more noble occupation is usury in grain, the lending
of grain to the starving peasants in the winter with the
stipulation that they will work in the summer at one-third
of the usual wage-rate. In the central black earth zone,
in which Orel Gubernia is situated, the landlords have
always engaged in this noble form of usury with particular
zeal. And in order to draw a distinction between noble and
ignoble usury, it is necessary, of course, to proclaim as
loudly as possible that the position of a bartender is a
degrading occupation for a nobleman.

"We must carefully cherish our calling which is expressed in the celebrated imperial manifesto by the words, unselfishly to serve the people. To serve for selfish motives would contradict this.... A social-estate that has to its credit such services as the valiant martial deeds of its ancestors and that had to bear the brunt of the great reforms of Emperor Alexander II still possesses opportunities for the future fulfilment of its duties to the state."

Yes, unselfish service! The distribution of lands, the granting of inhabited estates, i.e., gifts of thousands of dessiatines of land, together with thousands of serfs; the establishment of a class of big landowners possessing hundreds, thousands, and tens of thousands of dessiatines and by exploitation reducing millions of peasants to poverty—these are the manifestations of this unselfishness. The reference to the "great" reforms of Alexander II is particularly charming. Take, for example, the emancipation of the peasants. How unselfishly our noble aristocracy fleeced these peasants; compelling them to pay for their own land, at a price three times its real value; robbing them by cutting off various parts of their land; exchanging their own sandy wastes, gullies, and uncultivable land for the peasants' good land;—and now they have the insolence to boast of these exploits!

"There is nothing patriotic in the liquor trade.... Our traditions are not based on rubles, but on service to the state. The nobility must not become stockbrokers."

Sour grapes! The nobility "must not" become stockbrokers because large capital is required on the Stock Exchange, and our quondam slaveowners have squandered their fortunes. In the eyes of the broad masses they have long ago become, not stockbrokers, but the slaves of the Stock Exchange, the slaves of the ruble. And in their pursuit of the ruble, the "highest social-estate" has long been engaged in such highly patriotic occupations as the manufacture of raw brandy, the installation of sugar-refineries and other enterprises, participation in sundry dubious commercial and industrial undertakings, begging at the doors of high Court circles, grand dukes, cabinet ministers, etc., etc., in order to obtain concessions and government guarantees for such enterprises, in order to entreat for doles in the form of privileges for the Nobles' Bank, sugar-export bonuses, slices (thousands of dessiatines in extent!) of Bashkirian or other land, soft, lucrative jobs, etc.

"The ethics of the nobility bear the traces of history, of social position..."—as well as traces of the stable in which the nobles were trained to practise violence and indignities on the muzhiks. The age-long habit of command has bred in the nobles something even more subtle: the ability to clothe their exploiting interests in pompous phrases, calculated to deceive the ignorant "common people." Listen further:

"Why accelerate the vicissitude of the times? It may be a prejudice, but old traditions forbid us to help bring these things upon ourselves...."

These words, uttered by Mr. Naryshkin (one of the members of the council that advocated the state point of view), express a true class sense. Of course, to hesitate to accept the position of a collector (or even of a bartender) is, in these times, mere prejudice. But does not the unparalleled and shameless exploitation of the peasantry by the landlords in our rural districts rest on the prejudices of the benighted masses of the peasantry? Prejudices are dying out anyhow; why then hasten their death by openly bringing together the noble and the bartender, and in this way help the peasant to understand (which he is beginning to do, anyway) the simple truth that the noble landlord is a usurer and robber, a beast of prey, like any village bloodsucker, only immeasurably more powerful because of the lands he owns, his ancient privileges and his close relations with the tsarist government, his habit to command, and his ability to conceal his Judas[145] nature under a doctrine of romanticism and magnanimity?

Yes, Mr. Naryshkin is certainly a counsellor from whose lips political wisdom drops. I am not surprised that the Marshal of the Orel Nobility replied to him in terms so refined that they would do honour to an English lord. He said:

"It would be mere boldness on my part to object to the authorities whom we have heard here, were I not convinced that in arguing against their opinions, I am not arguing against their convictions."

Now, this is true, and, moreover, in a much wider sense than Mr. Stakhovich, who indeed accidentally let the truth slip, imagined. All the nobles, from the most practical to the most romantic, share the same convictions. All are fully convinced of their "sacred right" to possess the hundreds and thousands of dessiatines of land their ancestors grabbed or had granted to them by land-grabbers, the right to exploit the peasants and play the dominant role in the state, the right to enjoy the biggest (and if the worst comes to the worst, even smaller) slices of the state pie, i.e., the people's money. Their opinions differ only in regard to the expediency of undertaking this or that enterprise, and their discussions of these divergent opinions are as instructive for the proletariat as are all other domestic quarrels in the camp of the exploiters. Such disputes bring out the differences between the common interests of the capitalist or landlord class as a whole, and the interests of individual persons or separate groups. Not infrequently in the course of such disputes, one blabs what one has sought ever so carefully to conceal.

Besides this, however, the Orel episode throws some light upon the character of the notorious liquor monopoly. What benefits our official and semi-official press expected from it! Increased revenues, improved quality, and less drunkenness! But instead of increased revenues, all we actually have so far is an increase in the price of spirits, confusion in the budget, and the impossibility of determining the exact financial results of the whole operation. Instead of improvement in quality, we have deterioration; and the government is hardly likely to impress the public with its reports, displayed in the entire press, of the successful results of the "degustation" of the new "government vodka." Instead of less drunkenness, we have more illicit trading in spirits, augmented police incomes from this trading, the opening of liquor shops over the protests of the population, which is petitioning against their being opened,* and increased drunkenness in the streets.** But

* For example, it was recently reported in the newspapers that as far back as 1899 a number of villages in Archangel Gubernia adopted resolutions against the opening of liquor shops in their localities. The government, which at this very moment is introducing the liquor monopoly into that district, of course answered with a refusal, no doubt out of regard for the sobriety of the people!

** This is quite apart from the enormous amount of money the peasant communes have lost as a result of the liquor monopoly. Hith-

above all, what a new and gigantic field is opened for official arbitrariness, tyranny, favour-currying and embezzle-
ment by the creation of this new state enterprise, with a
turnover of many millions of rubles, and the creation of a
whole army of new officials! It is the invasion of a locust-
swarm of officials, boot-licking, intriguing, plundering,
wasting seas of ink and reams upon reams of paper. The Orel
project is nothing but an attempt to cloak in legal forms
the striving to grab the fattest possible slices of the state
pie, a desire which is so prevalent in our provinces, and which,
in view of the unrestrained power of the officials and the
gagging of the people, threatens to intensify the reign of
tyranny and plunder. A simple illustration: last autumn the
newspapers reported "a building incident in connection with
the liquor monopoly." In Moscow, three warehouses are being built for storing vodka to supply the whole of Moscow
Gubernia. The government appropriated a sum of 1,637,000
rubles for this purpose. It now appears that "it has been found
necessary to make a supplementary appropriation of *two-
and-a-half millions*."* Apparently the officials who had
charge of this state property pinched a little more than
fifty pairs of trousers and a few pairs of boots!

III. OBJECTIVE STATISTICS

Our government is in the habit of accusing its opponents, not only revolutionaries, but also liberals, of being
tendentious. Have you ever read the comments of the official press on the liberal (legal, of course) publications? *Vest-*

---

erto they obtained a revenue from liquor shops. The Treasury has
deprived them of this source of revenue without a kopek compensation! In his interesting book, *Das hungernde Russland* (*Reiseelndrücke,
Beobachtungen und Untersuchungen* [*Starving Russia* (Travel Impressions, Observations, and Inquiries).—*Ed.*] by C. Lebmann and Parvus,
Stuttgart, Dietz Verlag, 1900), Parvus justly describes this as *robbing
the rural commune funds*. He states that according to the calculations
of the Samara Gubernia Zemstvo, the losses incurred by the peasant
communes in the three years 1895-97 as a result of the introduction
of the liquor monopoly amounted to *3,150,000 rubles!*

   * Author's italics, see S. *Peterburgskiye Vedomosti* (*St. Petersburg Recorder*), No. 239, September 1, 1900.

nik Finansov,[146] the organ of the Ministry of Finance, would
at times publish reviews of the press, and each time the
official in charge of this column referred to the comments
of the (big) liberal magazines on the budget, on the famine,
or on some government measure, he always spoke with indignation of their "tendentiousness" and, by way of contrast,
pointed, "objectively," not only to "the seamy side," but
to the "gratifying features." This, of course, is only a minor example, but it illustrates the habitual attitude of
the government, its habitual tendency to brag of its "objectivity."

We shall endeavour to bring some satisfaction to these
strict and impartial judges. We shall endeavour to do this
in dealing with statistics. Naturally, we shall not take
statistics on this or that set of facts of public life: it is
well known that the facts are recorded by biased people and
generalised by institutions which are sometimes decidedly
"tendentious," like the Zemstvos. No, we shall deal with
statistics on ... laws. The most ardent supporter of the
government, we imagine, would hardly dare to assert that
there is anything more objective and impartial than statistics on laws—a simple calculation of the decisions made by
the government, quite apart from any consideration of the
divergence between word and deed, between promulgation
and execution, etc.

And now, to the matter.

The State Senate publishes, as is known, a *Compendium
of the Laws and Edicts of the Government,* a periodical that
announces the measures adopted by the government. We shall
examine these facts, and note *what* the laws and edicts are
about. Precisely: what they are about. We dare not criticise the official edicts; we shall merely compute the number issued in this or that sphere. The January newspapers reprinted from this government publication the content
of Nos. 2905 to 2929 of last year and Nos. 1 to 66 of the
current year. Thus, in the period from December 29, 1900,
to January 12, 1901, the very threshold of the new
century, ninety-one laws and edicts were promulgated. The
character of these ninety-one laws renders them very convenient for "statistical" analysis. None of them is outstanding; there is nothing that puts everything else in

the shade and lays a special impress upon the present period of domestic administration. All of them are relatively petty and answer to current requirements continuously and
regularly arising. We thus see the government in its everyday garb, and this serves as a further guarantee of the objectivity of the "statistics."

Of the ninety-one laws, thirty-four, i.e., more than a
third, deal with one and the same subject: extension of the
call dates for payment of capital on shares or of payment of
purchases of stock in various commercial and industrial
joint-stock companies. These laws can be recommended
to newspaper readers as a means of refreshing their memory
in regard to the list of our industrial enterprises and the
names of various firms. The second group of laws is entirely analogous to the first in content. It deals with changes
in the articles of association of commercial and industrial
companies. These include fifteen acts revising the articles
of association of K. and S. Popov Bros., tea dealers;
A. Nauman & Co., cardboard and tar-paper manufacturers;
I. A. Osipov & Co., tanners, and leather, canvas and linen
merchants; etc., etc. To these must be added eleven more
acts, of which six were passed to meet certain requirements
of trade and industry (the establishment of a public bank
and a mutual credit society; the fixing of prices of securities to be taken as deposit for state contracts; rules for
the movement of privately-owned cars on the railways;
regulations governing brokers on the Borisoglebsk Corn Exchange), while five deal with the appointment of six additional policemen and two mounted police sergeants to four
factories and one mine.

Thus, sixty out of ninety-one of the laws, i.e., two-
thirds, directly serve the various practical needs of our
capitalists and (partly) protect them from the discontent
of the workers. The impartial language of figures tells us
that our government, judging by the very nature of most of
its everyday laws and edicts, is a loyal servant of the capitalists and that, in relation to the capitalist class as a
whole, it functions in exactly the same way as, say,
the head office of an iron trust, or as does the office of a
sugar-refining syndicate in relation to the capitalists in
the individual branches of industry. Of course, the fact

that special laws have to be passed in order to introduce some trifling alteration in the articles of association of a company or to extend the call dates for payments on shares simply shows the unwieldiness of our state machinery; only a slight "improvement in the machinery" is necessary for all this to come under the jurisdiction of the local authorities. On the other hand, the unwieldiness of the machine, the excessive centralisation, the necessity for the government itself to poke its nose into everything—this is a feature of the whole of our public life, not merely of the sphere of commerce and industry. Hence, the examination of the number of enacted laws of this or that kind gives us a pretty fair insight into what the government interests itself in, into what it thinks and does.

But the government displays considerably less interest in private associations that do not pursue aims so honourable from the moral point of view, and safe from the political point of view, as profit-making (except that it displays interest in order to hamper, prohibit, suppress, etc.). In the period "under review"—the writer of these lines is in the civil service, and he hopes, therefore, that the reader will forgive his employment of bureaucratic terms— the articles of association of two societies were sanctioned (those of the Society for the Aid to Needy Students in the Vladikavkaz Boys' Gymnasium, and of the Vladikavkaz Society for Educational Excursions and Tours); by imperial grace permission to change the statutes was authorised for three others (the Saving and Mutual Aid Societies of the office employees and workers of the Lyudinovo and Sukreml Works and of the Maltsov Railway, the First Hop-Cultivation Society, and the Philanthropic Society for the Encouragement of Female Labour); fifty-five laws were passed pertaining to commercial and industrial companies; and five, in relation to various other societies. In the sphere of commercial and industrial interests, "we" exert our best efforts for the task and strive to do everything possible to facilitate association between merchants and manufacturers (strive, but do nothing, for the unwieldiness of the machine and the endless red tape considerably restrict the "possibilities" in the police state). In the sphere of non-commercial associations, we stand in principle for homeopathy. Now, hop-growing

societies and societies for the encouragement of female labour are not so bad, but educational excursions.... God knows
what may be discussed on these excursions! And will not
the constant surveillance of the inspectors be made difficult?
Now, you know, one must be careful in handling fire.

Schools. As many as three new schools have been established. And what schools! An elementary school for farmyard workers in the village of Blagodatnoye on the estate
of His Imperial Highness, the Grand Duke Pyotr Nikolaye-
vich. That the villages belonging to the Grand Dukes are
all paradises* I have long ceased to doubt. But neither do
I now doubt that even the highest personages may sincerely
and whole-heartedly interest themselves in the education
of the "younger brother." Moreover, the rules of the Derga-
chi Rural Handicraft School, and of the Asanovo Elementary Agricultural School have been confirmed. I regret that
I have not a reference book at hand to inform me whether
or not some highly-placed personage owns these village paradises, in which popular education—and landlord farming
are being cultivated with such zeal. But I console myself
with the thought that such inquiries do not enter into the
duties of a statistician.

This, then, is the sum total of the laws that express
"the government's solicitude for the people." As the reader
will observe, I have made the greatest possible allowances
in grouping these laws. Why, for example, is the Hop-Cultivation Society not a commercial enterprise? Perhaps because commerce is not the only thing that is discussed at
its meetings. Or take the school for farmyard workers.
Who can tell whether it is a school or an improved
stockyard?

We have still to deal with the last group of laws that
shows the government's solicitude for itself. This group
consists of three times as many laws as we assigned to the
last two categories, twenty-two laws, dealing with administrative reforms, each one more radical than the other—changing the name of the village Platonovskoye to Nikolayev-
skoye; modifying the articles of association, staffs, rules,

---

* A play on the name of the village Blagodatnoye which implies
an earthly paradise.—*Ed*.

lists, hours for sessions (of certain uyezd conferences), etc.;
increasing the salary of midwives attached to army units
in the Caucasus military area; determining the sums for shoe-
ing and veterinary treatment of Cossack mounts; changing
the by-laws of a private commercial school in Moscow; defining the rules of the scholarship grants endowed by Privy
Councillor Daniil Samuilovich Polyakov at the Kozlov Commercial School. I am not sure whether I have classified these
laws correctly. Do they really express the government's
solicitude for itself, or for commercial and industrial interests? If I have classified them wrongly, I beg the reader's indulgence, since this is the first attempt that has
been made to compile statistics on laws. Hitherto no one
has attempted to raise this sphere of knowledge to the level
of a strict science, not even the professors of Russian state
law.

Finally, one legislative act must be treated as a special, independent group, both because of its content and because of its being the first governmental measure in the new
century. This is the law concerning the "increase in the
area of forests to be devoted to the development and improvement of His Imperial Majesty's hunting." A grand *début*
worthy of a great power!

Now, to strike a balance. Statistics would be incomplete without it.

Fifty laws and edicts devoted to various commercial and
industrial companies and enterprises; a score of administrative name-changes and reforms; two creations and three
reorganisations of private societies; three schools for the
training of landlords' employees; six policemen and two
mounted sergeants appointed to factories. Can there be any
doubt whatever that such richly varied legislative and
administrative activity will guarantee our country rapid and
undeviating progress in the twentieth century?

THE DRAFTING
OF 183 STUDENTS INTO THE ARMY*

The newspapers of January 11 published the official announcement of the Ministry of Education on the drafting into the army of 183 students of Kiev University as a punishment for "riotous assembly." The Provisional Regulations of July 29, 1899—this menace to the student world and to society—are being put into execution less than eighteen months after their promulgation, and the government seems to hasten to justify itself for applying a measure of unexampled severity by publishing a ponderous indictment in which the misdeeds of the students are painted in the blackest possible colours.

Each misdeed is more ghastly than the preceding one! In the summer a general students' congress was convened in Odessa to discuss a plan to organise all Russian students for the purpose of giving expression to protests against various aspects of academic, public, and political life. As a punishment for these criminal political designs all the student delegates were arrested and deprived of their documents. But the unrest does not subside—it grows and persists in breaking out in *many* higher educational institutions. The students desire to discuss and conduct their common affairs freely and independently. Their authorities—with the soulless formalism for which Russian officials have always been noted—retaliate with petty vexations, rouse the discontent of the students to the highest

---

* We were going to press when the official announcement was published.

pitch, and automatically stimulate the thoughts of the youths who have not yet become submerged in the morass of bourgeois stagnation to protest against the whole system of police and official tyranny.

The Kiev students demand the dismissal of a professor who took the place of a colleague that had left. The administration resists, provokes students to "assemblies and demonstrations" and—yields. The students call a meeting to discuss what could make possible so horrendous a case— two "white linings"[147] (according to reports) raped a young girl. The administration sentences the "ringleaders" to solitary confinement in the students' detention cell. These refuse to submit. They are expelled. A crowd of students demonstratively accompany the expelled students to the railway station. A new meeting is called; the students remain until evening and refuse to disperse so long as the rector does not show up. The Vice-Governor and Chief of Gendarmerie arrive on the scene at the head of a detachment of troops, who surround the University and occupy the main hall. The rector is called. The students demand—a constitution, perhaps? No. They demand that the punishment of solitary confinement should not be carried out and that the expelled students should be reinstated. The participants at the meeting have their names taken and are allowed to go home.

Ponder over this astonishing lack of proportion between the modesty and innocuousness of the demands put forward by the students and the panicky dismay of the government, which behaves as if the axe were already being laid to the props of its power. Nothing gives our "omnipotent" government away so much as this display of consternation. By this it proves more convincingly than does any "criminal manifesto" to all who have eyes to see and ears to hear that it realises the complete instability of its position, and that it relies only on the bayonet and the knout to save it from the indignation of the people. Decades of experience have taught the government that it is surrounded by inflammable material and that a mere spark, a mere protest against the students' detention cell, may start a conflagration. This being the case, it is clear that the punishment had to be an exemplary one: Draft hundreds of students into the army! "Put

the drill sergeant in place of Voltaire!"[148]—the formula
has not become obsolete; on the contrary, the twentieth
century is destined to see its real application.

This new punitive measure, new in its attempt to revive
that which has long gone out of fashion, provokes many
thoughts and comparisons. Some three generations ago, in
the reign of Nicholas I, drafting into the army was a natural punishment entirely in keeping with the whole system of
Russian serf-owning society. Young nobles were sent to the
army and compelled to serve as private soldiers, losing
the privileges of their estate until they earned officer's
rank. Peasants were also drafted into the army, and it
meant a long term of penal servitude, where "Green Street"[149]
with its inhuman torment awaited them. It is now more than
a quarter of a century since "universal" military service
was introduced, which at the time was acclaimed as a great
democratic reform. Real universal military service that is
not merely on paper is undoubtedly a democratic reform; by
abolishing the social-estate system it would make all citizens equal. But if such were the case, could drafting into
the army be employed as a punishment? When the government converts military service into a form of punishment,
does it not thereby prove that we are much nearer to the
old recruiting system than to *universal* military service?
The Provisional Regulations of 1899 tear off the phari-
saical mask and expose the real Asiatic nature even of those
of our institutions which most resemble European institutions. In reality, we have not and never had universal military
service, because the privileges enjoyed by birth and wealth
create innumerable exceptions. In reality, we have not and
never had anything resembling equality of citizens in military service. On the contrary, the barracks are completely
saturated with the spirit of most revolting absence of
rights. The soldier from the working class or the peasantry
is completely defenceless; his human dignity is trodden
underfoot, he is robbed, he is beaten, beaten, and again
beaten—such is his constant fare. Those with influential
connections and money enjoy privileges and exemptions. It
is not surprising, therefore, that drafting into this school
of tyranny and violence can be a punishment, even a very
severe punishment, amounting almost to deprivation of rights.

The government thinks it will teach the "rebels" discipline in this school. But is it not mistaken in its calculations? Will not this school of Russian military service become the military school of the revolution? Not all the students, of course, possess the stamina to go through the whole course of training in this school. Some will break down under the heavy burden, fall in combat with the military authorities; others—the feeble and flabby—will be cowed into submission by the barracks. But there will be those whom it will harden, whose outlook will be broadened, who will be compelled to ponder and profoundly sense their aspirations towards liberty. They will experience the whole weight of tyranny and oppression on their own backs when their human dignity will be at the mercy of a drill sergeant who very frequently takes deliberate delight in tormenting the "educated." They will see with their own eyes what the position of the common people is, their hearts will be rent by the scenes of tyranny and violence they will be compelled to witness every day, and they will understand that the injustices and petty tyrannies from which the students suffer are mere drops in the ocean of oppression the people are forced to suffer. Those who will understand this will, on leaving military service, take a Hannibal's vow[150] to fight with the vanguard of the people for the emancipation of the entire people from despotism.

The humiliating character of this new punishment is no less outrageous than its cruelty. In declaring the students who protested against lawlessness to be mere rowdies—even as it declared the exiled striking workers to be persons of depraved demeanour—the government has thrown down a challenge to all who still possess a sense of decency. Read the government communication. It bristles with such words as disorder, brawling, outrage, shamelessness, licence. On the one hand, it speaks of criminal political aims and the desire for political protest; and on the other, it slanders the students as mere rowdies who must be disciplined. This is a slap in the face of Russian public opinion, whose sympathy for the students is very well known to the government. The only appropriate reply the students can make is to carry out the threat of the Kiev students, to organise a determined general student strike in all higher educational

institutions in support of the demand for the repeal of the
Provisional Regulations of July 29, 1899.

But it is not the students alone who must reply to the
government. Through the government's own conduct the incident has become something much greater than a mere student affair. The government turns to public opinion as though
to boast of the severity of the punishment it inflicts, as
though to mock at all aspirations towards liberty. All
conscious elements among all strata of the people must take
up this challenge, if they do not desire to fall to the level
of dumb slaves bearing their insults in silence. At the
head of these conscious elements stand the advanced workers
and the Social-Democratic organisations inseparably linked
with them. The working class constantly suffers immeasurably greater injuries and insults from the police lawlessness with which the students have now come into such sharp
conflict. The working class has already begun the struggle
for its emancipation. It must remember that this great
struggle imposes great obligations upon it, that it cannot
emancipate itself without emancipating the whole people
from despotism, that it is its duty first and foremost to
respond to every political protest and render every support
to that protest. The best representatives of our educated
classes have proved—and sealed the proof with the blood of
thousands of revolutionaries tortured to death by the government—their ability and readiness to shake from their
feet the dust of bourgeois society and join the ranks of
the socialists. The worker who can look on indifferently
while the government sends troops against the student youth
is unworthy of the name of socialist. The students came to
the assistance of the workers—the workers must come to the
aid of the students. The government wishes to deceive the
people when it declares that an attempt at political protest
is mere brawling. The workers must publicly declare and
explain to the broad masses that this is a lie; that the real
hotbed of violence, outrage, and licence is the autocratic Russian Government, the tyranny of the police and the
officials.

The manner in which this protest is to be organised
must be decided by the local Social-Democratic organisations and workers' groups. The most practical forms of protest

are the distribution, scattering, and posting up of leaflets, and the organisation of meetings to which as far as possible all classes of society should be invited. It would be desirable, however, where strong and well-established organisations exist, to attempt a broader and more open protest by means of a public demonstration. The demonstration organised last December 1, outside the premises of the newspaper *Yuzhny Krai*[151] in Kharkov, may serve as a good example of such a protest. The jubilee of that filthy sheet, which baits everything that aspires to light and freedom and glorifies every bestiality of our government, was being celebrated at the time. The large crowd assembled in front of *Yuzhny Krai*, solemnly tore up copies of the paper, tied them to the tails of horses, wrapped them round dogs, threw stones and stink-bombs containing sulphuretted hydrogen at the windows, and shouted: "Down with the corrupt press!" Such celebrations are well deserved, not only by the corrupt newspapers, but by all our government offices. If they but rarely celebrate anniversaries of official benevolence, they constantly deserve the celebration of the people's retribution. Every manifestation of governmental tyranny and violence is a legitimate motive for such a demonstration. The people must not let the government's announcement of its punishment of the students go unanswered!

Written in January 1901   Published according to
Published in February 1901   the *Iskra* text
   in *Iskra*, No. 2

THE WORKERS' PARTY AND THE PEASANTRY[152]

Forty years have passed since the peasants were emancipated. It is quite natural that the public should celebrate with particular enthusiasm February 19, the anniversary of the fall of old feudal Russia and the beginning of an epoch which promised the people liberty and prosperity. But we must not forget that besides genuine loathing of serfdom and all its manifestations, there is also much unctuousness in the laudatory orations delivered on the occasion. The now fashionable estimation of the "great" Reform as "the emancipation of the peasantry accompanied by a grant of land *with the aid* of state compensation" is utterly hypocritical and false. Actually, the peasants were emancipated *from* the land, inasmuch as the plots they had tilled for centuries were ruthlessly cut down and hundreds of thousands of peasants were deprived of all their land and settled on a quarter or beggar's allotment.[153] In point of fact, the peasants were doubly robbed: not only were their plots of land cut down, but they had to pay "redemption money" for the land left to them, and which had always been in their possession; the redemption price, moreover, was far above the actual value of the land. Ten years after the emancipation of the peasantry the landlords themselves admitted to government officials investigating the state of agriculture that the peasants had been made to pay, not only for their land, but for their personal liberty. Yet, although the peasants had to pay redemption money for their liberation, they were not granted real freedom; for twenty years they remained "temporarily bound"[154]; they were left—and have remained to this day—the lowest social-estate, subject to flogging;

liable to special taxes; bereft of the right freely to leave the semi-feudal commune, freely to dispose of their own land, or freely to settle in any part of the country. Our peasant Reform, far from manifesting magnanimity of the government, on the contrary, serves as a great historical example of the extent to which the autocratic government befouls everything it touches. Under pressure of military defeat, appalling financial difficulties, and menacing discontent among the peasantry, the government was actually *compelled* to liberate the peasants. The tsar himself admitted that the peasants had to be emancipated from above, lest they emancipate themselves from below. But in embarking on emancipation, the government did everything possible and impossible to satisfy the greed of the "injured" serf-owners; it did not even stop at the base device of reshuffling the men who were to carry out the Reform, although the men selected had come from among the nobility itself! The first body of mediators was dissolved and replaced by men incapable of refusing to help the serf-owners cheat the peasantry in the very process of demarcating the land. Nor could the great Reform be carried out without resort to military punitive action and the shooting-down of peasants who refused to accept the title-deeds to the land.[155] It is not surprising, therefore, that the best men of the time, muzzled by the censors, met this great Reform with the silence of condemnation.

The peasant, "emancipated" from corvée service, emerged from the hands of the reformers crushed, plundered, degraded, tied to his allotment, so much so that he had no alternative but "voluntarily" to accept corvée services. And so he began to cultivate the land of his former master, "renting" from him the very land that had been cut off from his own allotment, hiring himself out in the winter for summer work in return for the corn he had to borrow from the landlord to feed his hungry family. The "free labour," for which the manifesto drawn up by a jesuitical priest called upon the peasantry to ask the "blessing of God," turned out to be nothing more nor less than labour-service and bondage.

To oppression by the landlords, which was preserved thanks to the magnanimity of the officials who introduced and carried out the Reform, was added oppression by capital. The power of money, which crushed even the French peasant, emancipated from the power of the feudal landlords, not by a miserable, half-hearted reform, but by a mighty popular revolution—this power of money bore down with all its weight upon our semi-serf muzhik. He had to obtain money at all costs—in order to pay the taxes which had increased as a result of the beneficent Reform, to rent land, to buy the few miserable articles of factory-made goods which began to squeeze out the home manufactures of the peasant, to buy corn, etc. The power of money not only crushed the peasantry, but split it up. An enormous number of peasants were steadily ruined and turned into proletarians; from the minority arose a small group of grasping kulaks and enterprising muzhiks who laid hands upon the peasant farms and the peasants' lands, and who formed the kernel of the rising rural bourgeoisie. The forty years since the Reform have been marked by this constant process of "de-peasantising" the peasants, a process of slow and painful extinction. The peasant was reduced to beggary. He lived together with his cattle, was clothed in rags, and fared on weeds; he fled from his allotment, if he had anywhere to go, and even *paid* to be relieved of it, if he could induce anyone to take over a plot of land, the payments on which exceeded the income it yielded. The peasants were in a state of chronic starvation, and they died by the tens of thousands from famine and epidemics in bad harvest years, which recurred with increasing frequency.

This is the state of our countryside even at the present time. One might ask: What is the way out, by what means can the lot of the peasantry be improved? The small peasantry can free itself from the yoke of capital only by associating itself with the working-class movement, by helping the workers in their struggle for the socialist system, for transforming the land, as well as the other means of production (factories, works, machines, etc.), into social property. Trying to save the peasantry by protecting small-scale farming and small holdings from the onslaught of capitalism would be a useless retarding of social development; it would mean deceiving the peasantry with illusions of the possibility of prosperity even under capitalism, it would mean disuniting the labouring classes and creating a privileged position for the minority at the expense of the majority. That is why Social-Democrats will always struggle against senseless and vicious institutions such as that which forbids the peasant to dispose of his land, such as collective liability, or the system of prohibiting the peasants from freely leaving the village commune or freely accepting into it persons belonging to any social-estate. But, as we have seen, our peasants are suffering not only and not so much from oppression by capital as from oppression by the landlords and the survivals of serfdom. Ruthless struggle against these shackles, which immeasurably worsen the condition of the peasantry and tie it hand and foot, is not only possible but even necessary in the interest of the country's social development in general; for the hopeless poverty, ignorance, lack of rights, and degradation, from which the peasants suffer, lay an imprint of Asiatic backwardness upon the entire social system of our country. Social-Democracy would not be doing its duty if it did not render every assistance to this struggle. This assistance should take the form, briefly put, of *carrying the class struggle into the countryside*.

We have seen that in the modern Russian village two kinds of class antagonism exist side by side: first, the antagonism between the agricultural workers and the proprietors, and, secondly, the antagonism between the peasantry as a whole and the landlord class as a whole. The first antagonism is developing and becoming more acute, the second is gradually diminishing. The first is still wholly in the future; the second to a considerable degree already belongs to the past. And yet, despite this, it is the second antagonism that has the most vital and most practical significance for Russian Social-Democrats at the present time. It goes without saying it is an axiom for every Social-Democrat, that we must utilise all the opportunities presenting themselves to us to develop the class-consciousness of the agricultural wage-workers, that we must pay attention to the migration of urban workers to the countryside (e.g., mechanics employed on steam threshing-machines, etc.) and to the markets where agricultural labourers are hired.

But our rural labourers are still too closely connected with the peasantry, they are still too heavily burdened with the misfortunes of the peasantry as a whole to enable the movement of the rural workers to assume national significance, either now or in the immediate future. On the other hand, the question of sweeping away the survivals of serfdom, of driving the spirit of social-estate inequality and degradation of tens of millions of the "common people" out of the whole of the Russian state system is already a matter of national significance, and the Party which claims to be the vanguard in the fight for freedom cannot ignore it.

The deplorable condition of the peasantry has now become (in a more or less general form) almost universally recognised. The phrase about "the defects" of the Reform of 1861 and the need for state aid has become a current truism. It is our duty to point out that peasant distress arises precisely from the class oppression of the peasantry; that the government is the loyal champion of the oppressing classes; and that those who sincerely and seriously desire a radical improvement in the condition of the peasantry must seek, not aid from the government, but deliverance from its oppression and the achievement of political liberty. There is talk of the redemption payments being excessively high, and of benevolent measures on the part of the government to reduce them and extend the dates of payment. Our reply to this is: all payment of redemption money is nothing more nor less, than robbery of the peasantry by the landlords and the government, screened by legal forms and bureaucratic phrases; it is nothing more nor less than tribute paid to the serf-owners for emancipating their slaves. We will put forward the demand for the immediate and complete abolition of redemption payments and quit-rents, and the demand for the return to the people of the hundreds of millions which the tsarist government has extorted from them in the course of the years to satisfy the greed of the slaveowners. There is talk of the peasants not having sufficient land, of the need for state aid to provide them with more land. Our reply to this is: it is precisely *because of* state aid (aid to the landlords, of course) that the peasants in such an enormous number of cases were deprived of land they vitally needed. We put forward the demand for restitution to the peasants of the land of which they have been deprived, a condition that still binds them to forced labour, to the rendering of corvée service, i.e., that virtually keeps them in a state of serfdom. We will put forward the demand for the establishment of peasant committees to remove the crying injustices perpetrated against the emancipated slaves by the Committees of Nobles set up by the tsarist government. We will demand the establishment of courts empowered to reduce the excessively high payment for land extorted from the peasants by the landlords who take advantage of their hopeless position, courts in which the peasants could prosecute for usury all who take advantage of their extreme need to impose shackling agreements upon them. We will utilise every opportunity to explain to the peasants that the people who talk to them about the tutelage or aid of the present state are either fools or charlatans, and are their worst enemies; that what the peasants stand most in need of is relief from the monstrous oppression of the bureaucratic power, recognition of their complete and absolute equality in all respects with all other social-estates, complete freedom of movement from place to place, freedom to dispose of their lands, and freedom to manage their own communal affairs and dispose of the communal revenues. The most common facts in the life of any Russian village provide a thousand issues for agitation in behalf of the above demands. This agitation must be based upon the local, concrete, and most pressing needs of the peasantry; yet it must not be confined to these needs, but must be steadily directed towards widening the outlook of the peasants, towards developing their political consciousness. The peasants must be brought to understand the special positions occupied in the state by the landlords and the peasants respectively, and they must be taught that the only way to free the countryside from tyrannical oppression is to convene an assembly of representatives of the people and to overthrow the arbitrary rule of the officials. It is absurd to assert that the demand for political liberty would not be understood by the workers: not only the workers who have engaged the factory owners and the police in direct battle for years and who constantly see their best fighters subjected to arbitrary arrests and persecution—

not only these workers, who are already imbued with socialism, but every sensible peasant who thinks at all about the things he sees going on around him will understand what the workers are fighting for, will understand the significance of a Zemsky Sobor which will emancipate the whole country from the unlimited power of the hated officials. Agitation on the basis of the direct and most urgent needs of the peasants will fulfil its purpose—i.e., carry the class struggle into the countryside—only when it succeeds in combining every exposure of some "economic" evil with definite political demands.

But the question arises whether the Social-Democratic Labour Party can include in its programme demands like those referred to above. Can it undertake to carry on agitation among the peasantry? Will it not lead to the scattering and diversion of our revolutionary forces, not very numerous as it is, from the principal and only reliable channel of the movement?

Such objections are based on a misunderstanding. We must definitely include in our programme demands for the emancipation of our countryside from all the survivals of slavery, demands capable of rousing the best section of the peasantry, if not to engage in independent political action, then at all events consciously to support the working-class struggle for emancipation. We should be making a mistake if we defended measures that would have the effect of retarding social development or of artificially shielding the small peasantry against the growth of capitalism, against the development of large-scale production; but we should be committing a much more disastrous mistake if we failed to utilise the working-class movement for the purpose of spreading among the peasantry the democratic demands of which the Reform of February 19, 1861, fell short because of its distortion by the landlords and the officials. Our Party must include such demands in its programme if it is to take the lead of the whole people in the struggle against the autocracy.*

* We have drafted a Social-Democratic programme which includes the above-mentioned demands. We hope—after this draft has been discussed and amended with the participation of the Emancipation of Labour group—to publish it as the draft programme of our Party in one of our forthcoming issues.

But the inclusion of these points does not mean that we would call active revolutionary forces from the towns to the villages. Such a thing is out of the question. There can be no doubt that all the militant elements of the Party must concentrate on work in the towns and industrial centres; that only the industrial proletariat is capable of conducting a steadfast and mass struggle against the autocracy, of employing such methods of struggle as organising public demonstrations, or of issuing a *popular* political newspaper regularly and circulating it widely. We must include peasant demands in our programme, not in order to call convinced Social-Democrats from the towns to the countryside, not in order to chain them to the village, but to guide the activities of those forces that *cannot* find an outlet anywhere except in the rural localities and to utilise for the cause of democracy, for the political struggle for freedom, the ties which, owing to the force of circumstances, a good many faithful Social-Democratic intellectuals and workers have with the countryside—ties that are necessarily increasing and growing stronger with the growth of the movement. We have long passed the stage when we were a small detachment of volunteers, when the reserves of Social-Democratic forces were limited to circles of young people who all "went to the workers." Our movement now has a whole army at its command, an army of workers, engaged in the struggle for socialism and freedom—an army of intellectuals who have been taking part in the movement and who can now be found over the whole length and breadth of Russia—an army of sympathisers whose eyes are turned with faith and hope towards the working-class movement and who are prepared to render it a thousand services. We are confronted with the great task of organising all these armies in such a manner as will enable us, not only to organise transient outbreaks, not only to strike casual and sporadic (and therefore not dangerous) blows at the enemy, but to pursue the enemy steadily and persistently, in a determined struggle all along the line, to harass the autocratic government wherever it sows oppression and gathers a harvest of hatred. Can this aim be achieved without sowing the seeds of the class struggle and political consciousness among the many millions of the peasantry? Let no one say it is impossible

to sow these seeds! It is not only possible, it is already
being done in a thousand ways that escape our attention
and influence. This process will evolve much more widely
and rapidly when we issue a slogan that will bring our influence to bear and when we unfurl the banner of the emancipation of the Russian peasantry from all the survivals of shame-
ful serfdom. Country people coming to the towns even today
regard with curiosity and interest the workers' struggle,
incomprehensible to them, and carry news of it to the remotest parts of the land. We can and must bring about a
situation in which the curiosity of the bystanders is replaced,
if not by full understanding, then at least by a vague consciousness that the workers are struggling for the interests of the whole people, by a growing sympathy for their
struggle. And when that has been done, the day of the
victory of the revolutionary workers' party over the police
government will come with a rapidity exceeding our own
anticipation.

Written in January 1901   Published according to
Published in February 1901   the *Iskra* text
    in *Iskra*, No. 2

NOTES

[1] The article, *"On the Question of Our Factory Statistics (Professor Karyshev's New Statistical Exploits)*," was written in August 1898 and published in the collection *Economic Studies and Essays* that appeared early in October 1898. Lenin made extensive use of the material and the conclusions of this article for his *The Development of Capitalism in Russia* (Chapter V, "The First Stages of Capitalism in Industry"; Chapter VI, "Capitalist Manufacture and Capitalist Domestic Industry"; and Chapter VII, "The Development of Large-Scale Machine Industry," Section II, "Our Factory Statistics").   p. 13

[2] *Russkiye Vedomosti (Russian Recorder)*—a newspaper published in Moscow from 1863 onwards, it expressed the views of the moderate liberal intelligentsia. Among its contributors in the 1880s and 1890s were the democratic writers V. G. Korolenko, M. Y. Saltykov-Shchedrin, and G. I. Uspensky. It also published items written by liberal Narodniks. In 1905 it became the organ of the Right wing of the Constitutional-Democratic (Cadet) Party. Lenin said that *Russkiye Vedomosti* was a peculiar combination of "Right-wing Cadetism and a strain of Narodism" (see present edition, Vol. 19, "Frank Speeches of a Liberal"). In 1918 the publication was closed down together with other counter-revolutionary newspapers.   p. 17

[3] *Yuridichesky Vestnik (The Legal Messenger)*—a monthly magazine, bourgeois-liberal in trend, published in Moscow from 1867 to 1892.   p. 24

[4] *Mir Bozhy (The Wide World;* literally, *God's World)*—a monthly literary and popular-scientific magazine, liberal in trend, it was published in St. Petersburg from 1892 to 1906. In 1898 the magazine carried Lenin's review of A. Bogdanov's *A Short Course of Economic Science* (see p. 46 of this volume). From 1906 to 1918 the magazine appeared under the title *Sovremenny Mir (Contemporary World)*.   p. 27

[5] The reference is to Lenin's *The Development of Capitalism in Russia* (see present edition, Vol. 3).   p. 28

[6] *Zemstvo*—the name given to the local government bodies introduced in the central gubernias of tsarist Russia in 1864.

The powers of the Zemstvos were limited to purely local economic problems (hospital and road building, statistics, insurance,
etc.). Their activities were controlled by the provincial governors
and by the Ministry of Internal Affairs, which could overrule any
decisions disapproved by the government.   p. 36

[7] The results of the first general census of the population of the
Russian Empire, taken on January 28 (February 9), 1897, were
published as a series between 1897 and 1905; in the second edition of his *The Development of Capitalism in Russia* Lenin made
use of them, correcting the data on the population of a number of
places.   p. 41

[8] *Narodism*—a petty-bourgeois trend in the Russian revolutionary movement; it began to manifest itself in the sixties and seventies of the nineteenth century and comprised mainly progressive intellectuals from the lower estates. With the objective of rousing the peasantry to struggle against absolutism, the revolutionary youth "went among the people," to the village, gaining there,
however, no support. The Narodniks held to the view that
capitalism in Russia was a fortuitous phenomenon with no prospect of development, and that for this reason there would be no
growth and development of a Russian proletariat. The Narodniks
considered the peasantry to be the main revolutionary force and
regarded the village commune as the embryo of socialism. The
Narodniks proceeded from an erroneous view of the role of the
class struggle in historical development, maintaining that history
is made by heroes, by outstanding personalities, who are followed
passively by the popular masses.   p. 44

[9] *Katheder-reformers* or *Katheder-Socialists*—representatives of a
trend in bourgeois political economy in the 1870s and 1880s who
under the guise of socialism, advocated bourgeois-liberal reformism
from university chairs (*Katheder* in German). The fear aroused
among the exploiting classes by the spread of Marxism and the
growth of the working-class movement, as well as the efforts of
bourgeois ideologists to find fresh means of keeping the working
people in subjugation, brought *Katheder*-Socialism into being.

The *Katheder*-Socialists, among whom were Adolf Wagner,
Gustav Schmoller, Lorenz Brentano, and Werner Sombart, asserted
that the bourgeois state is above classes, that it can reconcile
mutually hostile classes, and that it can gradually introduce
"socialism" without affecting the interests of the capitalists, while
giving every possible consideration to the demands of the working
people. They suggested the legalisation of police-regulated wage-
labour and the revival of the medieval guilds. Marx and Engels
exposed *Katheder*-Socialism, showing how essentially reactionary
it was. Lenin called the *Katheder*-Socialists the bed bugs of "po-
lice-bourgeois university science" who hated Marx's revolution-

ary teachings. In Russia the views of the *Katheder*-Socialists were disseminated by the "legal Marxists."   p. 49

[10] Lenin refers to the liberal Narodniks headed by N. M. Mikhailovsky; he criticised the views of the "school" in his *What the "Friends of the People" Are and How They Fight the Social-Democrats* (see present edition, Vol. 1).   p. 49

[11] *Russkaya Mysl (Russian Thought)*—a monthly literary and political magazine published in Moscow from 1880 to 1918; until 1905 it was liberal Narodnik in its views, the editor from 1880 to 1885 was V. M. Lavrov. During the struggle between the Marxists and the liberal Narodniks in the nineties the magazine occasionally carried articles by Marxists. In this period *Russkaya Mysl* published the democratic writers D. N. Mamin-Sibiryak, G. I. Uspensky, V. G. Korolenko, A. M. Gorky, A. P. Chekhov, and others. After the Revolution of 1905 it became the organ of the counter-revolutionary liberals and was edited by P. B. Struve. It was an advocate of nationalism, reaction, and clericalism, and it defended landlordism. Lenin termed the journal "Black-Hundred Thought" (see present edition, Vol. 13, "Police-Patriotic Demonstration to Order").   p. 49

[12] Karl Marx, *Capital*, Vol. III, Moscow, 1959, pp. 709-10.   p. 52

[13] *Coloni*—tenant farmers renting small parcels of land from big landowners in the Roman Empire. The *coloni* paid in cash or kind for the right to use the land. The *coloni* later became bound serfs by virtue of their indebtedness to the landowners.   p. 53

[14] Karl Marx, *Capital*, Vol. III, Moscow, 1959, pp. 763-93.   p. 53

[15] Karl Marx, *Capital*, Vol. II, Moscow, 1957, p. 470   p. 57

[16] Karl Marx, *Capital*, Vol. III, Moscow, 1959, pp. 299-300.   p. 57

[17] Karl Marx, *Capital*, Vol. III, Moscow, 1959, pp. 239-40.   p. 58

[18] Karl Marx, *Capital*, Vol. III, Moscow, 1959, pp. 299-300.   p. 59

[19] Karl Marx, *Capital*, Vol. III, Moscow, 1959, p. 244.   p. 59

[20] Karl Marx, *Capital*, Vol. III, Moscow, 1959, pp. 472-73.   p. 59

[21] Karl Marx, *Capital*, Vol. II, Moscow, 1957, p. 316.   p. 60

[22] *Novoye Slovo (New Word)*—a monthly scientific, literary, and political magazine, published in St. Petersburg from 1894 by liberal Narodniks. Early in 1897 it was taken over by the "legal Marxists" (P. B. Struve, M. I. Tugan-Baranovsky, and others). *Novoye Slovo* published two of Lenin's articles when he was in exile in Siberia—"A Characterisation of Economic Romanticism" and "About a Certain Newspaper Article." The magazine also

presented writings by G. V. Plekhanov, V. I. Zasulich, L. Martov,
A. M. Gorky, and others. It was closed down by the tsarist authorities in December 1897.   p. 60

23 Karl Marx, *Capital*, Vol. II, Moscow, 1957, pp. 362-89.   p. 61

24 Karl Marx, *Capital*, Vol. II, Moscow, 1957, p. 17.   p. 64

25 *Nauchnoye Obozreniye* (*Science Review*)—a scientific magazine
issued in St. Petersburg from 1894 to 1903 (when it became a literary magazine). It published Lenin's three articles: "A Note on
the Question of the Market Theory" and "Once More on the Theory
of Realisation" (see present volume, pp. 55-64, 74-93); and "Uncritical Criticism" (see present edition, Vol. 3, pp. 609-32). p. 64

26 Karl Marx, *Capital*, Vol. III, Moscow, 1959, pp. 708-10.   p. 66

27 *Nachalo* (*The Beginning*)—a monthly literary and political magazine that was published in St. Petersburg during the first months
of 1899 by "legal Marxists"; its editors were P. B. Struve, M. I. Tugan-Baranovsky, and others. It published articles by G. V. Plekhanov, V. I. Zasulich, and others. The magazine was closed down
by the tsarist authorities in June 1899.   p. 66

28 *The village* (*land*) *commune* (Russ. *obshchina* or *mir*) was the communal form of peasant use of land characterised by compulsory
crop rotation and undivided woods and pastures. Its principal
features were collective liability, the periodical redistribution
of the land without the right to refuse the allotment, and prohibition of purchase or sale of the allotted land.
     The Russian village commune dates back to ancient times and
in the course of its historical development it gradually became one
of the mainstays of feudalism in Russia. The landlords and the
tsarist government used the village commune to intensify feudal
oppression and to squeeze land redemption payments and taxes
out of the people. Lenin pointed out that the village commune
"does not save the peasant from turning into a proletarian; actually
it serves as a medieval barrier dividing the peasants who are as
if chained to small associations and- to categories that have lost
all "reason for existence" (see "The Agrarian Question in Russia Towards the Close of the Nineteenth Century," present edition, Vol. 15).
     The problem of the village commune aroused heated debates
and brought an extensive economic literature into existence.
Particularly great interest in the village commune was displayed
by the Narodniks, who saw in it the guarantee of Russia's evolution to socialism by a special path. By tendentiously gathering
their material, falsifying facts, and employing so-called "average
figures," the Narodniks sought to prove that the commune peasantry
in Russia possessed a special sort of "steadfastness," that the village
commune protected the peasants against the penetration of capitalist relations into their lives and "saved" them from ruin and class
differentiation. As early as the 1880s, G. V. Plekhanov   showed

that the Narodnik illusions about "commune socialism" were unfounded and in the 1890s Lenin completely refuted the Narodnik
theories. Lenin made use of a tremendous amount of statistical
material and countless facts to show how capitalist relations were
developing in the Russian village and how capital, by penetrating
into the patriarchal village commune, was splitting the peasantry
into two antagonistic classes, the kulaks and the poor peasants.

In 1906 the tsarist minister Stolypin issued a law favouring
the kulaks which allowed peasants to leave the commune and sell
their allotments. This law marked the beginning of the official
abolition of the village commune system and intensified the differentiation of the peasantry. In the nine years following the adoption
of the law, over two million peasant families withdrew from the
communes.   p. 67

[29] *Allotment land*—land left for the use of the peasants after the
abolition of serfdom in 1861. The allotted land was not permitted
to be sold by the peasants. It was held by the village commune
and was periodically redistributed among the peasants.   p. 67

[30] *Collective liability* was a compulsory measure making the peasants of each village commune collectively liable for timely and
full payments and for the fulfilment of all sorts of services to the
state and the landlords (payment of taxes and land redemption
instalments, provision of recruits for the army, etc.). This form
of bondage was retained after serfdom had been abolished and remained in force until 1906.   p. 67

[31] *Winter hiring*—the hiring of peasants for summer work by landlords and kulaks in the winter, when the peasants were particularly
in need of cash and were willing to agree to extortionate terms.
                                                               p. 68

[32] *Physiocrats*—representatives of a trend in bourgeois classical
political economy in the fifties and sixties of the eighteenth century when the French Revolution was being prepared ideologically.
The school was founded by F. Quesnay. The physiocrats formula
for economic policy was *"laissez faire, laissez passer,"* which aimed
at providing the most favourable conditions for developing bourgeois relations. The physiocrats proclaimed the principle of the
unlimited rule of private property; they rejected protectionism,
struggled against the limitations of the guilds, and demanded
free trade and free competition.

The physiocrats transferred the investigation of the sources
of wealth and the surplus-product from the sphere of circulation
to that of production, but confined it to agricultural production.
They were the first to attempt a study of the laws of the reproduction and distribution of the aggregate social product. Quesnay's
Tableau économique was an attempt to depict the capitalist production process as a whole. The physiocrats, however, did not
understand the nature of value and did not realise that surplus-

value is congealed surplus-labour but regarded it as a peculiar
gift of nature ("the net product"). p. 75

[33] Frederick Engels, *Anti-Dühring*. Lenin refers to the chapter "From
the *Critical History*" (Part II, Chapter X). p. 75

[34] Karl Marx, *Capital*, Vol. I, Moscow, 1958, p. 591. p. 75

[35] Karl Marx, *Capital*, Vol. II, Moscow, 1957, pp. 359-60. p. 75

[36] Karl Marx, *Capital*, Vol. II, Moscow, 1957, pp. 360-89. p. 76

[37] Karl Marx, *Capital*, Vol. II, Moscow, 1957, p. 389. p. 77

[38] *Volume IV of Capital*—the designation given by Lenin, in accordance with the view expressed by Engels, to Marx's *Theories of
Surplus-Value*, written in the years 1862-63. In the preface to
Volume II of *Capital*, Engels wrote: "After eliminating the numerous passages covered by Books II and III, I intend to publish
the critical part of this manuscript as Book IV of *Capital*" (Karl
Marx, *Capital*, Vol. II p. 2). Death prevented Engels from preparing Volume IV for the press; it was first published in German,
after being edited by Karl Kautsky, in 1905-10. In this edition
basic principles governing the scientific publication of a text were
violated and there were distortions of a number of the tenets of
Marxism.

The Institute of Marxism-Leninism of the C.C. of the C.P.S.U.
is issuing a new (Russian) edition of *Theories of Surplus-Value*
(Volume IV of *Capital*) in three parts, according to the manuscript
of 1862-63. Part I appeared in 1955 and Part II in 1957. p. 78

[39] Karl Marx, *Capital*, Vol. III, Moscow, 1959, p. 820. p. 78

[40] Karl Marx, *Capital*, Vol. I, Moscow, 1958, pp. 589-91. p. 78

[41] Karl Marx, *Capital*, Vol. III, Moscow, 1959, p. 819. p. 78

[42] *Neo-Kantians*—adherents of Neo-Kantianism, a trend in bourgeois
philosophy that arose in Germany in the latter half of the nineteenth century; it was a resuscitation of the more reactionary, idealist concepts of Kant's philosophy. Neo-Kantianism opposed
dialectical and historical materialism with the slogan of "Back
to Kant!" In his book, *Ludwig Feuerbach and the End of Classical
German Philosophy*, Engels called the Neo-Kantians "theoretical
reactionaries" and "cobweb-spinning eclectic flea-crackers." The
Neo-Kantians among the German Social-Democrats (Eduard Bernstein, Karl Schmidt, and others) subjected to revision the Marxist
philosophy, Marx's economic theory, and the Marxist theory of
the class struggle and the dictatorship of the proletariat. Russian supporters of Neo-Kantianism included the "legal Marxists,"
Socialist-Revolutionaries, and Mensheviks. Lenin subjected the

reactionary philosophy of the Neo-Kantians to a comprehensive criticism in his *Materialism and Empirio-Criticism* (see present edition, Vol. 14).   p. 81

[43] Lenin refers to G. V. Plekhanov's *Development of the Monist View of History*, published legally in St. Petersburg in 1895 under the pen-name of N. Beltov, and to his *Essays on the History of Materialism* published in German.   p. 81

[44] Karl Marx, *Capital*, Vol. II, Moscow, 1957, p. 470.   p. 86

[45] Karl Marx, *Capital*, Vol. III, Moscow, 1959, p. 810.   p. 86

[46] Lenin refers to his work, "The Economic Content of Narodism and the Criticism of It in Mr. Struve's Book" (see present edition, Vol. 1, pp. 333-507).   p. 90

[47] *Entailed estates*—a system of inheritance that has been preserved in some capitalist countries from feudal times. Under this system estates are inherited undivided by the eldest in the family or by the eldest son of the holder.   p. 97

[48] A translation of one of the chapters of Karl Kautsky's *The Agrarian Question* was published in *Nauchnoye Obozreniye*, No. 8, for 1899, under the title "Modern Agriculture."   p. 99

[49] Lenin's study "*Capitalism in Agriculture (Kautsky's Book and Mr. Bulgakov's Article)*," was intended for publication in *Nachalo* but upon the closing-down of that magazine it was published in *Zhizn*.

Zhizn (*Life*)—a literary, scientific, and political magazine published in St. Petersburg from 1897 to 1901; in 1902 it was published abroad. From 1899 onwards the magazine was in the hands of the "legal Marxists."   p. 105

[50] Karl Marx, *Capital*, Vol. III, Moscow, 1959, p. 603.   p. 116

[51] *Russkoye Bogatstvo* (*Russian Wealth*)—a monthly magazine published in St. Petersburg from 1876 to the middle of 1918. In the early 1890s it became the organ of the liberal Narodniks and was edited by S. N. Krivenko and N. K. Mikhailovsky. The magazine advocated conciliation of the tsarist government and waged a bitter struggle against Marxism and the Russian Marxists. In 1906 it became the organ of the semi-Cadet "Popular Socialist" Party.   p. 121

[52] The reference is to Marx's article criticising an essay by E. de Girardin, "*Le Socialisme et l'impôt*" ("Socialism and Taxes").

The article was published in issue No. 4 of the journal *Neue Rheinische Zeitung. Politisch-ökonomische Revue* (*New Rhenish Gazette, Political-Economic Review*), issued in May 1850. The journal was published by Marx in Hamburg in 1850 and was a continuation of the *Neue Rheinische Zeitung*.   p. 136

[53] This is a reference to *The Influence of Harvests and Grain Prices on Certain Aspects of Russian Economy*, in two volumes, compiled by a group of authors of the liberal-bourgeois and Narodnik trend and edited by Professor A. I. Chuprov and A. S. Posnikov (1897). Lenin read this book when he was in exile and criticised it in his *The Development of Capitalism in Russia*.   p. 139

[54] Karl Marx, *Capital*, Vol. III, Moscow, 1959, pp. 600-793.   p. 139

[55] *Fideicommissum*—entailment of an estate. Under this system a landed estate passed to the eldest son of the testator and could not be mortgaged, divided, or sold *in parte* or *in toto*.

Anerbenrecht—a peasant variant of *fideicommissum* which gave the landed proprietor a somewhat greater right in respect of the inherited estate but which forbade the division of the inheritance.   p. 146

[56] Karl Marx, *Capital*, Vol. III, Moscow, 1959, p. 622.   p. 152

[57] Karl Marx, *Capital*, Vol. III, Moscow, 1959, p. 240.   p. 163

[58] Karl Marx, *Capital*, Vol. III, Moscow, 1959, p. 299.   p. 163

[59] "A Protest by Russian Social-Democrats" was written by Lenin in August 1899 when he was in exile and when he received the manifesto of the "economists—which A. I. Ulyanova-Yelizarova sent him from St. Petersburg and which she called the *Credo* of the "Young." The author of the *Credo* was Y. D. Kuskova, at the time a member of the Union of Russian Social-Democrats Abroad. The manifesto of the group of "economists" was not intended for the press; as Lenin said, it was published "irrespective of, and perhaps even against, the wishes of its authors," because the "economists" feared public criticism of their opportunist views.

The draft of the "Protest" which Lenin prepared to oppose the manifesto of the Russian Bernsteinians was discussed at a meeting of seventeen Marxists in exile in Minusinsk Region at the village of Yermakovskoye. The "Protest" was adopted unanimously. A colony of exiles in Turukhansk also subscribed to the "Protest." Another colony of 11 exiled Social-Democrats in the town of Orlov, Vyatka Gubernia, also came out against the *Credo* of the "economists."

The "Protest" was sent abroad and immediately upon its receipt G. V. Plekhanov sent it to the press for inclusion in the current number of *Rabocheye Dyelo*. The "young" members of the Union Abroad, engaged in editing *Rabocheye Dyelo*, however, published the "Protest" as a separate leaflet in December 1899 without Plekhanov's knowledge. The "Protest" was followed by a postscript stating that the *Credo* represented the opinion of individuals whose position did not constitute a danger to the Russian working-class movement and denying that "economism" was current among members of the Union of Russian Social-Democrats Abroad. Early in 1900 Plekhanov reprinted the "Protest" in the *Vademecum*,

a collection of essays against the "economists." Plekhanov wel-
comed the appearance of the "Protest" as evidence that the Russian
Social-Democrats had recognised the serious danger of "economism"
and had emphatically declared war on it.   p. 167

[60] *Rabocheye Dyelo* (*The Workers' Cause*)—the magazine of the "economists" which appeared irregularly in Geneva between April
1899 and February 1902 as an organ of the Union of Russian Social-Democrats Abroad. For a criticism of the *Rabocheye Dyelo*
group see Lenin's *What Is to Be Done?* (see present edition,
Vol. 5).   p. 167

[61] *The Emancipation of Labour* was the first Russian Marxist group.
It was founded in Geneva by G. V. Plekhanov in 1883 and included P. B. Axelrod, L. G. Deutsch, V. I. Zasulich, and V. N. Igna-
tov among its members.
    The group did much to spread Marxism in Russia. It translated
such Marxist works as *The Manifesto of the Communist Party*
by Marx and Engels, *Wage-Labour and Capital* by Marx, *Socialism: Utopian and Scientific* by Engels, etc., published them
abroad and organised their distribution in Russia. Plekhanov and
his group seriously undermined Narodism. In 1883 and in 1885
Plekhanov wrote two draft programmes of the Russian Social-
Democrats; these were published by the Emancipation of Labour
group and marked an important step towards the establishment
of a Social-Democratic party in Russia. Plekhanov's *Socialism
and the Political Struggle* (1883), *Our Differences* (1885), and *The
Development of the Monist View of History* (1895) played a considerable part in disseminating Marxist ideas. The group, however,
made some serious mistakes. It clung to remnants of Narodnik
views, underestimated the revolutionary role of the peasantry,
and overestimated the part played by the liberal bourgeoisie.
These errors were the germs of the future Menshevik ideas espoused
by Plekhanov and other members of the group. The group had no
practical ties with the working-class movement. Lenin pointed
out that the Emancipation of Labour group "only theoretically
founded the Social-Democratic Party and took the first step in
the direction of the working-class movement" (see present edition,
Vol. 20, "Ideological Struggle in the Working-Class Movement").
    At the Second Congress of the R.S.D.L.P., held in August
1903, the Emancipation of Labour group announced its dissolu-
tion.   p. 171

[62] *Bernsteinism*—a trend hostile to Marxism in international Social-Democracy. It emerged in Germany at the end of the nineteenth century and became connected in name with the Social-
Democrat Eduard Bernstein who attempted to revise Marx's revolutionary theory in the spirit of bourgeois liberalism. The Russian Bernsteinians were the "legal Marxists," the "economists,"
the Bundists, and the Mensheviks.   p. 172

[63] *The International Working Men's Association* (First International)—the First international organisation of the proletariat, founded

by Karl Marx in 1864 at an international workers' meeting convened in London by English and French workers. The foundation of the first International was the result of many years of persistent struggle waged by Marx and Engels to establish a revolutionary party of the working class. Lenin said that the First International "laid the foundation of an international organisation of the workers for the preparation of their revolutionary assault on capital," "laid the foundation for the proletarian, international struggle for socialism" (see present edition, Vol. 29, "*The Third International and Its Place in History*").

The central, leading body of the International Working Men's Association was the General Council, of which Marx was a permanent member. In the course of the struggle against the petty-bourgeois influences and sectarian tendencies then prevalent in the working-class movement (narrow trade-unionism in England, Proudhonism and anarchism in the Romance countries), Marx rallied around himself the most class-conscious members of the General Council (Friedrich Lessner, Eugène Dupont, Hermann Jung, and others). The First International directed the economic and political struggle of the workers of different countries and strengthened their international solidarity. The First International played a tremendous part in disseminating Marxism, in connecting socialism with the working-class movement.

Following the defeat of the Paris Commune, the working class faced the task of creating mass national parties based on the principles advanced by the First International. "As I view European conditions," wrote Marx in 1873, "it is quite useful to let the formal organisation of the International recede into the background for the time being" (Marx to Sorge, London, September 27, 1873). In 1876 the First International was officially disbanded at a convention in Philadelphia.   p. 175

[64] Karl Marx, *The Poverty of Philosophy*, Moscow, 1959, pp. 187-97.
                                                                      p. 176

[65] Lenin criticises the well-known Lassallean thesis that all other classes constitute a reactionary mass with respect to the working class. This thesis was included in the programme of the German Social-Democrats that was adopted at the Gotha Congress in 1875, the Congress which united the two hitherto separately existing German socialist parties, the Eisenachers and the Lassalleans.

Marx exposed the anti-revolutionary nature of this thesis in his *Critique of the Gotha Programme* (see Marx and Engels, *Selected Works*, Vol. II, Moscow, 1958, pp. 25-26).   p. 177

[66] *The North-Russian Workers' Union*, organised in 1878 in St. Petersburg, was one of the early revolutionary political organisations of the Russian working class. The leaders of the Union were Stepan Khalturin, a joiner, and Victor Obnorsky, a mechanic. The Union organised strikes and issued a number of proclamations. It had a membership of over 200. In 1879 the Union was suppressed

by the tsarist government. In February 1880 the members of the Union who remained at liberty published one issue of *Rabochaya Zarya* (*Workers' Dawn*), the first working-class newspaper in Russia.   p. 178

[67] *The South-Russian Workers' Union*, founded in 1875 in Odessa by Y. O. Zaslavsky, was the first workers' revolutionary political organisation in Russia. The Union was suppressed by the tsarist government after having been in existence for eight or nine months.
                                                                                   p. 178

[68] *Rabochaya Mysl* (*Workers' Thought*)—the newspaper of the "economists," published from October 1897 to December 1902; altogether 16 issues appeared (under the editorship of K. M. Takhtarev and others).

Lenin criticised the views of *Rabochaya Mysl* in his "A Retrograde Trend in Russian Social-Democracy" (see pp. 255-85 of this volume), in articles published in *Iskra*, and in his work *What Is to Be Done?* (see present edition, Vol. 5).   p. 179

[69] *S. Peterburgsky Rabochy Listok* (*St. Petersburg Workers' Paper*)— an illegal newspaper, organ of the St. Petersburg League of Struggle for the Emancipation of the Working Class. Two numbers appeared: No. 1 in February (dated January) 1897, which was mimeographed in Russia, some 300-400 copies having been run off; No. 2 in September 1897, in Geneva (printed).

The paper advanced the aim of combining the economic struggle of the working class with extensive political demands and stressed the necessity for the foundation of a working-class party.   p. 179

[70] *Rabochaya Gazeta* (*Workers' Gazette*)—the illegal organ of the Kiev group of Social-Democrats. Two issues appeared—No. 1 in August 1897 and No. 2 in December (dated November) of the same year. The First Congress of the R.S.D.L.P. adopted *Rabochaya Gazeta* as the Party's official organ. The newspaper did not appear after the Congress, the print-shop having been destroyed by the police and the members of the Central Committee arrested. Concerning the attempts to resume its publication made in 1899 see present volume, pp. 207-09.   p. 179

[71] The First Congress of the R.S.D.L.P. was held in March 1898 in Minsk. The Congress was attended by nine delegates from six organisations—the St. Petersburg, Moscow, Ekaterinolsav, and Kiev Leagues for the Emancipation of the Working Class, the *Rabochaya Gazeta* (Kiev) editorial group, and the Bund.

The Congress elected a Central Committee, adopted *Rabochaya Gazeta* as the official organ of the Party, published a *Manifesto*, and declared the Union of Russian Social-Democrats Abroad to be the Party's representative abroad. Soon after the Congress the Central Committee was arrested.

The First Congress of the R.S.D.L.P. was important for
its decisions and its *Manifesto* which proclaimed the formation
of the Russian Social-Democratic Labour Party.   p. 180

[72] *Narodnaya Volya (People's Will)*—a secret political organisation
of Narodnik terrorists that came into being in August 1879 as a
result of a split in the ranks of the Narodnik organisation *Zemlya
i Volya* (Land and Liberty). The Narodnaya Volya was headed by
an Executive Committee whose membership included A. I. Zhe-
lyabov, A. D. Mikhailov, M. F. Frolenko, N. A. Morozov, V. N. Fig-
ner, S. L. Perovskaya, and A. A. Kvyatkovsky. The Narodnaya
Volya clung to the utopian socialism of the Narodniks, but took
the path of political struggle, considering its most important task
to be the overthrow of the autocracy and the winning of political
liberty. Its programme envisaged the organisation of a "permanent
popular assembly" elected on the basis of universal suffrage, the
proclamation of democratic liberties, the transfer of the land to
the people, and the elaboration of measures for the transfer of the
factories to the workers. "The Narodovoltsi (members and followers of the Narodnaya Volya)," wrote Lenin, "made a step forward
in their transition to the political struggle, but they did not succeed in connecting it with socialism" (see present edition, Vol. 8,
"Working-Class and Bourgeois Democracy").

The Narodovoltsi carried on a heroic struggle against the autocracy. They based their activities on the fallacious theory of active
"heroes" and the passive "mass" and expected to recast society
without the participation of the people, employing only their own
forces and attempting to overawe and disorganise the government
by means of individual terror. After the assassination of Alexander
II on March 1, 1881, the government undertook brutal repressions
and by executions and provocations broke up the Narodnaya Volya organisation. Many attempts were made to reconstitute the
Narodnaya Volya throughout the eighties, but all were unsuccessful. In 1886, for instance, a group that followed the traditions of
the Narodnaya Volya was organised under the leadership of A. I.
Ulyanov (Lenin's brother) and P. Y. Shevyrev. After an unsuccessful attempt on the life of Alexander III in 1887, the group was
exposed and its active members were executed.

Although Lenin criticised the fallacious, utopian programme
of the Narodnaya Volya, he had a great respect for the selfless
struggle of its members against tsarism and placed a high value
on their secrecy technique and their strictly centralised organisation.   p. 181

[73] Lenin's review of Prokopovich's *Working-Class Movement in the
West. An Experiment in Critical Investigation. Vol. I. Germany.
Belgium* (St. Petersburg, 1899) was written at the end of 1899.
The first three pages and the end of the manuscript have been
lost; apparently the manuscript was prepared for the press, for
it contains some slight corrections made by Martov. The present
translation has been made from Lenin's original text without the

corrections. Lenin's review was not published at the time, in view
of the fact that Prokopovich's book was held up by the St. Petersburg Censorship Committee on May 22, 1899, and did not appear
until the end of January 1900.   p. 183

[74] *Novoye Vremya (New Times)*—a newspaper published in St. Petersburg from 1868 to October 1917; at first it was moderately liberal, but from 1876 onwards it became an organ of the reactionary
circles among the aristocracy and bureaucracy. The newspaper
opposed not only the revolutionary, but the bourgeois-liberal
movement. From 1905 onwards it was an organ of the Black
Hundreds.   p. 191

[75] *Zur Kritik*—Marx's *Zur Kritik der politischen Ökonomie (A Contribution to the Critique of Political Economy)*. Lenin's references
are to the Russian edition of the book published in 1896.   p. 195

[76] *Rheinische Zeitung für Politik, Handel und Gewerb (Rhenish Gazette for Politics, Trade, and Manufacture)*—a daily newspaper
that appeared in Cologne from January 1, 1842, to March 31, 1843.
The paper was founded by representatives of Rhineland bourgeois
who were opposed to Prussian absolutism. Certain Left Hegelians
were invited to contribute to the paper. Marx became a collaborator
in April 1842 and was one of the paper's editors from October of
that year. The *Rheinische Zeitung* also published a series of articles
by Frederick Engels. Under Marx the paper began to take on a
more definite revolutionary-democratic character. The course
taken by the *Rheinische Zeitung*, and the great popularity it achieved
in Germany, caused alarm and discontent in government circles and led to the vicious persecution of the paper by the reactionary press. On January 19, 1843, the Prussian Government issued
an order to close down the *Rheinische Zeitung* from April 1, 1843,
and to establish a particularly strict, double censorship for the
remaining period of its existence.   p. 195

[77] Lenin refers to the *Manifesto of the Communist Party*.   p. 196

[78] Karl Marx, "Preface to *A Contribution to the Critique of Political
Economy*" (Marx and Engels, *Selected Works*, Vol. I, Moscow, 1958,
p. 365).   p. 196

[79] See Note 78.   p. 196

[80] Lenin wrote *"Our Programme," "Our Immediate Task,"* and *"An
Urgent Question"* during his exile. He intended the articles for *Rabochaya Gazeta*, which had been adopted as official organ
of the Party at the First Congress of the R.S.D.L.P. An attempt
to renew the publication of the newspaper was made in 1899 and
the editorial group proposed to Lenin that he assume the editorship; later it invited him to collaborate. Lenin sent the articles with
the letter to the editorial group. The attempt to renew publication
was unsuccessful and the articles were never printed.   p. 205

[81] Russian opportunists, the "economists" and the Bundists, were in agreement with Bernstein's views. In his *Premises of Socialism*, Bernstein represented their agreement with his views as being that of the majority of the Russian Social-Democrats. p. 208

[82] This is a reference to the split in the Union of Russian Social-Democrats Abroad at its first conference held in Zurich in November 1898. p. 208

[83] The collection, *Proletarskaya Borba* (*Proletarian Struggle*), No. 1, published by the Social-Democratic group of the Urals, was printed in the winter of 1898-99 at the group's own press. The writers who prepared the collection adopted an "economist" position, denied the necessity for an independent working-class political party and believed that the political revolution could be effected by a general strike. Lenin characterised the views of the authors of this collection in an assessment in Chapter IV of *What Is to Be Done?* (see present edition, Vol. 5). p. 208

[84] The reference is to "A Draft Programme of Our Party" (see pp. 227-54 of this volume). p. 208

[85] This refers to the Second Congress of the R.S.D.L.P., which was to have been convened in the spring of 1900. For Lenin's attitude to the convening of a congress at this time see pp. 323 and 353 of this volume. p. 208

[86] *F. P.*—one of Lenin's pen-names. p. 209

[87] The reference is to Plekhanov's article, "Bernstein and Materialism," published in issue No. 44 of *Neue Zeit* (*New Times*), organ of the German Social-Democrats, in July 1898. p. 211

[88] The *Hannover Congress* of the German Social-Democrats was held in 1899 from September 27 to October 2 (October 9-14). In the discussion of the chief point on the agenda, "The Attack on the Fundamental Views and Tactics of the Party," the Congress voted against Bernstein's revisionist views, without, however, subjecting them to an extensive criticism. p. 211

[89] The law of June 2 (14), 1897, establishing an eleven-and-a-half-hour day for industrial enterprises and railway workshops. Prior to this the working day in Russia had not been regulated and was as long as fourteen or fifteen hours. The tsarist government was forced to issue the June 2 law because of pressure on the part of the working-class movement headed by the Leninist "League of Struggle for the Emancipation of the Working Class." Lenin made a detailed analysis and criticism of the law in a pamphlet entitled *The New Factory Law* (see present edition, Vol. 2, pp. 267-315). p. 213

[90] Marx and Engels, *The Manifesto of the Communist Party* (*Selected Works*, Vol. I, Moscow, 1958, pp. 42-43). p. 216

[91] *The Exceptional Law Against the Socialists* was promulgated in Germany in 1878. The law suppressed all organisations of the Social-Democratic Party, mass working-class organisations, and the labour press; socialist literature was confiscated and the banishing of socialists began. The law was annulled in 1890 under pressure of the mass working-class movement.   p. 224

[92] *Vorwärts (Forward)*—the central organ of German Social-Democracy; it was first published in 1876 and was edited by Wilhelm Liebknecht and others. Engels made use of its columns for the struggle against all manifestations of opportunism. From the middle nineties, however, after the death of Engels, *Vorwärts* began regularly to print articles of the opportunists, who predominated in German Social-Democracy and in the Second International. p. 224

[93] Lenin wrote *"A Draft Programme of Our Party"* when he was still in exile, as can be seen from the date "1899" which he inscribed on the manuscript and from the letter to the editorial group of *Rabochaya Gazeta* (see p. 207 of this volume. The mention of the year 1900 in the text is evidently due to the fact that the issue of *Rabochaya Gazeta* for which it was intended was to have appeared that year.

"A Draft Programme of Our Party" represented a continuation of Lenin s work on programmatic questions which he had begun in prison in 1895-96 (see present edition, Vol. 2, "Draft and Explanation of a Programme of the Social-Democratic Party," pp. 93-121).   p. 229

[94] Karl Marx, *Critique of the Gotha Programme* (Marx and Engels, *Selected Works*, Vol. II, Moscow, 1958, p. 16).   p. 229

[95] Karl Marx, *Capital*, Vol. I, Moscow, 1958, p. 763.   p. 233

[96] *The Erfurt Programme* of German Social-Democracy was adopted in October 1891 at a congress in Erfurt in place of the Gotha Programme of 1875; the errors in the latter were exposed by Marx in his *Critique of the Gotha Programme*.   p. 233

[97] Lenin refers to the leaflets distributed by the government during the strikes of 1896 and 1897. In the leaflet issued on June 15, 1896, S. Y. Witte, Minister of Finance, appealed to the workers not to listen to "agitators" (socialists) and to await better living conditions and improved working conditions from the government to whom "the affairs of the factory owners and the workers are alike dear." Witte threatened to punish the workers for the unauthorised cessation of work as "an illegal act."   p. 236

[98] Lenin refers to the "Provisional Regulations Governing the Military Service of Students of Higher Educational Institutions Expelled from Those Institutions for the Joint Organisation of Disorders." Under these regulations, approved on July 29 (August 10), 1899, students who participated in actions directed against the police

regime obtaining in institutions of higher learning would be expelled from universities and drafted into the tsarist army as
privates for a term ranging from one to three years. The students
of all higher educational institutions demanded the repeal of the
"Provisional Regulations" ("The Drafting of 183 Students into
the Army" in the present volume, pp. 414-19).   p. 236

[99] *Rural Superintendent* (*Zemsky Nachalnik in Russian*)—an administrative post instituted by the tsarist government in 1889 to
strengthen the authority of the landlords over the peasants. The
Rural Superintendents were appointed from among the local landed
nobility and were granted very great powers, not merely administrative, but also judicial, which included the right to arrest peasants
and administer corporal punishment.   p. 243

[100] Land redemption payments were established by the "Regulation
Governing Redemption by Peasant Who Have Emerged from Serf
Dependence..." adopted on February 19, 1861. The tsarist government compelled the peasants, in return for the allotments assigned
to them, to pay redemption to the landlords amounting to several
times the real price of the land. When the deal was concluded, the
government paid the landlord the purchase price, which was
considered a debt owed by the peasant to be repaid over a period
of 49 years. The instalments to be paid annually by the peasants
were called land redemption payments. These were an intolerable
burden on the peasants and caused their impoverishment and ruin.
The peasants formerly belonging to landlords alone paid nearly
2,000 million rubles to the tsarist government, whereas the market
price of the land that the peasants received did not exceed 544
million rubles. In view of the fact that the adoption of the redemption scheme by the peasants did not take place at once, but dragged
on until 1883, the redemption payments were not to have ended
before 1932. The peasant movement during the first Russian revolution (1905-07), however, compelled the tsarist government
to abolish the redemption payments as from January 1907.   p. 245

[101] *Law of easement*—the right to make use of the property of others.
In the present case Lenin refers to survivals of feudal relations in
the Western Territory. After the Reform of 1861 the peasants
were compelled to render supplementary services for the benefit
of the landlords for the right to use common roads, meadows,
pastures, water, etc.   p. 245

[102] Karl Marx, *The Eighteenth Brumaire of Louis Bonaparte* (Marx
and Engels, *Selected Works*, Vol. I, Moscow, 1958, p. 335).   p. 246

[103] *Royal demesne*—lands belonging to members of the tsar's family.
                                                               p. 248

[104] *Cut-off lands* (*otrezki*)—the pasture lands, woods, etc., which the
landlords "cut off," i.e., of which they deprived the peasants when
serfdom was abolished in Russia.   p. 249

[105] *Gubernia Committees of Nobles* were set up by the tsarist authorities in 1857-58 to draw up plans for the "Peasant Reform," for the "emancipation" of the peasants.

The plans put forward by the Committees of Nobles envisaged an "emancipation" that would benefit only the landlords; the committees effected the "legal" plunder of the peasants in the sixties.   p. 249

[106] *The League of Struggle for the Emancipation of the Working Class*, organised by Lenin in the autumn of 1895, united about twenty Marxist workers' circles in St. Petersburg. The work of the League was based on the principles of centralism and strict discipline. The League was headed by a central group consisting of V. I. Lenin, A. A. Vaneyev, P. K. Zaporozhets, G. M. Krzhizhanovsky, N. K. Krupskaya, L. Martov (Y. O. Zederbaum), M. A. Silvin, V. V. Starkov, and others. The entire work of the League, however, was under the direct leadership of five members of the group headed by Lenin. The League was divided into several district organisations. Such leading class-conscious workers as I. V. Babushkin and V. A. Shelgunov connected the groups with the factories where there were organisers in charge of gathering information and distributing literature. Workers' circles were established in the big factories.

For the first time in Russia the League set about introducing socialism into the working-class movement, effecting a transition from the propagation of Marxism among small numbers of advanced workers attending circles to political agitation among broad masses of the proletariat. It directed the working-class movement and connected the workers' struggle for economic demands with the political struggle against tsarism. It organised a strike in November 1895 at the Thornton Woollen Mill. In the summer of 1896 the famous St. Petersburg textile workers' strike, involving over 30,000 workers, took place under the leadership of the League. The League issued leaflets and pamphlets for the workers and prepared the ground for the issuance of the newspaper *Rabocheye Dyelo*. Its publications were edited by Lenin.

The League's influence spread far beyond St. Petersburg, and workers' circles in Moscow, Kiev, Ekaterinoslav, and other cities, and other parts of Russia followed its example and united to form Leagues of Struggle.

Late in the night of December 8 (20), 1895, the tsarist government dealt the League a severe blow by arresting a large number of its leading members, including Lenin. An issue of *Rabocheye Dyelo* ready for the press was seized. The League replied to the arrest of Lenin and the other members by issuing a leaflet containing political demands in which reference was made, for the first time to the existence of the League of Struggle.

While in prison, Lenin continued to guide the League, helped it with his advice, smuggled coded letters and leaflets out of prison, and wrote the pamphlet, *On Strikes* (the original of which has

not yet been found), and the "Draft and Explanation of a Programme of the Social-Democratic Party."

The League was significant, as Lenin put it, because it was
the first real beginning of a revolutionary party based on the working-class movement to guide the class struggle of the proletariat.
                                                                p. 256

[107] *The Kiev League of Struggle for the Emancipation of the Working
Class* was formed in March 1897, under the influence of the St.
Petersburg League of Struggle, by a resolution adopted at the Kiev
conference which proposed that all Russian Social-Democratic
organisations call themselves Leagues of Struggle for the Emancipation of the Working Class, following the example of the St.
Petersburg Social-Democratic organisation. The League united Russian and Polish Social-Democratic groups and a group of the Polish Socialist Party, altogether more than 30 members. The Kiev
League of Struggle maintained connections with the St. Petersburg League (through personal contacts and through acquaintance
with the St. Petersburg proclamations and Lenin's writings on
programmatic questions: Lenin's "Tasks of the Russian Social-
Democrats" was sent to Kiev in manuscript and was known to the
leaders of Kiev Social-Democratic organisations).

The activities of the Kiev League of Struggle began with the
May Day proclamation of 1897 which was widely distributed in
the southern cities of Russia. In that year the Kiev League
distributed 6,500 copies of proclamations at more than 25 Kiev
factories. That same year a special group of the League published
two issues of *Rabochaya Gazeta* as an all-Russian Social-Democratic
newspaper. The First Congress of the R.S.D.L.P., in March 1898,
adopted *Rabochaya Gazeta* as the Party's official organ. The
League's illegal literature was distributed mainly in the South-
Russian towns. In addition to its agitational work the League
carried on propaganda in workers' circles and at factory meetings.

The Kiev League of Struggle carried on active preparations
for the convening of the First Congress of the R.S.D.L.P. Shortly
after the Congress the League was suppressed by the police (the
Rabochaya Gazeta printing-press that had been transferred from
Kiev to Ekaterinoslav and a large quantity of illegal literature
was seized). Arrests were carried out in Kiev and in many big
Russian cities.

The Kiev League of Struggle played an important role in the
development and organisation of the working class in Russia for
the formation of a Marxist revolutionary party. The members
of the Social-Democratic groups that remained at liberty soon re-
stablished the underground organisation which took the name of
the Kiev Committee of the R.S.D.L.P.   p. 256

[108] *The General Jewish Workers' Union of Lithuania, Poland, and
Russia (The Bund)* was formed by a founding congress of Jewish
Social-Democratic groups held in Vilno in 1897; it was an asso-
ciation mainly of semi-proletarian Jewish artisans in the Western

regions of Russia. The Bund joined the R.S.D.L.P. at the First
Congress (1898) "as an autonomous organisation, independent only
as far as questions affecting the Jewish proletariat are concerned."
    The Bund brought nationalism and separatism into the working-
class movement of Russia. After the Second Congress of the
R.S.D.L.P. rejected its demand that it be recognised as the only
representative of the Jewish proletariat, the Bund left the Party.
In 1906 the Bund again entered the R.S.D.L.P. on the basis of a
resolution of the Fourth (Unity) Congress.
    Within the R.S.D.L.P. the Bundists persistently supported
the opportunist wing of the Party (the "economists," the Mensheviks, the liquidators) and struggled against the Bolsheviks and
Bolshevism. The Bund countered the Bolsheviks' programmatic
demand for the right of nations to self-determination by a demand
for cultural-national autonomy. During the period of the Stolypin
reaction, it adopted a liquidationist position and was active in
forming the August anti-Party bloc. During the First World War
(1914-18) it adopted the position of the social-chauvinists. In
1917 it supported the counter-revolutionary Provisional Government and fought on the side of the enemies of the Great October
Socialist Revolution. In the years of foreign military intervention
and civil war the Bund leadership joined forces with the counter-
revolution. At the same time, a change was taking place among
the rank and file of the Bund in favour of collaboration with Soviet
power. In 1921 the Bund decided to dissolve itself and part of
its membership entered the Russian Communist Party (Bolsheviks) on the basis of the rules of admission.   p. 256

[109] The pamphlet referred to is L. Martov's *Red Flag in Russia*, published abroad in October 1900.   p. 258

[110] *Sotsial-Demokrat (The Social-Democrat)*—a literary and political review, published by the Emancipation of Labour group in
London and Geneva between 1890 and 1892. Four issues appeared.
Sotsial-Demokrat played an important part in spreading Marxist ideas in Russia. G. V. Plekhanov, P. B. Axelrod, and V. I. Zasulich were the chief figures associated with its publication. p. 271

[111] *Balalaikin*—a character from M. Y. Saltykov-Shchedrin's *Modern Idyll*; a liberal windbag, adventurer, and liar.   p. 279

[112] *Moskovskiye Vedomosti (Moscow Recorder)*—one of the oldest
Russian newspapers, originally issued (in 1756) as a small sheet
by Moscow University. In 1863 it was taken over by M. N. Katkov
and became a monarchist-nationalist organ, reflecting the views
of the most reactionary sections of the landlords and the clergy.
In 1905 it became one of the leading organs of the Black Hundreds
and continued to appear until the October Revolution in 1917.
                                                                 p. 290

[113] *Grazhdanin (The Citizen)*—a reactionary magazine published in
St. Petersburg from 1872 to 1914. From the eighties of the last

century it was the organ of the extreme monarchists and was edited by Prince Meshchersky and financed by the government. It
had a small circulation, but it was influential in bureaucratic
circles.   p. 290

[114] *Johann of Kronstadt* (I. I. Sergeyev)—the priest of Kronstadt
Cathedral, an obscurantist notorious for his pogrom incitements
directed against non-Russian nationalities.   p. 291

[115] *Marshal of the Nobility*—in tsarist Russia, the elected representative of the nobility of a gubernia or uyezd. The Marshal of the
Nobility was in charge of all the affairs of the nobility; he occupied
an influential position in the administration and took the chair
at meetings of the Zemstvo.   p. 303

[116] *Factory affairs boards*—bodies supervising factory affairs in
tsarist Russia. As a rule, the boards consisted of the provincial
governor, the public prosecutor, the chief of the police administration, the factory inspector, and two factory owners.   p. 303

[117] Lenin wrote "*On Strikes*" for *Rabochaya Gazeta* when he was in
exile (see the "Letter to the Editorial Group," p. 207 of this
volume). Only the first part of the article is in the archives of the
Institute of Marxism-Leninism; it is not known whether the other
parts were written.   p. 310

[118] Frederick Engels, *The Condition of the Working Class in England*
(Marx and Engels, *Selected Works*, Vol. II, Moscow, 1958, p 260).
                                                                p. 315

[119] Lenin quotes a statement made by the Prussian Minister of the
Interior, von Puttkamer.   p. 317

[120] *Iskra* (*The Spark*) was the first all-Russian illegal Marxist newspaper; it was founded by Lenin in 1900 and it played an important
role in building the Marxist revolutionary party of the working
class in Russia.
It was impossible to publish the revolutionary newspaper in
Russia on account of police persecution, and, while still in exile
in Siberia, Lenin evolved a plan for its publication abroad. When
his exile ended (January 1900) Lenin immediately set about putting his plan into effect. In February, in St. Petersburg, he nego-
tiated with Vera Zasulich (who had come from abroad illegally)
on the participation of the Emancipation of Labour group in the
publication of the newspaper. At the end of March and the beginning of April a conference was held—known as the Pskov Conference—with V. I. Lenin, L. Martov (Y. O. Zederbaum), A. N. Potresov, S. I. Radchenko, and the "legal Marxists" P. B. Struve
and M. I. Tugan-Baranovsky participating, which discussed the
draft declaration, drawn up by Lenin, of the Editorial Board of the
all-Russian newspaper (*Iskra*) and the scientific and political

magazine (*Zarya*) on the programme and the aims of these publications. During the first half of 1900 Lenin travelled in a number of Russian cities (Moscow, St. Petersburg, Riga, Smolensk, Nizhni-Novgorod, Ufa, Samara, Syzran) and established contact with Social-Democratic groups and individual Social-Democrats, obtaining their support for *Iskra*. In August 1900, when Lenin arrived in Switzerland, he and Potresov conferred with the Emancipation of Labour group on the programme and the aims of the newspaper and the magazine, on possible contributors, and on the editorial board and its location. The conference almost ended in failure (see pp. 333-49 of this volume), but an agreement was finally reached on all disputed questions.

The first issue of Lenin's *Iskra* was published in Leipzig in December 1900; the ensuing issues were published in Munich; from July 1902 the paper was published in London, and from the spring of 1903 in Geneva. Considerable help in getting the newspaper going (the organisation of secret printing-presses, the acquisition of Russian type, etc.) was afforded by the German Social-Democrats Clara Zetkin, Adolf Braun, and others; by Julian Marchlewski, a Polish revolutionary residing in Munich at that time, and by Harry Quelch, one of the leaders of the English Social-Democratic Federation.

The Editorial Board of *Iskra* consisted of: V. I. Lenin, G. V. Plekhanov, L. Martov, P. B. Axelrod, A. N. Potresov, and V. I. Zasulich. The first secretary of the board was I. G. Smidovich-Leman; the post was then taken over, from the spring of 1901, by N. K. Krupskaya, who also conducted the correspondence between *Iskra* and the Russian Social-Democratic organisations. Lenin was in actuality editor-in-chief and the leading figure in *Iskral*, in which he published his articles on all basic questions of Party organisation and the class struggle of the proletariat in Russia, as well as on the most important events in world affairs.

Iskra became the centre for the unification of Party forces for the gathering and training of Party workers. In a number of Russian cities (St. Petersburg, Moscow, Samara, and others) groups and committees of the R.S.D.L.P. were organised on Leninist *Iskra* lines and a conference of *Iskra* supporters held in Samara in January 1902 founded the Russian *Iskra* organisation. *Iskra* organisations grew up and worked under the direct leadership of Lenin's disciples and comrades-in-arms: N. E. Bauman, I. V. Babushkin, S. I. Gusev, M. I. Kalinin, P. A. Krasikov, G. M. Krzhizhanovsky, F. V. Lengnik, P. N. Lepeshinsky, I. I. Radchenko, and others.

On the initiative and with the direct participation of Lenin, the *Iskra* Editorial Board drew up a draft programme of the Party (published in No. 21 of *Iskra*) and prepared the Second Congress of the R.S.D.L.P., held in July and August 1903. By the time the Congress was convened the majority of the local Social-Democratic organisations in Russia had adopted the *Iskra* position, approved its programme, organisational plan, and tactical line, and recognised the newspaper as their leading organ. A special resolution of the Congress noted *Iskra*'s exceptional role in the struggle to build the Party and adopted the newspaper as the central organ of the R.S.D.L.P. The Congress approved an editorial board consisting of Lenin, Plekhanov, and Martov. Despite the Congress decision, Martov refused to participate, and Nos. 46-51 of *Iskra* were edited by Lenin and Plekhanov. Later Plekhanov went over to the Menshevik position and demanded that all the old Menshevik editors be included in the Editorial Board of *Iskra*, although they had been rejected by the Congress. Lenin could not agree to this and on October 19 (November 1), 1903, he resigned from the *Iskra* Editorial Board. He was co-opted to the Central Committee, from where he conducted a struggle against the Menshevik opportunists. Issue No. 52 of *Iskra* was edited by Plekhanov alone. On November 13 (26), 1903, Plekhanov, on his own initiative and in violation of the will of the Congress, co-opted all the old Menshevik editors to the Editorial Board. Beginning with issue No. 52, the Mensheviks turned *Iskra* into their own organ.   p. 320

[121] *Zarya (Dawn)*—a Marxist scientific and political magazine published legally in Stuttgart in 1901-02 by the *Iskra* Editorial Board. Altogether four numbers (in three issues) appeared: No. 1—April 1901 (it actually appeared on March 23, New Style); No. 2-3—December 1901; and No. 4—August 1902.   p. 320

[122] Lenin refers to the "Announcement on the Renewal of Publications of the Emancipation of Labour Group" published at the beginning of 1900 in Geneva, after the appearance of Lenin's "A Protest by Russian Social-Democrats." In their "Announcement" the Emancipation of Labour group supported Lenin's appeal in the "Protest" for decisive struggle against opportunism in the ranks of Russian and international Social-Democracy.   p. 322

[123] By *groups and organisations* Lenin means the Social-Democrats grouped round the newspaper *Yuzhny Rabochy (Southern Worker)*, the Bund, and the Union of Russian Social-Democrats Abroad, the leadership of which had been transferred from the Emancipation of Labour group to the "young" supporters of "economism." These organisations planned to call the Second Congress of the Party in Smolensk in the spring of 1900. The circumstances surrounding the preparation for the Congress are discussed in Chapter 5 of Lenin's *What Is to Be Done?* (see present edition, Vol. 5).   p. 323

[124] Lenin refers to "A Draft Programme of Our Party" which he wrote at the end of 1899 for No. 3 of *Rabochaya Gazeta* that never came to be published (see present volume, pp. 227-54). A draft programme of the Party was elaborated for the Second Congress of the R.S.D.L.P., on Lenin's suggestion, by the Editorial Board of *Iskra* and *Zarya* and was printed in *Iskra*, No 21, on June 1, 1902; it was adopted by the Second Congress of the R.S.D.L.P. in August 1903.   p. 3

[125] Lenin quotes the basic postulate of the "General Rules of the International Working Men's Association" (First International) drawn up by Karl Marx (Marx and Engels, *Selected Works*, Vol. I, Moscow, 1956, p. 386).   p. 327

[126] The split in the Union of Russian Social-Democrats Abroad, referred to in this passage, occurred at the Second Congress of the Union in April 1900. At the First Congress of the R.S.D.L.P., the Union was recognised as the representative of the Party abroad; the majority of its members, however, adopted the "economist" position, on account of which the Emancipation of Labour group and their supporters left the Congress, broke off relations with the Union, and formed an independent organisation of Russian Social-Democrats abroad under the name of Russian Revolutionary Organisation *Sotsial-Demokrat*.   p. 333

[127] By saying that he had been "ordered" not "to shoot" at P. B. Struve in 1895 (in this case he is hinting at A. N. Potresov), G. V. Plekhanov was trying to justify his conciliatory attitude towards the revisionist position of the "legal Marxists." Lenin considered Plekhanov's behaviour to be incorrect, because he not only failed to criticise the bourgeois-liberal views of Struve but took the latter under his protection.   p. 334

[128] Lenin is apparently referring to Struve's article, "Again on Free Will and Necessity," published in 1897 in issue No. 8 of the magazine *Novoye Slovo* (*New Word*). In this article Struve declared himself openly against the Marxist theory of the proletarian revolution. On June 27 (July 9), 1899, Lenin wrote to Potresov: "One thing I do not understand—how could Kamensky (Plekhanov.—*Ed.*) leave unanswered the articles by Struve and Bulgakov against Engels in *Novoye Slovo*! Can you explain this to me?"   p. 334

[129] This passage refers to *Vademecum*, a collection of articles and documents for the *Rabocheye Dyelo* Editorial Board (1900) in which Plekhanov published, among other documents, three private letters from Z. M. Kopelson of the Bund and from an "economist" leader, Y. D. Kuskova.   p. 334

[130] "*Our third man*" was L. Martov (Y. O. Zederbaum) who was in the South of Russia at the time Lenin and Potresov conducted their negotiations with the Emancipation of Labour group and who did not go abroad until March 1901.   p. 335

[131] *Bobo*—P. B. Struve.   p. 336

Die Neue Zeit (*New Times*)—theoretical publication of German Social-Democracy. Appeared in Stuttgart from 1883 to 1923. Several articles by Frederick Engels appeared in its columns between 1885 and 1895. Engels frequently offered points of advice to the editors of *Die Neue Zeit* and severely criticised them for departing from Marxism. In the late 1890s, after Engels' death, the journal, which expounded Kautskian views, made a practice of publishing articles by revisionists. During the First World War (1914-18) the publication adopted a Centrist position and actually supported the social-chauvinists.   p. 337

[133] These were former members of the Union of Russian Social-Democrats Abroad who, after the split at the Second Congress of the Union, in April 1900, broke with the opportunist majority and united with the Emancipation of Labour group to form the *Sotsial-Demokrat* group.   p. 339

[134] *N.*—the city of Nuremberg which Lenin visited on his way from Geneva to Munich after the conference between the *Iskra* and the Emancipation of Labour groups.   p. 349

[135] This *"special agreement"* was apparently written later. The following document is now in the archives of the Institute of Marxism-Leninism, Central Committee of the C.P.S.U.; it is in an envelope bearing the inscription by N. K. Krupskaya: "Documents relating to the earliest period. Agreement on the publication of *Zarya* and *Iskra*:

"1. The collection *Zarya* and the newspaper *Iskra* are published and edited by a group of Russian Social-Democrats, the Emancipation of Labour group participating in the editorial work.

"2. All articles on matters of principle and those of special significance will be communicated to all members of the Emancipation of Labour group, if that is not made impossible by editorial and technical circumstances.

"3. The members of the Emancipation of Labour group will vote on all editorial questions—personally, if they are present in the place where the editorial office is located, and by mail when articles are communicated to them.

"4. In the event of differences of opinion between the editors and the Emancipation of Labour group, the editors undertake to publish in full the special opinion of the group or of each of its members individually.

"5. Only point 1 of this agreement is to be published. October 6, 1900."

The document is typewritten, has no heading, and is unsigned.   p. 350

[136] *The Self-Emancipation of the Working Class group* was a small circle of "economists" that came into being in St. Petersburg in the autumn of 1898 and existed for a few months only. The group issued a manifesto announcing its aims (printed in the magazine *Nakanune* [*On the Eve*], published in London), its rules, and several proclamations addressed to workers.

Lenin criticised the views of this group in Chapter 2 of his book, *What Is to Be Done?* (see present edition, Vol. 5).   p. 353

[137] See Note 125.   p. 368

[138] *Pyotr Alexeyev*—a worker-revolutionary in the seventies of the last century whose speech, made before a tsarist court on March 10 (22), 1877, in St. Petersburg, was first printed in London in the irregularly appearing collection *Vperyod! (Forward!)*. The speech was afterwards repeatedly published illegally and was very popular among Russian workers.   p. 371

[139] The reference is to the uprising for national liberation that began in India in 1857. The insurrection was suppressed by British troops in 1859.   p. 373

[140] *The Fifth International Socialist Congress of the Second International* was held from September 10 to September 14 (23-27, New Style), 1900, in Paris. The Russian delegation consisted of 23 members. Among its other decisions the Congress acted to establish a standing International Socialist Bureau composed of representatives of the socialist parties of all countries, its secretariat to be in Brussels.   p. 379

[141] *Arsenyev*—A. N. Potresov; *Velika*—V. I. Zasulich; *"the twin"*— P. B. Struve; *"the wife"*—N. A. Struve, wife of P. B. Struve.
                                                                        p. 380

[142] *The comrade and friend of P. B. Struve*—M. I. Tugan-Baranovsky.
                                                                        p. 381

[143] *Derzhimorda*—the name of a policeman in N. V. Gogol's comedy *The Inspector-General*; a boorish, insolent oppressor, a man of violence.   p. 390

[144] Lenin quotes from Gleb Uspensky's "Fyodor Mikhailovich Reshetnikov."   p. 402

[145] Lenin refers to Porphyry (nicknamed Judas) Golovlyov, a sanctimonious, hypocritical landlord serf-owner described in M. Saltykov-Shchedrin's *The Golovlyov Family*.   p. 406

[146] *Vestnik Finansov, Promyshlennosti i Torgovli (Finance, Industry and Trade Messenger)*—a weekly journal published by the Ministry of Finance in St. Petersburg from November 1883 to 1917 (until January 1885 it was called *Ukazatel Pravitelstvennykh Rasporyazheny po Ministerstvu Finansov—Record of Government Instructions, Ministry of Finance*). It carried government regulations, economic articles, and reviews.   p. 409

[147] *"White linings"*—the name given in tsarist Russia to monarchist-minded students from aristocratic and bourgeois circles who conducted a struggle against the democratic section of the students, supporters of the revolutionary movement. The name derived from white silk linings of their uniforms.   p. 415

[148] The words of Colonel Skalozub, a character in A. S. Griboyedov's
comedy *Wit Works Woe*.   p. 416

[149] *"Green Street"*—a form of corporal punishment employed in the
army of feudal Russia. The condemned man was tied to a rifle and
made to run the gauntlet between two ranks of soldiers who beat
him with sticks or green switches. This form of punishment was
particularly widespread under Tsar Nicholas I (1825-55).   p. 416

[150] *Hannibal's vow*—unwavering determination to fight to the end.
The Carthagenian general, Hannibal, made a vow not to cease
the struggle against Rome until his dying day.   p. 417

[151] *Yuzhny Krai (Southern Region)*—a daily newspaper dealing
with social, literary, and political problems founded in Kharkov
in 1880. The paper, published and edited by A. A. Yuzefovich, an
extreme reactionary, upheld conservative, royalist views.   p. 419

[152] The article, *"The Workers' Party and the Peasantry,"* was written
in connection with the elaboration of the agrarian programme of
the R.S.D.L.P., published in the name of the Editorial Board
of *Iskra* and *Zarya* in the summer of 1902 and adopted by the
Second Congress of the R.S.D.L.P. in 1903.   p. 420

[153] *A quarter or beggar's allotment*—a quarter of the so-called "maximum" or "decree" allotment, the amount established by law for
a given district at the time of the Reform of 1861. Some of the peasants received these tiny parcels of land from the landlords without
payment of redemption money. Such allotments were, therefore,
also called "gift allotments" and the peasants who received them
were called "gift peasants."   p. 420

[154] *Temporarily bound peasants*—peasants who were still compelled
to carry out certain duties (payment of quit-rent or performance
of corvée service) for the use of their land even after the Reform
and until they started paying redemption money to the landlord
for their allotment.
    From the moment the redemption contract was concluded, the
peasants ceased to be "temporarily bound" and joined the category
of "peasant property-owners."   p. 420

[155] These *title-deeds* were documents defining the land-owning relations of temporarily bound peasants and landlords upon the abolition of serfdom in 1861. The title-deed indicated the amount of
land used by the peasant before the Reform and the land and other
properties that remained in his hands after "emancipation"; the
deed also listed the duties the peasant had to perform for the landlord. The amount of redemption money to be paid by the peasant
was determined on the basis of this title-deed.   p. 421

THE LIFE AND WORK
OF
V. I. LENIN

Outstanding Dates
(1898-April 1901)

1898

Prior to January 24 (prior to February 5)	Lenin writes two letters to N. Y. Fedoseyev in Verkholensk (Siberia), the organiser and leader of the first Marxist circles in Kazan.
Between February 7 and February 17 (19-26)	Lenin writes his review of A. Bogdanov's *A Short Course of Economic Science.*
End of February (beginning of March) to August	Lenin translates Volume I of Sidney and Beatrice Webb's *Industrial Democracy.*
End of May (beginning of June)	Lenin and N. K. Krupskaya leave the village of Shushenskoye for Minusinsk. They take part in a meeting of exiles.
July 10 (22)	V. I. Lenin and N. K. Krupskaya are married.
August 9 (21)	Lenin completes the draft of his work, *The Development of Capitalism in Russia.*
Prior to August 26 (prior to September 7)	Lenin writes his article, "On the Question of Our Factory Statistics (Professor Karyshev's New Statistical Exploits)."
September 11-25 (September 23-October 7)	Lenin goes to Krasnoyarsk, works in a library, and meets local political exiles.
October 9-15 (21-27)	The first collection of Lenin's writings, *Economic Studies and Essays*, published in Russia, under the signature of Vladimir Ilyin.

Autumn	Lenin's pamphlet, *The Tasks of the Russian Social-Demokrats*, published in Geneva.
December 24, 1898-January 2, 1899 (January 5)	Lenin and Krupskaya go to Minusinsk. Lenin attends a meeting of exiled Marxists from different parts of the Minusinsk area.

1899

January 30 (February 11)	Lenin completes the preparation for the press of his *The Development of Capitalism in Russia*.
January	Lenin's "A Note on the Question of the Market Theory (Apropos of the Polemic of Messrs. Tugan-Baranovsky and Bulgakov)" is published in *Nauchnoye Obozreniye*, No. 1.
February	Lenin reviews R. Gvozdev's book, *Kulak Usury, Its Social and Economic Significance*, Parvus' *The World Market and the Agricultural Crisis*, and the handbook, *Commercial and Industrial Russia*.
First half of March	Lenin writes "Once More on the Theory of Realisation," an article against Struve.
Prior to March 21 (prior to April 2)	Lenin writes a review of Kautsky's *The Agrarian Question*.
March 24-31 (April 6-12)	Lenin's *The Development of Capitalism in Russia* is published, under the signature of Vladimir Ilyin.
April 4 (16)-May 9 (21)	Lenin writes two articles under the common heading, "Capitalism in Agriculture (Kautsky's Book and Mr. Bulgakov's Article)."
May 2 (14)	Lenin's house in the village of Shushenskoye is searched and Lenin is interrogated when the police establish the fact of his correspondence with exiled Social-Democrats.
May	Lenin's review of Hobson's work, *The Evolution of Modern Capitalism*, is published in *Nachalo*, No. 5.
Prior to May 29 (prior to June 10)	Lenin writes his "Reply to Mr. P. Nezhdanov," an article against revisionism.

Prior to August 22 (prior to September 3)	Lenin writes "A Protest by Russian Social-Democrats" against the *Credo*, the manifesto of the "economists."
	In the village of Yermakovskoye Lenin organises a conference of 17 Marxist political exiles which approves his "A Protest by Russian Social-Democrats."
September 9-15 (21-27)	Lenin's translation of Volume I of the Webbs' *Industrial Democracy* is published, under the signature of Vladimir Ilyin.
September 10 (22)	Lenin attends the funeral in Yermakovskoye of A. A. Vaneyev, an exiled member of the St. Petersburg League of Struggle for the Emancipation of the Working Class, and speaks at the graveside.
Beginning of September 1899- January 19 (31), 1900	Lenin and Krupskaya edit the Russian translation of Volume II of the Webbs' *Industrial Democracy* sent them from St. Petersburg.
Not earlier than October	Lenin accepts the proposal to edit Rabochaya Gazeta, which was recognised at the First Congress of the R.S.D.L.P. as the official organ of the Party, and, somewhat later, a further proposal to contribute to the newspaper. Lenin writes three articles for *Rabochaya Gazeta* and a "Letter to the Editorial Group."
End of the year	Lenin writes a review of S. N. Prokopovich's book, *The Working-Class Movement in the West*.
	Lenin writes a review of Kautsky's book, *Bernstein and the Social-Democratic Programme. A Counter-Critique.*
	Lenin and Krupskaya translate Kautsky's book, Bernstein and the Social-Democratic Programme. A Counter-Critique. Lenin's "A Protest by Russian Social-Democrats" is published in Geneva as a reprint from *Rabocheye Dyelo*, No. 4-5.
	Lenin writes the articles: "A Draft Programme of Our Party"; "A Retrograde Trend in Russian Social-Democracy"; "Apropos of the *Profession de foi*"; "Factory Courts"; "On Strikes."
1898-99	Lenin corresponds with F. V. Lengnik, who was in exile (the correspondence is devoted mostly to a discussion of philosophical questions).

1900

January 29	Lenin's term of exile ends.
(February 10)	Lenin and Krupskaya leave Shushenskoye for European Russia. Forbidden to live in the metropolitan cities, university towns, and big industrial centres, Lenin chooses the town of Pskov as being most convenient for contact with St. Petersburg.
First half of February	On his way from Siberia, Lenin stops at Ufa, where Krupskaya remained until the end of her term of exile. Lenin meets Social-Democrats in exile at Ufa (A. D. Tsyurupa and others).
Middle of February	Lenin visits Moscow illegally and stays with his relatives.
	From I. K. Lalayants, a representative of the Ekaterinoslav Committee, Lenin learns of the preparations for the convocation of the Second Congress of the R.S.D.L.P. and receives a proposal to participate in it as well as to undertake the editing of *Rabochaya Gazeta*.
Prior to February 26 (prior to March 10)	Lenin comes illegally to St. Petersburg, where he meets V. I. Zasulich, who has come from abroad, and conducts with her negotiations on the participation of the Emancipation of Labour group in the publication of an all-Russian Marxist newspaper and magazine abroad.
February 26 (March 10)	Lenin arrives in Pskov, where he is kept under the secret surveillance of the police.
Spring	Lenin establishes contact with Social-Democratic groups and individual Social-Democrats in various Russian towns and conducts negotiations for their support for the future *Iskra*.
	Lenin goes illegally to Riga to establish contact with local Social-Democrats. In Pskov Lenin takes part in a meeting of the local revolutionary and oppositional intellectuals; he speaks in criticism of revisionism.
End of March-beginning of April, prior to 4th (17)	Lenin draws up the draft declaration of the Editorial Board on the programme and the objectives of the all-Russian political newspaper (*Iskra*) and the scientific and political magazine (*Zarya*).

Lenin conducts a conference between revolutionary Marxists and "legal Marxists" (P. B. Struve, M. I. Tugan-Baranovsky) on the question of support for the publication of *Iskra* and *Zarya* (the Pskov Conference).

April-May — Lenin writes a report for the contemplated Second Congress of the R.S.D.L.P. and receives a mandate from the Emancipation of Labour group to attend the Congress.

May 6 (18) — Lenin obtains a passport to go to Germany.

May 20 (June 2) — Lenin goes illegally to St. Petersburg to establish contact with local Social-Democrats.

May 21 (June 3) — Lenin is arrested and interrogated in St. Petersburg,

May 31 (June 13) — Lenin is released from custody.

June 1-7 (14-20) — Lenin lives with relatives at Podolsk, near Moscow.
On Lenin's invitation a number of Social-Democrats (P. N. Lepeshinsky, S. P. and S. P. Shesternin, and others) come to Podolsk and Lenin comes to an agreement with them on their support for the future *Iskra*.

June 7 (20) — Lenin goes to N. K. Krupskaya in Ufa via Nizhni-Novgorod (now Gorky).

June 8 or 9 (21 or 22) — Lenin comes to an agreement with the Nizhni-Novgorod Social-Democrats on their support for *Iskra*.

Second half of June — In Ufa Lenin comes to an agreement with the local Social-Democrats in exile on their support for *Iskra*.

Later than July 2 (15) — Lenin leaves Ufa for Podolsk.

Between July 2 and 10 (15 and 23) — Lenin stays in Samara (now Kuibyshev), where he comes to an agreement with the local Social-Democrats on their support for *Iskra*.

July 10 (23) — Lenin returns to Podolsk.

July 16 (29) — Lenin leaves for abroad.

Beginning of August	Lenin stays in Zurich for two days and discusses with P. B. Axelrod the publication of *Iskra* and *Zarya*.
	Lenin has talks with G. V. Plekhanov in Geneva on the publication of *Iskra* and *Zarya*; differences of opinion with Plekhanov in connection with Lenin's draft statement "In the Name of the Editorial Board."
	At Bellerive (near Geneva) Lenin has talks with N. E. Bauman and other Social-Democrats on their participation in the work of *Iskra*.
August 11-15 (24-28)	Lenin takes part in a conference with the Emancipation of Labour group at Corsier (near Geneva) on the question of the publication and joint editing of *Iskra* and *Zarya*..
August 20 (September 2) and later	Lenin records the circumstances connected with his talks with Plekhanov ("How the 'Spark' Was Nearly Extinguished").
August 22 or 23 (September 4 or 5)	Lenin draws up a draft agreement between the *Iskra* group and the Emancipation of Labour group on the question of the publication of *Iskra* and *Zarya* and on the relation of the groups on the Editorial Board of the publications.
Between August 23 and September 2 (between September 5 and 15)	In his correspondence with an unknown Russian Social-Democrat Lenin emphatically rejects any agreement with the Union of Russian Social-Democrats Abroad, an organisation of "economists."
August 24 (September 6)	Lenin travels from Nuremberg to Munich.
Between September 27 and October 5 (between October 10 and 18)	The "Declaration of the Editorial Board of *Iskra*," composed by Lenin, is published as a separate leaflet. The statement is sent to Russia for distribution among Social-Democratic organisations and workers.
October 13 (26)	In a letter to A. A. Yakubova, Lenin, in the name of the *Iskra* group, emphatically refuses to accept the invitation to collaborate with *Rabochaya Mysl*, organ of the "economists."
Beginning of November	Lenin writes the preface to the pamphlet, *May Days in Kharkov*.

November	Lenin edits the first issue of *Iskra* and prepares it for the press.
End of November (first half of December)	Lenin organises the preparation and the publication of the first number of *Zarya* in Stuttgart.
Between December 1 and 10 (between December 19 and 23)	Lenin goes from Munich to Leipzig to prepare the first issue of *Iskra* for the press.
December 11 (24)	The first issue of *Iskra* appears carrying Lenin's articles: "The Urgent Tasks of Our Movement" (leading article); "The War in China"; "The Split in the Union of Russian Social-Democrats Abroad."
Between December 16 (29), 1900, and mid-February 1901	Lenin takes part in the negotiations between the Editorial Board of *Iskra* and *Zarya* and P. B. Struve, on the latter's arrival in Munich, on the conditions for Struve's collaboration with those publications. Lenin is emphatically against an agreement with Struve.

1901

January-March	The work of the "groups supporting *Iskra*" and its agents in Russia (St. Petersburg, Moscow, Pskov, Poltava, Samara, South Russia, etc.) develops under Lenin's guidance.
First half of February	The second issue of *Iskra* appears, carrying Lenin's article, "The Drafting of 183 Students into the Army."
Mid-February	Lenin goes to Prague and Vienna to arrange for N. K. Krupskaya to go abroad.
End of February-first half of March (March)	Lenin conducts negotiations for the establishment of an illegal printing-press for *Iskra* in Russia (in Kishinev).
March 10 (23)	The first issue of *Zarya* appears carrying three of Lenin's articles under the heading, *Casual Notes*.
April 12 (25)	Lenin places before the Emancipation of Labour group a plan for the unification of Russian revolutionary Social-Democratic organisations abroad, grouped round *Iskra*, into a League of Russian Revolutionary Social-Democracy.

April 19 (May 2)	The third issue of *Iskra* appears, carrying Lenin's article "The Workers' Party and the Peasantry."
Between April 24 and May 1 (between May 7 and 14)	The Conference in Munich of the Editorial Board of *Iskra* and *Zarya* discusses Lenin's plan for the formation of the League of Russian Revolutionary Social-Democracy Abroad, as well as provisional rules for the League.